# Practical Aspects of
# Interview and Interrogation

CRC SERIES IN
## PRACTICAL ASPECTS OF CRIMINAL AND FORENSIC INVESTIGATIONS

VERNON J. GEBERTH, BBA, MPS, FBINA *Series Editor*

**Practical Homicide Investigation: Tactics, Procedures, and Forensic Techniques, Second Edition**  Vernon J. Geberth

**The Counter-Terrorism Handbook: Tactics, Procedures, and Techniques**  Frank Bolz, Jr., Kenneth J. Dudonis, and David P. Schulz

**Forensic Pathology**  Dominick J. Di Maio, MD, and Vincent J.M. Di Maio, MD

**Interpretation of Bloodstain Evidence at Crime Scenes**  William G. Eckert and Stuart H. James

**Tire Imprint Evidence**  Peter McDonald

**Practical Drug Enforcement: Procedures and Administration**  Michael D. Lyman

**Practical Aspects of Rape Investigation: A Multidisciplinary Approach**  Robert R. Hazelwood and Ann Wolbert Burgess

**The Sexual Exploitation of Children: A Practical Guide to Assessment, Investigation, and Intervention**  Seth L. Goldstein

**Gunshot Wounds: Practical Aspects of Firearms, Ballistics, and Forensic Techniques**  Vincent J.M. Di Maio, MD

**Friction Ridge Skin: Comparison and Identification of Fingerprints**  James F. Cowger

**Footwear Impression Evidence**  William J. Bodziak

**Practical Fire and Arson Investigation**  John J. O'Connor

**The Practical Methodology of Forensic Photography**  David R. Redsicker

**Practical Aspects of Interview and Interrogation**  David E. Zulawski and Douglas E. Wicklander

# Practical Aspects of Interview and Interrogation

DAVID E. ZULAWSKI
DOUGLAS E. WICKLANDER

Wicklander–Zulawski & Associates, Inc.
Lombard, Illinois

Rock Valley College
Educational Resources
Center
WITHDRAWN

CRC Press
Boca Raton   Ann Arbor   London   Tokyo

**Library of Congress Cataloging-in-Publication Data**

Zulawski, David E.
    Practical aspects of interview and interrogation / David E.
Zulawski, Douglas E. Wicklander.
    p.   cm.
    Originally published: New York : Elsevier, c1992. (Elsevier series
in practical aspects of criminal and forensic investigations)
    Includes index.
    ISBN 0-8493-9520-8
    1. Police questioning--United States.   I. Wicklander, Douglas E.
II. Title.   III. Series: Elsevier series in practical aspects of
criminal and forensic investigations.
HV8073.Z85   1993
363.2'54--dc20                                                    93-21679
                                                                      CIP

No claim to original U.S. Government works
International Standard Book Number 0-8493-9520-8
Library of Congress Card Number 93-21679
Printed in the United States of America          8 9 0
Printed on acid-free paper

This book is dedicated to my wife, Annette,
children Jennifer, Jonathan, Patrick, Katherine, and Kelly,
and of course Mom and Dad.

**David E. Zulawski**

This book is dedicated to my wife, Debbie,
children Matthew, Andrew, and Ann,
and my mother.
Not enough can be said about their love and support.

**Douglas E. Wicklander**

# Contents

Preface                                                    xix
Acknowledgments                                            xxi
Editor's Note                                             xxiii

## 1  Introduction/Overview of the Process                  1

Good Guy/Bad Guy Approach                                    2
Factual Approach                                            2
Emotional Approach                                          2
Public versus Private Sector Approaches                     5
Legal Issues                                               7
Overview of the Interview and Interrogative Process         7
  Part One: Preparation and Strategy                        7
  Part Two: Interviewing                                    7
  Part Three: Establishing Credibility                      9
  Part Four: Reducing Resistance                            9
  Part Five: Obtaining the Admission                       10
  Part Six: Developing the Admission                       10
  Part Seven: Professional Close                           11

## 2  Preparation and Strategy                             13

Interview Goal                                             13
Evidence Considerations                                    14
Background Information                                      15
Selection of the Interviewer                               16
Case File and Props                                        17
Privacy                                                    18
Location—Planned Field Interview                           19
Room Setting                                               19

Distractions                                                     21
Roles of the Interviewer/Interrogator                            23
Language                                                         24
Taking Notes                                                     27
Strategies                                                       28


3    **Legal Aspects**                                          **31**
Who Are You?                                                     31
Constitutional Amendments                                        33
    Fourth Amendment                                             33
    Fifth Amendment                                              33
    Sixth Amendment                                              33
    Fourteenth Amendment                                         33
Public Sector Rules                                              34
Voluntariness                                                    35
The *Miranda* Rule                                               36
The Warnings                                                     36
Suspect Waiver                                                   38
The *Massiah* and *Escobedo* Rules                               39
Youths and Incompetents                                          39
Alcohol or Narcotics Intoxication                                40
Tricks and Promises                                              41
Public Employers                                                 41
Private Employers                                                42
Sixth Amendment: Right to an Attorney                            43
Federal Statutes                                                 44
Unions/Weingarten Rights                                         44
State Law                                                        45
Common Law                                                       45
    False Imprisonment                                           46
    Defamation                                                   46
    Malicious Prosecution                                        47
Assault and Battery                                              49
Intentional Infliction of Emotional Distress                     49


4    **Interpretation of Verbal and Physical Behavior**         **51**
Common Terms                                                     52
Faking Behavior                                                  53
Rules for Evaluating Behavior                                    54
    Evaluate the Suspect Against Himself                         54
    Evaluate the Suspect's Behavior Against
        that of the Population                                   55
    Evaluate Behavior in the Context of the Situation            56

Behavioral Clusters                                              56
Interviewer Behavior                                            57
Timing/Consistency                                              58
Cautions in the Evaluation of Behavior                          59
    Role of the Environment                                     59
    Interviewer–Suspect Attitudes                               60
    Mental Capacity of Suspect                                  60
    Medical Condition, Drug/Alcohol Usage                       61
    Cultural, Ethnic, and Geographic Differences                61
    Professional Criminals, Actors, and Politicians             62
    Fear of Detection                                           63
Fight or Flight                                                 64
Emotion                                                         65
Typical Attitudes Displayed by Suspects                         66
    The Truthful Suspect                                        66
    The Untruthful Suspect                                      66
    Attitudes Common to Both Truthful and
        Untruthful Suspects                                     67
Interpretation of Nonverbal Behavior                            69
    Trunk, Shoulder Position, and Posture                       69
        Truthful Individual                                     70
        Untruthful Individual                                   71
    Hand and Arm Positions                                      73
        Truthful Individual                                     74
        Untruthful Individual                                   74
        General Considerations                                  77
        Arm Barriers                                            79
    Leg and Feet Positions                                      80
        Truthful                                                85
    Head and Neck Positions                                     87
    Head Positions                                              88
        Truthful                                                88
        Untruthful                                              89
    Eye Movements                                               90
        Truthful                                                90
        Untruthful                                              90
    Mouth Positions                                             91
        Truthful                                                91
        Untruthful                                              91
    Nose                                                        92
    Neck                                                        92
Verbal Behavior                                                 93
    Truthful                                                    93
    Untruthful                                                  93

Unsolicited, Premature Excuses or Explanations          95
Uncheckable Sources                                     95
Focusing on Irrelevant Points                           96
Excessive Politeness or Respectfulness                  97
Helpfulness                                             97
Delays                                                  98
    Physical Behavior                                   99
    Repeating the Question                              99
    Responding with a Question                          100
    Hanging Sentences                                   101
    Nonresponses                                        101
    Giving a Minor Admission                            102
    Gallows Laughter                                    102
Political Answers                                       102
Emphasis on Truthfulness                                103
Memory Problems                                         104
The Admission of Guilt and Offer of Restitution         105
Verbal Slips                                            107
Strength of Denials                                     108

**5   Causes of Denials                                 109**
Environment                                             113
    Privacy                                             113
    Supportive Environment                              113
    Positioning                                         114
Interviewer/Interrogator                                115
    Interrogator's Personality                          115
    Interrogator's Attitude                             115
    Interrogator Reputation                             116
    Tentativeness and Unconvincing Behavior
        of the Interrogator                             116
    Perception of Interrogator                          117
    Wrong Rationalizations Used by the Interrogator     118
    Personalizing Rationalizations too Early            119
    Highlighting Consequences                           119
    Interrogator Silence                                119
    Interrogator Strategy                               120
    Wrong or Incomplete Evidence                        120
    Perceived Lack of Proof                             121
    Compromised Investigation                           121
    Questioning Techniques                              122
    Denial to Stall for Time                            122
    Poorly Timed Question                               124

Waiting too Long                                         124
Failing to Reaccuse                                      124
Suspect                                                  124
Seriousness of the Lie                                   124
Lack of Rules                                            126
Cultural Differences                                     126
Drugs and Alcohol                                        127
Consequences versus Justifications                       127
Involvement of Others                                    128
Truthful Denials                                         128

# 6  Interviewing                                        131

Preplanning the Interview                                138
Supporting Tactics                                       138
Rapport                                                  139
Establishing Management Rapport                          140
Establishing Rapport with the Victim,
  Witness, or Suspect                                    141
Common Ground                                            141
Appearance and Demeanor                                  142
Behavior                                                 142
Mirroring                                                143
Verbal Neurolinguistics Techniques                       146
Visual Mode                                              146
Auditory Mode                                            146
Kinesic Mode                                             146
Physiological Neurolinguistic Techniques                 147
Selling the Interview                                    149
Allowing a Narrative                                     150
Hearing the Untainted Story                              151
Evaluating Neurolinguistic Eye Movement                  153
Leading the Interview                                    157
Challenging the Untruthful Witness, Victim,
  or Suspect                                             158
Using Rationalizations                                   158
Shifting to Interrogation                                159
Using Cognitive Interview Techniques                     160
Using the Selective Interview Technique                  161
Questions Asked                                          162
Using Questions of Enticement                            165
Purpose                                                  165
Presentation of the Question                             166
Examples of Enticement Questions                         167

Implying an Eyewitness                                        167
Implying Handwriting Evidence                                 168
Implying Physical Evidence such as Fingerprints,
   Footprints, Tire Tracks                     168
Implying Closed Circuit Camera Evidence                       168
Asking the Suspect to Remember                                168
Obtaining the Suspect's Biographical Information              168
Obtaining a Written Statement                                 169
Closing Professionally                                        169

7   Establishing Credibility/The Accusation                  171
Positioning                                                   172
Attitude                                                      172
Introduction                                                  172
Impressions Given by the Interrogator                         172
Selection of the Accusation                                   173
  Factual Approach                                   174
  Direct Accusation                                  175
    Relate the Issue                       177
    Make Clear, Simple Accusations         178
    Pause                                  178
    Repeat the Accusation                  178
    Lead into Rationalizations             179
    A Problem with Direct Accusation       179
  Introductory Statement Approach                    179
    Interrogator's Behavior                181
    Suspect's Behavior                     181
    Introductory Statement Options         182
  Construction of the Introductory Statement for
    Loss Prevention—Private Sector         182
  Explanation of the Interrogator's Role             183
  Explanation of How Losses Occur                    183
  Explanation of How Investigations
    Are Conducted                           185
  Discussions of Why Employees Make
    Mistakes—Rationalizations              185
  Transition Statement                               186
  Soft Accusation/Assumptive Question                186
  Follow-up Question                                  187
  Length of the Introductory Statement               187
Participatory Accusation                                      188
  Construction of the Participatory Accusation        189
  Introduction                                        189

Establishing the Suspect's Alibi and
　　Actions on the Job                                          189
Promoting Cooperation through a Story              190
Discussing How Investigations Are Conducted      191
Creating Rationalizations                                191
Offering the Soft Accusation/Assumptive Question  192
Transcript of a Tape                                        192
Interrogation Time Limit                                   198
Countering Suspect Interruptions                       199

8　**Reducing Resistance—Rationalizations**          **201**
Concept of Rationalization                                202
Determining Which Rationalization to Use           204
　Motive of the Crime                                        204
　Background of the Offender                             205
　Behavior of the Suspect                                  207
　　Receptive Behavior                                      207
　　Nonreceptive Behavior                                 207
Minimizing the Seriousness of the Offense          210
Focusing the Suspect's Attention on the Future or Past  210
Offering a Positive Outlook                               211
Relating Personal Stories                                   211
Illustrating with Current Events and Publications   212
Avoiding Threats or Promises                             213
Examples of Rationalizations                            214
　Job Pressures                                               214
　Financial Pressure                                         214
　Minimization                                               214
　Focusing on the Future                                   215
　Positive Outlook                                          215
Examples of Rationalizations with Choice Questions  215
　General                                                       215
　Suggest Accident                                          216
　　Use                                                         216
　　Choice Questions                                        216
　Suggest Impulse                                           216
　　Use                                                         216
　　Choice Questions                                        217
　Blame Victim (Company or Supervisor)            217
　　Use                                                         217
　　Choice Questions                                        217
　Blame Poor Pay                                            218
　　Use                                                         218

Choice Questions                                         218
Blame Fellow Worker or Friends                           218
Use                                                      218
Choice Questions                                         218
Blame Poor Security                                      218
Use                                                      219
Choice Questions                                         219
Blame the Economy (Politicians, Creditors)              219
Use                                                      219
Choice Questions                                         219
Blame Peer Pressure                                      220
Use                                                      220
Choice Questions                                         220
Exaggerate Loss, Frequency, or Seriousness               220
Use                                                      220
Choice Questions                                         221
Propose Loss of Control                                  221
Use                                                      221
Choice Questions                                         221
Blame the Use of Alcohol/Drugs                           221
Use                                                      222
Choice Questions                                         222
Emphasize Borrowing                                      222
Use                                                      222
Choice Questions                                         223
Play One Against the Other                               223
Use                                                      223
Choice Questions                                         223
Identify the Hurdle                                      223
Correcting the Rationalizations                          224

# 9  Denials                                             227

Types of Denials                                         227
Emphatic Denial                                          228
Explanatory Denials                                      228
Where Denials Occur                                      228
Emphatic Denials                                         229
Suspect's Behavior                                       229
Physical Behavior                                        229
Verbal Behavior                                          230
Handling Emphatic Denials                                230
Use the Suspect's First Name                             231
Discuss Important Areas                                  231

Tell the Suspect That He Will Have
a Chance to Talk 232
Advise the Suspect That It Is Better to Say
Nothing Than to Lie 232
Interrupt the Suspect and State the Denial
for Him 232
Use Behavior to Control the Interrogation 233
Change the Psychology of the Room 234
Use an Enticement Question to Stop
a Suspect's Denial 236
Truthful Emphatic Denials 237
Explanatory Denials 239

## 10 Obtaining the Admission 243

Mindset of the Suspect in Submission 243
Behavior of the Suspect in Submission 244
Shortening and Repeating Rationalizations 244
Closing Physically with the Suspect 245
Controlling the Suspect 246
Avoiding Physical Contact 246
Using the Assumptive Question 248
Testing the Waters 248
Transition Statement 249
Choice Question/Soft Accusation 249
Suspect's Behavioral Shift 250
Asking Assumptive Questions 250
The Soft Accusation 251
Construction of the Soft Accusation 251
Wording of the Soft Accusation 252
Suspect's Response to Soft Accusation 252
Follow-Up Question 253
The Choice Question 254
Acknowledging Acceptance of the Assumptive
Question by the Suspect 256
Observing Behavioral Clues of an Admission 257
Sample Introductory Statements 259
Loss Prevention 259
Part One: What We Do and How We Do It 259
Part Two: How Losses Occur 260
Part Three: How Investigations Are Conducted 261
Part Four: Discussion of Why Mistakes Are Made 262
Impulse 262
Peer Pressure 263

Financial Problems                                              264
Part Five: The Soft Accusation/Assumptive Question              266
Law Enforcement                                                 266
Part One: Who We Are and What We Do                             266
Part Two: Different Types of Crimes                             267
Part Three: How We Investigate                                  267
Part Four: Discussion of Why Mistakes Are Made                  269
Part Five: The Soft Accusation/Assumptive Question              270

## 11 Development of the Admission                                271

Acceptance of the Soft Accusation/Choice Question
  by the Suspect                                                272
Techniques to Expand the First Admission                        275
  The Worksheet                                                 275
  Resistance-Reducing Techniques                                275
  The Assumptive Question                                       276
  Use of Exaggeration to Encourage Admission                    277
  Use of the Investigation as a Wedge                           277
  Substantiation of Amounts                                     278
    The Length of Involvement                                   278
    The Most Taken at Any One Time                              279
    The Average Amount Taken Each Time                          279
    The List of Items                                           280
    The Total Dollar Figure                                     281
    The Repetition of Topics                                    282
    The Mental Review of Places                                 283
Behavioral Peak of Tension                                      284
Change of Interrogators                                         286
The Use of Evidence/The Absolute Denial                         287
Development of Knowledge                                        288
  Request for Names                                             288

## 12 The Statement                                              291

Types of Statements                                             294
  Narrative                                                     294
  Question and Answer                                           294
  Formal Statements                                             295
  Audio or Video Recordings                                     295
Interrogator Control                                            297
Timing of Taking the Statement                                  297
Potential Problems                                              299
  The Suspect Alleges That the Statement
    Was Dictated to Him                                         299

The Suspect Says That He Cannot Read or Write          300
The Recording of a Statement May Be Questioned        300
The Suspect Alleges That He Was not Advised
    of His Rights                                             301
The Suspect Alleges Coercion in Writing
    the Statement                                            301
The Suspect Refuses to Make a Written Statement       301
The Interrogator Believes That the Suspect May Be
    Unwilling to Make a Written Statement                  303
The Suspect Avoids Admitting Elements or
    Details of the Crime                                     303
Statement Format                                             304
    Part One: Introduction                                   304
    Part Two: The Admission                                  305
    Part Three: Substantiation                               305
    Part Four: Voluntariness                                 306
    Part Five: Signature and Correcting Errors               307
Protection of the Statement                                  308
Transcription of the Statement                               309
Witnessing the Written Statement                             309
Completion of Other Documents                                310
The Written Report                                           310

13  **Ending the Interview**                                **313**
Professional Close                                           314
The Unsuccessful Interview/Interrogation                     314
Support for the Suspect                                       317
The End of the Interview                                      318
Final Report                                                  318
Ethical Considerations                                       318

**About the Authors**                                       **321**
**Index**                                                   **323**

# Preface

From the beginning, people have wrestled with the problem of identifying and inducing a liar to divulge information. For years, the art of interviewing and interrogation has been passed informally between the experienced and the inexperienced investigators as they worked together. As sophistication in investigative and evidence techniques improved, so did the teaching of interview and interrogations. Numerous books and articles were published by successful interrogators discussing techniques and their application to the criminal suspect. Kidd, Reid, Arthur, and other interrogators began to look at how they identified and caused a suspect to confess.

The observation of behavior, the use of structured questions, and a series of steps during the interrogation were the common denominators in the identification and interrogation of the criminal suspect.

With the special problems and needs of both the public and private sectors, modifications of the technique are warranted. Differing resources, experience, and training require the reader to change techniques based on his needs—needs that may alter in the next job or case.

It is our intention to present, through a structured format, an approach to interview and interrogation that has proven successful time and time again. We ask only that the reader keep an open mind to the techniques we will be discussing. Compare it to past experience and apply it to the specific problems and constraints you presently face.

David E. Zulawski
Douglas E. Wicklander

# Acknowledgments

We wish to thank our friends in both the private and public sectors for their support. Their comments, suggestions, and feedback were invaluable in molding the concept and presentation into a usable form. The value of their years of experience can never be underestimated.

We particularly wish to thank attorney Terry Sullivan and his staff for their review of Chapter 3, Legal Aspects. And we thank Mercedes Balcer for her efforts at typing and retyping drafts of the manuscript while never losing her sense of humor.

David E. Zulawski
Douglas E. Wicklander

# Editor's Note

This textbook is part of a series entitled, "Practical Aspects of Criminal and Forensic Investigations."

This series was created by Vernon J. Geberth, a retired New York City Police Department Lieutenant Commander, who is an author, educator, and consultant on homicide and forensic investigations.

The series has been designed to provide contemporary, comprehensive, and pragmatic information to the practitioner involved in criminal and forensic investigations by authors who are nationally recognized experts in their respective fields.

# Practical Aspects of
# Interview and Interrogation

# Introduction/Overview of the Process

1

There's one way to find out if a man is honest—
*ask him.*
*—Groucho Marx*

It is appropriate that this book on interview and interrogation begin with a quotation from a comedian. Comedians are perceptive individuals who can see humor and truth in people, two things that sometimes are one and the same. We, as interrogators, are attempting to be as perceptive as comedians—looking for the truth in people. In the following chapters, we are going to follow Groucho Marx's advice and ask suspects whether or not they are telling the truth. The suspect's truthfulness can be evaluated by their verbal and physical behavior as well as by their attitudes toward the interrogator and the investigation.

Although many of the readers of this book may be experienced in interview and interrogation, we hope to put into perspective aspects of the process that may benefit them also. We are going to attempt to categorize suspects' actions that the experienced reader may have already observed. At the same time, we want to identify for the new interrogator phases and actions that can act as a foundation during the interview/interrogation process.

There are many different forms and derivations of the interrogative process. History has shown us that interrogation in times of war has taken the route of torture and killings to elicit information from suspects. Currently a number of nations still practice torture and beatings as a means of eliciting confessions from those unfortunate enough to be perceived as suspects. Narcotic interrogation using resistance-weakening drugs is also a method employed by some governments to obtain information.

Although torture and drug-influenced interrogations may have very high confession rates they are, simply stated, illegal. The Constitution of the United States and the Bill of Rights have preserved the rights of the individual during a criminal investigation, thereby rendering these inhumane techniques unlawful. The Supreme Court, through several landmark decisions, has reinforced the rights of an accused guaranteed by our democratic process.

## Good Guy/Bad Guy Approach

In the United States, several methods of interrogation are typically used to elicit information from a suspect. One method made famous by television and Hollywood is the good guy/bad guy routine. In this type of confrontation with the subject, one interrogator plays the heartless, uncompromising role while a second interrogator, in contrast, plays the soft, understanding role. The contrast between these two individuals encourages the suspect to take the sympathetic ear of the second interrogator and confess to the incident. The exposure this technique has received in television and movies and its having been used in an unprofessional manner has made it largely ineffective against suspects. Additionally, depending on the role of the hard interrogator, it may verge on intimidation and coercion, which could render a suspect's statement unusable.

## Factual Approach

Another form of interrogation is the factual approach. The use of a factual approach requires an extensive investigation into the circumstances surrounding the incident and the activities of the suspect. In addition, the answers to most of the investigative questions of who, what, when, where, how, and why must be available to the interrogator.

Unfortunately, this type of interrogation lends itself only to those situations that have been intensively investigated because of the serious nature of the incident. In most instances, this factual approach is ineffective because the scope of the investigation has not been sufficient to counter the suspects' explanations or stories. Often, a factual interrogation may also lack the inclusion of "rationalization" by the interrogator, which allows the suspect to save face while making an admission.

## Emotional Approach

In the emotional approach to interrogation the interrogator confronts the subject not on the circumstances or details surrounding his involvement in the issue, but rather on the reasons why the subject did what he did. It is here that the interrogator rationalizes with the suspect by offering reasons or excuses that allow the suspect to save face while admitting his involvement in the incident. This form of interrogation does not require the extensive investigation into the incident that a factual attack requires. The use of rationalization in an emotional appeal is effective on all but the most street-hardened individuals. By allowing the suspect to save face, it makes it easier for him to talk about his guilt. Rationalizations offer a means for the suspect to save face and make his reasons for becoming involved appear to be understandable under the circumstances.

The emotional approach can be made more effective in many cases when modified by incorporating a factual component. This factual component establishes the credibility of the interrogator's investigation before the interrogator expresses his understanding of why the suspect committed the offense. Modifying the emotional approach through the use of a factual component allows the interrogator to quickly reduce the resistance of a suspect by first establishing the suspect's guilt and then offering him an easy way out that allows him to save face while confessing.

The discussions in this text will focus primarily on using an emotional appeal to the suspect, justifying his or her actions and minimizing the seriousness of the incident under investigation. Even in situations where the factual approach is deemed the most appropriate method, the emotional interrogation, using rationalizations to justify and minimize the seriousness of the suspect's involvement, can enhance the results achieved.

Even though the interview and interrogation process is an art rather than a science, it can still be learned. However, some interviewers will, because of their own personality, perception, perseverance, and practice, be better at interviewing and interrogating than others.

Many of us have had the good fortune to learn from expert interrogators as they worked. These men and women have a natural flair for interview and interrogation of suspects. This book will offer new interrogators advice and experience to which they would not otherwise have access.

Unfortunately, many of the things that have been learned by expert interrogators are not passed on because the experts do not or are not able to understand how they interrogate or encourage a suspect to confess. The techniques discussed in the following chapters are not always going to identify the guilty or cause him to confess. There will always be a certain percentage of suspects who will never confess, no matter what evidence is available, or what is said to them.

The interview and interrogation techniques that will be discussed in the following chapters are not a substitute for a good investigation. That investigation is essential to discover the factual basis behind the issue under investigation, narrow the scope of the suspect population, and learn the background of all possible suspects. The interviewer/interrogator's job is made easier and produces more effective results when proper investigative techniques have developed evidence.

Certainly, the purpose of the interview and interrogation process is to identify the guilty party and obtain a legally admissible confession. This is, without question, the most satisfying of all interrogations. The case is satisfactorily resolved with a signed statement attesting to the suspect's involvement and perhaps the development of additional evidence.

Unfortunately, in the real world there are suspects who will not confess; therefore, the second purpose of the interview and interrogation process must then be to establish convincingly to ourselves that a particular suspect was, indeed, involved. In doing so, we have narrowed the scope of the investigation and focused the entire investigative resources of the company or department on the investigation of a single individual or group of individuals. At the same time, and more importantly, we have eliminated a very large percentage of the innocent suspects within the scope of the investigation. In private sector investigation, it is imperative that this narrowing of focus be done to maintain the morale of the employees and their image of the company. The public sector must do this simply to have a manageable number of suspects.

The third and equally important purpose of the interview and interrogation process is to clear other related cases and recover evidence or assets of the company or victim. Whereas the security or loss prevention department is rarely viewed as a profit-making function of the company, it does not have to be that way. Restitution in the form of cash payments can be added to the bottom line profits of the company and justify security expenditures and operations. One of the authors' clients obtained several hundred thousand dollars in theft confessions from employees during a recent year. Almost half of this amount was actually recovered in the form of cash repayment to the company. Certainly, recoveries of this nature can help justify some of the company's security expenditures. As in any company, the ability to make a profit is paramount; security can contribute with loss prevention and restitution programs.

Public law enforcement can enhance a prosecutable case by providing a solid foundation of additional evidence of the subject's guilt. Other investigations can be resolved by the suspect's admitting involvement or having knowledge of those responsible.

Defining several terms will aid in clarifying the information in following chapters:

INTERVIEW: a nonaccusatory, structured interview during which specific behavior-provoking questions are asked with the purpose of eliciting interpretable behavior symptoms that are typical of innocence or guilt. Additional factual information concerning the case and/or suspects may also be developed during this nonaccusatory interview.

INTERROGATION: a conversation between the interrogator and suspect, during which the suspect is accused of involvement in a particular incident or group of incidents. Many companies use the word *interview* as a substitute for the word *interrogation*. For the sake of clarity in this text, the term interview will be used to indicate a nonaccusatory conversation while interrogation will represent the change to an accusatory tone.

INTERVIEWER/INTERROGATOR: an individual skilled in the nature of interview and interrogation process and the interpretation of verbal and physical behavior. As above, the terms interviewer and interrogator will be used to differentiate between a nonaccusatory and accusatory environment.

SUSPECT: any individual within the scope of the case who has not yet been cleared by the investigation. A suspect under this definition can be either truthful or untruthful.

WITNESS: an individual who can provide direct or indirect evidence to the case. This individual may or may not be providing truthful information and may or may not be the victim.

The need to interview and interrogate victims, witnesses, and suspects encompasses both public law enforcement and the private sector. The development of information is fundamental to the process of investigations. However, it is worth noting that there are significant differences between the investigative techniques and strategies employed by public law enforcement and those of the private sector. Differences in resources and operational strategies between the public and private sector require each to use methods and procedures specifically designed to enhance the success of the process.

## Public versus Private Sector Approaches

A fundamental difference between the public and private sectors is the use of investigations. Public law enforcement prepares a case specifically for prosecution and trial. The private sector prepares its case to present to Personnel for termination of the suspect's employment and defense of the company in an unemployment, arbitration hearing, or in some other form of litigation. Under certain circumstances, the private sector investigator might also take the case the next logical step, prosecution.

There are significant differences in the levels of proof needed, depending on the choice of end result. Business, by its very nature, is profit-oriented and clearly weighs the return on its investigative dollar. Many corporate officers who note a significant shortage after reviewing figures want and demand results, not today, but yesterday. They may not accept an investigation that will resolve the case in six months to a year. Only on major cases do police feel that type of pressure. A random murder, burglary, or robbery does not generally stir public sentiment and pressure like a serial killing or an entire block of houses being burglarized. Now, public sentiment and pressure are focused to resolve the case. This pressure can alter the interview and investigative process.

The public law enforcement officer typically has the resources and time to conduct in-depth investigations of suspects to ascertain their involvement. It is not unusual for public law enforcement investigations to continue for months or even years to develop the information necessary to convict in a court of law. Additionally, the vast amount of information available to public law enforcement is significantly different from that available to the private sector. Often, wiretap, surveillance, physical evidence, and other forensic techniques can independently identify the suspect as the person responsible for the incident even without a confession. Legal avenues using search warrants, subpoena, and grand jury hearings open doors to information that the private sector could never hope to obtain. Only rarely will these type of resources be allocated to a private sector investigation.

The types of cases also vary significantly, the private sector handling primarily economic crimes such as theft, fraud, and embezzlement. Less often, drug, burglary, or other criminal activities may be investigated but generally as part of an ongoing theft investigation. In the private sector, the goal is not only the prosecution and/or termination of the dishonest employee, but also recovery of company assets through restitution, civil recovery, or insurance claims.

The public sector's goal is the suspects' conviction, with restitution or compensation to the victim far down on its list of priorities. Private sector cases typically are related to incidents that have occurred within the company and/or at a single location. The number of potential suspects is generally already limited to any employees assigned to that location. The public law enforcement investigator often has to deal with cases that may cover multiple jurisdictions and numerous states. Thus, the scope of the investigation is broader in the public sector, perhaps encompassing thousands of potential suspects.

Private sector investigators generally deal with cases at a single location with smaller suspect groups. The incidents being investigated may continue over a longer period of time, however, whereas the public law enforcement more typically investigates single-issue incidents and the circumstances surrounding them, with larger groups of potential suspects.

## Legal Issues

The legal constraints also differ between public law enforcement and the private sector. The *Miranda* decision, custody, Exclusionary Rule ("fruit of the poisonous tree"), and the courts' view of the totality of circumstances to determine the voluntariness of the confession are some of the more common issues raised by the public sector when discussing interview and interrogation. Private industry must contend with management, personnel, company policy, and hearing officers when conducting their interviews or interrogations.

There are still many fundamental similarities between private and public sectors in the interview and interrogation process. For example, it is conducted in privacy, generally on a one-on-one basis, possibly with a witness present—for example, when a woman is being interviewed, when an employee requests union representation, when an interpreter is needed to conduct the interview or interrogation, or as a matter of department policy. On occasion, a novice interviewer/interrogator may accompany the experienced interrogator to gain valuable experience.

## Overview of the Interview and Interrogative Process

This text is in a building block style: Information from previous chapters is used as a foundation for subsequent chapters (see Figure 1.1).

### Part One: Preparation and Strategy

Part one deals with the preparation and strategy that effectively counter the suspect's resistance to confessing. Here, discussion takes into account differing legal constraints facing the public and private sectors. Then, the foundation for the interrogation is laid by considering why and how people lie, a discussion of verbal and physical behavior symptoms, and finally, the reasons for denials by suspects.

### Part Two: Interviewing

Part two considers the nonaccusatory interview in a number of ways—fact gathering, the heart of the investigation; Cognitive Interviewing, a method to enhance witness recollection; and the Selective Interview, a means to evaluate the truthfulness of a potential witness or suspect.

8

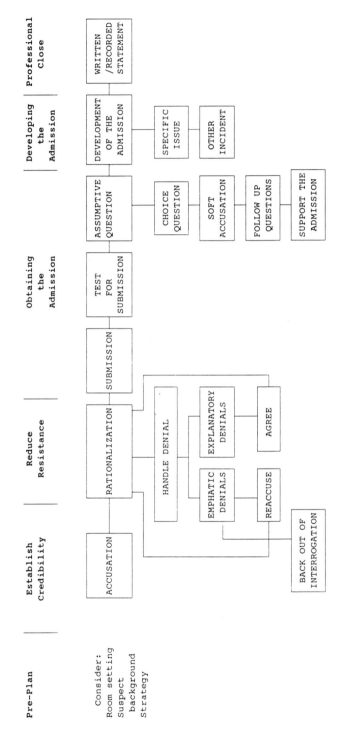

1.1. Chart illustrating the flow of information from preplanning to conclusion.

| Pre-Plan | Establish Credibility | Reduce Resistance | Obtaining the Admission | Developing the Admission | Professional Close |

We will also consider Neurolinguistics as it relates to the process of communication and evaluation of truth and deception. Each of these topics will be considered in light of the differences between victims, witnesses, and suspects.

This last step before interrogation is the identification of individuals responsible for incidents and/or the gathering of factual information from informants and witnesses using the *Selective Interview Technique.* The Selective Interview Technique can be used in both specific incidents or general loss incident investigations. It offers the interviewer a structured format using questions that elicit verbal and physical behavior typical of innocence or guilt. During the Selective Interview, the techniques necessary to identify the guilty and eliminate the innocent from the investigation will be discussed.

## *Part Three: Establishing Credibility*

Part three deals with the interrogation of a guilty suspect. Once the guilty party has been identified through the interview or investigative process, the interrogation of the suspect is ready to begin. In any interrogation, an accusation of wrongdoing must be made at some point so that the suspect understands that the interrogator believes that he is involved in the incident under investigation.

The accusation can take one of several forms, depending upon the purpose of the interrogation, the background of the suspect, the factual nature of the case, and the restraints under which the interrogator must work. The purpose or direction of the overall interrogation will be dictated by the desired result and preinterrogation strategy selected by the interrogator.

In this section the interrogator learns to establish the credibility of the investigation in the suspect's mind. Here the interrogator convinces the suspect that the investigation has clearly identified him as the perpetrator of the crime.

## *Part Four: Reducing Resistance*

Following the accusation, the interrogator must use techniques that reduce a suspects resistance to confession. The interrogator may get a denial from the suspect. This denial can take one of two forms: emphatic or explanatory. The *emphatic denial* is a physical behavior, such as shaking the head, or could be a verbal response such as, "No, I did not do it," where the suspect refuses to acknowledge the truthfulness of the accusation. The explanatory denial, which usually follows the emphatic denial, is any response from the suspect that offers an excuse or reason why the suspect could not or would not be involved in the incident. A suspects' explanatory denial may be the first time that the interrogator recognizes that he is making progress in the interrogation. Examples of explanatory denials are "I wouldn't kill my wife... I loved her," and "I wouldn't take that money... I don't need it."

Throughout the course of the interrogation, the interrogator is controlling and directing the conversation. During this conversation, the interrogator offers the suspect rationalizations (reasons or excuses) why the suspect became involved in the incident that will psychologically minimize the seriousness and make the suspect's actions understandable. The interrogator takes the blame away from the suspect and focuses it on someone or something else. Thus, the suspect's attention is focused on resolving the problem rather than any consequences for his actions. It is during rationalizations that the subject may interrupt the interrogation with emphatic and explanatory denials.

## Part Five: Obtaining the Admission

When the interrogator is making headway in reducing the suspect's resistance to confess, the suspect begins to go into the behavioral phase of submission. That is, he enters a behaviorally recognizable phase of the interrogation that indicates his susceptibility to making an admission. This phase is typified by a suspect who has stopped all denials and has come to grips with the realization that he is going to admit his involvement.

Once the suspect displays the behavioral manifestations of submission, the interrogator continues with the rationalization but shortens its length and prepares to present the suspect with a choice question. This question offers the suspect two choices. One choice appears harsh and unacceptable, whereas the second seems to be understandable or more socially acceptable—for example, "Did you use the money for drugs or for bills?" "Did you mean to hurt her or was it an accident?" Although the interrogator does not care which of the choices the suspect chooses, he is encouraging the suspect to choose the more acceptable, face-saving choice. The interrogator is simply looking for the suspect to pick one of the two choices, which in turn is the first admission of guilt.

## Part Six: Developing the Admission

Once the suspect has made an initial admission by selecting one of the two choices, the interrogator then prepares to develop this admission into an acceptable confession. This development may follow one of two directions. In a single, specific-issue case, development will first focus on the incident in question—for example, "How did you get the $1,000 out of the safe?"

"What did you spend the money on?" "What bills did you pay?" "What did you start the fire with?" "Where did you put the gun?"

During development of admission in a case in which general theft activity is being investigated, the focus will also be on the total amount of the suspect's involvement in the theft of money or merchandise and/or on his knowledge of others' involvement in dishonesty at the company. This avenue will also be followed when a suspect has made an admission in a specific incident and the interrogator expands into involvement in other types of criminal or procedural wrongdoing.

## Part Seven: Professional Close

Part seven deals with the professional close, the written statement, and treatment of the suspect. The suspect, having made admissions, puts these admissions into writing. The discussion here deals with the form and content of the written statement and techniques to insure the suspect's cooperation in writing the statement. Finally, the authors discuss how to end the process, i.e., how the suspect should be treated and strategies to ensure continued cooperation.

It is not necessary that the reader become exactly like the authors in their approach to the interview and interrogation process. Rather, an interviewer/interrogator should select portions of the techniques described that he feels fit well with his personality or position and utilize them to his advantage.

# Preparation and Strategy

# 2

*Two minutes of preparation can save hours
of interrogation.*

Although interviews typically may take place outside of a formalized setting, proper preparation for the interview or interrogation is essential for its successful conclusion. Many field interviews taking place on the street or at a place of business outside the control of the interviewer/interrogator must rely on the locations at hand to provide a proper setting. The decision to interview a witness or suspect should be handled with a careful eye toward the ultimate goal of the conversation.

## Interview Goal

Often, key interviews have generated a considerable amount of information because the interviewer gave thought to the type and quality of information that the witness or suspect could potentially provide. When interviewing a witness for any incident, the scope of the interview should be broadly based enough to allow information that is not actively solicited from the suspect to come out. In addition, whenever possible, the elements necessary to prove the crime being investigated should have been carefully reviewed by the interviewer.

In situations where the interviewer is interviewing an individual who could be a suspect, the guidelines as to what will allow for an arrest of the individual or his termination in an employment setting should be considered. An interviewer/interrogator who has these boundaries clearly in mind will understand the elements necessary for a criminal prosecution in the public sector, or for a termination of employment in the private sector. In the public law enforcement sector, the actual interview may be designed simply to elicit an alibi or a sequence of events that can be later proved or disproved by an investigation. However, in the private sector, the interview is more typically designed simply to elicit the factual circumstances surrounding a case or specific loss and establish the behavioral clues necessary to clear the suspect or focus the investigation on him.

## Evidence Considerations

Another element that the interviewer/interrogator should consider is the available evidence concerning the incident under investigation.In identifying the evidence and how it fits into the incident, an interviewer/interrogator can preplan a suspect's plausible explanations for the evidence. These plausible explanations by the suspect, while false, still afford the suspect an opportunity to explain away key damaging elements of the case. By anticipating the suspect's explanations of damaging evidence, a skilled interviewer/interrogator can have the suspect lock himself into a story or sequence of events that can later be disproved. Additionally, a suspect's lying about his activities increases the impact of any evidence developed during the investigation that disproves the story he has concocted.

### Case Example

A security manager for a large national retailer was suspected of stealing $900 in cash from the store's safe during an audit of the cash. During the investigation, it was learned that the suspect had made a deposit into his account at the bank across the street from the store and that he was having financial problems.

The seemingly damaging evidence of the deposit could be plausibly explained or excused away by the suspect. By anticipating that the suspect might use his girlfriend, also an employee, as an alibi to verify his story, it was decided to interview her simultaneously. She was mentally walked moment by moment through the day of the theft. By locking her into a sequence of events, her value as an alibi to the suspect was seriously diminished.

Several probable suspect explanations were anticipated by the interrogator:

1. The suspect omits the bank deposit entirely from the sequence of events he recounts.
2. The suspect explains that he won the money gambling or in another untraceable activity.
3. The suspect says the money was a loan or gift from a family member.
4. The suspect relates that the money had been saved over time and the suspect's decision to deposit it was a coincidence.

The suspect was asked to recount the events on the day of the theft from the time he arrived until he left work. Surprisingly, the suspect admitted that a deposit of $900 was made into his account in the early afternoon of the day of the theft saying, "I know this looks suspicious." His attempt to stay close to the truth was to his benefit. The best liars generally attempt to stick closely to the truth. A denial of the deposit or its omission while recounting the day's events would be incriminating. When asked where the money came from, he related that it was a loan from his mother and uncle. He said he had been saving the loaned money at home for some time, again a good move because family members will often back up a relative's story or be uncooperative during the investigation.

Having anticipated this as a possible explanation, however, a trap was already prepared: "When your mother loaned you the money, what bank was the check drawn from?" His reply, "First National of _____." Then the second trap was sprung: "Did your uncle send you a check or money order?" The reply, "Money order." "Was it a Visa or American Express?" He replied, "American Express."

The preplanned interview, which anticipated the suspect's responses, allowed the suspect to be trapped well before any interrogation even started. There were no documents to match the story the suspect told, which helped establish clear evidence of his guilt.

## Background Information

Prior to any interview or interrogation, the interviewer should review the background information on the subject. It is during the study of the suspect's background that relevant information may have been developed that would assist the interrogator during the interview/interrogation. It may also allow the interrogator an opportunity to begin developing preliminary thoughts regarding rationalizations that might be effective with this particular individual if an interrogation is contemplated.

Background information is also useful during interviews where the subject may have a hidden agenda that would taint the information that he or she is willing to provide the interviewer/interrogator. The interviewer/interrogator should also consider the order in which the subjects should be interviewed. This could be a particularly important consideration should the interviewer anticipate that one suspect might provide critical evidence against other suspects.

The impact on a primary suspect of having a coconspirator interrogated at the same time may add stress and concern about what is being said about him. In the early stages of an investigation, where a primary suspect has not been identified, there may be no basis for a particular order of interviews until the investigation begins to focus on a suspect.

In larger cases where multiple suspects are involved, such as the closure of a sting or undercover operation, the interrogation takes on as much of an administrative tone as an interrogational one. The organization of the files and choreography of the movement of suspects to and from the interview, the assignment of interrogators, the feeding of suspects, and establishing an evidence-holding room, all play a critical part in the successful conclusion of the process. An excellent discussion of handling large case closures can be found in J. Kirk Barefoot's book, *Employee Theft Investigations.*[1]

One preliminary issue not to be overlooked is the question of how the suspect has reacted during previous interviews or interrogations. If the interrogator could ask only one question regarding the subjects background it should be, "How has he acted when he's either been disciplined or confronted on previous occasions?"

The skilled interrogator realizes that people tend to fall into patterns when they respond to confrontation. The suspect who has in the past reacted aggressively is likely to react exactly as he did before. This information often is available from other officers, loss prevention personnel, the employee's supervisor, teachers, or personnel department. By knowing in advance a previous problem or a likely attitude response of the suspect, an interrogator can anticipate tactics that will beat the suspect at his own game.

## Selection of the Interviewer

Another consideration prior to conducting any interview should be the selection of the interviewer/interrogator. In many cases, the individual who actually develops the case may not be the best person to conduct the interview/interrogation. Even though he may have the best overall knowledge of the case, an investigator may never fully appreciate the complexities of the interview or interrogation of suspects.

Consideration should be given as to whether past experience with the person to be interviewed would be beneficial or not. In some cases, previous contact and its resulting rapport will benefit the interviewer in getting additional admissions. However, this may not always be the case. For example, there may have been a personality conflict, disagreement, or an arrest that resulted in hard feelings against the interviewer/interrogator. In situations where the interviewer would be a subordinate of the person to be interviewed, thought should be given to changing the interviewer. A store loss prevention manager attempting to interview a store or district manager or senior executive whose level

---

1. Butterworth Publishers, Stoneham, Mass., 1980.

of responsibility is far above his, might present an insurmountable barrier to a confession.

Selection of the interviewer in the private sector may be based upon the job level and areas of responsibility of the suspect. Whereas the public law enforcement sector has the legal system and its support to back up an investigator's right to interview or interrogate a suspect, the private loss prevention representative does not have this same legal status. The relative position of the loss prevention investigator in the company will thus dictate those he should interview. In many cases, company policy dictates who will interview upper level management. This is something the public sector must rarely consider.

## Case File and Props

In an interrogation of a suspect, the use of a case file can facilitate a suspect's confession. The case file, which may be nothing more than a file folder containing papers, is the embodiment of the investigation. It is something tangible that the interrogator can touch, look at, and review to add credibility that an in-depth investigation has been conducted, regardless of whether or not it has been in fact undertaken. It is not in the best interests of the interrogator to overplay the case file with props, forms, or video tape cassettes in an attempt to add credibility to the investigation. Overplaying the file can lead to denials by the suspect, or worse, having the suspect ask to be shown the proof of his involvement. It is preferable to keep the file simple, and let the suspect reach erroneous conclusions regarding what it may contain.

In many instances, interrogation of suspects may be conducted with less than absolute proof of their involvement in the issue under investigation. In these situations, the case file can be used as a prop to gesture toward and review when appropriate. At the very least, the case file should contain the materials necessary to complete an interrogation without leaving the room. It should contain paper for notes, consent-to-search forms, statement forms, restitution forms, evidence to be presented to the suspect, and any other pertinent material. The interrogation of a suspect is something that should not be interrupted, and the interrogator should have all the tools necessary to complete his task so that the psychological mindset of the suspect is not diverted from his decision to confess.

It may also be beneficial to have present any evidence that could be identified by a suspect to further implicate himself in the incident under investigation—for example, documents establishing fraud, such as fraudulent refunds or credits, forged checks, or other paperwork needed to commit the crime, weapons, articles of clothing, or pictures. Anytime evidence is brought within reach of a suspect, it should be safeguarded.

*Never leave a case file or evidence unattended with a suspect.* Valuable evidence can be easily destroyed or tampered with, thereby ruining an otherwise airtight case.

## Privacy

Generally, interviewers and interrogators have an opportunity to pre-plan both the time and the location of the interview. The field interview conducted in response to suspicious behavior by suspect(s) is generally conducted at the location of the stop. In these situations, the officer has little, if any, control of the surroundings of his interview. However, the officer should, whenever possible, attempt to establish a zone of privacy in which he can communicate with the suspect. In a field interview the surrounding distractions may interfere with the suspect's concentration on the officer's questions. In addition, the potential for danger through intervention of associates or passers-by complicates the problem. During a field interview in threatening circumstances, an officer's safety is paramount.

The zone of privacy that a field officer establishes can be beneficial in eliciting information from a suspect. In certain situations, a zone of privacy can be established simply by moving the suspect a few feet into an area where the conversation cannot be overheard. This can also be attained by allowing the suspect to join the officer in his squad car. However, department policy may preclude or discourage this practice, unless the suspect has been searched prior to getting into the vehicle with the officer.

In a "stop-and-frisk" interview and a planned field interview, privacy plays a major role in obtaining information from a suspect. Consider for a moment that we are asking a suspect to tell something that perhaps nobody else knows about—a deep, dark secret in his life, a secret, that if found out, might cost him his freedom, his job, or reputation. For example, consider your own preferences if you were to have done something that was either wrong or shameful, and then decided you wanted to talk about it. What would be easier for you to do—Talk to a single person and confide in him about that most embarrassing moment in your life, or to admit to that same embarrassing incident in front of a group of people? Secrets are disclosed in moments of intimacy. It is the single interviewer/interrogator who has established a significant rapport with a suspect who can gain the secret.

Although this noncustodial stop-and-frisk interview in response to suspicious activity is designed to elicit information concerning the reasons for and circumstances surrounding the suspicious behavior, it has several major differences from a formalized interview or interrogation:

1. The spontaneity of the stop and lack of preparation for it
2. The uncertainty of the guilt of the suspects being interviewed
3. Uncertainty of the incident under investigation
4. The necessity to broaden the scope of the interview in an attempt to identify other information that could be used as grounds to establish probable cause for a search or arrest
5. The semiarrest status surrounding a stop-and-frisk interview

In a field interview, the two keys are officer safety and establishing a zone of privacy where the discussion between the officer and the suspect can take place without being overheard.

## Location—Planned Field Interview

In many instances during an investigation, the interviewer will interview victims and potential witnesses in the field. During these interviews, the location of the interview is often out of the hands of the interviewer. In many cases, the interviews are conducted in the supportive environment of the witnesses' homes or places of business. Often, these interviews have multiple distractions, such as phone calls or interruptions by children, that break the continuity of the interview. These distractions often disrupt the interviewer's flow of thought and can allow a suspect time to manufacture a plausible story or explanation. For witnesses, these distractions may cloud an already uncertain memory of the incident.

An integral part of the investigation, the planned field interview can be made more effective with preparation and preplanning. Often, calling ahead to arrange for a convenient time will reduce distractions and may make the witness more receptive to an interview.

On occasion, a suspect will be interviewed in a supportive environment either because he has not yet been identified as the primary suspect in the incident or because it is still in the very earliest stages of the investigation when it is necessary to obtain the suspect's alibi. Regardless of the reason for the interview's being conducted in a supportive environment, the interviewer should still attempt to reduce surrounding distractions and create a zone of privacy that will make the individual more comfortable in talking.

## Room Setting

The privacy and intimacy that an interrogator creates in the interrogation is enhanced by a private setting. This private setting should be arranged so that interruptions and distractions will be minimized and so that a suspect can focus his somewhat divided attention on the interrogator and his words. The interrogator attempts to build a mindset that focuses the suspect's attention on the resolution of the problem and away from the consequences of his actions. Interruptions during a dialogue only reduce the likelihood of success.

In selecting a location for the interrogation or planned interview, the interrogator should consider several points. First, the interrogator should consider the privacy of the particular location in which he has planned to do the interview. The room should be one that will be available for the duration of the interview and that will not allow frequent interruptions by others. Second, the room should be arranged to appear as nonthreatening as possible. The days of the bleak, stark, cold interview room should have passed. Such an environment is alienating to a suspect who is already apprehensive about his presence at the interview. The cold, stark setting only aggravates the suspect's defensiveness and fear of what may happen. Instilling fear into the suspect only increases the likelihood that the suspect will move into a denial phase and makes it even more difficult for the interviewer/interrogator to obtain the information he is after.

An office is a comfortable place where most people have either worked or visited. It is essentially a neutral, nonthreatening environment. Although the office has certain distractions that a "classic" interrogation room may not have, it also provides certain benefits to the interviewer/interrogator. The warmth and comfort of an office tend to reduce the defensiveness of the suspect and remove some resistance to the process of communication. An essential point in the practice of interrogation is not to put a suspect into a defensive posture such that he will want to dig in and defend himself with denials. The office (see Figure 2.1) should be private and have enough chairs for all the participants. An office also has the benefit of reducing the interview's level of seriousness and gives it the appearance of a business meeting rather than a serious confrontation between adversaries, as an interrogation room would connote.

Although the comfortable feeling of the office has a definite impact on the defensiveness of the suspect, the office should not be cluttered. The desk should be cleared of items that the subject may use to distract himself. The room setting should be evaluated for items or distractions that might influence a suspect's behavior and make it difficult for the interviewer to ascertain the reason behind the suspect's behavior. For example, when we discussed how privacy makes it easier for the suspect to confess, it also makes it easier to read a suspect's behavior. A field interview, for example, may be conducted on an open street. Here the officer has little or no control over the surroundings. In such a situation, the breaking of eye contact may be the result of the suspect's lying to the officer, a car's passing, or light going on in a window across the street.

**2.1.** The interrogator (left) should establish a neutral unthreatening environment that reduces the level of seriousness of the meeting.

Thus, the interpretation of the behavior in areas where distractions are allowed adds a variable that makes an accurate determination of the suspect's truthfulness or deception more difficult for the investigator.

## Distractions

If we allow a suspect to smoke or indirectly offer him an opportunity to smoke by leaving an ashtray out, we have added a variable to the interview that complicates our interpretation of his behavior. If, in response to a question, the suspect reaches into his pocket and withdraws a pack of cigarettes, takes one out, and lights it, how does one interpret it? Was this act designed to buy the suspect time to concoct a response, or was it merely his desire for a cigarette?

Leaving pencils, paper clips, or other items on the desk where a suspect can reach over and begin to play with them can create a similar set of variables for the investigator. Does the suspect's attention to the created job of bending the paper clip mean he cannot look at you because he is lying, or is he simply playing with the item? In many cases, a suspect will utilize these methods in an attempt to buy himself time after being asked a question so that he can determine which answer is going to help him.

An additional source of distraction can be reminders of punishment.

These can take many forms, from plaques on the wall to articles of clothing worn by law enforcement officials. In many instances, the gun, badge, handcuffs, or certificates of training can create in the suspect's mind an understanding of the seriousness of the investigation and its consequences.

A detective for a midwestern police department came into the authors' office with a suspect who was suspected of sexually abusing his 18-month-old daughter. While the authors were involved in the interview of the father, the investigator was invited to have a cup of coffee and relax while doing his paperwork. The offices were well lighted and at a comfortable temperature so the officer kept his sport coat on while he awaited the outcome of the interview. During the next hour and a half, he occupied himself doing paperwork and having coffee. One of the authors returned to report on the suspect's confession to the sexual abuse of the child and asked the investigator to come in and witness the suspect's verbal statement. The investigator immediately rose, took off his sport coat and picked up his file to walk into the interview room. This action displayed the officer's badge, handcuffs, and weapon. Whether this action was an indication that he intended to get down to work and resolve the case or whether it was a need on his part to display his authority was never ascertained. However, before he entered the room he was asked to put his coat back on so that the suspect was not faced with the visual impact of the seriousness of his actions.

The discussion of distractions during the interview could be carried out to infinite detail. However, if the interviewer/interrogator merely places himself in the position of the suspect and views the room from the suspect's vantage point, he will easily be able to determine the distractions that may influence the interview or interrogation. Closing the blinds, unplugging the phone, and removing items from the top of the desk can certainly be done without any inconvenience.

In many instances, the interviewer is not lucky enough to have a private office but has to make do with a stockroom in a store, a conference room, or other temporary facility not designed for an interview. Using those facilities requires the same planning as for private office interviews. Preparing for privacy by putting up "Do Not Disturb" signs, taking items off the desk, and arranging the furniture in such a way that the interview can begin as soon as the suspect or witness walks in the door can all be done in advance.

The authors have had an opportunity to interview and interrogate in many different locations, ranging from the street corner to the police department, to the board room of major corporations. The interview and interrogation of suspects is a task with which we are comfortable; however, there have been many occasions when our surroundings were less than adequate. The least favorite interview site is the police interrogation room. The cold, hard feel of the room and the starkness of the surroundings are alienating to a degree that even a veteran interrogator can find uncomfortable. Is it any wonder that a suspect would feel uncomfortable and perhaps defensive in this environment? Although these types of interview holding rooms have their place in the police environment, especially when a suspect is in custody and his freedom of movement has to be limited, it may be beneficial to move the suspect to another office to do the actual interview or interrogation. Obviously, care should be taken to prevent a dangerous or escape-prone prisoner from gaining access to items that could be used as weapons against the interviewer/interrogator.

## Roles of the Interviewer/Interrogator

Recently, a client's husband asked us during dinner, "In five words or less, can you describe what it is that you really do?" After pondering this question for a short time, the response was, "I'm a confident negotiator." The more that we consider this statement, the truer we believe it is. The role of the interviewer/interrogator has traditionally been viewed as adversarial in nature, interrogator versus suspect.

In the traditional view of the interrogator versus the suspect, the two become opponents who can challenge each other. A suspect may in fact direct his anger or frustrations toward the interrogator. The interrogator may be frustrated by the suspect's unwillingness to confess and direct sarcastic or unkind comments toward the suspect.

The interviewer/interrogator has to understand that it is the suspect's job during the interrogation to omit, evade, conceal, lie, and attempt to deceive in every way possible the interviewer/interrogator. By understanding the roles played by the participants in an interview/interrogation, it becomes evident that taking the roles as opponents is counterproductive. The role of the confident mediator allows the interrogator/interviewer to direct hostile feelings, frustrations, and blame away from the interrogator, to the law, the criminal justice system, the company, or some other entity.

The successful interrogator takes on the role of the mediator–negotiator, negotiating from a position of confidence, confidence not only that he can resolve the problem, but also that he can understand the suspect and believe in the facts of the case. The mediator acts as a go-between, someone who can find common ground in any situation without appearing to take sides. Think of the interview/interrogation process as a well-planned play. The interrogator/interviewer has an opportunity to choreograph the movements, the setting, and some of the dialogue of the play about to be acted out. He considers and arranges the room setting and location of the interview to his advantage.

He thinks about his appearance. Many interrogators have the mistaken belief that they should be dressed in a suit and tie and look the absolute professional at all times. Although this may be true in certain circumstances, the interrogator must also give consideration to the needs of the suspect. The interrogator should have the ability to change his appearance depending upon the person to whom he is speaking. For example, if the authors were going to interrogate a senior vice president of purchasing on a kickback scheme, they are dealing with someone of power and must dress as well as, if not better than, the suspect to make them equals. In other instances, such formal dressing only increases the defensiveness of the suspect and may not be in the best interest of the interrogator.

In his book *Spy vs. Spy*,[2] Ronald Kessler discussed counterintelligence activities and security breaches in the United States. It is interesting to note the preparation of the setting, demeanor, and dress of the agents as they planned for a confrontation with a suspected traitor. The Behavioral Science Unit of the FBI helped plan the interview approach that took these factors into account.

In dealing with a younger person who is perhaps less educated than the interrogator, it may not be in the best interest of the interviewer/interrogator to be dressed in a suit and tie. In this situation, it might be to their advantage to appear in shirt sleeves with the tie loosened or even in a sport shirt and pair of slacks or skirt.

Consider what attitude is likely to be taken by the suspect. By anticipating what the attitude will be, the interviewer can often counter the suspect. In anticipating behavior such as anger, suspicion, sullenness, or contempt, the interviewer can plan to fit his image to the needs of the suspect and modify his actions and dress appropriately.

## Language

Looking at the process of interview and interrogation reveals many similarities to a sales function. In selling, the salesperson must identify the needs of his customer. These needs could include the image, financial, or emotional needs of the customer or his corporation. Once the salesperson has identified the needs of the client, he now highlights the benefits of his product that answer the client's needs. If the product's benefits outweigh any objections that the client has, and the product meets his needs, both personal and corporate, he will make the purchase. If not, he won't buy. Similarly, in an interrogation, if the perceived benefits of giving the information, either from a witness or suspect's

---

2. Pocket Books, New York, 1980.

point of view don't override his objections to giving this information, he won't talk.

Central to selling a suspect on confessing is the level of rapport and communication that the interviewer/interrogator achieves with the suspect. When we communicate with other individuals, it is imperative that they understand what we are talking about. It is always preferable to speak simply. People will never look down on another individual because he talks clearly and simply. What does cause problems is when someone talks above the educational level of another person or uses words improperly during a conversation.

An interviewer or interrogator who attempts to talk above a suspect's intellect faces the problem that the suspect may not understand what is being asked. This compounds the problems of an already difficult situation during which the interviewer has been attempting to establish rapport and read a suspect's behavior for deception. Should the suspect fail to understand what is being asked and therefore delays answering to consider the question, the interviewer is forced to decide whether the delay is an attempt at deception or not. In addition, the witness or suspect may interpret the interviewer/interrogator as trying to be superior, thus alienating that person.

Many interviewers/interrogators attempt to use street language or street slang in an attempt to establish a rapport with the suspect. In our experience, only rarely does this have positive benefits, primarily because few interviewer/interrogators can successfully pull it off. In most instances when an interviewer or interrogator attempts to use street language, it only diminishes their credibility in the eyes of the suspect. The suspect views this use of language as a phony front by the interviewer/interrogator. They recognize that it is unlikely the interviewer or interrogator actually speaks in this manner in day-to-day conversations.

The suspect or witness has to make a decision on whether or not to talk about what they know. Part of their decision and, often the critical part, is the suspect's evaluation of the person who is questioning them. In instances where they see a phoniness or dialogue that obviously does not match the person seated in front of them, they become suspicious. This only undermines the role that the interviewer/interrogator is attempting to achieve.

The interviewer/interrogator maintains his professional role, and his language should match the level of professionalism he has attained. The use of curse words or derogatory terms during an interview/interrogation often is counterproductive. Even if a suspect repeatedly curses and uses vile language, the interviewer/interrogator should refrain from doing likewise. The suspect's behavior is often an attempt to provoke a similar response in the interviewer to which he can then take exception and become angry. If the suspect can draw the interrogator into making a response to which he can take exception, the suspect has then succeeded in making the interviewer/interrogator an opponent rather than the mediator.

A final note on language and communications with a suspect: Consider the process of interview and interrogation as psychologically reducing the seriousness of the incident under investigation and justifying the actions of a suspect. This allows a suspect to perceive a reduction in the seriousness of his violation. The interrogator, during the interview and/or interrogation, can unwittingly reinforce the seriousness of the incident by his tone of voice and selection of words. In any conversation, the tone of voice can transmit to the other party an underlying meaning that may be totally opposite of the words used.

Consider the example in which a husband comes home and asks his wife, "How was your day?" She responds, "Fine."

Verbally, the word that she has chosen indicates that her day has been successful and nothing out of the ordinary has happened. If the tone of voice chosen by her was lilting and lighthearted, it substantiates the fact that she has in fact had a good day.

That same response "Fine," used in a short and clipped manner, however, contradicts the meaning of the word itself. She has given an appropriate response that her day was fine, but the tone of voice accompanying the word was a contradiction that would lead us to believe that her day has not gone well. This initial conclusion may be further validated by other physical gestures and behaviors accompanying the response, "Fine." Sharp, jerky movements and rattling of pans would support the conclusion that all has not gone well.

In the same way, an interviewer/interrogator can be seen by the suspect as being accusatory, rude, or frivolous in a serious manner when the interviewer has no intention of being any of those. Since a vast amount of human communication occurs below the surface of the actual words through the tone of voice, speed of delivery, and the physical behaviors associated with the spoken word, an interviewer/interrogator can convey meanings both intentional and unintentional along with the spoken word. In some instances these tones can provide a valuable communication tool for the interviewer/interrogator who can convey another meaning without actually having to say the words that might otherwise inflame a volatile situation.

Think for a moment about the way in which you speak to another person when you want to display disbelief, ask a question, make an accusation, or restate a fact. A valuable exercise in communication, which can be done quite simply by the reader, is to speak into a tape recorder and listen to the tone of voice, speed of delivery, and word selections that are used. Many times, people are surprised to hear their own voice and may at first not recognize it. Imagine for a moment that it is not you speaking, but an interviewer. Ask yourself, how does the voice sound, what meaning is actually being conveyed. One of the finest learning tools available to an interviewer is to tape actual interviews and interrogations. The review of these tapes provides valuable insight into the ways he can improve. Before doing this, however, the interviewer should review department policy and state law to ascertain whether or not taping is permitted.

Consider also the choice of words utilized by the interviewer/interrogator. Harsh words that attach connotations of punishment recreate the seriousness of the incident under investigation. Using words like kill, rape, embezzle, fraud, and theft, all recall in the suspect's, victim's, or witness's mind, the seriousness of the issue.

The process of rationalization is designed to minimize the seriousness of the incident in the suspect's or witness's mind. An interviewer/interrogator who repeatedly utilizes harsh words only defeats this purpose. As interrogators, we should take a lesson from the suspects and reduce the seriousness of the incident by using less descriptive terms. We might, for example, use terms such as, "this thing," "it," "took," or "did him."

A cardinal rule is to attempt to communicate on the same level as your suspect. If he is in fact attempting to minimize the seriousness of what he has done through the use of these words, it only benefits the interrogator to follow suit and attempt to minimize the crime's seriousness as well.

The guilty tend to use words that justify what they have done: "borrowed" instead of steal; "done" instead of killed. This is the same thing the media does when describing a story. During a war, to make the losses of human life more palatable, they called it a "body count" rather than the death of human beings. If the media wants to highlight the viciousness of the crime, they use words like "massacre," or "brutalize," words that highlight the seriousness of what has actually happened.

## Taking Notes

A common occurrence during the interview and interrogation process is for the interviewer/interrogator to take notes. In the earliest stage of an interview, note-taking is generally not in the best interest of the interviewer. It is essential that the interviewer gain a rapport with a suspect, victim, or witness before he attempts to write down any of the information obtained. Most people, through TV and media exposure, expect an interviewer to take some notes during the interview. It is generally preferable to have gained the information first, then go back over and recreate your notes with the suspect during a second review of the facts.

The notes taken during a nonaccusatory interview may have evidentiary value and should be comprehensive in reporting what was said. During note-taking, the interviewer should note who was present, the time and place of the interview, and the correct spelling of the names of all present. The correct spelling of names and addresses should be obtained at the conclusion of the interview. Writing down a witness's or suspect's name and address immediately may be likely to reduce their cooperation.

Should an interview turn into a situation where the interrogator is attempting to elicit information of an adverse or incriminating nature from the suspect, the note-taking should cease and the pen and paper be put away. Taking notes at this point can remind the suspect that everything he says is on permanent record. Instead of note-taking, the interrogator focuses on offering the suspect face-saving rationalizations. Note-taking can resume after the confession has resulted and the interrogator has developed the admission into the totality of the circumstances surrounding the incident(s) in which the suspect was involved.

## Strategies

The person responsible for conducting any interview or interrogation should have the overall responsibility for establishing a strategy for it. This strategy should consider the order of interviews, the timing of the interviews, and the plans for handling simultaneous multiple interviews.

One of the most difficult types of interrogations is that of a single suspect who has no coconspirators. This is because the single suspect alone is fully aware of his exposure based on what he has or has not told others.

In collusion cases where multiple suspects are acting together, it is usually easier to interrogate because the interrogator can play one suspect against another, none of whom has the full knowledge of what has or will be said. Collusion cases tend to be similar to knocking down a row of dominoes. Once you are able to push one over, the others generally follow by falling in order.

Deciding who should be interrogated first is usually approached by two separate strategies. The first strategy consists of identifying the individual who, based on his background and personality, appears most likely to confess. By confronting the weak link in the chain initially, the interrogator hopes that information this suspect provides can be used against the stronger personalities or more street-sharp individuals. The second strategy consists of identifying the most difficult suspects, the ones that the interviewer feels will be least likely to confess during an interrogation.

With especially difficult suspects the investigation close is timed to coincide with the suspect's being apprehended in the act. In doing so, their resistance is significantly weakened due to the circumstances of their apprehensions.

### Case Example

During an undercover operation at an electronics and appliance warehouse, a number of employees were identified as being involved in a theft ring. These employees, working with drivers, would move merchandise onto the dock. At the end of the day, they would load the merchandise that was to be stolen onto the now empty trucks for delivery to an apartment that had been rented as a storage facility.

Based on the information available, it was decided that the investigation would be closed at a time when two opportune investigative objectives could be achieved: first, that one of the more difficult primary suspects would be caught in the act, and second, that the apprehension would take place at the apartment being utilized for storage. This way, two results would be achieved: first, the initial resistance of a difficult suspect would be overcome, and second, there would develop an opportunity either to look into the apartment or to establish the grounds for a search of the apartment.

The apprehension was made as the primary suspect and helper attempted to carry a 25-inch color TV into the apartment. At that time, the suspect and the driver's helper were separated and returned to the warehouse to be interviewed.

The primary suspect's first words were, "The paperwork is in the truck." On returning to the truck with the TV, the other stolen merchandise—a freezer, washer and dryer—were recovered. When the suspect was unable to produce the paperwork for the stolen goods, he immediately denied stealing anything. Shortly thereafter, he admitted that he had stolen these items and it was his first time. He also stated that the other individual with him had no knowledge of what was transpiring.

During a subsequent interview back at the warehouse, the suspect acknowledged additional theft activities and implicated other employees in the warehouse. The two suspects were turned over to the local police for prosecution. During the remainder of the case closure, approximately twelve other employees were interviewed regarding their involvement in theft activity at the warehouse. These interviews resulted in six additional felony prosecutions and terminations of twelve employees.

Anticipating a suspect's response to an accusation and planning for it as a preinterrogation strategy will often allow an interrogator to obtain a confession from people who would not ordinarily confess.

# Legal Aspects

3

*Legal precedents change and the interviewer
must constantly be aware of decisions that
have an impact on his job.*

This chapter is intended to review the key areas of law that form the guidelines that define the boundaries of how an interview or interrogation must be conducted. This chapter is not meant to cover all the details of law, but rather to highlight general principles applicable to the process. Legal precedents change and the interviewer must constantly be aware of decisions that have an impact on his job. The interviewer/interrogator should regularly ask for interpretation and direction from prosecutors or corporate counsel. Asking for clarification is preferable to proceeding without direction. Textbooks cannot remain current with the ever-changing court decisions, so the professional interviewer/interrogator must constantly update himself on the ever changing local and federal laws and company policy.

## Who Are You?

The first step in determining which rules an interviewer/interrogator is to play by is to define what, in fact, his job is. Traditionally, those individuals employed by local, state, and federal agencies are deemed to be in the public sector and are required to follow the rules and regulations set down by the law relating to arrest, search, seizure and interrogation. In most cases these same rules and court decisions apply to private sector employees who have been granted special powers of arrest. For example, this applies to railroad police officers, university campus police, or any private employee who has been empowered with special police powers by the local jurisdiction. Also bound by these rules are private sector employees who act as agents for the police during an investigation. Acting as an agent for the police would entail performing some type of action at the direction of a law enforcement officer. As an agent of the police then, the employee is required to follow the arrest and search and seizure decisions of the courts and legislature.

Those individuals employed in the private sector who have no affiliation with a public law enforcement agency typically do not have to concern themselves with the issues of *Miranda*, right to counsel, or search issues. The private sector interrogator who intends to prosecute cases that he develops should contact the local prosecutor to determine any special requirements he may have for case preparation. Some local prosecutors require private sector interrogators to give *Miranda* to a suspect even though it is not required under the *Miranda* decision. However, off-duty law enforcement officials "moonlighting" in the private sector must still comply with the restrictions placed on public sector employees. Private sector employees involved in investigations may be less concerned with the ultimate prosecution of an individual and focus instead on the termination of his employment and recovery of the assets of the company. The private sector interviewer/interrogator must be concerned with the policies and procedures set down by company management and the personnel department as well as the rulings of labor arbitrators in conducting interviews and interrogations with employees.

Some private sector investigators such as railroad police officers, special agents for utilities, campus police, and others have the public law enforcement officer's power of arrest, search, and seizure. However, they are also directed by policies and procedures set by their employer and potentially by the contracts with the unions servicing the company's employees. Thus, they may have the additional responsibility of presenting a case to a labor arbitrator regarding a policy or procedural violation of company rules. For example, railroad special agents might present evidence gathered during an investigation into an employee's drinking alcohol during working hours. Discipline, as a result of the investigator's findings, could result in suspension or termination of the employee's employment. Because of union contracts, any discipline might later be appealed to an arbitrator for review. The interviewer/interrogator employed by the private sector, yet having the powers of arrest granted them by statute, may face a conflict in objectives due to their special status.

The scope of the case also differs between the public and private law enforcement sectors. Generally, public sector law enforcement is specifically focused on a particular act or group of acts that are clearly defined by the investigation (i.e., the victim was raped and murdered on

January 29). In the private sector the scope of the investigation may be equally well defined, such as focusing on the theft of $7,000 deposit on a specific date, or be less clearly defined, such as looking into acts that are committed in violation of a number of company policies (i.e., a store has an inventory shortage of 5.2% since the last inventory. This means that 5.2% of its inventory in relation to its sales at that location are missing for any of a variety of reasons: paperwork errors, shoplifting, or employee theft). There may also be issues that are not necessarily criminal in nature, but rather violate company policy, such as a sexual harassment claim made by one employee of the company against another.

## Constitutional Amendments

The basis for the legal decisions in the United States is the Constitution and its amendments. The Supreme Court of the United States reviews cases in light of the guarantees granted by the constitution and legal precedents. The following excerpts from the Fourth, Fifth, Sixth, and Fourteenth Amendments provide an understanding for some of the court's basic rulings relating to interview and interrogation.

### Fourth Amendment

The right of the people to be secure in their persons, houses, papers and effects, and against unreasonable searches and seizures, shall not be violated, and no warrant shall issue, but upon probable cause, supported by oath or affirmation, and particularly describing the place to be searched, and the person or things to be seized.

### Fifth Amendment

No person...shall be compelled in any criminal case to be a witness against himself, nor be deprived of life, liberty, or property without due process of law...

### Sixth Amendment

In all criminal prosecutions, the accused shall enjoy the right...to be confronted with Witnesses against him; have compulsory process for obtaining witnesses in his favor, and to have assistance of counsel for his defense.

### Fourteenth Amendment

All persons born or naturalized in the United States, and subject to the jurisdiction thereof, are citizens of the United States and of the state wherein they reside. No state shall make or enforce any law which shall abridge the privileges or immunities of citizens of the United States; nor shall any state deprive any person of life, liberty, or property, without due process of law; nor deny to any person within its jurisdiction the equal protection of the laws...

These four amendments provide the basis for the courts' rulings in many of the landmark cases. The Fourth Amendment is the basis for the Exclusionary Rule, which excludes evidence that has been improperly or illegally seized. The Fifth grants the citizen the right to remain silent, and the Sixth gives him the right to counsel to represent him in proceedings against him. The Fourteenth Amendment grants each citizen the due process of the law.

## Public Sector Rules

One of the earliest cases that directly related to the interrogation of a criminal suspect by police was *Brown v. Mississippi*.[1] The United States Supreme Court found in this case that the police had obtained the confession from Brown through the use of "third degree tactics." The Court ruled that the resulting confession was inadmissible as evidence in the case. In its decision, the Supreme Court applied the Fourteenth Amendment Due Process Clause, ruling that a confession is admissible only if it is voluntary. Therefore, to admit an involuntary confession into evidence is to deprive a citizen of his liberty without due process of law. This decision does not deal with the trustworthiness of the suspect's statement, but whether it was voluntarily given by the suspect. *Brown v. Mississippi* was the first state confession case that used the federal constitutionally guaranteed rights and made them applicable to the states and thus, state and local investigators. An accused is deprived of due process if his conviction rests partially or completely on an involuntary confession, as in *Lego v. Twomey*.[2] The deprivation of due process could occur even if the suspect's statement was true, as in *Rogers v. Richmond*,[3] and even if there was substantial corroborating evidence of the suspect's guilt (see *Payne v. Arkansas*[4]).

Once the United States Supreme Court applied the Fourteenth Amendment Due Process Clause to the states, the Fifth and Sixth Amendments to the United States Constitution were also made applicable to the states. This application created decisions that were especially pertinent to the public law enforcement officer. These rulings

---

1. Brown v. Mississippi, 297 U.S. 278 (1936)
2. Lego v. Twomey, 404 U.S. 477 (1972)
3. Rogers v. Richmond, 365 U.S. 534 (1961)
4. Payne v. Arkansas, 356 U.S. 560 (1958)

related to the suspect's privilege against self-incrimination and his right to counsel. What followed were rules that were applicable to the states. Today, the landmark decisions of *Escobedo* and *Massiah*, both Sixth Amendment right-to-counsel issues, and *Miranda*, the Fifth Amendment right against self-incrimination, are all applicable to the state and local law enforcement officers as they interview and interrogate.

In these three landmark cases, the court set down specific rules and guidelines that a public law enforcement officer had to follow to protect the rights of a suspect.

## Voluntariness

Although *Escobedo*, *Massiah*, and *Miranda* overshadowed the voluntariness rule for testing the admissibility of a confession, it is still the voluntariness of the confession that is the fundamental issue in determining the admissibility of a confession. Unfortunately, although the courts have provided guidelines for the officer in *Escobedo*, *Massiah*, and *Miranda* decisions, determining the voluntariness of a confession is much less clear. To determine whether a confession is voluntary, there are no specific rules to follow or apply. Rather, the court has used as a test the "totality of circumstances." Here the courts view the circumstances and environment surrounding a suspect who gives a confession. The courts take into account the methods employed in obtaining the confession, the suspect's physical and mental condition, the length of time over which questioning took place, and the suspect's age, education, and previous experience with law enforcement agencies before making a determination of whether the confession was voluntary.

The courts have made it very clear that the use of physical force or physical abuse or even the threat of this type of conduct on the part of police will render a confession involuntary. Depriving a suspect of sleep, rest, food, or drink for substantial periods while he is being interrogated would make any resulting confession highly questionable.

However, the courts have also ruled that the use of trickery or lying by an officer to obtain a confession does not necessarily invalidate the confession. In the case *Frazier v. Cupp*,[5] the court upheld a conviction based on a confession where the officer used trickery and lying to elicit a confession. The defendant who was suspected of a homicide was told that his accomplice had confessed. This was completely untrue. The Supreme Court ruled in its opinion that the mere fact that the police had misrepresented a statement, i.e., that the suspected accomplice had

---

5. Frazier v. Cupp, 394 U.S. 731, 89 S.CT. 1420 (1969)

confessed, was insufficient to make the confession involuntary. The court also stated that the voluntariness of a confession must be decided on a case-by-case basis, viewing "the totality of circumstances" surrounding the confession made by a suspect.

The danger to a prosecution in obtaining an involuntary confession goes past its exclusion at trial. Evidence developed as a result of the confession may also be inadmissible because of the Exclusionary Rule. As a "fruit of the poisonous tree," evidence developed as a result of an inadmissible confession may also be excluded, unless it can be shown that it would have been discovered independent of the confession.

### The *Miranda* Rule

Simply described, *Miranda* could be said to be warnings to a suspect administered during a custodial interrogation. For *Miranda* to be applicable to an interrogation, it must meet two criteria. First, the setting must be custodial in nature. The court has defined custodial to mean that the suspect's freedom of action has been curtailed in some significant way. Second, the individual conducting the interrogation must be a law enforcement officer or acting as an agent for a law enforcement officer.

Should a custody situation arise, the suspect must be advised of the following: his right to an attorney, his right against self-incrimination, and his right to remain silent. If a suspect is taken into custody by police and questioned without advising him of his *Miranda* rights, his responses cannot be used in evidence against him to establish his guilt.[6] However, the court ruled in *Harris v. New York* that statements made by a suspect after questioning without advising him of the *Miranda* warnings, may still be used to later impeach a defendant's credibility should he elect to testify at trial.[7]

### The Warnings

After each warning, the officer must determine whether the suspect has understood what he has been told. The suspect has the following rights[8]:

1. He has the right to remain silent
2. Anything he says may be used against him
3. He has the right to an attorney

---

6. Estelle v. Smith, 451 U.S. 454 (1981)
7. Harris v. New York, 401 U.S. 222 (1971)
8. Note: The exact wordings of the warnings should be read from a card, or form approved by the officer's department or prosecutor. Because of local variations in wording, as well as the inclusion of a fifth warning by some departments, the exact wordings have been omitted.

4. Should he not be able to afford an attorney, one would be provided for him without charge

Only upon the waiver of these rights by the suspect can an interrogation occur. Awareness of these rights will help to ensure the courts that the confession is a knowing and intelligent decision by the suspect.

The Supreme Court ruling in *Miranda* also found that a suspect could waive these rights at any time during the interrogation. As a result of this portion of the decision, many agencies added a fifth warning that was not required by the court. This fifth warning basically asked the suspect to acknowledge that he understood the rights he had available and that he could stop talking to the officer at any time and demand a lawyer at any time. Many departments also have taken the stance that the suspect should sign a written waiver on which he initials each of the warnings signifying his understanding of them and then signs the entire document. This, however, was not required by the court, but rather is an attempt by departments to help show that there was a knowing and intelligent waiver by the suspect.

A commonly held misunderstanding is that the mere focusing of suspicion on a suspect required that the *Miranda* warnings be administered. In *Beckwith v. United States*,[9] the court found that the issue of custody was the test and not merely the focus of suspicion on an individual.

The focus of suspicion issue was carried a step further in the case of *Oregon v. Mathiason*,[10] where a suspect was invited into a police station to discuss his involvement in a burglary. During the course of this discussion at the police station, he was told that he was not under arrest and could leave at any time. Subsequently, the suspect made a confession to the burglary. He was then allowed to leave the station after making his damaging admissions. The detective later obtained a warrant and arrested Mathiason for the burglary. In this case, the court ruled that since the suspect was not in custody at the time of the confession, the need to give *Miranda* warnings was not present. However, if the suspect would have been arrested had he elected to leave, this then would generally require that the *Miranda* warnings be given.

In the strict sense, if a suspect is not under arrest, there is no need for an officer to advise a suspect of his rights. However, from a practical standpoint, it may be advisable to warn the suspect. Defense counsels often use *Miranda* as a smoke screen to confuse the issue once in court. Also, the interrogation of a suspect on a serious issue such as homicide might make it preferable for the officer to advise a suspect because of

---

9. Beckwith v. United States, 425 U.S. 341
10. Oregon v. Mathiason, 429 U.S. 492 (1977)

later advantages it might give the prosecutor. In serious crimes, the prosecutor should be consulted if there is a question as to whether to advise a suspect of his rights before questioning.

## Suspect Waiver

As a general rule, it is preferable that the accused verbalize his understanding of the *Miranda* warnings. The nodding of the accused's head *might* also be acceptable, but it is usually preferable for the suspect to respond verbally. Depending on the suspect's age, education, and experience with the criminal justice system, it may also be beneficial to ask additional questions that will help satisfy the court's need to establish that the suspect understood his rights prior to the waiver and knowingly waived them.

At any time during an interrogation following the reading of the waiver of the *Miranda* rights, a suspect may make a demand for counsel or assert his right of silence. Once either of these rights is invoked, all questioning must cease. The officer can make no attempts to convince the accused to give up the constitutional rights that he has elected to exercise. Some officers in the past have at a later point asked a suspect if he has changed his mind about talking; however, this is dangerous ground and could easily result in a confession's being ruled inadmissible. In *Edwards v. Arizona,*[11] the court made it abundantly clear that once a suspect invokes the right of counsel, all questioning must cease, unless the suspect's attorney is present or the suspect initiates any subsequent conversation. In December 1990, the Supreme Court extended the protection of *Miranda* even further in its decision of *Minnick v. Mississippi.*[12] Minnick was arrested for murder and his interrogation ended when he requested an attorney. He was allowed to meet with his attorney two or three times. He later confessed to a deputy sheriff and was convicted and sentenced to death. The court held that once counsel is requested the interrogation must cease and may not begin again until counsel is present. Even after the suspect has had an opportunity to consult with his attorney no questioning can resume without his attorney's being present. This new rule makes it almost impossible for the police to urge a suspect who has invoked *Miranda* to change his mind. Once a suspect invokes *Miranda,* a permanent prohibition against interrogation begins, unless counsel is present.

Failure to administer a *Miranda* warning will not always result in the suppression of a confession. Currently, there is only one single public safety exception to the *Miranda* rule. This exception is in *New York v.*

---

11. Edwards v. Arizona, 451 U.S. 477 101 S.CT. 1880 68 L. ED. 2d 378 (1981)
12. Minnick v. Mississippi, 89-6332, Cited 51CCH S.Ct. BULL. p. B313-336

*Quarles.*[13] Here, the court adopted a public safety exception that covers situations where the concern for public safety must override the officers adherence to the rule of *Miranda.*

*New York v. Quarles* dealt with a rape suspect's being questioned about the location of a gun that the victim said he had. Because there was an immediate need for the police to locate the gun to protect themselves and the public from harm, the court ruled that this overrode the failure of the officer to immediately administer *Miranda* warnings before he asked questions regarding the location of the weapon. In this ruling, the court determined that no matter what the officer's actual intent in asking the question might be, if the question could reasonably be prompted by a concern for his own or the public's safety then the response would be deemed admissible by the court. This exception allows the street officer to respond to the needs of public safety when circumstances warrant, but still protect the suspect's rights with an objective test the courts can apply. It would be a mistake for the officer to use this as a crutch to avoid the administration of a suspect's rights.

## The *Massiah* and *Escobedo* Rules

The difference between *Massiah, Escobedo,* and *Miranda* lies in the right to counsel. In *Miranda,* the right to counsel is significant in that it assists a suspect in exercising his right to silence. However, in *Massiah* and *Escobedo,* the suspect's right to silence is secondary to the suspect's right to counsel.

*Massiah* concerns the right to counsel after the suspect has been indicted; however, this has expanded through other cases and makes it clear that *Massiah* is now applicable any time counsel has entered the picture in defense of a suspect. Based on the *Massiah* and *Escobedo* rulings, it is evident that law enforcement officers must take extreme care when questioning any defendant who is represented by counsel. The waiver of rights made by a suspect after counsel has been retained will be difficult to show, unless it can be clearly established that it was done at the instigation of the accused and not the police (see Minnick v. Mississippi,[12] expansion of *Miranda* protection).

## Youths and Incompetents

When can a young person or a mentally incompetent individual give a knowing waiver of his constitutional rights? This question addresses two issues. The first is voluntariness, and the second the mental

---

13. New York v. Quarles, U.S. 104 S.CT. 2626 81L. ED. 2d 550 (1984)

capabilities of the youth. The courts have generally ruled that a person of young age can give a voluntary confession and knowingly waive his constitutional rights. However, the actual age of the suspect is not necessarily the critical factor. In determining whether or not the waiver was voluntary, the court looks at prior experience with police or the judicial system. This prior experience with law enforcement and the judicial system can overcome the suspect's young chronological age. A youth's age does, however, become a factor when there is a lack of experience with the criminal justice system. The lack of experience and immaturity bring into question whether he can evaluate the ramifications of a confession.

Although many youths will not have had any experience with the law enforcement community, their education can take the place of contact with the law. Given a school-acquired understanding of the governmental process and the rights he can exercise under the Constitution should allow the youth to make the same competent decision an adult or delinquent would under similar circumstances.

Many states have legislated juvenile acts that place certain requirements on public law enforcement officers to notify the parent or legal guardian, without any unnecessary delay, when a juvenile has been taken into custody. In many instances, the juvenile acts also require the officer to turn the minor over to a juvenile officer who has been specifically designated to handle juvenile problems. A confession by a youth prior to either of these circumstances' taking place may bear on the voluntariness of the confession given by a juvenile.

Whether or not a suspect is mentally incompetent is a decision for the court to judge during a competency hearing. The suspect who is judged mentally incompetent cannot knowingly understand and/or waive his constitutional rights. If, in fact, this was the case, it would also be unlikely that he would be able to participate in his own defense prior to and during trial. The officer does not have any choice but to go through the *Miranda* procedures. The officer should maintain a detailed record of what was said to and by the suspect, along with notes concerning his condition and demeanor at the time that the confession was given. The ultimate determination of mental competency and whether a person was legally insane during the commission of the crime yet later competent to give a voluntary confession is up to the court. The officer's sole responsibility is to gather evidence and accurately report that evidence to the court.

## Alcohol or Narcotics Intoxication

Intoxication is not generally a defense, although it may speak to the lack of a specific intent to commit a crime. The real question addresses the mental competency of the suspect. Simply because an individual is more likely to confess if intoxicated does not mean he is mentally incapable of giving a valid confession. The burden falls on the suspect to show that his confession was involuntary and untrue. He also must prove that he was intoxicated to the point of being unconscious of the meaning of the words he used when confessing. For example, in *People v. Sleboda*,[14] the defendant was able to stand and answer questions following an automobile accident. In addition, he was concerned for other family members and showed an awareness of the accident that had taken place.

The suspect attempted to use the defense that he was so intoxicated that he could not knowingly waive his rights. The court found that for the defendant to be able to use this defense, he would have to be so grossly intoxicated that he could not waive his rights. However, in light of the factual testimony relating to his concern shown for family members and his awareness of the circumstances surrounding the accident, the court found that the defendant's statements were knowingly and voluntarily given.

A suspect should *never* be given any alcoholic beverages or illegal drugs prior to or during the course of an interrogation. Administering alcohol or illegal drugs to a suspect is unprofessional and may open the department and officer to litigation as a result of this action. Typically, the administration of any medications should be done only on the instructions of competent medical staff.

### Tricks and Promises

An officer's promise to a suspect of more lenient treatment or sentence, based on cooperation, could provide an innocent person an opportunity to confess when there is strong circumstantial evidence. The courts have established a general rule that the promise of leniency to a suspect will nullify any subsequent confession. However, a promise by the interrogator to discuss the suspect's cooperation with the prosecutor is permissible. Other examples of promises that would not make a confession inadmissible would be an interrogator's promise to seek psychiatric treatment for the suspect or recommend a lower bail for the suspect.

Some states have enacted specific statutes regarding the use of promises during an interrogation. These constitutional statutes would supersede any other court rulings.

### Public Employers

The United States Supreme Court in a series of decisions has forced public employers to apply the Fifth Amendment right against self-in-

---

14. People v. Sleboda, 166 Illinois APP. 3d 42, 519 N.E. 2D512 116 Illinois DEC.620 (1988)

crimination to their employees. Public employers cannot force employees to choose between their Fifth Amendment rights of silence and losing their jobs. The first case relating to this issue was a New Jersey case, *Garrity v. New Jersey*.[15] In *Garrity v. New Jersey*, police officers were subjected to dismissal if they refused to answer questions on the grounds that the answers to those questions could tend to incriminate them.

In *Garrity*, the police officers answered the questions and were subsequently prosecuted for conspiracy to obstruct the administration of traffic laws. At trial they sought to exclude the statements that they had made from any criminal proceedings on the grounds that the statements had been coerced in violation of the Fifth Amendment. The United States Supreme Court found that the statements were, in fact, coerced and as a result should be excluded at trial.

In 1968, the United States Supreme Court once again looked at the Fifth Amendment and the coercion of a statement from a public employee. In *Gardner v. Broderick*, [16] a police officer was to appear before a grand jury investigation, but the police officer refused to sign a waiver of immunity from prosecution. As a result of this refusal to sign the waiver, he was subsequently discharged from the force. The Supreme Court saw a significant difference between this case and *Garrity*. The primary difference between the two was the officer's refusal to testify after he was told that he would not be subject to prosecution for any incriminating statements he made to the grand jury, as opposed to the circumstances in *Garrity* where the threat of termination coerced the officer's statements.

Determining whether or not the Fifth Amendment right against self-incrimination is applicable is directly related to whether or not a prosecution is contemplated. In instances where the officer is to be disciplined administratively rather than through the criminal justice system, the officer has no right to remain silent without its affecting his employment. Once the decision has been made to approach the case from a criminal prosecution standpoint, the public employer must advise the employee of his rights. Therefore, the officer should be alerted that any incriminating statements he makes can be used against him at trial.

### Private Employers

The United States Supreme Court has made a distinction between public and private employers in the application of the Fifth Amendment. As long as the private employer or its employees are not acting as agents

---

15. Garrity v. New Jersey, 385 U.S. 493, 17 L Ed 2d 562, 87 S Ct 616 (1967)
16. Gardner v. Broderick, 392 U.S. 273, 20LEd2d 1082, 88S Ct1913 (1968)

for public law enforcement, the Supreme Court has ruled that the Fifth Amendment generally does not apply to private employers. In the first case relating to this issue, *Gardner v. Broderick,*[16] the court clearly distinguished the difference between a public and private sector employee. The court ruled that there are few employment situations where the employee does not agree to take the employment on the terms that are offered him; thus, the constitutional rights are generally not protected when dealing with a private employer. However, the Supreme Court has clearly set up the guidelines under which *Miranda* warnings are required: The warnings are required when 1) questioning is begun by law enforcement officers; and 2) the individual has been taken into custody or has been deprived of his freedom in some significant way. A landmark case relating to the nonapplicability of *Miranda* warnings to the private sector came in a California case, *People v. Deborah C.,*[17] a juvenile.

In this case, a plain clothes store detective detained a 15-year-old female after observing her leaving the store without paying for some jewelry. She was taken to the loss prevention office and placed under a citizen's arrest without being given a *Miranda* warning.

The California Supreme Court distinguished in its decision between the state involvement created when loss prevention acts in the law enforcement sector and that same loss prevention investigator is interrogating someone. The interrogation of someone is an action that in and of itself is not illegal. The California Supreme Court looked upon the *Miranda* decision as the U.S. Supreme Court's response to "third degree" tactics used to obtain confessions. "Third degree" tactics are considered physical abuse or the threats of physical abuse, duress, coercion and length of the interrogation. The court found no evidence of abusive techniques by loss prevention agents that would require *Miranda.*

The court concluded that the private loss prevention or security function was not required to follow the *Miranda* warnings before eliciting an admission that could be used in a later trial. The noncustodial setting and the differences in psychological advantages between law enforcement and private sector investigators allowed the California Supreme Court to conclude that private and public employers who interview their employees about job-related events in a noncustodial setting need not administer the *Miranda* warnings.

## Sixth Amendment: Right to an Attorney

The employer, public or private, conducting an interview in a noncus-

---

17. People v. Deborah C., 30CAL3d 125, 177CAL RPTR852, 635P2d446 (1981)

todial setting does not have to advise the employee of his right to counsel. However, if the employee is protected by a collective bargaining agreement, the right to a representative may include the implied right to select an attorney to represent him during the subsequent grievance proceedings. The public employer who is faced with questioning an employee potentially to be charged criminally must provide for due process, as must the private employer with a union agreement that may require an attorney to be present. Private employers can force an employee to choose between having an attorney present or discontinuing the interview. If the interview is discontinued, the employee should be advised that any decision relating to his employment will be based on the information available to the company. However, the interrogator and the company should be aware that there may be some potential liability with this tactic since an employee may file suit for negligent discharge alleging that the company incompletely conducted their investigation.

## Federal Statutes

Under certain circumstances, other federal statutes will come into play concerning the interviewing or interrogation of the public or private employees. Some of the provisions of the National Labor Relations Act, Title VII of the Civil Rights Act of 1964, or other discrimination laws may be applicable.

For example, the National Labor Relations Act prohibits an employer from questioning an employee about his union affiliation or sympathies, organizing efforts, bargaining, or other union-connected activities. In addition, an employer, either public or private, cannot single out for interviews or interrogation a protected group under Title VII without risking a claim of discrimination. This is not to say that an employer cannot question a group of employees regarding wrongdoing who are all of the same age, race, or sex, but merely to point out the potential allegation that could later be raised.

In addition, the public and private employer may face a violation of federal or state statutes should they fail to fully investigate and discover the wrongdoing of an employee. The activities that the employer failed to uncover may have violated the Occupational Safety and General Health Act (OSHA), which requires the employer to provide a safe environment for work. Finally, the public or private employer might violate the Fair Labor Standards Act if the employee is not paid for the time spent in the interview.

## Unions/Weingarten Rights

The United States Supreme Court, in reviewing *NLRB v. J. Weingarten*,

*Inc.*,[18] has given the employees the right of union representation during certain interviews. The *Weingarten* case concerned a union retail employee who was suspected of dishonesty. The employee was interviewed and, during the course of the interview, requested that her union steward be present. The interviewer denied this request, and following the interview, the employee filed an unfair labor practices charge with the National Labor Relations Board (NLRB). The NLRB found that the employer had, in fact, violated the employee's right to have a union steward present during the interview. On appeal, the United States Supreme Court agreed with this finding.

The *Weingarten* rule is applicable only if the employee requests representation and only if the employee reasonably believes that the interview could result in disciplinary action against him. The employee representative can act as an observer and advise the employee regarding his rights under the collective bargaining agreement but cannot act as an investigator. The union employee can waive the right of union representation during any interview. Generally, the offer of union representation does not have to be made to an employee prior to the interview, unless it is required by company policy or the collective bargaining agreement.

At one time, the NLRB had ruled that the *Weingarten* rule was also applicable to nonunion employees. However, at the present time the National Labor Relations Board has reversed itself with respect to the Weingarten rule as it applies to nonunion employees.[19] Because the NLRB has fluctuated on their position relating to Weingarten, the company's corporate counsel should monitor any changes in the NLRB's position.

## State Law

Most of the states have state constitutional provisions that follow the U.S. Constitution. In many cases, the restrictions imposed by the state constitutions will be similar to those imposed by the Constitution of the United States. The interviewer/interrogator should familiarize himself with any specific state laws or regulations relating to the interview and interrogation process.

## Common Law

The following are common law causes of action that an employer or interviewer must be aware of before he conducts any interviews. Even though the employee has common law rights, the public and private

---

18. NLRB v. J. Weingarten, Inc., 420 U.S. 251, 43 L Ed 2d171, 95 S CT 959 (1975)
19. Sears, Roebuck & Company, 274NLRB55 (1985)

employer has the right to investigate and to expect loyalty from the employee.

## False Imprisonment

This cause of action generally requires that an employee be detained without his consent or a legal justification to restrain him. A false imprisonment is a detention where no arrest warrant has been issued, or if one has been issued, it is void. For an employee to prove a case of false imprisonment, he must prove the following: first, that an arrest or forcible detention took place; second, that the arrest or imprisonment was caused by the company; third, that the detention was unlawful or made without a warrant; and fourth, that there was malice on the part of the company.

An employer is entitled to interview an employee on its premises about violations of company policy without liability for false imprisonment, as in *Faniel v. Chesapeake & Potomac Telephone Company*[20] and *Lansburgh's Inc. v. Ruffin.*[21] Although an employee may have a fear of losing his employment during an interview, and though it might seem coercive, this will not make an employee's submission to an interview become involuntary.[20] In viewing whether or not false imprisonment has occurred, the courts look to the length of the interview/interrogation and the manner in which it was conducted.

In a number of cases where false imprisonment was found to have occurred, the employee was physically restrained from leaving. In other cases, the interrogator yelled, beat on the desk, or made threats that the suspect would be sent to the penitentiary or never let out of the room.

## Defamation

The allegation of defamation of character is the most often occurring allegation made by a suspect regarding an incident of misconduct. The defamation of character may occur in the form of a slander or libelous statement. Slander is a false statement that was not written down but was spoken to one or more individuals. Libel is an untrue statement that was written down and was communicated to others.

In order for the employee to establish that he has suffered a defamation of character, he must prove first that particular words were actually spoken, including proving both the time and place that the activity took place. Second, the employee must also prove that these words were spoken or published to third persons. The third proof that the employee

---

20. Faniel v. Chesapeake & Potomac Telephone Company, 404 A2d174 (DCApp1979)
21. Lansburgh's Inc. v. Ruffin, 372 A2d561 (DCApp1977)

must show is that the words written or spoken were actually false. Finally, the employee must also show other facts that prove that the words are libelous or slanderous. This would include that there was malice on the part of the company or investigator and that the libel or slander was not privileged in any way.

The defense for an allegation of defamation of character is that the truth is always a complete defense regardless of the motives of the person saying it. A comment made by an investigator or company is fair when it is based on facts that have been truly stated and is free of motives, either real or imagined by the employees. There is also a defense against defamation of character if the company can establish that it had a qualified privilege to communicate the information to third parties. An employer has a qualified privilege to communicate allegations during an investigation. However, this qualified privilege is lost if false communications were made out of spite or malice with knowledge that the statements were, in fact, false. In addition, these knowingly false statements must have been communicated to an excessive number of people. The interviewer, during the course of investigative interviews, should avoid repeating any information or allegations to third parties of which he is uncertain. As a practical matter, the interview process is one of gathering rather than giving information to the interviewee.

An investigator should limit communicating allegations to those who have a need to know as part of the investigation or decision-making process relating to the consequences of the suspects actions. An investigator can establish the qualified privilege by noting on investigative reports that the document is privileged for counsel. This establishes an attorney–client privilege and protects many documents during an investigation.

The interviewer/interrogator should understand that a qualified privilege exists to express oral charges to superiors, police, prosecutors, or other persons having a need to know within the company. Care should be taken that the report of what happened during the investigation, interview, or interrogation is fair and that statements made are fair and done without malice to the suspect.

## Malicious Prosecution

Companies investigating employee theft, illegal drug use, or other illegal activities within a company must decide whether or not it is in their best interest to contact a law enforcement agency. A number of factors may come into play relating to the decision to contact a law enforcement agency. These factors might include an assessment of the investigative abilities of the company, a decision on whether a prosecution is desired, and any legal requirement to make a report with a public law enforcement agency. Certain businesses such as financial institutions are required to report thefts to the FBI. Illegal activities such as the theft of firearms or controlled substances are also closely monitored by federal and state agencies. Since most companies do not have a requirement to notify public law enforcement of problems within their company, they generally do not do so because of the cost of prosecution and the difficulty of proving circumstantial cases. A corporation's bonding company may also need to be made aware of loss to keep the insurance contract in force.

Once the company has decided to prosecute an employee, the company can be opening the door to potential liability for an allegation of malicious prosecution and false arrest. Malicious prosecution involves the use of a legal authority such as the police or prosecutor's office to have a person arrested and brought to trial. For an employee to establish a malicious prosecution claim against the company, the employee must prove that 1) the employer instituted or continued a criminal proceeding; 2) the proceeding was terminated in the employee's favor; 3) no probable cause existed for initiating a proceeding; and 4) the employer's motive in initiating the proceeding was malice or some other purpose other than bring the employee to justice.[22]

By the action of simply informing a prosecutor or law enforcement agency of the facts of the case and leaving the decision to prosecute to them, a company reduces any potential liability. An exception to this would be if the company or its agents knowingly provided false information or attempted to influence the prosecution of the employer. Thus, if the company obtains a valid arrest warrant for an employee that has been legally authorized, it cannot be held liable for the arrest by police but could be liable should the company have misused the legal process.[23] If the employee is found guilty, the company has a complete defense against liability for a malicious prosecution; however, any termination of criminal proceedings in the favor of the employee can create a potential for liability. Liability can also be created if the company files a complaint against the employee and later withdraws it. This action on the part of the company has established one of the elements necessary for a malicious prosecution claim. A commonly contested issue is whether or not probable cause for a criminal proceeding existed when it was initiated by the employer. Probable cause is a reasonable belief in the guilt of the employee. Whether or not probable cause existed is determined by evaluating the information available to the company at the time a complaint was made.

---

22. Prosser & Keeton on Torts (1977)
23. Prosser & Keeton on Torts (Fifth Edition 1984)

A private sector investigator can limit his and the company's potential liability for a malicious prosecution allegation by allowing the prosecutor or police officer to make the decision to prosecute. The fourth element in a malicious prosecution claim is malice, which can be differentiated from an employer's having probable cause. Malice on the part of the company or an employer may be shown through personal animosity between the person making the accusation and the accused employee. It can also be inferred from the lack of a complete investigation on the part of the company. Furthermore, the company may show the element of malice, if the company conveys facts that are untrue or withholds facts that might mitigate the conclusion reached by police investigators.

## Assault and Battery

Although assault and battery are related, they are fundamentally different. Battery is bodily contact that either causes harm or is offensive to a reasonable person's sense of dignity;[23] assault is words or actions that place the employee in fear of receiving a battery. Actual physical contact is not an element of assault, but violence either threatened or offered, is required. An assault can occur when the person uses threatening words or gestures and has the ability to commit the battery.[23]

## Intentional Infliction of Emotional Distress

In this tort, the company or its agents must deliberately and outrageously conduct activities toward a person that would inflict emotional harm. The elements incorporated in this claim are 1) outrageous conduct by the defendant; 2) intent to cause emotional injury to the employee; and 3) the occurrence in fact of emotional injury to the employee.

This conduct, on the part of the employer or its agents, must be outrageous and extreme. This would include any activity that would not generally have been tolerated by society. It also must have been meant to cause severe emotional distress to the suspect. This action against the employer is also often combined with alleging a wrongful termination. However, the termination of an employee's employment is not outside the reasonable bounds of conduct and thus does not result in an intentional infliction of emotional distress.

The employee alleging intentional infliction of emotional distress must also prove that he suffered from severe emotional distress. This must be shown in some way other than simply by his own testimony. In addition, the employee must prove malice. In many investigations, an employer may make accusations based on reasonable suspicion.

Once an employer is able to show reasonable suspicion, the burden of proof to prove malice or disregard of the employee's rights now shifts to the employee.[24]

Courts frequently have rejected these suits based on the fact that simply firing an employee is not extreme and outrageous conduct beyond what would be normally found in society. However, when the courts or juries have found that employees were abusively treated, the damages awarded have been considerable.

---

24. Aerosmith v. Williams, 174 GA. pp.690, 331 S.E.2d30,33 (1986)

# Interpretation of Verbal and Physical Behavior

# 4

*All behavior is meaningful; it is only the true meaning that may not be evident to the observer.*

The seasoned investigator often refers to his "gut feelings" when identifying a suspect. "I've got a gut feeling that it's him" or "I know in my gut that it's him" are phrases used often by investigators. The investigators have identified behavioral characteristics or investigative similarities that allow them to make an often accurate determination that a particular individual is responsible for an incident. The discussion of behavior symptoms and detecting lies from a suspect's words, actions, and attitude is the next step in the professional interviewer's pattern of growth.

The purpose of this chapter is to take the seasoned interviewer/interrogator from the level of the gut feeling to the next level of being able to articulate the behavioral clues that lead him to believe that the suspect or witness is truthful or untruthful. By being able to articulate the behavioral clues and their meaning, an interviewer/interrogator can begin to use other investigators in a more systematic way. By being able to recreate an interview with a suspect both verbally and physically, the investigator can elicit opinions from other similarly trained interviewer/interrogators. The ability of interrogators working as a group to recognize deception allows for the input of others into the interview.

In discussing behavior, it is important that the interviewer/interrogator recognize that behavior symptoms do not occur by chance. All behavior is meaningful; it is only the true meaning that may not be evident to the observer. Each time a victim, witness, or suspect manifests a particular behavior, it is caused by something, has a reason, or has an objective. In many cases, the victim, witness, or suspect is not even aware that he is reacting and providing the interviewer/interrogator with behavioral clues.

In this discussion we will deal with two styles of behavior:

1. VERBAL: Verbal behavior encompasses the words that are actually spoken, the choice of words used, and tone of voice and speed of delivery.
2. NONVERBAL: This behavior consists of facial expressions, body positioning, posture, and movements used to express the words that were chosen. In some cases movements or gestures (emblems) take the place of the words.

Studies vary in the percentage of communication that takes place in each one of these channels. However, the dominant communication channel between individuals is the nonverbal channel, accounting for between 55% and 65% of the communication between individuals. Between 30% and 40% of communication is done using the tone of voice. Less than 10% of communication between people actually is the result of the words that are spoken.

Simply listening to an everyday conversation should quickly convince anyone that the above percentages are true. The pauses, the movements of the hand, and shifts of the body at certain points in a conversation tell a story that adds depth and fullness to the words that were spoken.

## Common Terms

The following are some commonly used terms that are necessary to understand prior to a discussion of the meaning of behavior.

1. LEAKAGE: Leakage occurs when the true feelings or attitudes of an individual leak out through uncontrolled body language. In the deceptive individual, the behavior leaked may be contrary to the attitudes and words the individual is attempting to portray.
2. EMBLEMS: Emblems are nonverbal gestures that can be directly translated into or substituted for words. The following are some common examples of emblems: shaking the head no, shaking the head yes, shrugging the shoulders with the hands turned up, index finger touching the thumb forming a sign for okay, palm extended out for stop.
3. ILLUSTRATORS: Illustrators are hand and arm movements that are used when speaking to illustrate or additionally describe what is being said by the individual. An example of this would be a movement that adds emphasis to the words that are spoken.
4. CONGRUENCE: Congruence means equal or the same—for exam-

ple, truthful verbal behavior corresponding with truthful physical behavior. Verbal and physical behaviors are thus in congruence.

5. INCONGRUENCE: Any words that do not match the nonverbal behavior. Truthful verbal behavior spoken in conjunction with untruthful nonverbal behavior is incongruent or not equal.

Several excellent texts are available to individuals who wish to acquire an in-depth scientific view of verbal and nonverbal clues to deception. You may read *Telling Lies* by Paul Ekman,[1] *Face Language* by Robert Whiteside,[2] and *Reading Faces* by Leopold Bellak, M.D., and Samm Sinclair Baker.[3] Investigation into the study of deceit and how people lie is still in its earliest stages of evolution. It has only been in the last twenty years that it has received significant laboratory study. As the scientists search for scientifically acceptable parameters that will identify a lie, they are reviewing ground covered by interviewer/interrogators over years of interviewing/interrogating suspects. Many of the research paths currently being explored hold future promise for the successful identification of lies by suspects, victims and witnesses. The difficulty of many of these paths is their application to the field investigator. It is extremely rare that an investigator has the ability to measure and time facial movements or photograph expressions that last less than a quarter of a second to evaluate whether or not he is being told a lie or the truth. However, this research has only scratched the surface and may yet provide the field interviewer/interrogator with methods as yet undreamed of.

The interviewer/interrogator is faced with a complex situation. In an interview or interrogation, the interviewer must assess an abundance of information. In fact, the information received during the interview and interrogation is often so overwhelming that the interviewer cannot observe everything. *The skilled interviewer/interrogator realizes that there is no single behavioral clue that is always a reliable indicator of truth or deception in all people.*

Each individual may have different behavioral norms and methods of lying. In most cases, the interviewer/interrogator must assess behavioral clues over a very short interaction with the suspect, or witness making it difficult to know where to focus one's attention.

## Faking Behavior

Can an individual in an interview successfully fake truthful behavior? The answer to this is generally that he cannot, because the suspect must

---

1. Berkley Books, New York, 1985.
2. Fell, Hollywood, Florida, 1984.
3. Holt, Rinehart, and Winston, New York, 1981.

pay attention to too many different signals, behaviors, and emotions. The timing of the behavior must also keep them congruent to the behavior a truthful person would utilize. Although an individual might be able to create certain behaviors that appear to be truthful, he is just as likely to allow a leakage of other behaviors that contradict his truthful behavior. Witnesses or suspects who are attempting to lie to an interviewer/interrogator are generally more successful when the interviewer or interrogator is unobservant or who wants to believe the story he is told. It is also easier to fake behavior when the body can be hidden from the observer. The use of a desk, a wall, or an interview by telephone allows the untruthful suspect to conceal all or a significant part of his body that may leak behaviors not congruent with his truthful words. It is also more likely that an experienced liar, a professional actor, or politician will be more difficult to detect. These individuals consciously practice how they look when they talk and eliminate the gestures that do not help convince the listener of their truthfulness. It is generally easier to catch people who rarely lie than those who lie as a matter of course.

It is also difficult for the guilty to fake behavior successfully because the subconscious mind acts independently of the conscious mind. Because of this, the nonverbal behavior is often in stark contrast to the words that portray innocence.

## Rules for Evaluating Behavior

To successfully evaluate an individual's behavior, the interviewer/ interrogator use certain guidelines that put the behavior in context.

### Evaluate the Suspect Against Himself

The interviewer/interrogator must recognize that verbal and nonverbal behavior is very individualized. Although generalizations can be made about behaviors that are more likely to be truthful or deceptive, each individual is to a certain extent unique when he attempts to deceive. As people grow, they each have a unique environmental, financial, and parental situation that gives them a significant diversity of experiences. We may generalize and formulate hypotheses regarding typical behaviors that indicate deceptions, but they may or may not be true when read against the individual suspect himself.

The interviewer/interrogator should attempt to identify a behavioral norm for the victim, witness, or suspect. This behavioral norm provides a baseline for the individual and corresponds to how they react in situations where they are not under stress. Observing the individual while gathering background information and during the rapport-establishment phase will give the interviewer/interrogator an average behavior baseline that will serve as a reference point for comparison. This comparison will be made when the interviewer/interrogator later discusses the incident under investigation. Does the witness or suspect significantly change under interrogation?

The interviewer/interrogator should recognize that in any situation that is unusual or potentially threatening, an individual's stress level may rise. Consider the reaction of most people when stopped for a traffic violation. The level of nervousness, quivering in the voice, etc., becomes apparent because of the stress of the situation. Simply being in this type of position causes an individual to undergo some behavioral changes. However, the observant investigator will recognize that although people who are being interviewed or questioned may be nervous, this nervousness may have nothing to do whatsoever with deception. It may be simply their uncertainty because of the situation.

In assessing an individual's reaction to the interview/interrogation, the observant interrogator knows that truthful suspects may be nervous at the beginning of the interview, but as soon as they sense there is nothing to fear, they become more relaxed. The untruthful suspect or witness recognizes that they are in a dangerous position and the fear of detection increases, thereby increasing the stress level that they are under during the interview. As a result, rather than becoming more comfortable as the interview proceeds, the untruthful individual tends to become more nervous or maintain the nervousness that they showed at the beginning of the interview.

## Evaluate the Suspect's Behavior Against that of the Population

Although the evaluation of the individual's behavioral norm is an important factor in assessing whether or not we are seeing deceptive behavior, another practice that is often successful for the interviewer/interrogator is to read the suspect's behavior against the average of the population. In these situations, the interviewer/interrogator assesses the normalcy of a behavior as it relates to the population as a whole. By this, we mean looking at what most people would do in a similar set of circumstances.

The interviewer/interrogator commonly introduces himself and shakes hands with the witness or suspect. The interviewer/interrogator should evaluate the hand shake of the witness or suspect compared to all the other people to whom he has been introduced. Does the hand tremble as it is extended? Is the suspect reluctant to extend the hand? How does the hand feel? Is it warm and dry or cold and clammy? Although none of these particular responses means absolute deception, any could be the first indication for an interrogator that something outside the ordinary is happening with the suspect. Often an individual will react in an unusual attitude toward the interviewer/interrogator. Take, for example, the case of the homicide of a small child in a suburb of a major metropolitan area. The child was allegedly abducted from her home overnight while the parents were asleep. Shortly after the parents reported their child missing, she was found dead in a wooded area several miles from her home. As the investigation progressed, the parents were reluctant to cooperate with the police investigation of the homicide. This included refusing to give police access to the residence and child's room. In addition, they were reluctant to talk with police investigators.

It is highly unlikely that any parent whose child was abducted would fail to cooperate totally in a police investigation into the incident. However, in this case, the parents refused to cooperate with the investigation and the police ultimately had to obtain a search warrant for the residence. The parents obtained counsel and they refused to talk to police. The father was subsequently convicted of the homicide and is currently incarcerated in a state penitentiary.

The interviewer/interrogator should ask himself, how would I react if my child were abducted and killed? Certainly not as these parents did. In certain situations, however, this reluctance might not be at all unusual. If the parents had had numerous brushes with the law or had repeatedly been questioned about crimes in which they were not involved, they might legitimately be reluctant to talk with the police or cooperate in the investigation. When a parent who has had no previous brushes with the law acts differently from what most of us would consider normal behavior, the interviewer/interrogator should suspect deception. The individual's own behavioral norm now should take precedence over the responses of the average population.

### Evaluate Behavior in the Context of the Situation

The behavioral clues presented by an individual can be read only in the context of the situation. For example, the eye contact of a young boy meeting older friends of his parents may be somewhat limited. This lack of eye contact is in all likelihood due to the shyness he feels at meeting older adults. However, in another situation, it could mean that he is lying. Another twist of this scenario could be that the day before he had been caught ringing the doorbell and running away from his parent's friend's home, so the boy's lack of eye contact could be a result of many different reasons. Thus, the exact same behavioral clues may be judged differently based on the circumstances surrounding the interview.

### Behavioral Clusters

The behavior that is observed during the course of an interview or an interrogation are more likely to be valid when clusters of different types of behavior occur. For example, in a deceptive individual, the interviewer could observe a lack of eye contact, closed body posture, and grooming gestures. At the same time, there may be deceptive verbal behavior with delays in the speech pattern. The clustering of similar behaviors when evaluated globally leads the interviewer/interrogator to the conclusion that the individual is likely to be truthful or deceptive.

Rarely is it sufficient for a single behavior to be interpreted as truth or deception. The accuracy of the decision is enhanced when the behavior can be read in clusters that support one another, leading to the conclusion of truthfulness. Much like deception, truthful behavior can be read using clusters of behavior, such as direct spontaneous responses, good eye contact, open posture, and related fluid movements.

The interviewer/interrogator should recognize that, on occasion, an innocent person may do or say something that would be more likely to come from a deceptive individual. In the same way, the deceptive individual may on occasion respond in or appear to assume a truthful manner. The clusters of behavior occurring over time during the interview/interrogation will form a pattern that will enhance the likelihood of a correct decision about the suspect's truthfulness or untruthfulness.

## Interviewer Behavior

The interviewer/interrogator also must be concerned that he in no way project his beliefs or disbeliefs to a suspect. By projecting his feelings to the individual being interviewed or interrogated, the interviewer can effect a change of that individual's behavior. For example, the truthful suspect who fears that the interviewer does not believe him because of the behavioral clues the interviewer/interrogator has shown, may give behavior that is incongruent with his true status. The emotional fear of being disbelieved may in fact cause an innocent person to alter his behavior because of this stress. Conversely, a guilty suspect may reduce his fear of detection simply because he perceives that he is believed by the interviewer/interrogator. As the fear of detection diminishes, the guilty suspect is less likely to give himself away through the leakage of untruthful behavior.

Additionally, the interviewer/interrogator should be careful to avoid causing undue pressure on the suspect by sitting too close. In situations where an interviewer/interrogator initially sits too close to the suspect, he could cause the suspect to feel uncomfortable and modify his behavior. This could result in discomfort due to the interviewer/interrogator's proximity rather than any type of deception.

In the same way that the interviewer/interrogator evaluates the behavior of a suspect, so too does the suspect evaluate the behavior of the interviewer/interrogator. In normal conversations, eye contact between two parties ranges between 40% and 60%. In situations where an interviewer/interrogator looks too much at a suspect, the suspect may recognize that the interviewer/interrogator is acting beyond the normal guidelines and accuse the interrogator of disbelief. In each of these situations, the positioning and behavior of the interviewer/interrogator has modified the behavioral clues given by a suspect. In these situations, the behavior is not related directly to the incident under investigation but rather to the interaction between the interviewer and suspect.

The interviewer/interrogator should also refrain from identifying a particular deceptive behavior of the suspect to him. For example, an interrogator tells a suspect that he knows he is lying to him because he cannot look the interrogator in the eye. What happens next is a staring match between the suspect and the interrogator, with the suspect rarely, if ever, breaking eye contact. This change of behavior by the suspect is a result of the interrogator's statement. The suspect consciously alters and modifies his behavior to conceal a particular deceptive response from the interrogator. Interviewers/interrogators should never call attention to evidently deceptive behavior. This behavior is the interviewer/interrogator's "ace in the hole" and will allow him to effectively interpret and steer the interview/interrogation using the suspect's unmodified behavior. Once the suspect recognizes that his behavior is being evaluated, he may begin to modify it, which creates additional difficulty for the interviewer/interrogator.

## Timing/Consistency

Every suspect and witness will exhibit verbal and nonverbal behavioral clues to some extent. The interviewer must evaluate these behaviors based on their timing and consistency. For example, one common gesture of people who wear glasses is to push the glasses up or make an adjustment of the glasses on the face. This common gesture is done because the glasses are loose or because the face has become oily and the glasses have slid down. Thus, the adjustment of the glasses can be a common necessity for those individuals who wear them. This adjustment, however, can be interpreted differently depending upon the timing of the movement in relationship to a stressful question. For example, consider the following dialogue:

> INTERVIEWER: Larry, let me ask you this. Did you steal that missing deposit from the safe yesterday?
> SUSPECT: (Pauses, hand over the face, adjusts glasses) No, I didn't.

A second example with different timing of the movement:

*INTERVIEWER:*    Larry, let me ask you, did you steal that missing deposit from the safe yesterday?
*SUSPECT:*    No, I didn't. (Good eye contact. Direct spontaneous response. Ten seconds later suspect adjusts his glasses.)

In both of these cases the movement to adjust the glasses was accomplished in exactly the same manner, with only the timing of the movement changing. In the first example, the suspect, Larry, uses the movement of the glasses on his face to screen his face and eyes from the interrogator while he decided how to respond. In the second example, the suspect directly responded to the interviewer's question and only at a point of limited stress elected to adjust his glasses. In evaluating these two movements an interrogator would assess the first as probable deception because of its timing and the second less likely to be deception.

The suspect should consistently utilize a pattern of behavior that increases the likelihood of the accuracy of his interpretations. In the above dialogue, the interviewer might see Larry repeatedly put his hand to his glasses concealing his eyes and face at points where he was attempting to lie or where the stress of the questions was high. In the second example, the truthful suspect Larry might make adjustments to his glasses, but these adjustments are not directly related to the stressful questions and lack the consistency or timing necessary to judge them as being deceptive.

## Cautions in the Evaluation of Behavior

In interpreting a suspect's verbal and nonverbal behavior, the interviewer/interrogator must be conscious of pitfalls in the process of this evaluation. There are many individual, cultural, and environmental circumstances that can cause a suspect to change his behavior. These changes may have nothing to do with deception on the part of the suspect.

### Role of the Environment

The interviewer/interrogator must be conscious of the environment in which he conducts an interview or interrogation. The distractions surrounding a suspect may cause behavior that is unrelated to the question being asked. For example, if an interviewer is asking a question and the suspect breaks eye contact, it could mean one of two things in a situation where the environment was not controlled: 1) deception, or 2) distraction when a vehicle drove past or someone walked by. Ideally, the environment should reduce outside distractions so that the behavioral responses can be attributed directly to the questions being asked by the interviewer. In less controlled environments such as field interviews or interviews conducted in a less formal setting, the interviewer must consider whether or not the behavior has some cause other than his question.

## Interviewer–Suspect Attitudes

The interviewer/interrogator must also consider any personal biases he may have either for or against the individual being questioned. In situations where the interviewer has a bias in favor of the person, it is likely that this bias may cloud his observation of deceptive behavior. How many times during an investigation has an investigator heard, "I just can't believe Bill did it?" The individual who has a personal relationship with Bill does not want to believe that he was involved in the incident. This personal bias allowed them to overlook information and behavior that would have been indicative of Bill's guilt. This bias may also be reflected as a result of a physical resemblance to someone the interviewer/interrogator likes or dislikes. We all probably have an Aunt Marie who makes the best chocolate cake and always had an ice cold glass of milk for us whenever we stopped by. Now, whenever we see someone who reminds us of our Aunt Marie, we feel positive toward her. Conversely, when we encounter people who physically resemble somebody we do not like, we have negative feelings toward them simply because of that resemblance.

An interrogator must also take into account the attitude of the suspect when assessing his behavior. In situations where an interviewer/interrogator is dealing with somebody who does not like the law enforcement function, he typically receives negative feedback from that individual. None of us likes to be disliked and individuals tend to treat others the way others treat them. Thus, when we are dealing with a person who does not like us, we are more likely to judge the person to be deceptive based on his behavior owing to the bias we have against him. The interviewer/interrogator must constantly be aware of personal biases for and against individuals and recognize that these can jeopardize the accurate evaluation of a suspect's behavior.

## Mental Capacity of Suspect

A suspect's mental capacity may affect the type of behavior as well as behavioral clues. In situations where a suspect is of low intelligence, we may find that he delays before responding to the interviewer/interrogator's question. This delay typically would be interpreted as deceptive. However, because of the relatively low intelligence of the suspect, the interviewer/interrogator must consider the possibility that the pause was a function of intelligence rather than deception.

An individual's educational level may also play a part in determining the gestures that are used during a conversation. Research in linguistics has shown that people of a higher social status or who are better educated tend to be more verbal and use fewer gestures. The suspect who has a lower mental capacity or who is less well educated tends to rely more on gestures to explain himself.

## Medical Condition, Drug/Alcohol Usage

Individuals can respond in a behaviorally suspect or noticeable manner because they are being treated for a medical condition. The symptoms of the medical condition may result in actual changes in the body's physiology. These changes in physiology could also result from the side effects of prescribed medications. For example, an individual with a dry, clicky mouth may be lying or may be taking a diuretic for water retention. A side effect of the diuretic is a dryness in the mouth that results in a dry, clicky sound. The dry, clicky mouth is also a recognized sign of deception. Other individuals may have a tremor in the hand because of a muscle strain or even as a side effect of chemotherapy. The physical behavior observed has nothing whatsoever to do with deception but is simply a reflection of the individual's medical condition. These medical conditions or medication side effects can cause behavior symptoms similar to those of a deceptive individual.

Other individuals will be under the influence of drugs or alcohol at the time of an interview or interrogation. The use of behavior to identify their true status is unlikely because the behavioral responses may be due to the drug and alcohol ingestion alone. The pattern of slurred speech, unsteadiness on the feet, confused thought process, and the inability to stay on the topic are common side effects of someone under the influence of drugs or alcohol. An individual in a state of intoxication, be it from drugs or alcohol, is unsuitable for a behavioral assessment relating to truth or deception.

## Cultural, Ethnic, and Geographic Differences

The interviewer/interrogator must also be aware that cultural, ethnic, and geographic differences can cause behavior variations in people. Eye contact between individuals, in a normal conversation, is generally 40% to 60%. However, in an Oriental population, the eye contact may be significantly less because in Oriental society, it is inappropriate to make eye contact with someone in authority. Gestures and behaviors may also be typical for specific cultures and very appropriate for their ethnic group. For example, in the Middle East, it is not inappropriate for two men to walk hand in hand, whereas this is an unusual behavior in most areas of the United States. In the United States, when men hold hands, it is often associated with their sexual preference. In the Middle East, the hand-holding between men has nothing to do with their sexual preferences.

There also may be geographical differences in speech patterns and social norms. By recognizing that these differences occur, the interviewer/interrogator can take them into consideration when evaluating an individual's behavior for truth or deception.

## Professional Criminals, Actors, and Politicians

The interviewer/interrogator must always be conscious of the skill with which people interact with others. Criminals, actors, and politicians are people who are typically conscious of their behavior. Each of these individuals must have a knowledge of human behavior and the ability to mimic in order to be successful. These types of individuals can be extremely difficult to catch in a lie because of their ability to mask and cover their incongruent behavioral leakage.

The professional criminal (not necessarily someone in organized crime, but rather someone who has actively pursued a criminal career) can also be difficult to assess behaviorally. These individuals generally began lying at an early age. They began with their parents and teachers and continue with their employers and the police. Because of their success in deception and their practiced ability to deceive, their behavioral characteristics are often unreliable.

The difficulty with experienced criminals is that they often look truthful when in fact they are involved in the incident under investigation. An additional difficulty that the interviewer/interrogator can face with this type of individual is that he may appear deceptive when he is truthful because of past involvement in similar situations. This can be especially relevant in crimes that occur repeatedly such as burglary or theft. In addition, this type of conflicting behavior may be displayed because the individual has no respect for law enforcement and "doesn't care."

Con men who ply their trade through their ability to deceive can be extremely difficult to assess behaviorally. These individuals have often successfully beaten the system and so view the process as much as a game as a serious encounter. Because they consider it a game, they often take great delight in lying and showing their cleverness at fooling an investigator.

Many actors and politicians can successfully create emotions. They do so by recreating a past moment of their life in their mind and allow their body to display the appropriate behavior of that emotion. As a result, the emotion shown in the circumstances tends to look extremely real because it is directly related to past experience. Many actors are trained to show emotion by this very method. Consider the TV evangelists who can cry at the drop of a hat to show their sincerity.

## Fear of Detection

The behavior displayed by a suspect in an interview or interrogation is often directly related to the fear of detection. The greater the fear of detection that an individual has, the greater the likelihood that a behavioral slip will occur or leakage will show their true status. The investigator should not assume that the fear of detection is directly related to the seriousness of the incident. In many cases the seriousness of the incident has little or nothing to do with the fear of detection. For example, an employee steals five dollars out of the register and nobody catches him. He continues to steal in any number of ways for a period of a year before finally deciding to steal a large deposit. At this point, he is questioned regarding the theft of the deposit. Does he have a fear of detection? In all probability, the fear of detection is greatly diminished because he has been successfully involved in theft over a long period without being caught. Why should he be concerned now? On the other hand the individual may show significant behavioral changes simply because, for the first time, he did steal a large amount using a method that he was not used to. It is the perception of the individual of the likelihood that he has been detected that comes into play in assessing whether or not there will be significant behavioral changes.

In certain instances, as when questioning a suspect about multiple criminal acts, there may be significantly different patterns of behavior to each different act. Take for example an individual who has been stealing from his company using fraudulent credits. The deceptive behavior associated with stealing using fraudulent credits is significantly more threatening to the suspect than asking about biographical information. Thus the behavioral change should occur on the more emotionally stressful issue.

Suspects often react to different crimes. For example, some suspects view a rape preceding a homicide as significantly more serious than the killing itself. Thus, the fear of detection is greater on the rape than it would be on the homicide. As such, it would be likely that the individual would show more significant behavioral changes in the rape inquiry than in the homicide inquiry simply because it has a greater emotional impact and stimulates as a result a greater fear of detection. However, it might be easier to obtain a confession from a suspect by concentrating on the less emotional issue. The fear of detection may also be increased when there are larger punishments for one rather than another issue. In the previous instance, while the homicide is significantly harsher in terms of punishment than the rape, the suspect could still view the rape as the more emotionally volatile issue.

Although the behavioral changes observed by the interviewer/interrogator may give us an indication that the suspect is untruthful, they do not necessarily tell us the particulars of the untruth. In some instances, the deceptive behavior may be related to a side issue such as the theft of other money or the knowledge of who actually perpetrated the crime. The behavioral changes could also be a result of the fear of not being believed.

A lie fails because the suspect allows the attendant emotion to leak out and be observed. The stronger the emotion felt by the suspect, the greater the likelihood of a behavioral leak. The fear of detection can also be directly related to a suspect's beliefs about the circumstances of the crime. The interviewer/interrogator should remember that a lie that is told over and over can actually become the foundation of a belief on the part of the suspect.

## Fight or Flight

Self-preservation is one of the primary needs of an individual. The body, as it evolved, developed a system of self-preservation called the autonomic nervous system. The autonomic nervous system is the body's defense mechanism. When the mind recognizes a danger to its well-being, the autonomic nervous system changes the body's physiology to prepare it to either fight or flee the perceived threat.

Consider walking down a dark street and having somebody step out of the shadows in front of you. Without having to think about it, the body's autonomic defense system kicks in and begins to prepare the body to fight or flee from the threat. Adrenaline is secreted into the circulatory system, which increases the heart rate. As the heart rate increases the body needs to put more oxygen into the system. The respiratory pattern of the individual changes becoming deeper and more rapid.

The body begins to build up heat with all the movement occurring in the heart and the lungs. To dissipate this heat, the body begins to perspire and diverts the blood from the digestive track in the abdominal cavity to the surface of the skin. As the blood is diverted to the surface of the skin, a flushing begins to occur. The perspiration begins to evaporate from the surface of the skin, thereby cooling it. As this happens, the blood now begins to cool and release its heat. The body is a dynamic system that is not consciously controlled by the individual in these types of situations.

In the same way that the body protects a person when he feels threatened, similar physiological changes occur when an individual has a fear of detection. The body undergoes physiological changes of which the individual is not consciously in control. The corresponding behavioral changes are often observable to the interviewer/interrogator. The pulsation of the carotid artery on either side of the neck or the blood vessels in the temple are directly reflective of increased blood pressure. The flushing or blanching of the skin may be related to the body's diversion of the blood from the digestive tract to the surface of the skin. The change in the respiratory pattern can also be noted. These physiological changes in the body tend to be relatively uncontrolled by the individual, and thus make excellent indicators showing a suspect's stress or strong emotion, such as the fear of detection.

## Emotion

The stronger an emotion felt by a suspect attempting to lie, the greater the likelihood of significant leakage of behavior. The difficulty for the interviewer/interrogator is that emotions are rarely in their pure form. The emotions may be several different types. For example, on a roller-coaster ride, an individual may have the emotion of fear of being killed on one of the high speed turns and at the same time excitement and laughter as a result of the fun of having lived through the turn. Suspects feel these combined emotions also. On the one hand they have the fear of detection, but on the other hand in many cases they enjoy the game of conning their adversary into believing their noninvolvement. The problem the guilty face is that they want to conceal the emotion associated with the fear of detection. The easiest way to do this is to mask that emotion with another. They may use anger or a smile to conceal their emotions. Often the interviewer/interrogator will notice a suspect's attempting to win him over with a smile. This is often accompanied by inappropriate laughter. The use of the smile is an attempt by the suspect to conceal one emotion with another and use it as a mask. The suspect may also commonly use anger to mask other emotions.

Probably the technique used most often to mask emotions by the suspect is the smile. It is relatively easy for the suspect to smile and it is socially appropriate. In addition, studies have shown that people who smile are judged to be more trustworthy and honest, whereas those who scowl or frown were judged to be less trustworthy or honest.

Using the mask of emotions will help confuse the interviewer/interrogator and make the true meaning of any leakage questionable. The difficulty the interviewer/interrogator has is in differentiating which emotion is in play at the current time. Is it fear of detection or fear of being disbelieved? Is it embarrassment or anger? Regardless of the emotion, the stronger the emotion felt by the suspect, the greater the amount of leakage likely to occur for the interviewer's observation.

## Typical Attitudes Displayed by Suspects

The interviewer/interrogator should remember that extremes in behavior are often indicative of deception. At the very least, the observant interviewer/interrogator should recognize that the stress of lying often causes changes in attitudes and verbal and nonverbal behavior. These changes should be compared with what is normal for the individual and the population in general.

### The Truthful Suspect

Truthful individuals generally are calm, relaxed, and cooperative while being interviewed by police or loss prevention. Even though innocent, the suspect may be concerned that he is being questioned and this concern may cause some stress. However, as he becomes more comfortable with the situation, this stress typically reduces and his behavior becomes more comfortable and relaxed with the situation.

The truthful suspect generally is sincere in both word and action. His smiles look genuine because they are sincere. The truthful individual is inflexible in the stories that he tells. However, the interviewer does need to be careful about truthful witnesses and victims who may embellish or add to a description to be even more helpful. Overall, the truthful individual is cordial, friendly, and relatively easy to handle.

Knowing that these observations are generally true, experienced investigators have often interviewed individuals who were innocent but were less than friendly because of their dislike for the police or loss prevention personnel. The experienced interviewer can recognize this attitude and still make considerable inroads in establishing information.

### The Untruthful Suspect

The attitude displayed by untruthful suspects may be impatience, both in word and action. The guilty will often look at their watch and suggest that they need to be somewhere else. They also are tense and defensive. An example of defensiveness can be illustrated in the following dialogue. A store manager was interviewed regarding the theft of several deposits. The interviewer greeted the manager and introduced himself: "Hi, I'm Dave Zulawski. How are you today?" The manager's response was, "What do you want to know for and why are you asking me all these questions?"

Comparing the response from the manager to what one might expect from the population as a whole, this certainly is an inappropriate response, which indicates an unusual amount of stress and defensiveness. This unusual response and her defensiveness were the first indications of the manager's guilt.

Some guilty suspects will attempt to portray an outwardly unconcerned attitude. They attempt to convince the interviewer that this meeting between themselves and the police or loss prevention is nothing out of the ordinary and absolutely no threat to them whatsoever. Although this surface attitude is generally supported by their lounging style posture, inwardly they are in a state of panic.

Guilty suspects often attempt to take an overly friendly, polite, or cooperative attitude toward the interviewer/interrogator. The guilty suspect uses this tactic in an attempt to keep the interviewer/interrogators as a friend rather than as an enemy. The guilty hopes this cooperative attitude will get them a break or even that they will be overlooked as a suspect. Excessive friendliness and politeness by the suspect should immediately alert the interviewer/interrogator to the probable deception of the suspect. Even when the guilty person employing this attitude is confronted about his involvement in the incident, he will remain extremely friendly. In fact, many times an individual will apologize for not being involved in the crime. "I'm sorry but I really didn't do this" is a typical guilty response to the interrogator.

Another attitude that is commonly used by the guilty suspect is that of being defeated. The suspect has done the hard work for the interrogator and reduced his own resistance to giving an admission by believing that he has already been detected and caught. Individuals having this type of an attitude typically confess fairly rapidly because they already believe that their guilt is known for certain.

Some guilty suspects will attempt to take the offensive by portraying a surly, nasty, aggressive attitude toward the interviewer/interrogator. This surly attitude is designed to put the interviewer/interrogator on the defensive and cause him to back off from the confrontation with the suspect. The suspect's belief that a good defense begins with an aggressive offense is true if this causes the interviewer/interrogator to back off. The interviewer should consider whether or not this individual may only have an extreme dislike for the police or loss prevention functions. If the suspect has an extreme dislike for the police, then the surly behavior may not necessarily be untruthful.

## Attitudes Common to Both Truthful and Untruthful Suspects

In certain situations, the interviewer/interrogator may find that there are attitudes that are common to both the truthful and untruthful suspect. For example, nervousness may be evidenced by a truthful person who has been put into a position of being questioned by someone in authority. The unusualness of this interview may in fact cause nervousness in a truthful suspect. The guilty suspect, however, is nervous because of his involvement in the incident and his belief that the interviewer/interrogator has focused on them as the primary suspect. Whereas the truthful individual will become calmer as the interview continues, the nervousness of the guilty will continue or increase.

Anger is another attitude that may be common to both the truthful and untruthful suspect. The truthful suspect may be angry because of his perception of being railroaded or a past experience with the police or loss prevention. The guilty suspect may use feigned anger in an attempt to take the offensive and force the interviewer/interrogator to back off from any confrontation. It has been the experience of the authors that anger displayed at the beginning of the interview/interrogation is typical of a guilty suspect. However, if anger is displayed later in the interview or interrogation, it may in fact be from a truthful suspect who has now become annoyed.

### Case Example

An example of anger based on the perception of the investigation can be seen in a theft of $20,000 in rings from a jewelry counter in metropolitan St. Louis.

The jewelry counter was attended by two sales clerks, a white female and a black female. The black female sales clerk went on break and left the area to get coffee. Behind the counter on top of a safe was a tray of rings valued at approximately $20,000 that was supposed to have been secured in the jewelry case. Shortly after the black sales clerk left the department for her break, two male blacks entered the department. One occupied the white sales clerk with questions while the other reached across the counter and took the rings. The sales clerk observed the theft and called for loss prevention and the police. The two offenders left the area taking the $20,000 in rings with them.

An investigation into the theft was initiated by police and store loss prevention. The rings were in a place where they were not supposed to be and this was in complete violation of company policy relating to the handling of high value merchandise. Investigators elected to interview the black sales clerk first because of the possibility of collusion along racial lines. The investigators made an investigative assumption that if there was help from one of the employees to commit the theft, it would have occurred along racial lines. However, when the female black sales clerk was asked to be interviewed she was extremely upset because of her perception of the investigation. She felt that she was being singled out for the interview simply because she was black and the two offenders were also black. This anger, which was legitimate, created significant problems in interpreting her behavior. The black sales clerk was subsequently cleared of any involvement in the incident, but the order in which the interviews were conducted created investigative problems.

In other cases, the truthful and untruthful suspect may just quietly wait and listen for the interviewer to lead him. The quiet behavior is to the benefit of the guilty because they do not have to do any talking unless they are asked. The quiet truthful suspect may be quiet simply because this is his personality trait.

## Interpretation of Nonverbal Behavior

The interviewer/interrogator should remember that the entire body must be considered when observing nonverbal behavior. For the purpose of discussion, the body will be divided into zones. In addition, behaviors will be divided into those that are typically truthful or untruthful. Remember that no single behavior, either verbal or nonverbal, is always indicative of deception. The interviewer must look for differences against the suspect's normal, against the population, and then put the behavior in the context of its occurrence.

## *Trunk, Shoulder Position, and Posture*

One of the first behavioral indications that an interviewer/interrogator is likely to observe is how the suspect sits in his chair. The interviewer/interrogator's chair is positioned three to four feet across from the suspect's chair. After introductions, the truthful suspect will, without hesitation, walk in and sit down in the chair that is offered to him. The guilty, however, often walk to their chair and then move it. This movement will provide one of several benefits to them. First, by pulling the chair slightly away from the interviewer, the suspect will reduce some of the stress that he feels. Second, the movement of the chair often changes its alignment so that the suspect no longer has to directly face the interviewer. This allows the suspect to protect the abdominal region of the body by turning away from the interviewer/interrogator so his shoulders are no longer parallel to that of the interviewer. In some instances, the guilty will not move the chair, but will sit side-saddle, which takes the shoulders out of the position parallel to the interviewer/interrogator and provides a defensive area for the abdomen. Some younger males may in fact turn the chair and straddle it using the back as a barrier to separate themselves from the interviewer/interrogator. This is generally interpreted as a deceptive position assumed by the guilty.

**4.1.** Truthful individuals usually have good posture and appear relaxed while talking with the interviewer/interrogator.

*Truthful Individual.* Usually, the truthful individual will have good posture (see Figure 4.1). When they seat themselves in the chair across from the interviewer's chair, they sit in an upright position with their shoulders squared and parallel to the shoulders of the interviewer/interrogator. They are relaxed and keep their arms loose and away from the body. Imagine a small cone starting at the suspect's waist and moving up to encompass the shoulders. The truthful person generally will stay within this imaginary cone. As a result of remaining within this cone, their posture tends to remain good and any movements that they make during the course of the interview tend to be minimal.

**4.2.** Untruthful individuals will often position themselves in a defensive posture that makes them feel more comfortable by protecting the abdominal region of the body.

*Untruthful Individual.* Because the untruthful suspect is uncomfortable and has a fear of detection, he will often attempt to take a defensive posture that makes him feel more comfortable and conceals vulnerable parts of the body (see Figure 4.2). When an individual feels uncomfortable, he tends to protect the abdominal region of the body, which is the most vulnerable. The shoulder blades, rib cage, and collar bone protect the upper body, but it is in the abdominal region where most people feel uncomfortable. This discomfort translates into movements and a posture or position that covers this portion of the body.

The untruthful person may position his shoulders in such a way that it turns the trunk of the body so it is not exposed to the interviewer. This positioning reduces the discomfort felt from the fear of detection.

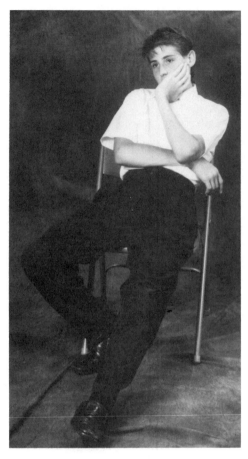

**4.3.** Untruthful individuals may posture themselves in a slumping position, extending the legs toward the interviewer/interrogator.

The untruthful individuals will also posture themselves in a slumping position (see Figure 4.3), extending the feet and legs toward the interviewer/interrogator to put a greater distance between themselves and the person they fear may detect their deception. Recall the imaginary cone extending from the waist to the shoulder of the truthful person; it is helpful in understanding the attempted deception. The deceptive individual is not restricted by this cone and can engage in huge, gross body shifts. These shifts may span several feet of space and take several seconds to actually complete. These large gross shifts of the body are not in any way restricted by the cone, and as a result, the trunk will lean excessively. The suspect who is in a position to lean on a desk or table may slump over and put all their weight on the table, supporting his head in his hand.

The guilty also may perspire excessively, particularly in the area of the trunk of the body. This perspiration should be considered in context with the actions immediately before arrival and the temperature of the room. In a comfortable room, where the suspect has not engaged in any physical exertion immediately prior to his arrival, it will be indicative of the autonomic nervous system psychological responses in the body. The perspiration may not be a relevant clue if the suspect has engaged in strenuous activity or come from an extremely hot environment just prior to the meeting.

There may also be significant changes in the respiratory pattern of the deceptive individual. Most people at rest breathe between eighteen and twenty-two cycles per minute. The respiratory pattern in a guilty suspect often changes dramatically as a result of his fear of detection. In about a third of the cases, the suspect's respiratory pattern increases and takes on almost a panting, labored look. Contributing to this labored respiratory pattern is the tension of the large upper chest muscles. Once they inhale, they are rarely able to take the full volume of oxygen that they need. As a result of this lack of oxygen, they increase the respiration pattern until it almost becomes a pant. Because of the need for additional oxygen, the suspect also may take large breaths to build the oxygen level in the blood up to the necessary levels and compensate for the muscular tension.

More commonly, the guilty individual's respiratory pattern tends to slow and become shallow or irregular. This irregularity may be highlighted by the taking of deep breaths periodically during the course of the interview and then releasing the breath slowly through a sigh or a cough.

## Hand and Arm Positions

The hands and arms are used for a number of purposes by truthful and untruthful suspects. The hands and the arms may provide the guilty with a barrier to protect the abdominal cavity and relieve the stress of sitting across from an interviewer/interrogator. The hands and the arms often are used to perform created jobs or grooming gestures. In Paul Ekman's book *Telling Lies*,[4] he refers to the grooming gestures and created jobs as *manipulators*. The grooming gestures and created jobs such as picking lint are part of our every day life. Again, the context and more importantly, the timing of these grooming gestures are critically

---

4. *Ibid*

important in evaluating whether or not they are related to deception. Dr. Ekman argues that these manipulators can be a sign that someone is upset, but an increase in the manipulator activity is not necessarily a reliable sign of deceit. Dr. Ekman believes that the prevailing belief among layman is that they erroneously believe grooming gestures do indicate deception.

Although the manipulators may not be a reliable sign of deceit, these grooming gestures and created jobs are often used by a guilty suspect in an effort to cover their uncertainty when asked a question they had not considered or prepared an answer for. The suspect's uncertainty requires that he pause to consider which response is truly in his best interests. This pause is often awkward and the guilty will use the created job or a grooming gesture to cover the delay while they formulate a response. It is not the gesture itself, but rather the context and timing of the gesture that need to be evaluated. We all at one time or another have picked a piece of lint off of our clothes or groomed our hair; however, these gestures can be considered as deceptive when they occur at certain times or cover a suspect's delay. For example, the hands and the arms are an extremely important part of any conversation. The movement of the hands and arms helps to relieve the stress of a situation. The movements may reflect the emotional turmoil of the individual or they may cover the guilty person's fear of deception. The hands and arms illustrate the conversation and expand the meaning of the actual words.

*Truthful Individual.* During his conversations with the interviewer/interrogator, the truthful suspect will generally have comfortable, relaxed movements. The truthful individual generally has no impairment of his fine motor coordination. His ability to write, gesture, and easily control the movement of objects remains essentially normal. The hands usually are warm and dry and remain that way through to the conclusion of the meeting. In some instances, because of the autonomic nervous system, a truthful person's hands may be cold and clammy, but at the conclusion of the interview, after they become more comfortable, the hands return to their normal warm and dry state. The truthful individual who holds his head during the interview tends to do so very lightly. The hand merely rests lightly on the chin or on the cheek. The trunk of the body remains upright and, as a result, the weight of the head is held directly on the neck.

*Untruthful Individual.* The deceptive individual tends to hold extensive tension in the muscles. This creates movements that appear jerky and abrupt. These jerky, abrupt movements also may be inappropriately timed to the words spoken by the suspect. These movements used to emphasize words arrive early or late, thus appearing awkward. When extending the hand to make a gesture, the guilty must overcome the muscular contraction of the arm. As they overcome the muscle's contractions, they overcompensate, which causes the arm to move more rapidly than normal. As a result, the guilty often have difficulty with fine motor coordination.

This loss of fine motor coordination can be observed in a number of places during an interview or interrogation. The interviewer who uses a Miranda or other release form often notes that the signature of the suspect differs from times when the suspect was not under stress. The guilty suspect's signature often becomes illegible or has a spiky appearance. The muscular tension is also evidenced in the movements a suspect may make during the interview. The quick shift of the body, jerky head movements, or his difficulty in simply taking a pen out of his pocket and putting it back illustrates his tension.

The deceitful suspect may also have cold and clammy hands. Although the cold and clammy hands may not always be a reliable indicator, it is a behavior that is controlled by the autonomic nervous system. The interviewer/interrogator may find that the suspect has warm, dry hands at the beginning of the interview and upon shaking hands at the close, discovers that the suspect's hands have become sweaty and cold. This change may be the result of their fear of detection and the engagement of the autonomic nervous system. The suspect who has cold, sweaty hands will attempt to wipe them off on their clothes, lap, handkerchief, or tissue. Many suspects who attempt to use a handkerchief or tissue turn it into a created job where it is not only wiping the hands, but also is now being rolled into small balls or being played with. The change in the warmth of the hands is but a small piece of the puzzle in determining if the suspect is deceptive. In the search for truth and deception, the interviewer must look at the context of the behavior, habits of the suspect, and the timing of the events.

The hands also can be used to cover the mouth. Generally, it is the guilty who cover the mouth when they put the hand to their face (see Figure 4.4). The hand over the mouth serves two purposes. First, the hand muffles the voice and makes it difficult for the interviewer/interrogator to hear what the suspect has said. This benefits the suspect by helping him to avoid saying things clearly that may not be in his interest. Second, this gesture may be an unconscious attempt to stop the mouth from actually making inappropriate statements.

In one case, the hand over the mouth was done purposely by the guilty to avoid detection. The company lunchroom had been the location of repeated thefts of the food brought by employees for their lunch. The perpetrator simply consumed another's lunch, which created turmoil among the employees.

In an attempt to identify the perpetrator, a bait lunch containing a

**4.4.** The untruthful suspect often puts a hand over his mouth to muffle his words and to conceal his facial expressions.

nontoxic dye was placed in the refrigerator. This dye turned purple on contact with moisture. After the lunch was stolen, it was readily apparent who was responsible. However, the suspect attempted to avoid detection by concealing her stained lips, gums, and teeth behind her hand.

There are other reasons a suspect might put his hands over the mouth besides deception. The individual may think he has bad breath, has braces, or his teeth may be in need of dental care.

The movements and gestures used by the guilty tend to diminish when they lie. In attempting to control their behavior, the guilty tend to diminish their movements and eliminate those that do not easily cover the deception.

Consider the sixth grade book report. The child who has not read the book or practiced for the oral report tends to stand very stiffly at the front of the class, whereas the student who read the book, and is prepared, is confident. As a result of the confidence in his knowledge, he reacts in a much more comfortable manner. This analogy applies to the criminal case. The guilty have only read the dust jacket of the book, and as a result, are prepared to talk about the high points of their alibi. The truthful read the entire book and are confident of all the details because they know the story completely.

The hands may also be used to screen the eyes during deception. The suspect often is uncomfortable looking at the interviewer/interrogator while he lies. In an effort to conceal his eyes and prevent the interviewer/interrogator from noting his lack of eye contact, the guilty person will use the hands to cover the eyes. Scratching the nose, rubbing the brow, or adjusting the glasses could also be used as a ruse to cover the actual purpose of the hand movement.

*General Considerations.* The hands can also convey other messages to the interviewer/interrogator. The drumming of fingers often indicates the impatience of the suspect. Clenched fists may show the suspect's frustration or a negative attitude toward the discussion or interviewer/interrogator.

The hand's holding the head may indicate boredom, either real or feigned, or evaluation. If displaying boredom, the suspect holds the weight of the head up because the trunk of the body has slumped out of the upright position. In a position of evaluation or consideration, the hand is lightly held on the chin or cheek and there may be some stroking of the face as he considers what is being said.

The hand may also be used to scratch portions of the body. Many guilty individuals undergoing an autonomic nervous system response have a need to scratch. As the blood is diverted from the digestive tract it is rerouted to the surface of the skin. The capillaries expand to take this additional volume of blood and the nerve endings located on the skin's surface are sensitized, that creates a tingling. Many guilty individuals begin to itch and scratch immediately after the introduction of a stressful topic. Desmond Morris, author and behavioral observer, noted that telling a lie often causes a tingling in the face or neck that must be scratched. This is especially evident in the nose because of the large number of capillaries and its sensitivity.

This scratching can be observed in areas of the body that contain large volumes of blood, the scalp, nose, arms, and upper trunk. It is interesting to note that people usually scratch an itch five times. It is rarely more or less than five times. However, a pretend itch used to cover discomfort may be done less than five times. The fake itch designed to cover a delay

4.5. The steepling of the hands generally accompanies a confident attitude of the individual.

or break of eye contact may be scratched much lighter than a real itch. Women often scratch the face more lightly than men because they do not want to smear their makeup.

The hands may also be "steepled," where the tips of the fingers of each hand are touched together (see Figure 4.5). This steepling displays a generally confident attitude on the part of the individual. The rubbing of the hands together can be a positive expectation such as one would do when anticipating a good meal. A slower movement is usually judged as an indication of dishonesty, such as the con man who slowly rubs his hands together and says he has a great deal for you.

Finally, the suspect may use the thumbs to indicate a defensive or

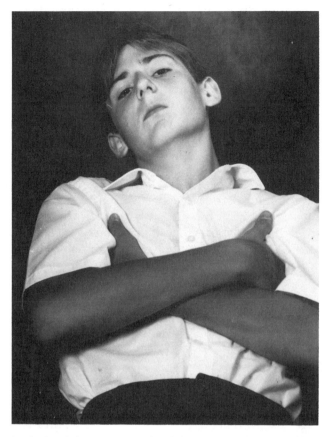

**4.6.** The individual with his arms crossed and thumbs extended upwards often displays a defensive or superior attitude.

superior attitude. Generally, when a suspect takes this posture, he will be leaning back in the chair, arms crossed and fingers tucked underneath the armpits with the thumbs extended upwards (see Figure 4.6). This is the posture often taken by young males as they sprawl out in the chair, feet extended to show that they are not in any way intimidated by the interviewer/interrogator. Although the positioning of the thumbs does not necessarily indicate deception, it may be an indicator of the attitude the suspect is going to attempt to use during the course of the interview/interrogation.

*Arm Barriers.* A deceitful suspect may use the arms as a means of providing a barrier to protect the abdominal region. Crossed arms often indicate negative thoughts or displeasure with the conversation. This arm positioning may also be used in situations where an individual feels uncertain or insecure. The crossed arms are also used when an individual feels cold. The positioning of the hands often helps in the interpretation of crossed arms. If an individual is cold, the hands are flattened and placed under the armpits and the trunk of the body is hugged, whereas anger may be displayed by crossing the arms and clenching the fists under the arms. Sometimes, the hands will not be tucked, but will instead be used to grasp the biceps of the upper arm. Generally, this can be interpreted as a negative posture. The suspect displaying this position is usually very resistant to changing his mind.

The crossed-arm barrier may be modified by an individual to conceal defensiveness. Public speakers, when they are asked questions or challenged, use a modified barrier to defend themselves. Rather than positioning themselves with a full arm-cross barrier, they will use a less obvious barrier that still allows them some protection. For example, the hand may come across to touch the watch or a ring on the other hand. This still provides a barrier protecting the abdominal cavity and reducing the stress that the individual feels. These types of gestures are often used to cover nervousness or apprehension without having to go into the full arm-crossed position.

## Leg and Feet Positions

Legs and feet are often used to provide a defensive barrier for the suspect against the threat posed by the interviewer/interrogator. This behavior has more validity with men than with women. Women are taught to sit with their legs crossed. Their mothers and fathers taught them that this was an appropriate position socially. Younger women, with the advent of pants, do not always use the crossed leg position. Some individuals will not cross their legs because their clothing is too tight or they are in pain from arthritis or an injury. Often, the crossing of the legs is done in conjunction with a crossing of the arms. Women often show displeasure by crossing both the arms and the legs when talking to a husband or boyfriend who has displeased them.

There are two basic methods of crossing one's legs. The first method, generally used by women and older men, is the knee-over-knee (see Figure 4.7). The second type of leg cross is the ankle-over-knee (see Figure 4.8). Although many people say that sitting with their legs crossed is comfortable and that is why they sit that way, the interviewer/interrogator should remember that it is comfortable because of how they feel emotionally at the moment. Crossing the ankles or legs typically provides a defensive barrier against the interviewer/interrogator. As a general rule, the more defensive an individual becomes, the higher the knee rise to protect the abdominal region (see Figure 4.9). In

4.7. The knee-over-knee crossed-leg position is often used by women and older men.

the ankle-over-knee position, the knee rises to screen more of the abdominal region and may even have an arm draped across it to provide an additional barrier for a suspect who feels threatened (see Figure 4.10). In the knee-over-knee crossing of the legs, it is the positioning of the foot that indicates an increased defensiveness (see Figure 4.11). The foot, rather than being held off to one side, is pointed directly at the interviewer to keep him even further away, and reduces the suspect's stress level.

The leg and arm barriers can be seen in everyday interactions between people. These barriers are used when people are dealing with strangers or with others whom they do not know well. Take, for example, the positioning of people in elevators. Typically, they position themselves with their back to the wall, cross their ankles and their arms. This

**4.8.** Another common crossed-leg position is the ankle-over-the-knee.

posturing shows the discomfort of the individual in this environment. By observing the interactions among small groups, the keen observer can begin to identify relationships among the groups in terms of who is dominant and whether or not people know each other well.

The guilty will often extend the legs and feet toward the interrogator to keep him physically at a distance. This may be done using an ankle lock, where the feet are crossed at the ankles. This indicates a negative attitude, nervousness, or fear. By increasing the distance between the interviewer/interrogator and themselves, the suspect reduces the tension and discomfort that he feels.

Changing posture in response to an emotionally significant question in many cases will cause a suspect to cross or uncross his legs. When an interviewer asks a witness if he knows who is responsible for a crime,

**4.9.** A defensive individual may use the knee to screen the abdominal region of the body.

and suddenly observes a shift of the witness's upper body, turn of the shoulders, crossing of the legs, and draping an arm across the abdomen, he recognizes that this question has caused a significant amount of stress in the suspect. Our conclusion, in all likelihood, the suspect knows or has a strong suspicion of who is responsible for the crime.

The positioning of the feet may also indicate to the interviewer/interrogator when a suspect is ready to leave. The suspect positions both feet in a runner's starting block position, twists, and leans toward the door. The hands will move to the arms of the chair or the suspect's knees to help move him into an upright position (see Figure 4.12).

This is commonly used by the host when his guests have overstayed

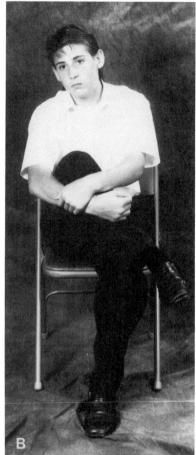

**4.10.** An arm draped over the knee may provide an additional defensive barrier to the crossed legs. The arms may also be used to hold the leg barrier in place.

their welcome. Once the interviewer/interrogator observes these behavioral clues, he should not be surprised when the suspect begins to leave.

Some people will circle or tap their foot during the course of the interview. This is more commonly observed with female suspects or witnesses. Sometimes, this is done as a sign of impatience on the part of the suspect. Some individuals use this as a signal that they need to use the washroom. However, in certain circumstances this activity can signify something in terms of a suspect's truth or deception. Many times this activity will cease completely when a suspect has been asked a particularly stressful question. However, the activity can also start at the point where a stressful question was asked. Thus, the cessation of

**4.11.** The position of the foot helps keep the interviewer/interrogator farther from a defensive suspect. Note also the closed upper body position with crossed arms and twisted shoulder.

this activity or the beginning of this activity may in fact indicate that the individual is under stress as a result of that question.

*Truthful.* A truthful person may use some form of a barrier because he feels uncomfortable about being asked about his involvement or knowledge of a particular crime. However, a truthful individual's crossing of the legs tends to provide less of a barrier than those individuals who are deceitful. The truthful individual often positions the ankle over the knee with the calf almost parallel to the ground. In deceptive suspects, the knee typically rises to provide even more of a barrier for the abdominal cavity (see Figure 4.9). Truthful individuals comfortable with the situation often use no barrier whatsoever and simply place their

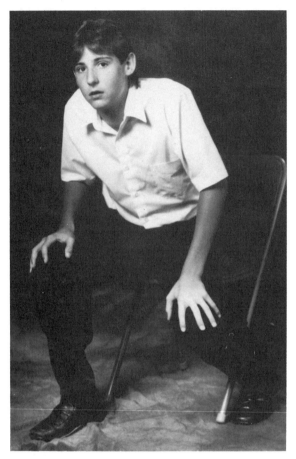

**4.12.** The positioning of the feet in a starting block position, a leaning trunk, and the hands on the knees indicates the individual is ready to leave.

feet flat on the floor with their legs open. This position is somewhat unusual for women, but when they do use it, the feet are placed close together. The positioning of the feet flat on the floor is also very likely to occur when a suspect decides to confess.

This positioning of the feet on the floor appears to provide some emotional stability for the suspect or anyone making a decision. Studies of negotiations in major corporations have shown that when the ultimate deal was agreed upon, over 90% of the key participants in the negotiation had their feet flat on the floor. The feet-flat-on-the-floor position then can take one of two meanings: an openness to discuss and

**4.13.** Truthful individuals generally hold their heads upright. A slight tilt of the head can indicate interest.

come to an agreement, or a behavioral indication of a suspect's willingness to confess.

## Head and Neck Positions

The head and the face are probably the most expressive part of the body. The face is capable is displaying hundreds of different expressions and movements to illustrate and add depth to the words that are spoken. Although the face is capable of giving significant information to the interviewer/interrogator, it is also where most guilty suspects attempt to focus their deceit. In preparing their lies, the guilty often work on the words and the facial expressions that will accompany the words. The authors on numerous occasions have had an opportunity to observe suspects attempting to prepare lies. The facial expression planned by suspects played a keen role in the attempt to deceive. Generally, the guilty would begin by practicing the words they intended to use and the

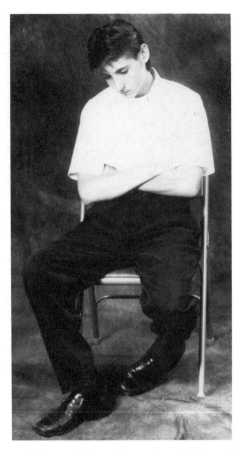

**4.14.** The head-down position can indicate a negative attitude or submission on the part of the suspect.

way they would sound. Then, the guilty suspects incorporated facial expressions and finally some minor hand movements in an effort to convey the message of truthfulness.

## Head Positions

*Truthful.* There are general positions that the head may be in (see Figure 4.13). The first is upright, held straight with its weight supported on the neck. This is generally a neutral position. Tilting the head to either side shows interest. This tilting of the head is similar to the positioning of the head of an animal who is interested in something.

**4.15.** The head back with the individual looking down the nose often accompanies a dominant or superior attitude on the part of the person.

Puppies often do this when they hear their owner whistle or hear a sound about which they are uncertain.

*Untruthful.* The head down can indicate a negative attitude or submission on the part of the suspect (see Figure 4.14). Finally, the fourth position is the head back with the suspect looking down the nose. This head back looking down the nose is a dominant or superior position taken often by guilty suspects (see Figure 4.15). The untruthful individual tends to put the head back or forward out of the plane of the shoulders. The head also may be held up by the hand in the event the trunk of the body has slumped off to one side. The movements of the guilty's head are jerky or abrupt. Many times the guilty individual will roll the head around the neck to loosen the tension in the muscles of the neck and shoulder. In some cases, it is easier for the guilty suspect to nod his head by moving the entire trunk of his body forward and back than it is to move the head because of the muscular tension held in the shoulders and neck. By contrast, the truthful individual tends to nod very gently and fluidly.

## Eye Movements

*Truthful.* The truthful individual will generally have good eye contact with the interviewer/interrogator. Good eye contact is defined in two ways. First, that the eye contact is appropriate for the individual and/or falls within the 40% to 60% range that is normal in most conversations. Second, the suspect maintains eye contact with the interviewer/interrogator when he is asked questions of emotional weight. Although the eyes may offer a significant amount of information to the interviewer/interrogator, it is wise to be cautious because most liars recognize that poor eye contact is an indicator of deception. Therefore, many deceitful individuals will attempt to maintain eye contact even though it is uncomfortable. Generally, the truthful suspect's eyes also have warmth and depth to them and allows the interviewer/interrogator to look below the surface of his eyes.

*Untruthful.* Often the deceptive individual's eyes will be cold and hostile. They have a flat look to them that does not allow the interviewer/interrogator to look beneath the surface of the eyes. The movement of the guilty's eyes can also take on a hunted look. This may include rapid eye movement or the "bug-eyed" look commonly associated with fear. This bug-eyed look will usually allow the interviewer or interrogator to observe the whites of the eyes. These types of eye movements are similar to those observed when surprising a rabbit in the yard. The rabbit's eyes bulge to give it additional peripheral vision, and the rapid eye movement searches for an escape route.

The guilty suspect may fail to maintain eye contact with the interviewer/interrogator in several ways. The first type of poor eye contact is failure to look at the interviewer/interrogator during stressful questions. The suspect may break eye contact by looking away and then look back, or look away to supervise a created job or grooming gesture. Then, he may return to look the interviewer/interrogator in the eyes. Other forms of poor eye contact are eye contact that is nonexistent and eye contact that is too dominant. This dominant eye contact appears aggressive or overly intense. The guilty whose eye contact is nonexistent are extremely uncomfortable meeting the eyes of the interviewer/interrogator. This extreme lack of eye contact is an excellent indicator of deception. Nonexistent eye contact, with a corresponding emotional withdrawal, can also be an indication that the guilty suspect is in submission and ready to confess.

Eye contact may also be broken by the guilty by closing of the eyes when a denial is made or by placing the hand over the face covering the eyes. Additionally, some deceptive suspects may actually turn the entire head and look away to avoid eye contact with the interviewer/interrogator at moments of deception.

It is the eyes that will help us ascertain during the interrogation whether or not we are making headway with a suspect. The tension of eye muscles, softness of gaze, and the amount of the eye contact help the interrogator determine whether the suspect is accepting the rationalization he is being presented.

Many facial muscles are involuntary and can be moved only when an appropriate emotion is felt. Very often, the muscles around the eyes and mouth do not follow the feigned behavior. For example, the suspect who attempts a phony smile has difficulty doing so believably because he is not feeling the emotion of happiness or joy. Although the smile is partially there, it lacks the movement of certain muscles around the eyes and the mouth to make it appear genuine. Instead of appearing genuinely happy, the face has a forced expression appearance.

## Mouth Positions

The mouth also gives behavioral clues that can help the interviewer/interrogator determine whether or not a suspect is deceitful.

*Truthful.* The truthful individual generally has a sincere smile. Although there are any number of smiles an individual is capable of making, the failure to feel the emotion accompanying that smile will cause it to look phony. Usually, the face will have a comfortable, relaxed look, and the smile will be spontaneous and last for only a short period: Genuine smiles tend to be short in duration. The jaw line of the suspect will typically be relaxed and not holding tension.

*Untruthful.* With the guilty, the mouth plays a much larger role in situations where the suspect is attempting to deceive the interviewer/interrogator. Initially, the suspect may attempt phony smiles or smirks to show his sincerity or disbelief at what he is being told. The mouth may also be used to perform created jobs. These created jobs can be anything from picking of the teeth to chewing of the fingernails. Because these activities may be done at times unrelated to stress, their timing is extremely important in determining whether or not they were related to deception.

The mouth of deceptive individuals is often dry. This dryness results from a change in the saliva due to a natural diuretic being secreted into the circulatory system as a part of an autonomic nervous system response. This dryness causes the saliva to take on a tacky, stringy appearance and causes the tongue to stick to the roof of the mouth. As the tongue is extricated from the roof of the mouth, it often makes a dry, clicky sound. This particular physiological phenomena was observed hundreds of years ago by the Chinese and even our own native American Indians. Although there are other explanations beside deception for the dryness in the mouth, such as its being a side effect of medication, it is much more likely to be associated with deception if the dryness has its onset following the introduction of a stressful issue.

The dry, clicky mouth may also cause the suspect to continually lick and wet the lips during the interview. The stickiness of the saliva may require the suspect to clear his throat. In evaluating these behavior symptoms, the interviewer/interrogator should have observed whether they had their origins prior to the questioning about the significant incident or whether they were a result of questions only recently posed. The saliva changes also can cause a slight foaming to occur at the corners of the suspect's mouth.

Although any of these behaviors alone is insufficient to determine deception, in combination with other behavioral indicators they can increase the likelihood of ascertaining the suspect's true status in the investigation.

## Nose

The deceitful suspects often use the nose for created jobs. The hand-to-the nose gesture is often used to screen the eyes and face during the course of a lie. In addition, physiological changes due to the autonomic nervous system may result in an itching or increased nasal discharge. These typical behaviors are event-oriented responses to particularly stressful questions posed to the guilty suspect in contrast to actions of the suspect who comes to the interview with a stuffy nose.

## Neck

The neck can also give behavioral information to the interviewer/interrogator. The larynx or Adam's apple can be observed most clearly in men. In certain suspects, a quivering Adam's apple is due to the tension of the muscles in the shoulder and neck. This quiver may also be reflected in the guilty suspect's voice.

The large arteries and veins on either side of the neck or in the temple of the head often show an observable pulse. The interviewer/interrogator should recognize this physiological response of increased heart rate and blood pressure as being an autonomic nervous system response to stress or the fear of detention.

## Verbal Behavior

The difficulty in assessing verbal behavior is that the words spoken to interviewer/interrogator may be exactly the same for both the truthful and the untruthful suspect. It is only the differences in the nonverbal behavior, tone of voice, loudness, and speed of delivery that may differentiate truth from deception. The interviewer/interrogator must, at the onset of any interview or interrogation, begin by establishing both the suspect's normal verbal and nonverbal behavior. Establishing a normal tone, loudness, and speed of delivery will allow the observant interviewer/interrogator to note differences in responses made by the suspect.

### Truthful

Truthful individuals generally respond directly to questions and make timely responses. Because they are responding with a truthful answer, it is rarely necessary for them to delay to consider their answer. The truthful individual speaks understandably and uses realistic terms when discussing the incident. The truthful person is not afraid to say murdered, killed, stole, raped, fraud, or any other term that attaches a connotation of punishment. They are able to do so because the punishment does not apply to them, but rather to another individual.

### Untruthful

The deceitful individual is vague and stammering in his responses. There may be long pauses when speaking or answers that are too quick, too short, too long, or too elaborate. The guilty talk softly, mumble, and in many cases talk through their hand.

Although on the surface it seems that there is a significant difference between the dialogue of the truthful and untruthful, the interviewer/interrogator must look at the suspect's behavior in terms of both what is normal for the individual and what is normal for the population as a whole.

The deceitful individual and the truthful individual will vary in a number of ways in their use of verbal ploys. One that frequently comes up is complaints. A complaint may be voiced by the both the deceitful and truthful individual; however, the timing of the complaints may be significantly different. If a truthful person does complain, he usually waits until the latter part of the interview when the interviewer/interrogator has completed most of his tasks. At that point he will voice any complaints that he might have. Not so with the deceitful. They tend to form their complaints early in the interview alleging violation of rights, the inconvenience of the interview, the discomfort of the environment, or any other complaint that seems appropriate in the least.

### Case Example

The authors were called to investigate a $100,000 diamond shortage in a jewelry store. The loss had occurred over the six months prior to its discovery at inventory. An analysis of the case facts lead the authors to conclude that the theft was most likely to have been perpetrated by the manager or assistant manager because it required the inventory count to be manipulated. This manipulation of the count was necessary because the diamonds, owing to their value, were counted each day. Therefore, any diamonds that were missing would have been discovered during the evening count unless company documents had been altered. The most likely individual to carry out the manipulation was either the manager or his assistant.

Prior to beginning the interviews, the authors were standing in the store waiting for the assistant manager to arrive. While doing so, they noted a male enter the store. He looked at the authors and the regional manager and quickly turned his back. The regional manager was questioned as to his identity. The regional manager identified him as a full-time sales clerk at the store.

Because of the clerk's unusual behavior when he observed the regional manager and investigators, it was decided to interview him first. The suspect was greeted by one of the authors, who introduced himself. The employee immediately began a tirade. In a loud voice, he asked who we were, what we thought we were doing, how could we bring him in on his day off. He demanded identification and attempted to control the early portion of the interview. His complaints ranged from his displeasure at being there on his day off to complaints about the violations of his rights as an employee. This behavior was extremely unusual for this individual, who was normally quiet and reserved.

The onset of the complaints met the criteria for a deceptive individual. Additional behavioral clues during the interview lead the authors to believe that he was responsible for the $100,000 loss. His explanation for his animosity toward the interviewer was the fact that he had been brought in on his day off.

The next interview conducted was with a female employee also brought in on her day off. She was cooperative, pleasant, and allowed the interview to go to its conclusion. Once the interview concluded she related that she thought it was unfair that she had to come in on her day off, with no notice, to be questioned. She said that she understood the reasons for it, but hoped that in the future arrangements could be made to do any interviews during her regular work hours.

Thus, there were two suspects with the same complaint, both of whom voiced it, but the suspects' timing and attitude were significantly different. By looking at the timing of the complaints in this case, it is evident that the first individual did not want the interview to continue. Subsequent investigations revealed that the first salesman had been able to manipulate the inventory documents by deducting rings from the inventory log count. Since nobody was checking the register media to determine if the ring was actually sold, the first salesman simply deducted a piece of diamond jewelry from the count, indicating it had been sold. When the count of the diamonds was done that evening, the log matched the diamond pieces still present.

## Unsolicited, Premature Excuses or Explanations

Often, the guilty will attempt to get their story out before they are ever asked. They attempt to prove their innocence through a premature explanation, which typically highlights the reasons why they could not or would not do anything like that. This explanation might be totally unsolicited or may be in response to a question such as, "Did you steal the car?" The response begins with a denial and immediately goes into a dissertation of why the suspect could not be involved. The truthful response to this question is more likely to be very direct, "No, I didn't." At that point, the truthful individual waits to have another question directed toward him. The guilty suspect will often use this method to discount, in advance, any evidence he is aware of which is contrary to his claim of innocence.

## Uncheckable Sources

Truthful individuals rarely rely on an uncheckable source to substantiate their story. The truthful individual often does not even realize that he is a suspect or potential suspect in the case. He merely views himself as someone who has been asked to help out. The guilty person, however, views himself as much more than a witness. He sees himself as someone upon whom the investigation may focus. As such, he feels it is necessary to add credibility to his statements over and above the words themselves. The statements made by deceitful individuals often rely on an uncheckable source to back up their story:

You can ask my mom. Were she alive today, she would tell you...

You could ask my [priest, rabbi, minister, social worker] they would tell you...

You can ask my parole officer, he'll tell you I didn't or I wouldn't...

The use of these uncheckable sources is intended to bolster the believability of the suspect's statement. In reality, if an investigator were to check these sources, they would generally not find any derogatory information, simply because these would be the last people in the world to whom the suspect would confide his wrongdoing.

## Focusing on Irrelevant Points

This tactic is often employed by the guilty in an attempt to convince an interrogator of his innocence. In this technique, the guilty person identifies some irrelevant point of information that can be verified as a known truth witnessed by a named third person. The suspect offers the interviewer/interrogator an opportunity to verify his truthfulness on this specific point. He does this because it is in fact true. The suspect then uses this irrelevant known truth to tie the pieces of his deceptive story together. The interviewer/interrogator is asked to believe the alibi because he has been offered an incident that he can check on and find is indeed truthful. Therefore, the suspect would like the interviewer/interrogator to believe that everything else he has said is also the truth. A suspect who utilizes this tactic typically returns to the irrelevant known truth on a number of times to tie the deceptive story together.

The suspect may also focus on petty issues that are insignificant to the major investigation. Often, rather than talking about the primary incident under investigation, the suspect talks about how he was treated or rather mistreated by the officer during the course of the arrest. They will attempt to discredit their accuser through their accuser's alleged improper behavior. By discrediting the accuser, the suspect attempts to discredit any allegations that the accuser made. For example, the suspect will attempt to discredit the victim of a rape by calling her a "lying whore." By alleging that she is a prostitute and a liar, the suspect casts doubt on any allegations she may have made concerning her being raped. Suspects often accuse an interrogator or interviewer of mistreating them during the interview or interrogation. By casting a cloud over the propriety of the interviewer/interrogator's treatment of him, the suspect focuses attention away from his admission and the facts of the case.

A suspect may also use irrelevant points to prove his innocence. The driver in an accused arson discounted the witness's description of the vehicle and partial license number because the witness did not observe a for sale sign in the rear window of the truck. The suspect's argument was that if the witness did not see the sign it was not the suspect's vehicle.

## Excessive Politeness or Respectfulness

Many guilty suspects will attempt to win over the interviewer/interrogator by being overly polite and respectful. This politeness often seems quite out of place. For example, the 17-year-old street gang member who talks in a respectful tone of voice and calls the police officer "Sir." This attitude is out of character for this type of individual and is probably an attempt to deceive the officer or gain favor. This attempt to gain favor or deceive the interviewer/interrogator has one of two aims. First, the suspect hopes that, by being polite and respectful, he will predispose the interviewer/interrogator to believe his lies because the interviewer likes him. Second, the suspect hopes that if his deception is discovered, the interviewer/interrogator may give him a break because he was not a troublemaker. The overly polite and respectful manner of speech is a tip-off to the interrogator that the suspect is attempting to predispose him favorably toward the suspect.

However, individual differences may indicate that this is the suspect's normal behavior. Whereas the 17-year-old gang member would be unlikely to call an officer "Sir" except sarcastically, a suspect recently out of the military might do so as a matter of course. Certain areas of the country also encourage the use of "sir" and "ma'am" as part of their respect shown to elders. Obviously, in these cases, the interviewer/interrogator should consider that these may be appropriate geographic responses rather than a deceptive individual's attempt to curry favor.

## Helpfulness

In some instances, the guilty will attempt to deceive the interviewer/interrogator by being overly helpful. Generally, his helpfulness is an exaggerated attempt to give the interviewer/interrogator anything that he or she needs, but the helpfulness is a guise to lull the unwary interviewer/interrogator into complacency about the suspect. The suspect hopes that he will be overlooked because of his cooperation.

Observing the suspect following the interview is often beneficial in making a determination of their truth or deception. This observation may be conducted by police, loss prevention personnel, or the employee's immediate supervisor. Often what will be observed is an employee who is overly helpful. This overly helpful employee is overzealous in performing his work, cleaning, and caring for the tasks at hand. This overzealousness is generally out of character for the employee and should be noted as an indication of deception. The suspect may also return in a sullen or despondent manner as the realization of his predicament strikes home.

At other times, the suspect will return to talk to the interviewer/interrogator. This return to talk with the interviewer/interrogator is designed to test the water and see how his story was accepted. The suspect returns with a question, a minor bit of information, or to ask for directions. Using these as a ruse, he can evaluate the interviewer/interrogator's attitude toward him. The suspect is looking for behavioral changes that indicate belief or disbelief. For example, the suspect may ask for directions back to his house. This is hardly necessary since, in most instances, simply reversing ones tracks will take him back home. At other times, the suspect will come back to correct irrelevant information. This irrelevant information might be as simple as the suspect's starting date of employment. By correcting this information, the suspect can evaluate the interviewer/interrogator's behavior, plus show the suspect's helpfulness and cooperation with the investigation. The suspect who manifests this behavior is often deceptive.

## Delays

As a general rule, a delay in response to an interviewer/interrogator's question is a good indicator of a suspect's guilt. Innocent individuals rarely need to think about a response. They simply answer the question posed directly and promptly. The guilty, however, often pause or delay a response while they consider:

1. What is the truth?
2. What type of response is appropriate to deceive the interviewer/interrogator?
3. What might be the potential result of the response they make?

Ask yourself this question: "Did you have breakfast this morning?" The response to this question has little or no emotional impact on you. However, your response to the question is generally an immediate "yes" or "no." "Did you drive to work this morning?" Again, the response is an immediate "yes" or "no." The truthful suspect does not have to delay to consider his answer. The answer is obvious to the truthful and they have no reason to delay. It is possible, however, that an innocent person might delay for any of the following reasons:

1. The wording of the question
2. A significant delay in time between the incident and the interview
3. Mental confusion

As a general rule, the interviewer/interrogator should recognize that a delay or pause in a speech pattern is very often related to attempted deception by the guilty suspect.

The interviewer/interrogator must also recognize that a failure to delay by a suspect or witness could also be an indication of deception.

Some of the questions asked of a suspect requires that he give them some thought prior to making a response. For example, consider all the jobs that you had ever held, your immediate supervisor at each position, and out of those supervisors pick who was best and why. This compound question should legitimately result in an individual delaying before giving a response. This is not a simple yes or no question either in terms of the span of time covered or of its complexity. A delay to this question is appropriate and typical of an innocent individual. If the individual responded to this question immediately with an answer, the interviewer/interrogator should suspect deceit. It is the guilty who spend their time anticipating questions that they think might incriminate them.

Another explanation for an immediate response to the best supervisor question would be that the individual was looking for a job and had been just asked the question. It could also be that they are considering looking for a job, and are anticipating interview questions, or they could have had only one job and one supervisor.

It is usually the extremes in behavior that indicate deception. Answering a complex question without thought is just as likely to be deceptive as delaying in answering a very simple question.

Many deceptive suspects will utilize a series of verbal and physical ploys to cover the awkward pause while they decide what to say.

## Physical Behavior

The suspect may utilize any of a number of physical behaviors to cover the delay in his response. These could be coughing, taking a deep breath, clearing the throat, or sighing. The suspect also may use created jobs or grooming gestures such as picking lint to avoid an awkward appearance to the delay before they respond. Although these behaviors in and of themselves are not necessarily deceptive, when combined with a delay in response to a direct question such as, "Did you rob Marty's gas station last night?" they would be indicative of deception.

## Repeating the Question

Another tactic employed by the deceitful is repeating the question. The individual responds by repeating the interrogator's question and then responds with the answer. For example, an interviewer/interrogator asks the suspect, "Did you ever just think about breaking into a drug store even though you didn't actually do it?" The suspect responds by saying, "Did I ever just think about breaking into a drug store even though I didn't?" The suspect pauses and answers, "I would say no."

Repeating the interviewer's question allows the suspect a moment of time to consider his response and its implications. Simply repeating the question he was asked requires little or no work on the part of the suspect's conscious mind. While slowly repeating the question back to the interviewer/interrogator, the suspect can easily consider his alternatives and make an appropriate choice of a response. This is a conversational tactic used between people everyday while we consider a response. For example, if you were asked, "Did you ever consider returning to college to get a degree in psychology?" your response might easily be, "Return to school to get a degree, well, yes I have thought about it." Repeating the question allows you to consider your response and attempt to identify the asker's motivation. However, in an interview/interrogation, questions often do not require thought because they are simply factual recollections. Thus, the suspect who repeats the question, "Did I kill John Jones?" or "Did I steal merchandise?" before making a denial, is in all probability deceptive.

## Responding with a Question

Another ploy of the guilty is to avoid answering the interviewer/interrogator's question by asking a question. This evasiveness is accomplished by diverting the interviewer/interrogator's attention when the suspect responds with a question. This response is designed to avoid an answer that may tend to incriminate them. In conversations, individuals often use this tactic when they perceive that the conversation is moving in a direction that is potentially embarrassing or threatening to them. The change of topic is often accomplished through a question. The evasive device might simply be, "Did you hear what happened over in the fourth district last night?" The change in topic hopes to pique another's interest, causing them to forget about probing an area potentially threatening or embarrassing to the individual. Suspects use the same method in attempting to evade particularly intrusive or threatening questions.

The suspect may also utilize this type of a response in an attempt to draw the interviewer/interrogator into a direct accusation. Questions such as "Are you saying I stole?" "Are you saying I killed her?" "Are you calling me a thief?" are ploys by the suspect to force the interviewer/interrogator to take a position and defend it. If the interviewer says "no," the suspect can reasonably believe that the interviewer/interrogator does not know his guilt for sure. If the interviewer/interrogator responds affirmatively to these types of questions, the suspect can now make a denial and begin to defend his position. Dealing with this suspect's tactics will be discussed in a later chapter.

## Hanging Sentences

Often, an interviewer/interrogator's question will cause mental confusion on the part of the suspect. This mental confusion will result in hanging sentences. The suspect attempts to develop a response to the question asked by the interviewer/interrogator; however, as he begins talking, he realizes that his response is inappropriate. Once he realizes the inappropriateness of his response, he changes the direction of his answer and attempts to continue.

The interviewer/interrogator hears, "Well...," "You know...," "It could be that..." Often, the suspect will look sheepishly at the interviewer/interrogator in hopes that he will not be required to complete his answer, or the partial response may be finished with a shrug of the shoulder.

Hanging sentences are an excellent indicator of mental confusion. The inability of the suspect to answer the question directly and his display of a confused thought pattern should be of particular interest to the perceptive interviewer/interrogator. It may or may not be to the interviewer/interrogator's benefit to explore this particular area immediately. He should, however, recognize the hanging sentence as a point of confusion and stress, and, therefore, probably a point of deception by the suspect.

## Nonresponses

The tactic of nonresponsiveness can take one of two forms. First is evasiveness. The evasiveness by the suspect is simply interjecting some other statement and directing the conversation away from something that he did not want to talk about. Politicians utilize this type of response to avoid answering questions that they do not want to answer. Instead, they turn the conversation to points that they feel make them look better or they want to talk about. A nonresponsive answer fails to answer the interviewer/interrogator's question and instead leads him into areas that are either less threatening or more positive. The truthful individual, however, is less likely to respond this way since he tends to directly answer the question.

The second form of unresponsiveness occurs during the interrogation of a guilty suspect. During the submissive phase of the interrogation, the guilty suspect withdraws emotionally and begins having an internal conversation with himself weighing his options. In many instances, this withdrawal is so complete that the suspect actually does not hear the choice question posed by the interrogator. This requires that the interrogator repeat the question several times. It is not an unwillingness to answer, but rather the emotional withdrawal that causes the delay in answering. This will be discussed in more detail during submission and obtaining the admission.

## Giving a Minor Admission

Another tactic utilized by the guilty is to make a minor, less threatening admission in an attempt to convince the interrogator of his truthfulness. In the private sector, the suspect may make an admission to a policy violation in an attempt to cover his involvement in theft activity. In such cases, the suspect may make a minor admission to drug use in an attempt to convince the officer of his noninvolvement in a rape.

The minor admission by the suspect is supposed to convince the interviewer/interrogator of the suspect's truthfulness and candor. Usually, this derogatory revelation is a very minor admission that is not likely to result in any serious action being taken against the suspect. "Yeah, I tried grass" or "Maybe I didn't ring up the correct price," are examples of minor admissions that might be made by the suspect.

## Gallows Laughter

Inappropriate laughter (gallows laughter) by a suspect is an attempt to make the interviewer/interrogator's question seem petty. Generally, this gallows or forced laughter is inappropriate and fails to have the ring of authenticity. This laughter usually has a forced and uncomfortable sound. The laughter can also be used to cover the deceptive suspect's delay. In some cases, a suspect will use gallows laughter and then mockingly admit that they did the crime and exaggerate circumstances surrounding it.

> *INTERVIEWER:*  Did you have sex with Mary Smith?
> *SUSPECT:*  (Gallows laughter) Have sex with Mary Smith? I did it twelve times with her and then we laid on the beach naked drinking champagne.

The gallows laughter, mocking tone, and exaggeration by the suspect is designed to humiliate the questioner and ridicule him for the foolishness of his question. The interviewer/interrogator may be embarrassed at having posed a foolish question. As a result of the suspect's treatment the interviewer/interrogator may fail to follow up on the question because of the suspect's mockery.

## Political Answers

Political answers are attempts by a suspect to respond to the interviewer/interrogator's question without telling a complete lie. The political response allows the suspect to hedge his bet against potential evidence that the interviewer/interrogator may possess. These types of qualifying phrases are used by the suspect to evade, to avoid having to falsify and lie directly.

Some examples of political answers would be

To the best of my knowledge...

I believe...

If I recall correctly...

Kind of...

Sort of...

Not really...

At this point in time...

If my memory serves me correctly...

These types of responses are typically used by deceptive individuals. The guilty suspect may use these qualifiers when an interviewer/interrogator's question was not exactly on target. For example, the interrogator asks the suspect, "Bill, did you break into the house on Derby Lane?" The suspect responds, "No, not really."

The suspect's response leaves open the option that he did burglarize the residence, but did not break in. The suspect may have just walked into the house through an unlocked door. The suspect's response was a qualified denial. The qualified response is generally indicative of a deceptive individual. Truthful suspects respond directly and deny the crime generally, "I didn't steal any money." The guilty respond by denying specifically. "I didn't steal that $300." This leaves open the opportunity for the deceptive individual to evade the specific incident without confessing to a secondary involvement in a crime.

## Emphasis on Truthfulness

Often, deceptive individuals will attempt to convince the interviewer/interrogator of their veracity by continually referring to how truthful they have been. They will use phrases such as, "Honestly," "Honest to God," "Trust me on this one," or, "I swear on a stack of bibles," to increase their believability in the interrogator's eyes.

In addition, the guilty may point out how helpful they have been in previous investigations. They may even vaguely identify incidents in which they helped the police or loss prevention resolve a crime. The guilty may also point out his instances where he has turned in lost or stolen property. These instances may or may not be true.

However, the truthful individual who may have cooperated in the past generally does not find it necessary to highlight his cooperation with the police or loss prevention. The truthful individual believes that his past behavior is already known by investigators. The truthful individual usually does not consider himself a suspect, and therefore has no reason to enhance his believability. The guilty person, on the other hand, believes that all eyes are turned on him and he will utilize any effort to make himself look better.

## Memory Problems

Memory problems are often indicative of the deceptive suspect. Memory problems can take one of two forms. The first is selective inability to remember. They will use this faulty memory in an attempt to forestall any interrogation: "How can I tell you that I did it when I just don't remember," or, "I might have taken something but I just don't remember what it was."

Many interrogators find that the "I can't remember" defense is difficult to overcome. The interrogator is put into the position of having to prove that the suspect does remember. The difficulty here is that the interrogator has little chance of proving to a guilty suspect that he does recall his dishonesty. Even factual evidence that indicates the suspect's recollection can be overcome by the suspect feigning a memory loss.

The second form of memory problem is a selectively good memory. Here the suspect has the ability to recall specific incidents that support his noninvolvement in the incident, but he lacks the ability to recall information that may not be helpful to his case. This selective good memory can also be found in instances where a guilty suspect is able to recall information from a previous date with great detail. The recollection of this particular incident is recalled because it favors the suspect.

In general, the recollection of an event is predicated on a "hook" in the memory. There has to be some significance to the event or hook that causes a suspect to recall the details. For example, if you were asked what you were doing on July 1, 1989, most people would be unable to remember. However, if you were involved in a significant event such as an accident, had a death in the family, left on vacation, or had some other memory hook that you were able to tie the event to, the recollection is likely. Often, the ability to remember is affected by the significance of the event and the amount of time passing before the event has to be recalled.

With the passage of time, the memory can also become distorted. Usually, the truthful individual who is able to recall an event does so repeatedly with only minor changes. The deceptive individual who is manufacturing a story to enhance the believability of his innocence is often likely to tell the story with significant changes in the details. The deceptive individual is often reluctant to repeat his story to other investigators or to retell the story to the original investigator for fear that the details will not match. The liar needs a good memory.

During the investigation of a burglary, a suspect was questioned regarding the details of the suspect's whereabouts prior to, during, and after the crime. As he recounted his alibi for the third time, the interrogator began to point out the repeated changes and discrepancies in his story. The interrogator told the suspect that he couldn't keep changing his story and the suspect responded, "I can if I want." The suspect who changes his story repeatedly does so because he fails to recall the details he made up, perhaps only moments before. The adage "a liar needs a good memory" is never more true than when he attempts repeatedly to recount the details of his alibi.

Finally, some suspects will attempt to use the "I don't understand" tactic to discourage an interrogator from attempting to elicit a confession or information. Here, an otherwise intelligent suspect claims not to understand questions or the meanings of the questions and thus avoids responding to the interviewer/interrogator. Failing to understand a question might be acceptable if the suspect was of especially low intelligence and the interviewer/interrogator was not speaking to his level. However, this tactic is usually used by the guilty to evade a direct response to an interviewer/interrogator's question. Suspects who speak English as a second language frequently hide behind this ploy to foil answering questions.

The tenacity with which a suspect will stick with his story is also dependent upon his truthfulness. Truthful suspects are able to recount their story repeatedly with only minor changes and will rarely change significant details of the story. In evaluating a suspect's alibi, the interviewer/interrogator should look for subtle, minor differences that are likely to be found in a truthful suspect's story. It is the guilty who vary significantly in the details of the story and are willing to change the story to fit real or fictitious evidence presented by the interviewer/interrogator. For example, the suspect claims to have been home for the entire evening watching TV. When the interviewer/interrogator questions him regarding his being identified near the location of the robbery, the suspect suddenly recalls that he did run out to get a pack of cigarettes. This change of the suspect's alibi is typical of the guilty person's need to explain away seemingly damaging evidence presented by the interviewer/interrogator. Techniques to offer the suspect a chance to change his story can be found in Chapter 6 in the section "Questions of Enticement."

## The Admission of Guilt and Offer of Restitution

The innocent suspects refuse to admit involvement in an incident to which they were not a party. Their denials are generalized and they refuse to admit any guilt or make restitution for a loss in which they were not a party.

The guilty are much more likely to attempt the ploy that they are willing to admit guilt if it makes the interviewer/interrogator "happy." The guilty also may say, "Okay, if that's what you want me to say, I'll say it." This is said with a sarcastic voice and is rarely a genuine offer by the guilty to confess. The guilty however, use this ploy in an attempt to make the interrogator back off. This is a childlike approach to a difficult situation where the individual attempts to blame others for his difficulty.

The guilty may also offer to pay for things that they deny that they stole. Generally, they do this "just to be fair." In certain instances, a truthful suspect may offer restitution. In these situations, the individual tends to be long-term, conscientious members of the community, who because of a misguided feeling of responsibility, feel obligated to pay for the loss. The interrogator should view such offers of restitution carefully. These must always be tested by the interrogator to determine whether they are from the truthful or deceptive individual. To test such an offer, the interrogator offers a fictitious second amount or incident to see if the suspect is willing to pay that amount back too, even though we know that it was not stolen. The following dialogue illustrates the testing of the offer to make restitution.

> INTERROGATOR:   We're glad to hear you say that you're willing to pay this money back even though you didn't take it. That shows a lot of effort on your part and I think we're a long way toward getting this cleared up.
> SUSPECT:   Yeah.
> INTERROGATOR:   Now I'm not sure if you are aware, but besides the $151 loss, there was an additional $30 shortage that came up in the funds about a day later. Can we count on you to pay that back too?
> SUSPECT:   No!
> INTERROGATOR:   Why not?
> SUSPECT:   Because I didn't take that money.

In many cases, the guilty suspect realizes what he just said. He is willing to pay back $151, but not just $30 because he didn't steal that. Thus, some suspects are tricked into an admission or they give a vague refusal to pay the money.

A truthful individual, however, may also reluctantly agree to pay the fictitious $30 loss back. If the individual agrees to pay back a fictitious amount, the interrogator should view the agreement to make the restitution for the loss cautiously. The suspect may simply feel responsible

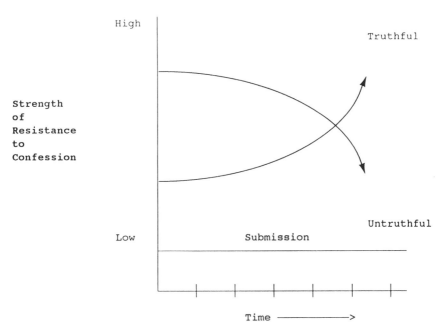

**4.16.** This chart illustrates the resistance of truthful and untruthful suspects. The truthful suspect's resistance to a confession increases as time passes in the interview, whereas the guilty suspect's resistance lessens until he is ready to confess.

but in no way had stolen the money. On the other hand, the suspect could have been involved in other thefts, which was the reason for the offer to pay back the fictitious loss.

## Verbal Slips

Another excellent indicator of deception is a verbal slip. Verbal slips are mental errors by the guilty suspect. While they recreate the image of involvement in their mind and attempt to formulate a deceptive answer, their verbal response becomes confused. In the confusion, they actually acknowledge their involvement in the incident. The interviewer/interrogator should consider the odds that a truthful person would respond in this way.

> *INTERROGATOR:* Mark, let me ask you, did you rob the 76 station in Des Plaines?
> *SUSPECT:* Yes..., I mean no...

The suspect has spoken the truth unconsciously. Before his conscious mind can take over with the contrived story, the mouth misspeaks the truth. Probably more common is the verbal slip that occurs during the phase of developing the admission. In these types of slips, the suspect is repeatedly attempting to minimize the seriousness of his involvement. Often, these verbal slips come when the suspect is asked how many items he has taken. Up to this time, the suspect has said a shirt, coat, jacket, VCR, and a radio. When asked later in the interrogation to again tell the interrogator the items he has stolen, several items now are spoken pluralized, such as jackets and radios. There are really two issues at play in this example. First, the unconscious mind's selection of the truth before the concocted story takes over, and second, the inability of the suspect to recall what he has previously told the interviewer/interrogator.

The guilty will also be particularly interested in what the punishment for the incident under investigation is going to be. He will often question the interviewer/interrogator regarding what is going to happen to the person responsible. The truthful suspect rarely does this because he has a good idea of what the end result will be: termination, prosecution, and embarrassment.

## Strength of Denials

If the interrogator confronts a truthful suspect, he usually receives initial denials that are direct and spontaneous. As the interrogator presses the interrogation and time passes, these denials get progressively stronger, and the truthful suspect becomes more and more dominant. Ultimately, the truthful suspect is able to stop the interrogator from making any headway and begins to convince the interrogator of his truthfulness.

The guilty suspect, on the other hand, may start off with denials that are equal in strength or even significantly stronger than those of the truthful suspect (see Figure 4.16). The feigned initial strength of denial may be coupled with contrived emotional acts that are overacted and unbelievable. The difference between the truthful and untruthful denials is that as the interrogator begins to offer rationalizations that allow the suspects to save face, the guilty's denials tend to diminish in strength and frequency. As the rationalizations begin to have their desired effect of reducing the suspect's resistance to a confession, the suspect becomes quiet, and slowly moves behaviorally to a submissive posture and ultimately a confession.

# Causes of Denials

5

*The greatest cause of denials is often the
interviewer/interrogator himself.*

Lying and the use of denials is a daily occurrence in many individuals' lives. Many people find that it is easier to lie than to tell the truth. Lies and denials vary in their seriousness from the "white lie" to the very serious. Denials are usually the guilty person's attempt to protect his deception from being uncovered by another. Although there are other forms of denials, this text will concentrate on those used to protect a deception.

An individual's use of denials is essentially a defensive or avoidance behavior. From childhood, we learned that an admission of wrongdoing generally results in unpleasant consequences. Young children easily learn that if they admit the damage to a fallen lamp, it will result in their being punished. After several incidents, the child has learned to deny his involvement to avoid the unpleasantness of a consequence. The punishment or consequences may be as minimal as a parent's disapproval or causing pain to another by telling them the truth.

Opposing an individuals' perception of the helpfulness of the lie in avoiding consequences is society's moral disapproval of lying. An individual's desire to avoid the consequences conflicts with religious, parental, and societal imperatives to tell the truth in spite of the consequences. On the one hand, parents, teachers, and religious leaders encourage truth telling and appropriate moral conduct, but on the other hand, they punish the child when inappropriate behavior is discovered. The inability of the individual to reconcile the two sides in his mind leads to a mental state called *dissonance*. Psychologists use the term dissonance to describe a stressful state where the mind is not in equilibrium. The stress is created by the knowledge of what is right versus the attempt to deceive, which violates society's moral and ethical codes. The emotional stress resulting from these conflicting views is guilt. Guilt is sometimes so overpowering that it alone can overcome an individual's fear of consequences.

When an individual begins to tell lies, he discovers that, on occasion, he may be successful in his deception. Thus, the successful perpetration of the lie becomes a learned behavior, and is used repeatedly to overcome situations of risk. The successful liar soon learns that this deception, if successfully carried out, gives him power. Gradually, the lies begin to accompany forms of wrongdoing, which range from theft, to murder, or to some other act.

However, lying to others has an effect upon an individual. First, the successful liar discovers that lies are becoming easier to tell and he begins to perceive them as less harmful to others. Second, the liar's perception regarding his chances of being caught begins to alter. He begins to believe that he cannot be caught lying. This changing perception skews the individual's judgement and he begins to lie more frequently. The liar believes that lying frequently reduces his chances of getting caught. Although this is completely untrue, it remains his perspective. The third effect lying has on a liar is his believing his own reasons or good motives for committing the crime under investigation. The suspect believes that to kill or steal is justified because of his altered reasoning.

Thus, socialized individuals develop a *benefit versus consequence* scale. The decision whether or not to lie is based upon the individual's assessment of whether the benefits of telling the truth outweigh the consequences resulting from an admission. The suspect's fear of consequences typically fall into one of five areas:

1. Fear of prosecution
2. Fear of termination
3. Fear of embarrassment
4. Fear of restitution
5. Fear for their own or another's physical safety

The following thought process illustrates the development of a denial:
Fear of consequences → fear of confession → defensiveness → denial

Youngsters often make decisions using the fun coefficient. The fun coefficient is the amount of fun that they will have doing something, divided by the amount of trouble they will get into if discovered. If the amount of fun outweighs the amount of trouble, the decision is easily made. In the event that the likelihood of discovery seems minimal, then the immediacy of the fun will outweigh discovery and they will elect to follow the wrong path. Very young children are not even this sophisti-

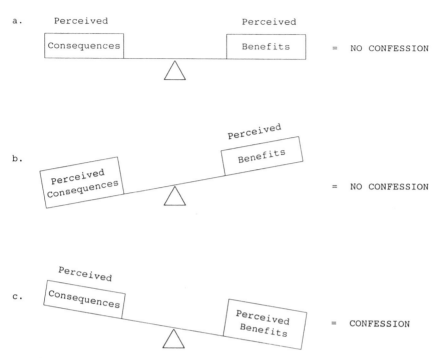

**5.1.** The suspect who perceives the consequences and benefits as equal generally takes the path of least resistance and does not confess. The suspect who believes the seriousness of the consequences outweigh any benefits of a confession will also not confess. It is the suspect who perceives a benefit that outweighs the consequences who confesses.

cated and often do not even consider the possibility of a consequence. As an individual matures, the consequences, or their perception of the consequences, take on a greater role in the decision making process.

In making a decision to deny, the individual weighs the consequences to himself and others, as well as the benefits. These benefits, however, may not necessarily be real or tangible. The benefits may simply be the individual's perception of how he will be perceived by others. His belief that he will be favorably perceived by others may or may not be true; however, it may overcome his fear of embarrassment.

The decision to confess, therefore, is to a large extent determined by the benefits perceived by the individual. This decision making process is illustrated in Figure 5.1.

Denials occur daily in each of our lives in the form of concealment, misrepresentation, avoidance, minimization, exaggeration, or falsification. The interviewer/interrogator can face the possibility of denials in both interviews and interrogations. During an interview, an interviewer must overcome the witness's resistance to giving information. The witness's or victim's resistance to giving information is a result of his perception of the consequences. The consequences of cooperation may be retribution from the criminal, having to testify in court, which takes time away from work or family to testify, embarrassment, or simply being viewed as an informant. Any of these may be a sufficient consequence for an individual to resist giving information.

On the benefits side of the equation is helping catch and punish the person responsible, doing their duty as a citizen, the publicity, and the need to feel important. All of these can be perceived as benefits. The perception of consequences and benefits is purely individual, but can be generalized across different types of witnesses and suspects. Each witness and suspect has his own set of needs that may influence his level of cooperation.

In an interrogation, the suspect sees consequences in a much more personal way. He recognizes that the loss of his job, prosecution, or personal embarrassment are directly related to his involvement in the issue under investigation. To a lesser degree there may be a fear of having to pay back what he has stolen or of suffering physical retribution from others involved. Even though the suspect internalizes these consequences in a much more personal way than a witness, benefits can be presented to overcome his perception of the consequences. For some suspects, simply the reduction of guilt that they feel as a result of their having been involved in the incident may be sufficient to overcome the process of denial. This is occasionally seen when an individual turns himself in after discovering he can no longer live with the guilt of knowing that he killed or stole from another person.

Some suspects simply cannot stand up emotionally to the overwhelming weight of evidence presented to prove their guilt and they confess. Other suspects perceive that there may be a benefit in how others will think of them. For them, it is important to be allowed to save face with family, friends, or coworkers. This face-saving provides the suspect a sufficient benefit to overcome the consequences.

Thus far, we have considered the causes of denials as a result of learned behavior. The fear of consequences results in defensiveness and that defensiveness manifests itself as a denial of involvement. Recognizing that the consequences can sometimes be an overwhelming concern to the suspect, the interviewer/interrogator must consider the suspect's view of three primary factors that can cause denials.

1. The environment
2. The interrogator
3. The suspect

An interrogator should consider the suspect's perspective as it relates to the causes of denials. The interrogator must look at the suspect's moral and ethical value system to understand the suspect's reasons for denial. How the suspect perceives the consequences, investigation, interrogator, environment, and himself can all have an impact on the likelihood of denial.

## Environment

Recognizing that the environment can play a major role in whether or not a suspect may deny or resist a confession is important to the interrogator. There are a number of environmental considerations that may precipitate a denial.

### Privacy

During the discussion of room setting, we equated privacy and the perception of privacy to the emotional impact that it has on a suspect. In an environment without privacy, the suspect may feel increased fear of embarrassment, which will result in a denial. The selection of the witness may also result in increased likelihood of denials. Where the witness has an emotional bond with the suspect or has developed a friendship or trust, this may result in an increased likelihood of denial because the suspect does not want to admit that he has violated another's trust. Remembering that an individual prefers to be perceived in the best possible light will enable the interrogator to anticipate situations where a witness may cause a denial because of his relationship with the suspect.

### Supportive Environment

Selecting an environment that is supportive to a suspect may also increase the likelihood of a suspect's denial. In these situations, because the suspect is in a familiar, supportive surrounding, he may feel emotionally secure and stronger, which results in his failure to understand the difficulty of his position completely. The higher the level of comfort, the more likely it is that the suspect will discount evidence against him with a denial. The supportive environment may also lead to denials because the suspect vividly sees the impact that a consequence will have on his normal life. The supportive environment of home or office also affords a suspect the day-to-day distractions, that he may use to avoid thinking about his guilt.

Interviewer/interrogators generally avoid interviewing or interrogating a suspect in a supportive environment, but this is often not the case with victims or witnesses. In many cases, seeking a supportive environment for a victim or witness will assist them in building a greater rapport with the interviewer. A supportive environment can be especially important when interviewing a small child. Emotionally insecure with adults, and frightened because of the situation, children are often uncooperative and denying. The interviewer who uses a supportive environment reduces the likelihood of the denial and increases the child's cooperation.

## Positioning

Finally, consider the positioning of the interviewer/interrogator in relation to the victim, witness, or suspect. Positioning oneself in ways that increase the individual's defensiveness, such as standing over or sitting too close to him, should be avoided. Each individual has elliptical behavioral zones surrounding his body in which he interacts with others. The intimate zone is the innermost zone, which generally extends out from the individual one to two feet. Into this zone, an individual typically allows family, close friends, lovers, and small children, people with whom he is particularly comfortable being close to physically. The second zone is the social zone of the individual. This generally extends from two to perhaps six feet. It is in this zone that the majority of an individual's social interaction takes place. It is here that the person conducts meetings, makes purchases, and holds discussions with others. The third zone is a public zone extending out six to ten feet, in which the individual will react to others, but to a lesser degree.

Studies of violent criminals have postulated that their intimate zones may extend further than normal from their body. This would explain why these violence-prone individuals often claim that the violence was sparked because "he was in my face" or "he was crowding me," even when the evidence suggested otherwise. Significant internal pressure can be felt simply by standing face-to-face with someone. The closer one moves forward, the greater the pressure or discomfort that is experienced. This discomfort is more pronounced when there is not a close personal relationship between the two individuals. When an interrogator invades a victim's, witness's, or suspect's personal zone, without allowing the individual to become accustomed to his presence, it will directly translate into an emotional discomfort. This discomfort can cause defensiveness and ultimately a denial by the individual.

An interviewer/interrogator's standing close or moving too quickly toward a suspect or witness often results in a suspect's corresponding movement away from the interviewer/interrogator. The emotional pressure caused by the proximity of the interviewer/interrogator can result in a suspect's or witness's even feeling physically threatened. This certainly could increase the likelihood of a denial and/or a failure to cooperate further.

### Interviewer/Interrogator

Not surprisingly, the greatest cause of denials is often the inter-viewer/interrogator himself. Denials are often not fully understood by interviewers and interrogators. Interviewers/interrogators often blame denials only on the suspect's fear of consequences. Although the sus-pect's fear of consequences and personality play a significant role, the interrogator may have caused denials because of strategies or tactics he employed during the interrogation. The suspect's perception of the interrogator and his strategy can often dictate whether the suspect will deny.

## Interrogator's Personality

The suspect's perception of an interrogator's personality can play a large part in determining whether the interviewer/interrogator will be able to overcome a suspect's fear of the consequences. Interrogators who are overbearing, aggressive, or nonempathic toward a suspect often increase the suspect's defensiveness, resulting in denial. An interrogator who displays this type of personality is judged by the suspect to be an opponent. The suspect counters the interviewer/interrogator's attitude with defensiveness, which leads to denial. The adage that you attract more flies with honey than vinegar is especially applicable when antici-pating the likelihood of denials.

When an interrogator is disliked by a suspect, the dislike often culminates in distrust and denial. Part of the suspect's decision to trust the interrogator is based on the interrogator's sincerity and certainty in the suspect's guilt. An interrogator's lack of sincerity encourages a suspect to deny because he fails to trust the interrogator.

## Interrogator's Attitude

The interrogator who appears to the suspect to be too-matter-of-fact, passive, robotic, or rushed in his handling of the case may cause a denial. In each of these cases, the suspect may determine it is in his best interest to deny because of his negative perception of the interrogator. In situ-ations where an interrogator is too passive, the suspect may view this as weakness and exploit it by denials and aggressive behavior. In in-stances where an interrogator attempts to rush the suspect into a confession, the suspect may elect to deny simply because he believes the hurried demeanor of the interrogator is a weakness he can exploit. Here, the interrogator's weakness is his lack of time to complete the interrogation. By making denials, and waiting the interrogator out, the suspect believes that he can win the encounter.

## Interrogator Reputation

In some instances, an interrogator's reputation may foster the suspect's denial. If the interviewer/interrogator has a reputation as being uncaring, rough, or unfair, it may encourage a suspect to deny because of his increased fear of having to deal with a nonempathic individual.

Denials also often occur when the interviewer/interrogator has had unsatisfactory encounters with the suspect previously. Personality conflicts resulting from earlier encounters, interviews, or interrogations are often sufficient to cause denials by the suspect.

If the interrogator has previously been fooled by the suspect, or the suspect has not confessed during previous interrogations, the suspect is likely to deny involvement because of those past experiences. The suspect has successfully held off the interviewer/interrogator during the previous interviews or interrogations, and he fully expects to be able to do so again. His presumption that this investigation is not conclusive is supported by his past experience, when he was neither arrested or terminated. The failure of the termination or arrest to materialize after his last confrontation bolsters his ability to hold up during future interrogations. If a suspect is able to hold up against a competent interrogator the first time, it is unlikely that other interrogators will gain an admission without strong conclusive evidence of the suspect's guilt.

## Tentativeness and Unconvincing Behavior of the Interrogator

The verbal and physical behavior displayed by the interrogator during the interrogation can also directly affect a suspect's decision to deny. In instances where the interrogator is perceived to be unsure, inconsistent, or weak, the suspect will often make a denial to test the interrogator's assertions. Because the suspect sees a lack of confidence by the interrogator, he denies because he does not believe the investigation is as conclusive as the interrogator would have him believe. Therefore he denies involvement to continue to avoid detection.

An interrogator's uncertainty of the case facts, misquoting of commonly known facts, or unprepared appearance can all encourage a suspect to deny. The suspect's decision to deny is based upon his belief that he has not been identified. The suspect is gambling that the interrogator's bumbling of the facts is directly related to the competency of the investigation. Most suspects recognize that an incompetent investigation will be unlikely to result in their being proved guilty of the offense.

The interrogator's tentativeness, evidenced by his lack of preparation and understanding of the case evidence, may convince the suspect that he is in a winning position. The interrogator's tentativeness may be reflected in his tone of voice. An interrogator's voice that is insincere, uncertain, or lacking confidence may bolster the suspect's belief that he has not yet been discovered, and contributes to his decision to deny.

A suspect consistently evaluates the language used by the interrogator to determine the viability of continued denials. An interrogator who uses tentative words such as might, could, perhaps, usually, or maybe when describing the suspect's involvement, encourages a suspect to believe he has not been caught. Consider the difference in emotional impact of the following two statements:

1. "With our investigative techniques, we can sometimes identify the person responsible for the incident. In this case we think that it is probably you."
2. "There is no question about the results of our investigation. It clearly indicates that you are responsible for the incident."

The tentativeness of the first statement encourages a suspect to attempt to evade detection by using a denial. The second statement may also result in a denial, because of its directness, but the suspect can also observe the confidence the interrogator displayed in the suspect's guilt.

## Perception of Interrogator

The suspect's initial evaluation of the interrogator may cause him to deny simply because he believes that the interrogator can be fooled. The suspect is encouraged to lie and deny his involvement in the incident because he believes that it is unlikely that the interrogator can or will detect his dishonesty or lies.

Inspector Columbo is television's answer to this type of interrogator. Columbo is portrayed as a bumbling, incompetent investigator. Columbo's incompetence is perceived by the suspect who denies and makes up lies to cover his tracks. The suspect's downfall, of course, are his own lies, as he discovers the bumbling inspector is merely a role played by the sharp, intuitive Lieutenant Columbo.

The suspect is encouraged to lie because he believes that the investigator is just another individual that can be successfully fooled. The origin of the suspect's belief that he could fool others began when he successfully duped parents, teachers, and employers. The suspect's perception of the interrogator's competence may be derived from his knowledge of the system and his having previously beat other incompetent interviewers and interrogators.

Recognizing the interrogator's bumbling ways, the suspect believes he will, in all likelihood, be successful in this deception as well. Therefore, he denies involvement.

## Wrong Rationalizations Used by the Interrogator

In Chapter 8 of this text, we will discuss the use of rationalizations to overcome a suspect's resistance to confessing. At this point, it is sufficient to say that a suspect who has not been offered an acceptable face saving device will be more reluctant to confess than one who has. In some instances, a suspect can be encouraged to confess simply because of the overwhelming evidence of his guilt. However, the confession could be more easily obtained if the interrogator transfers the suspect's guilt and minimized the seriousness of the incident through the use of rationalizations.

It is the interrogator's job, during the interrogation, to establish the credibility of the investigation that leads the suspect to believe he has been identified as being responsible for the incident. Developing a belief by the suspect that he has been caught is critical to the suspect's making an admission. However, factually overwhelming the suspect without allowing him to save face or failing to convince him that his guilt has been absolutely detected is likely to result in a denial. An interrogator who fails to allow a suspect to save face is really asking for multiple admissions from the suspect—one, that he did it and two, that he is a horrible person for having done it.

When the interrogator fails to offer the suspect a way to save face, the suspect denies because he cannot emotionally handle the negative image of himself and the consequences he faces. The lack of justifications for the suspect's actions only increases the emotional weight of the incident in the suspect's mind and encourages him to deny.

Offering the suspect a rationalization that he does not accept can also increase the likelihood of denial. The suspect may feel that economic reasons would justify his acts, but the interrogator talks instead about job performance. The interrogator's failure to meet the emotional needs of the suspect with a proper rationalization increases the probability of denial because the suspect has not adequately been given the opportunity to save face.

Rationalizations are always individualized for each suspect. In certain instances, a suspect will not accept a particular rationalization or justification for his behavior. For example, a suspect may rationalize and believe that economic reasons were a contributing factor for his committing a particular crime. If the interrogator fails to use that justification, however, he will find increased denials and resistance by the suspect. Once the interrogator discovers the reason favored by the suspect, the level of denials will decrease dramatically as the suspect accepts the face-saving devices. An interrogator who is faced with recurring denials should shift rationalizations in an effort to find one more acceptable to the suspect.

## Personalizing Rationalizations too Early

In the early stages of a confrontation with the suspect, an interrogator can cause the initial denial by utilizing rationalizations coupled with the pronouns you and you're or the suspect's name. In instances where the suspect has not yet accepted the rationalizations, the use of the personal pronouns you and you're is more likely to encourage a suspect to deny because the interrogator's words are hitting too close to home. During the early stages of an interrogation, where the interrogator has not made a direct accusation of involvement to the suspect, the use of third person pronouns (them, they, he, she) discourages the suspect from denying. The suspect listens to the rationalizations and allows them to have an impact on him but is not threatened by the rationalizations because they lack directness.

## Highlighting Consequences

The interrogator may also cause a suspect's denials by increasing the seriousness of the consequences. This is done by the interrogator's using realistic words that recreate the seriousness of the incident in the suspect's mind. An interrogator who uses words such as steal, theft, murder, rob, or rape encourages the suspect to reconsider the consequences. During the interrogation, the interrogator uses rationalizations to minimize the seriousness of the suspect's actions. However, by using words that attach consequences, the interrogator is encouraging the suspect once again to build his fear of detection, become defensive, and deny.

Some interrogators highlight the consequences in the hope of scaring a suspect into a confession. Only rarely does this tactic work. More often, it merely encourages additional resistance from the suspect whose fear of detection has increased.

## Interrogator Silence

The word choice of an interrogator may cause denials as might long pauses or silences. The use of silence by an interviewer/interrogator rarely enhances the likelihood of a confession. To the contrary, it allows the suspect an opportunity to think and assess other possibilities that might convince the interrogator of his innocence. In an interrogation, silence invites the suspect to join the conversation. Especially in the early stages of the interrogation when the suspect is still emotionally strong, this invitation will almost always result in denials. Although pauses by the interrogator have their place in highlighting a particular

statement or word, those pauses that extend beyond the need to emphasize a point or word invite a denial from the suspect.

Silence in an interview can sometimes be an effective tactic. Since
the victim or witness is talking much more, they tend to fill silence with
more conversation. This often results in additional information being
developed. By contrast, in an interrogation, the suspect will deny or lead
the interrogator astray.

## Interrogator Strategy

The interrogator's selection of a particular strategy in the interrogation
may also increase the likelihood of denials. Interrogators who immediately confront the suspect without establishing rapport or building the
credibility of the investigation often force the suspect to protect a
position and deny. In this case, the initial cause of denials is not
complicated. The directness of the interrogator's approach catches the
suspect off guard and the suspect's first instinct is to lie. Now the
suspect has not only committed the crime but also has lied by denying
his involvement. The interrogator who forces the suspect into a position
of having to lie about an incident typically encourages the suspect to lie
and deny further in order to protect what he has already said.

The interrogator who elects to use a strategy of interrogating a suspect
on his strongest defense may also face denials. The interrogator who
begins the interrogation by focusing on a single specific incident or
moment in time encourages a suspect to mount a defense. The suspect
perceives that his exposure is minimal, and he can protect himself with
a denial.

Once the suspect is able to grasp the focus and direction of the
interrogation, he can build his defenses. When the interrogator focuses
his attention on a single issue, this limits the suspect's exposure and
makes his defense easier to construct. If the interrogator cannot prove,
to the suspect's satisfaction, that the suspect is involved, he will
continue to deny. Often, because the interrogator lacks the necessary
proof, the suspect's denials grow in intensity when he recognizes the
investigation's weakness.

Because the interrogator has confronted the suspect on only a single
specific incident, the effects of denials can be very difficult for the
interrogator to overcome. Once the suspect discovers that his denials cause
the interrogator difficulty, he will continue with additional denials.

## Wrong or Incomplete Evidence

In many cases, an initial attack on a suspect's story was based on
incomplete or inconclusive evidence. Once an interrogator has used

incorrect facts to establish the credibility of the investigation, the suspect will gamble that the investigation is not conclusive in proving his guilt. If the suspect believes that the investigation is inconclusive, he will employ denials to defend himself and his position.

Investigative errors shake the suspect's belief that he has been caught and encourage him to take a chance that the interviewer/interrogator does not really know he is responsible. These errors in investigative facts may lead the suspect to specifically deny, "I didn't kill her with the bat." The suspect is denying the weapon, not the crime. In a theft, the suspect may say, "I didn't take those twenty VCRs." It may be that he took fifteen, and the victim inflated the loss to obtain a larger insurance claim.

These specific denials by the suspect are often a predecessor to the confession, if the interrogator recognizes that the suspect is not claiming innocence but just denying incorrect details. Recognizing a specific denial by the suspect often allows the interrogator to correct the wrong information that caused the denial and delayed the admission.

## Perceived Lack of Proof

Another cause of denials by a guilty suspect is his belief that the interrogator cannot prove his allegation. The interrogator who fails to establish the credibility of his investigation promotes a belief by the suspect that his guilt is not certain, which will certainly cause a suspect to deny. The suspect, in evaluating the risk–benefit scale, believes that he has not been clearly identified. The suspect who believes that his guilt is uncertain will continue to deny until the interrogator presents evidence to prove his involvement.

The liar believes that others have the same value system as he does and believes that they would attempt to deceive him. For this reason, he is unlikely or unwilling to believe the interrogator's statements regarding his involvement in the incident. Because he fails to believe the interrogator, he is likely to continue to make denials until he can evaluate the interrogator's proofs.

## Compromised Investigation

Denials are also likely from people who have had time to prepare for the interview or interrogation. Sometimes, the interrogation of a suspect has been compromised by third parties. The third party may have been a coconspirator previously interrogated or a well-meaning individual who gives the suspect information, leading him to believe that he will be interrogated. The suspect, having had time to develop a story and think through the probable questions he might be asked, believes he is likely to be able to convince the interrogator of his innocence. By preplanning his story, alibi, and defenses, the suspect believes he has concocted a plausible sequence of events that can answer all aspects of even a thorough investigation.

Because the suspect has had time to prepare, his behavior can appear more truthful because of a reduced fear of detection and/or time to practice the lie. Having time to prepare reduces the level of emotion he feels about the incident and his lie. The reduced level of emotion make it easier for the suspect to limit the leakage of deceptive behavior. An interrogator should be cautious when evaluating a suspect's behavior if the suspect had prior knowledge of the likelihood of an interview/interrogation.

Similarly, an interrogator who fails to pin down a suspect in his alibi or story before presenting evidence may find that he has encouraged the suspect to deny his involvement. The suspect's denial is encouraged because he has the latitude to make up incidents or circumstances that explain away the damaging evidence. The interrogator's failure to lock the suspect into a story allowed the suspect the freedom to make up lies more easily. Since it is easier for the suspect to lie than to tell the truth, he denies and then fabricates supporting alibis.

## Questioning Techniques

The questioning techniques used by an interrogator may also prompt denials from a suspect. The use of direct accusations almost always results in a denial by the suspect, especially if used in the very earliest stages of the interrogation. This direct accusation often begins the cycle of denials as the suspect uses more denials to protect himself and his original denial.

An interrogation beginning with this type of statement—"Our investigation indicates that you killed John Jones!"—will almost always result in a denial by the suspect. This denial occurs because the interrogator has not offered the suspect an opportunity to save face or has not established the credibility of the investigation in the suspect's mind.

## Denial to Stall for Time

On occasion, a guilty suspect will use denials as a means of stalling for time while he evaluates his situation and weighs his alternatives. The suspect who has been directly accused will often deny while he decides how to handle the situation. This is often employed as a first line of defense by the suspect who has been surprised with a direct accusation by the interrogator. The suspect employs a denial that refutes the interrogator's allegation simply because it requires little or no thought and buys him the time necessary to plan and evaluate further action.

An interrogator may also cause a suspect's denial by presenting evidence of the suspect's guilt too early in the interrogation. The presentation of evidence without providing a face-saving rationalization for the suspect encourages him to deny. He denies because he would be admitting that he was involved and that he was a horrible person for having participated in the incident.

Generally, interrogators who present their evidence early in the interrogation are attempting to bring the suspect quickly into submission. However, contrary to this widely held notion, it is more likely to encourage a suspect to deny, or at least to question the validity of the evidence presented by the interrogator.

The suspect is usually physically and emotionally strongest at the beginning of the interrogation. Because of his strength, even strong evidence will often be questioned by the suspect. This is particularly true in cases where the evidence is circumstantial. Circumstantial evidence is even more susceptible to attack by a suspect than direct evidence because, when viewed separately, it may seem weak or inconclusive to the suspect. Many a suspect believes that if there is no direct evidence, such as a witness or video of his involvement in the crime, then he has not been caught. This belief reduces the emotional impact of the circumstantial evidence against the suspect and increases the likelihood of a denial.

In the earliest stage of the interrogation, a suspect will often look for the interrogator to present them a question or statement that he can deny. When this question or statement is not forthcoming, suspects will often attempt to elicit it by asking, "Are you accusing me of stealing?" or "Are you saying that I did this?" The suspect has now laid a trap for the unwary interrogator. Should the interrogator respond, "Yes, that's exactly what I'm saying," the suspect has now drawn an interrogator into a direct accusation to which the suspect can appropriately respond with a denial. The suspect now has drawn the lines of engagement and will continue to protect his position with additional denials.

The stalling tactic is also employed by suspects who have used aggression and denials to get out of trouble in the past. This type of response allows a suspect to attack. The adage that says the best defense is a good offense certainly applies with this type of individual. The aggressiveness that the suspect had used in the past often forced weaker or uncertain opponents to back down from even strong positions. The success of his past experiences encourages the suspect to return to this pattern of behavior.

## Poorly Timed Question

The interrogator may also cause a denial by asking a poorly timed choice or assumptive question. The choice question offers the suspect an acceptable versus unacceptable choice for committing the crime, for example, "Did you use the money to buy drugs or was it for bills?" The interrogator will encourage the suspect to select one of the choices. In an interrogation where the suspect has not stopped his denials, this will only encourage additional ones. The interrogator may have asked the suspect, "Did you plan on doing this or did it happen on the spur of the moment without thinking?" The suspect who is not emotionally ready to confess responds with a denial such as, "I didn't do anything." If the interrogator follows up with another direct question, such as, "Well, has this happened a lot of times or just a few?" it only encourages another denial from the suspect. The failure by the interrogator to recognize the level of the suspect's resistance will result in poorly timed questions that cause the suspect to deny.

## Waiting too Long

In some situations, an interrogator may wait too long in an interrogation and pass the point of emotional susceptibility of the suspect to confess. Waiting past the optimum point to obtain a confession results in the suspect's once again becoming emotionally stronger and likely to defend himself with denials. Some suspects become emotionally stronger after crying and return to denials.

## Failing to Reaccuse

Finally, a suspect's denials can be encouraged if the interrogator does not reaccuse a suspect after the suspect makes an initial denial. Once a suspect makes a denial, and it goes unrefuted by the interrogator, the suspect recognizes that the case may not be as solid as alleged. The suspect thinks, "If the interrogator really did have what he says he has, he would reaccuse me. The fact that he didn't may indicate he's bluffing." This increases the suspect's perception that the interrogator may not be dealing from a position of strength, and increases the likelihood of resistance by the suspect.

## Suspect

## Seriousness of the Lie

The suspect also may evaluate the necessity to deny based on his perception of the seriousness of the lie or denial. Often, the liar is persuaded by his own rationalizations that no real harm was intended. People often evaluate the seriousness of a lie based on how much harm it does. A lie that does not do much harm is less serious than one that causes significant problems. The liar also sees a single lie as less serious than numerous lies. Similarly, planned lies are generally viewed as much more serious than lies told on the spur of the moment.

Regardless of the degree, all lies, in some ways, cause damage to the suspect and violate the trust of others. Initially, the damage to the suspect may simply be the personal dissonance caused by his guilt feelings. However, the need to lie may increase because the suspect has told one lie and now is required to support that lie with others. Thus, the individual also suffers from a diminished resistance to telling lies as he becomes more practiced and comfortable in their use.

In many cases, the suspect's moral and ethical guidelines will justify his telling a lie. These justifications for lying are in many cases actually believed by the suspect.

1. He will excuse a lie by stating that it was not a lie, but simply a joke, an evasion, or an exaggeration.
2. The suspect will claim that he was not really responsible for his actions and never meant to mislead, or was incompetent (mentally, or under the influence of drugs or alcohol) at the time the lie was told.
3. He will admit the lie but offers excuses for it.

Finally, the interrogator may focus his interrogation on what the suspect considers the most emotionally significant issue. If an interrogator attempts to obtain an admission to what the suspect perceives as the most threatening issue, it will often increase resistance and result in a denial by the suspect.

An example of this perception is illustrated in a case where a security guard was suspected of stealing women's high-heeled shoes from desks at a bankcard facility. Investigators also suspected that the shoes were being worn by the security officer during his shift.

The interrogator could elect to confront the suspect on any one of three levels, with each level having a greater emotional weight for the suspect. The greatest emotional weight in the suspect's mind would be an interrogation regarding a sexual deviance. Of lesser emotional weight, but still threatening, would be his wearing of the women's high-heeled shoes. The third and least threatening direction the interrogation could take would be to question the suspect on his having taken the shoes without reference to his wearing them or his sexual proclivities. The case was resolved when the suspect admitted removing the shoes from the women's desks.

The interrogation was conducted beginning with the issue of least emotional weight, that he removed the women's shoes from the desk.

When he had admitted the removal of the shoes, the next level, wearing the shoes, could be addressed. By looking at the emotional weight of the incident, the interrogator can pick portions of the issue that will be easier for the suspect to confess to and therefore be less likely to elicit a denial.

The emotional weight or seriousness of the issue is evident in many cases, the rape–homicide where the suspect admits killing but not raping the victim. The burglar admits the burglary but denies defecating on the hall floor. The suspect's view of an issue's seriousness will often result in denial when the interrogator attempts to obtain an admission in an area perceived by the suspect to have the greatest emotional weight.

## Lack of Rules

In certain instances, the suspect will make denials and justify his actions because of the "lack of rules" for his behavior or job. These procedural gray areas are perceived by the suspect as not being "wrong." The suspect's perception that he has not violated rules or regulations or that he is acting within the group norm allows him to justify his behavior. The belief in his correctness causes the subject to make a denial.

Often, this denial is fostered because the suspect knows the ins and outs of his job and/or the criminal justice system. The interrogator should remember that each person he interrogates is an expert at his job, be it stockboy, cashier, bank president, or professional criminal. Knowing the rules, regulations, policies, and procedures of his position allows the suspect to hide within gray areas to maintain his innocence. The ability of the suspect to justify his actions, based on his perception of the work, legal, and/or cultural environment, affords him an opportunity to explain away seemingly damning evidence. As he attempts to explain away damning evidence by using the gray areas, he utilizes denials to protest his innocence.

## Cultural Differences

Cultural differences may also play a role in precipitating a denial by the suspect. The cultural background and beliefs of the suspect may make it likely for him to deny. In certain cultures, the practice of lying to others during business is accepted. This form of denial, and even the perception of right and wrong, based upon cultural heritage, may even dissuade a suspect from believing he has done wrong.

In certain cultures, to take revenge on someone who has dishonored the family outweighs any legal prohibitions against killing. In other situations, the suspect's perception of social status may preclude his making an admission because the interrogator is perceived as being below him socially. This certainly is evident in the Arab or Middle Eastern society and their treatment of women. Asking a female interrogator to conduct an interview or an interrogation with a male from this background is likely to result in denials by the suspect. Their perception of women and their place in society is remarkably different than those commonly held in the western world.

## Drugs and Alcohol

The suspect who feigns drug or alcohol intoxication at the time of the crime may deny knowledge of involvement because he "just can't remember." This denial may be real, but it is more likely to be fabricated. The denial justified by intoxication is often used by victims of prostitutes. These victims will claim that they were "drugged" or "slipped a mickey" without their knowledge. Such an assertion allows the victim a face-saving device that explains how he was robbed but saves him from having to reveal what he had really been up to when he was taken advantage of. The denial is tempered by his inability to remember what actually happened.

## Consequences versus Justifications

Finally, in making the decision whether or not to admit or deny, the suspect must weigh the consequences of his actions and his justifications. In situations where the suspect faces extreme consequences (such as incarceration or death penalty) for his actions, he will often employ a denial. The suspect does so because he is emotionally unprepared to deal with the harshness of the consequences.

The suspect's realization process in an interrogation is comparable to the five stages of grief. In grief, the first stage is denial, then anger surfaces, followed by bargaining, depression, and finally, acceptance. Recognizing that an interrogation is a significant emotional crisis for the suspect to work through, the interrogator should expect that the suspect will deny because he does not want to believe that he has been detected.

Many suspects then use anger as a release or defense to support their denial or in an attempt to dissuade the interrogator. Next comes bargaining. The suspect looks at alternatives and attempts to work out what he considers will be the best deal for himself. Once that thought process has concluded, the suspect then goes into submission, similar to the depression of grief, and finally, acceptance. The suspect cognitively recognizes and then accepts that he has been detected.

When judging the consequences, the suspect must begin to justify to himself and the interrogator his reasons for committing the incident. In many cases, the suspect will have never verbalized these reasons to himself, whereas in others, he has clearly justified his behavior to himself. Although he may believe that everyone is doing it and it is not really harming anyone, he may have never clearly stated it in his mind.

In assessing the emotional impact of being caught, the suspect must now look for that elusive justification that this was the reason for his involvement in the act. Often, it is the interrogator who will help the suspect find the justification that allows the suspect to overcome the denial process. Once the justification or rationalization is firmly set in the suspect's mind, the risk–benefit equation that the suspect has set up in his mind begins to alter. As the risk–benefit scale begins to alter, the suspect will cease making denials and attempt to save face with the interrogator.

## Involvement of Others

Generally, a suspect is more likely to deny guilt if he acted alone than if he acted with others. When a suspect who acted alone is interrogated, he knows the full circumstances of the case, and whether anyone else has been told of his involvement. This suspect can clearly and accurately estimate his exposure in an investigation. Since he has a clear picture of the likelihood of discovery he will often feel confident in his position and his ability to defend himself.

Once a suspect has to evaluate what a coconspirator might have said or done it becomes more difficult to assess his position accurately. Wondering who else might know what the other suspect might have said creates many decision-making problems for the suspect. Now he has to consider if accurate information presented by the interrogator might have come directly from his partner in crime.

In other situations denials might occur because the suspect attempts to protect other suspects. The pressure of peers not to inform on each other can initially create denials. However, the primary weakness of the suspect is his uncertainty and distrust of the others involved. Interrogation of multiple suspects is usually an easier undertaking than attempting to gain an admission from a single perpetrator.

## Truthful Denials

On occasion an interrogator may mistakenly confront a truthful suspect and this will clearly result in a denial. This denial is a result of the suspect's innocence.

Typically, a truthful suspect's denials will be direct and spontaneous.

These denials may be of the specific variety, denying a particular detail of the incident, or may be broad, generalized denials of any involvement.

As a general rule, these types of denials become more dominant and numerous as the interrogation continues. They finally overcome an interrogator's ability to control the conversation. The persistence of these denials, including their spontaneity and intensity, will be a clue for the interrogator in evaluating the suspect's truthfulness to the incident under investigation.

# Interviewing

# 6

*The interviewer/interrogator should*
*understand that although a meeting between*
*a suspect and the interviewer may be*
*nonaccusatory for the purpose of simply*
*eliciting alibis or explanations, it can turn*
*into an interrogation at any time.*

This chapter will begin the discussion of different interviewing techniques by highlighting their differences from the process of interrogation. Generally, an interview is a fact-gathering process that attempts to answer the questions who, what, where, when, how, and why. Talking during the interview, unlike during interrogation, is dominated by the victim, witness, or suspect[1] who responds to questions posed by the interviewer.

During the interview, the suspect may be asked behavior-provoking questions by the interviewer to determine the suspect's truthfulness. The interviewer may be attempting to obtain interpretable behavior that is consistent with that of a truthful or deceptive individual. In doing so, he may be able to eliminate the interviewee as a suspect in the crime or identify him as a possible perpetrator, and thereby significantly narrow the focus of his investigation.

The setting of an interview also tends to be much less formal than that of an interrogation. In an interview, the interviewer may often pick a time and location convenient for the person being interviewed. In the

---

1. The person being interviewed may be a victim, witness, or suspect whose true status is unknown—each can be considered a suspect. That status changes once the interviewer has evaluated their truthfulness and relationship to the incident.

earliest stages of an investigation, the interview is necessarily broad-based, with the interviewer attempting to give direction to the investigation.

Since an interview is a noncustody situation, Miranda warnings are not necessary. There may be, however, situations in which a primary suspect is to be interviewed after the investigation has focused on him. This interview may be intended not to obtain a confession, but rather for the police to attempt to ascertain the suspect's alibi or explanations. In certain instances, because the scope of the interview has narrowed significantly, and identified a particular suspect, a police interrogator may want to consider the wisdom of giving the suspect Miranda warnings, in case the interview later changes into an interrogation and the suspect is taken into custody.

The interviewer/interrogator should understand that although a meeting between a suspect and the interviewer may be nonaccusatory for the purpose of simply eliciting alibis or explanations, it can turn into an interrogation at any time. The change in the process from nonaccusatory to accusatory can be very direct or very subtle. In either case, the amount of talking done by the interviewer and suspect changes dramatically. During the interview process, the investigator has made the majority of his questions broad and open-end to elicit a narrative response from the suspect. To clarify specific points, he may have used closed-end questions. For example, an open-end question might be, "What happened next?" and a closed-end question might be designed to elicit a specific piece of information: "What color was the car?" or "Did she tell you that she had done it?"

However, once the interviewer has elected to confront the suspect, he begins to do all the talking and offers face-saving rationalizations that minimize the seriousness of the suspect's involvement. The difficulty for police who go from an interview into an interrogation is that the suspect may refrain from any further conversations with the officer. This change in tactics may also cause a suspect to invoke his rights of silence and counsel, which stop any further communications with the suspect. In the private sector, such a tactic is less significant because the employee does not generally have a right to counsel or silence (see Chapter 3, Legal Aspects, for additional discussion on the subject).

By contrast, an interrogation is designed to obtain information that might be incriminatory from a suspect who may be reluctant to give the information. The purpose of the interrogation is to overcome the suspect's initial resistance and open a dialogue that will encourage the suspect to give information against his interests. An interrogator is still attempting to answer the six investigative questions (who, what, when, where, how, and why), but there are two basic differences between an interview and interrogation:

1. In interrogation generally, the suspect talks only when he is confessing.
2. The suspect resists telling the truth until he is convinced of the need to do otherwise.

While the interviewer/interrogator is talking with any suspect, victim, or witness, it is important that he look for personal agendas or reasons that may taint the information given during the interview. A sign of such a reason or agenda may even be in the form of the suspect's simple reluctance to cooperate during an interview. This lack of cooperation could be the result of many different reasons, for example, not wanting to be involved because the individual does not want to take time from work to testify in court. Certainly, this is not an unusual attitude because it requires the victim or witness to take the time to go to court and testify with little apparent benefit to themselves. Consider the arrival of a summons for jury duty. Although it is everyone's duty to assist in the criminal justice system, how many people are actually excited about the prospect of being selected for a jury, then having to take time away from work, family, and/or home to be part of a trial. Is it any wonder that witnesses are often reluctant to supply information valuable to an investigation?

The victim or witness may be reluctant to provide information simply because "to inform," "narc," or "rat on," is discouraged by friends, family, neighbors and other peer groups. Giving information may even result in their being shunned by the people most important to them.

Another form of reluctance may come into play when the witness or victim is asked to give information against the interests of a family member or close friend. Here, long term relationships may even outweigh a significant criminal act. In a recent case, the uncle of a child was alleged to have been involved in a series of molestations of his niece. These molestations took place over a number of years prior to the allegations. The niece finally came forward and told her mother about her uncle's activities. The case was turned over to the police and the uncle was arrested. The mother of the child was put under significant family pressure not to testify and to drop the charges against the uncle. The family's reasoning: The uncle had a good job, he was really a wonderful member of the family, and this would ruin his life. The pressure from family members in this case could have tainted the prosecution; however, the mother continued to press for prosecution.

The interview of victims and witnesses is typically done at a time and place convenient to them. If the interviewer/interrogator believes that the individual might ultimately be the suspect and an interrogation could ensue, he should have the suspect come to his office or a location where a more formalized setting can be arranged. Regardless of whether the interviewer plans a nonaccusatory interview or an interrogation of a suspect, the behavior displayed by the interviewer should be one of reasonableness and fairness. There is never room for mistreatment of a witness or suspect by an interviewer. Yelling, screaming, or pounding fists on the table to obtain information from a reluctant witness are reminiscent of the days of the third degree.

In the interview, the interviewer should open the lines of communication so that the victim, witness, or suspect will begin to talk about the incident under investigation. In the very earliest stages of an investigation especially, when a suspect does not yet feel that the investigation has focused on him, he may be inclined to talk at length with the police or investigator. It is during this time that the suspect may give incriminating statements that at first seem like nothing more than innocent remarks. Establishing the suspect's alibi or story in the earliest stages of the investigation can often be of value in a later interrogation, once his stories have been disproved.

The value of this tactic in the police setting is significantly different from that in private settings. In general, the public law enforcement investigators have the manpower and resources to conduct in-depth investigations into the suspect's story. In most cases in the private sector, there is a much more limited approach. The company may not have the resources, manpower, or expertise to conduct an in-depth investigation. In addition, the value of the lies told during the preliminary interview may have greater value in a trial than in a presentation to a personnel manager or company management.

In the private sector, a circumstantial case is rarely sufficient to obtain a termination. As a general rule, personnel departments require direct evidence in the form of an observation or a suspect's statement of involvement rather than circumstantial evidence that tends to prove one's guilt. In the public sector, a suspect's statements or his lies relating to an alibi may prove to be a valuable part of the prosecution's case in establishing the suspect's guilt.

The reliability of the eyewitnesses' or victims' testimony may also come into question because of their personal biases or perspectives. How many times have investigators found significant differences in descriptions of an offender at the scene of a robbery? These differences could be based upon the position of the witness making the observation, the age of the witness, the length of the observation or any number of other reasons. In many cases, the reliability of eyewitness testimony has been seriously questioned by investigators and the courts.

A witness or victim may provide inaccurate information without intentionally doing so. On the other hand, witnesses or victims may intentionally provide only a portion of the relevant information to the interviewer. This information could have been withheld so that the victim did not have to disclose his negligent actions, such as not locking the safe, that allowed the theft to take place.

Certain witnesses and informants are driven by the motive of revenge. They want to get even for a real or perceived insult that the suspect has done to them. In these cases, the interviewer needs to uncover the true motive to evaluate the information. In one case, a security officer stole $4,600 from a safe in the president's office of a manufacturing facility. The guard discovered the combination to the safe in a secretary's phone list. The case was ultimately solved when the security officer's father-in-law called the company to tell them what his son-in-law had done. In this case, the father-in-law was motivated by an intense dislike of the man his daughter had chosen to marry. In another case, a man on parole for burglary was implicated in a break-in at a catalogue showroom, where he stole thousands of dollars in precious stones. The informant was the man's wife. She discovered that while he was incarcerated, she enjoyed living alone. In order to return to the single life, she effected his arrest, prosecution, and reincarceration.

Certain individuals have a dislike for law enforcement, security, and loss prevention officials, and will for that reason fail to cooperate. In situations where the investigator finds a witness or suspect of this sort, there may be little or no usable information to be gained. Generally, such a resentful witness or suspect requires some leverage from the investigator to open a useful dialogue. It may be necessary for the witness or suspect to feel there is some benefit in his talking with the investigator. In certain cases, this benefit may take the form of a lower bond, reduction in charges, or a station adjustment of the criminal activity without formal charges being brought against the suspect or friend of the witness.

The reality of dealing with these resentful individuals is an everyday occurrence for the investigator. It is the desire to trade up for a more significant "catch" that encourages an investigator to attempt this form of barter arrangement. Although it is a common practice for investigators to "turn" a suspect because of their ability to prosecute him, care must be taken to assure that the information supplied by the informant is reliable.

### Case Example

In an investigation of a series of burglaries from railroad boxcars in transit, three suspects were observed attempting to burglarize a boxcar in a railroad yard. The three suspects were apprehended and interviewed about their involvement in the rash of burglaries. During the interviews, one of the suspects offered to trade information for a reduced bond. The information implicated another gang member in the earlier burglaries at the yard. The suspect identified "Tommy Lee" as being involved in the earlier burglaries. The suspect provided information of the whereabouts of stolen merchandise as well as the whereabouts of Tommy Lee.

Subsequent investigation into the information provided by the arrested suspect revealed that Tommy Lee was currently wanted for armed robbery and had two other outstanding theft warrants pending. With the assistance of the local police, a photo lineup was arranged to verify that the suspect, in fact, knew and could identify Tommy Lee. The suspect picked Tommy Lee's picture out of the photo lineup and verified other personal information with an investigator who was familiar with Tommy Lee. Further investigation of the information provided by the informant resulted in the apprehension of Tommy Lee and two other suspects.

The interviewer also needs to be aware that a suspect or victim may omit or evade questions in an attempt to conceal information that he may not want to answer. A victim, for example, might conceal the fact that he was robbed in a hotel room by a prostitute rather than face the embarrassment about his indiscretion. In other cases, the victim may conceal information because he himself was involved in something illegal or unethical. Consider the home owner who falsifies the inventory of items stolen from his home. He includes furs, jewels, and other valuables that he never owned to inflate the claim. At other times, an officer may unwittingly interview the perpetrator of the incident before the investigation has focused on him. During the interview, the offender may attempt to mislead or misdirect the investigation by providing information that is false or that will take considerable time and effort to discredit.

Considering the impact that a well organized and well conducted interview can have on an investigation, it is worth the time and effort to plan and prepare for the optimum results. In Chapter 2, we examined some of the elements necessary to prepare for the interview or interrogation.

We looked at the background information, the case facts, the location of the interview, and other factors that could create a supportive environment for the witness or suspect. Understanding the elements of the crime and what must be proved in order to obtain a conviction or a termination is critical in the interview process. The interviewer should think of himself as a sponge soaking up a pool of water. In this metaphor, the interviewer rarely puts water into the pool that is being soaked up. By not giving information derived from other sources to the person being interviewed, the interviewer can test the truthfulness of the suspect's information. It is also necessary for the interviewer to conceal what he knows in order to prevent information known only to the suspect from leaking out. An interviewer's failure to do this may hamper or taint further inquiries. The investigator must also be careful regarding allegations made against particular individuals while interviewing victims or witnesses. Repeated indiscrete allegations of misconduct during interviews could result in later allegations of slander by the suspect. This should not deter an investigation—the employer and investigator have the right to investigate—but the investigator does not have the right to spread unsubstantiated rumors or allegations.

Prior to interviewing a victim, witness, or suspect, the interviewer should consider which areas they may be able to provide information that is beneficial to the investigation.

### Case Example

In a recent case, $73,000 was embezzled from a firm by an employee "Mary" (a pseudonym), who used a weakness in the accounting system to have checks made out to her. Mary caused from one to three checks to be fraudulently issued to her each month for a period of about 18 months. The company was concerned that the checks and balances within its system had been circumvented. In looking at the employees involved in the checks and balances, it was of a particular concern to the company that Mary may have been in collusion with others. Mary's sister was in management capacity at the company and was responsible for customer service issues. While the older sister was a long-term and trusted employee, the sheer size of the loss indicated that she may have known of her sister's involvement in the theft. When the loss was discovered and Mary was identified as the individual responsible, an investigation was conducted to recover potential assets purchased with the funds. Mary was confronted and initially acknowledged her involvement in the theft of $3,000 from the company. Upon further investigation, the company found approximately $70,000 in other checks that were used to steal from the company.

Further interviews were planned to determine exactly how the system operated and the persons responsible for the checks and balances. A list of people to be interviewed was drawn up, in which each person was categorized by the types of information they would most likely be able to provide. This preplanning of the interview allowed the interviewer to focus specifically on employees who had information regarding the systems in place and their checks and balances. Additionally, the list highlighted employees who knew the suspect, her background and interests. The interviews were planned in such a way that the system and background information provided a picture of both Mary and her sister, "Barb." It had been planned that the final interview to be conducted was to be with Mary's sister because of the potential for collusion between the two. It was determined that Barb would be interviewed with two purposes in mind: 1) to determine whether or not Barb had direct knowledge of Mary's embezzlement taking place prior to its discovery and; 2) to ascertain the lifestyle and background information on Mary. Barb was exonerated of any knowledge of her younger sister's embezzlement activities and went on to supply significant information relating to the sister's lifestyle and off-work activities. This included insights into family relationships, social acquaintances, and interests.

## Preplanning the Interview

In preplanning areas of inquiry, it is often worth taking the time to make notes about specific areas of interest that the interviewer may want to ask about during the interview. It may be also worthwhile to prepare specific questions that may even be written out to assure the accuracy of the way that they were asked. Trial lawyers often use this tactic to ensure that the witness responds to a particular point that may help prove a point or establish a response for later appeal. Lawyers planning for the questioning of the witness during trial use specifically selected words in the question so that they can then evaluate the suspect's responses. Although we suggest that it may be in an interviewer's interest to have written out specific questions, we do not suggest that an interviewer go into an interview and read a list of questions. These questions should be included in the conversation in such a way that they do not seem out of the ordinary. Often, these particular questions may form the key elements of or be the reason for the interview. To place any undue importance upon these questions may alert a victim, witness, or suspect that the interviewer has particular interest in these areas of inquiry.

The key questions need to be camouflaged during the interview so that the interviewer does not highlight their importance. For example, when conducting a kickback investigation, an investigator may look at a buyer's phone records for investigative leads, but the request is not for the buyer's phone number alone. To conceal the target of the investigation, the entire buying department's phone records may be requested. Although an investigator may not be able to conceal the fact that he is looking, he can at least conceal who he is looking at.

## Supporting Tactics

The interviewer should also consider the use of face-saving rationalization, minimization, and justification tactics that will help the witness to feel more comfortable in giving information. These "supporting tactics" will make it easier for the witness to continue giving information since he feels he is doing the right thing. In each interview, a person may or may not need the "support" given him by the interviewer.

However, in cases where a key interview is to be conducted, the interviewer should consider which type of support the witness may need. The witnesses' background, interests, and personality, may offer clues to an interviewer's ways in which he can provide emotional support during the interview. These tactics are more fully explored in Chapter 8, Reducing Resistance—Rationalizations. With only slight modifications, these same tactics can be applied in both the interview and interrogation.

## Rapport

One of the first needs to be addressed is establishing a rapport with the victim, witness, or suspect. Almost any text on interviewing or interrogation encourages establishing a rapport with the interviewee but does not provide any direction on how to establish this rapport. The establishment of rapport is fundamental to the success of any interview; however, establishing rapport with someone is more than merely smiling.

In interviewing, an individual is more likely to confide in someone who he feels is supportive and with whom he is comfortable. Even the most cooperative, agreeable witness can be turned off by an interviewer who fails to establish rapport.

Many times, officers use the authority of their badge and the power of subpoena or a search warrant to encourage a witness to cooperate. Although this might be necessary under certain circumstances, it is not the optimum method for obtaining the desired information. For consumers, by comparison, the decision to buy is often positively influenced by a salesperson who makes them feel comfortable, not by a salesperson who is unlikable or seemingly uninterested.

In the private sector, the investigator does not generally have the ability to subpoena documents or records but must instead depend on the cooperation of the person to be interviewed. In many companies, this cooperation may be limited by the pressure that company management uses to conceal illegal acts or by company policies. Management often views an investigation in different light from the police, security, or loss prevention investigator. Management's perspective is based on need for profit and sales driving the organization. In their view, taking an employee off the sales floor or away from his duties affects the bottom line profit of the organization.

In many cases, company personnel policies restrict interviews without a specific allegation of misconduct against that employee. Thus, there are significant difficulties in conducting investigative or even fact finding interviews within the private sector. The level of cooperation from line management can often be directly related to the backing of the company's senior management.

## Establishing Management Rapport

The interviewer attempting to work within a corporate environment must first begin by "selling" upper level management on the need to conduct interviews. Recognizing that senior management tends to be dollars-and-results-oriented requires that the "sales presentation" focus on the benefits of interviewing. In planning for the interview and the presentation to management, the interviewer should have a clear purpose in mind for the interviews. The interviewer should plan to address managements objections, such as the potential for disrupting the sales function, potential morale problems, and the legal impact on the company as a result of interviewing or failing to interview.

One management consideration that typically comes up in the private sector is the impact of the interview on employee morale and the resulting job satisfaction. Often, management and the personnel department within the organization do not clearly understand the difference between interview and interrogation. Personnel is often hesitant to allow employees to be interviewed because of their fear of the interviewer's making unfounded or wholesale allegations against each person who is interviewed. Often, just taking the time to explain what is to be said and how it is planned can obtain management support for the process.

Clearly establishing the ground rules for the interviews with management and personnel offices before any nonaccusatory interviews are conducted will increase the likelihood of their support and the successful conclusion of the process. Although law enforcement officials can use their position to encourage management to cooperate, the in-house security or loss prevention representative generally does not have the same status within the organization. However, the failure of the law enforcement officer to take into consideration the business aspects of interviewing employees can create management resentment and make the process that much more difficult.

Complicating this issue further is the possibility that member(s) of management may be involved in some illegal activity at the company. Members of management thus involved may be reluctant to allow interviews with the associates because they are afraid that allegations of their wrongdoing may come to light.

In cases where the management at a particular location is weak or suspected of wrongdoing, the investigator may wish to obtain the cooperation of upper level management to overcome any reluctance to cooperate. By anticipating the possible reluctance of a manager to cooperate because of a lack of floor coverage, the interviewer can arrange for additional management to help operate the facility during the time the interviews are taking place. Since police tend to be less familiar with the private sector, they need to be especially sensitive to the needs of the business before interviews are scheduled. This awareness is nothing more than establishing a rapport and a working relationship with senior management to make sure the lines of communication remain open and the needs of each are being met.

## Establishing Rapport with the Victim, Witness, or Suspect

In establishing rapport with the victim, witness, or suspect, the interviewer can use several different tactics. Certainly, an authoritative, superior attitude on the part of the interviewer may cause some people to give information. However, it is more likely that this type of an attitude will increase the defensiveness of the person being interviewed and make him reluctant to cooperate. Preferably, the interviewer should assume a professional yet friendly approach to the person being interviewed. This can be done easily without attempting to be too familiar with the person being interviewed. Interviewers who are too blunt and to the point, who attempt to obtain information without establishing rapport, are often faced with a witness who is cold and uncooperative.

*Common Ground.* Initially, the interviewer should attempt to establish rapport by finding some common ground or interest about which he can speak to the individual. People tend to like people who have similar interests and personalities. By reading the witness's or suspect's personality, the interviewer can establish rapport by changing topics to discuss points of interest particular to them. Drawing a person out and making him talk about himself and his interests tend to establish a comfortable feeling and ease any apprehension. The interviewer must be able to read the individual's behavior to determine how long he should stay in the rapport-generating phase. With a senior executive who is a "get to the point" type of individual, this rapport-generating time may be extremely limited. The interviewer does not want to overstay his welcome, which might tend to affect further cooperation.

As with the presentations to senior management, a sales presentation must be made to each victim, witness, or suspect to secure their cooperation. This presentation highlights the benefits of providing information to the interviewer. The interviewer who knows of a previous complaint at the witness's residence may be able to use that as a benefit to encourage cooperation to assist in resolving this case. However, the witness may be reluctant to give information because the previous problem that he complained about was never resolved. The interviewer encounter a witness who is reluctant simply because the witness feels that since nothing was done before, they should not go out on a limb to help.

In any case, the interviewer who can provide a benefit for cooperation in the interview will increase the likelihood of the witnesses' cooperation. The benefit might be pride, case resolution, revenge, or anything else that returns something to the person interviewed. It may be as simple as showing respect for the individual.

*Appearance and Demeanor.* Often, the interviewer is first judged by his appearance and demeanor in his initial approach. During the first few seconds of the meeting, the victim, witness, or suspect often makes a decision about the interviewer. The interviewer should take care to conceal handcuffs, weapon, or radios, which may increase the seriousness of the incident in the individual's mind and create a sense of unease at giving information.

Words such as witness, victim, court, testimony, or slang terms used by police and loss prevention can also create an unacceptable image. The interviewer should also avoid any words that trigger negative responses. This can be as simple as avoiding the term *witness*. Just as the interrogator avoids words like steal, embezzle, fraud, kill, rape, or other words that attach consequences, the interviewer avoids using words that cause a witness to comprehend the consequences of giving information, such as lost time from work, attending court, or any number of other less than pleasant activities. The interviewer should also refrain from presenting any personal biases or expressing an outward disbelief of what the suspect has said.

Remember that a smile has opened many doors. In a recent study, participants were asked to determine a person's trustworthiness and honesty based on the appearance of his face. People who had a genuine smile were judged to be more honest and trustworthy than those who had scowling or expressionless faces. Is it any wonder that the harsh, cold interviewer may be less likely to produce desirable results than the interviewer who has a friendly demeanor?

*Behavior.* How often have you met someone and after only a short time felt like you have known him forever? With such an individual, an instant rapport opened the lines of communication and made us feel extremely comfortable and trusting. To discover why these feelings exist, one has to only look as far as the similarities in thinking and interests. If we focused on the differences between ourselves and our new-found friend rather than the similarities, we begin to break down and lose rapport with the individual. Recognizing similarities between ourselves and other people is not as difficult as one might think. For example, common ground with any individual might be found in the family, frustrations of work, bills, children, the need to own a car, or any of dozens of other similarities in our lives. Recognizing each of these similarities will assist us in forming a bond with the individual that we are addressing.

Thus, in looking at the victim, witness, or suspect, the interviewer must discover similar interests, dress, activities, friends, or beliefs, as a means to assist in opening a dialogue with the person to be interviewed. Consider how often a common acquaintance forms the beginning of a conversation or friendship.

*Mirroring.* The interviewer who uses only words to build rapport has failed to use all the avenues of communication available. The words spoken between two people account for less than 10% of the communication between individuals. The vast majority of communication takes place using the tone of voice and emphasis on words. In addition, almost half of the communication between individuals is based on physical behavior, posture, and gestures of the participants. Understanding other levels of communication enables the interviewer to incorporate the tone of voice, word emphasis, and physical behavior in his attempt to generate rapport.

By recognizing the fact that people like people who look, talk, and act similar to themselves, the interviewer can consciously begin to model the speech patterns, speed of delivery, breathing, posture, and the gestures of the individual he is speaking to. This is called *mirroring.*

Interestingly, people who have established a high level of rapport with each other tend to mirror each other's behavior (see Figure 6.1). This mirroring shows up as similar body positioning, physiology, tone of voice, and even choice of words used between the two parties. The interviewer who has achieved rapport often finds that the victim, witness, or suspect's body posture, position, and tone of voice is similar to his own.

When the interviewer mirrors an individual's posture, gestures, and physiology, he can create within himself the same emotions that the suspect is feeling. The emotions that a person feels, whether fear, happiness, anger, or something else, are tied to behavioral and physiological clues. If one were to emulate the posturing of a Super Bowl player who had just lost the big game—shoulders slumped, head down, tension released from the body—one could begin to feel the depression and sense of loss that this person is feeling. The ability to change emotions can be as simple as changing the posturing on the body. When a person cries, the head and eyes drop; when a person laughs, the head rises. Try to feel happy with your head down and feel the emotional difference. When a child has fallen and hurt themselves, the mother puts

**6.1.** People who have a high level of rapport tend to mirror each others' behavior.

her hand to the child's chin and raises the head to look into her eyes, and very shortly the child stops crying. The change in head position does not match crying behavior so it stops.

These learned physical actions that we have paired with our emotions are something that we unconsciously do when that emotion is dominant within us. An interviewer attempting to understand the emotional context of the individual he is talking to can develop within himself the same emotion by mirroring the suspect's behavior. By doing this, the interviewer can also create a sense of rapport with the person.

To understand the elements of mirroring and how we interact with others around us, the interviewer should begin to observe people in social settings. When three individuals are having a conversation, do their movements and gestures mirror one another or are they in contrast? If the three are all mirroring each other, there is complete communication going on. However, contrary posturing may mean that there are disagreements or that no rapport exists within the group.

The use of mirroring to establish rapport is merely one element of a science called *neurolinguistics*, essentially, the language of the mind. John Grinder, a linguist, and Richard Brandler, a therapist and mathematician, are primarily responsible for the development of neurolinguistics. It originally was developed to model people who were successful and teach them to be successful by having them model the successful patterns of others.

In certain instances, an interviewer will encounter a suspect or witness who is angry or suspicious of the interviewer's attempt to elicit information. In these cases, it is imperative that the interviewer establish rapport to ultimately alter this person's behavior. By beginning to mirror the voice, posturing, and behavior of the reluctant witness, the interviewer begins working on the subconscious level while the words spoken by the interviewer are having an impact on the individual's conscious mind. The individual consciously hears the words, and because of their similar tone, speed of delivery, and the interviewer's posture, he begins to feel a relationship of responsiveness toward the interviewer.

The interviewer at this point can begin to modify his behavior and lead the individual to a more open, cooperative posture. The ability to successfully mirror another individual is based on the interviewer's observation of gestures and voice patterns and personal flexibility in modifying his own behavior to mirror that of the person being interviewed. This requires practice for the interviewer just beginning to use the technique. It is usually preferable to begin using the mirroring techniques in a social setting. While doing these mirroring exercises, the interviewer should be consciously aware of how he feels towards the person he is mirroring. Once the interviewer has attempted these techniques in the social setting, he will discover that he is able to recognize the emotional state of the person with whom he's speaking.

## Verbal Neurolinguistics Techniques

In addition to mirroring posture, gestures, tone of voice, speed of delivery, and physiology of the individual, it is also necessary to understand that each one of us processes information and communicates on three verbal levels. While each person uses the three levels, visual, audio, and kinesic, to communicate his thoughts and feelings to others, he generally has one dominant channel that will be used. The interviewer can modify his use of language to appeal to the channel that the person is comfortable using at the time of interview.

*Visual Mode.* For example, if an individual generally communicates on a visual level, his conversation and word choices typically are visual in nature or they form a picture with the words. Such an individual uses language as if he were watching a video and describing it. The interviewer might hear this type of individual say, "When you see me say," or "When I see something like this," or "Come and look at this," or "Picture this," or "I'm not sure I see what you're saying," or "Look at it this way."

These individuals are using a visual mode to communicate and process information. Upon recognizing this mode of communication, the interviewer should begin to use similar words that would "paint a picture" for the person to whom he is speaking. The interviewer who uses the channel of communication similar to that of the interviewee considerably enhances the likelihood of rapport between himself and individual; this also results in clear communication between the two. Ask questions such as, "What did you see next?" "How did he appear to you?" "Try to look back and see if you can recall."

*Auditory Mode.* Another individual may use the auditory mode as his dominant channel. Such an individual uses words that express hearing in their conversation. From these types of people, we will hear, "Do you hear where I'm coming from?" or "When I hear something like this," or "This doesn't ring true to me," or "I don't like the sound of this." All of these indicate that the dominant channel is audio. The interviewer should ask questions such as, "What did you hear next?" "What did it sound like?" "Who talked next?" "What did he say?"

*Kinesic Mode.* The final method of processing information is kinesics. Examples of words or phrases that indicate this channel's use might be, "Get in touch with," "Get a handle on," "Let me get the feel of this," "I don't feel good about this," or "Let me get a grasp on this situation." The interviewer might ask questions of this individual like, "How did you feel when you saw this happen?" or "How do you think they felt?" or "Let's get a handle on how this happened."

## Physiological Neurolinguistic Techniques

In addition to utilizing the mirroring and verbal clues to establish rapport and communication, the interviewer can also use the body's physiology to discover the channel of most effective communication. The respiratory pattern of individuals can give an indication of the dominant channel. When people breathe high in the chest, they tend to be in a visual representation mode. If the breathing is relatively even and uses the entire chest and stomach area, they are typically in an auditory mode. Finally, an individual who is using his stomach when breathing is most likely in a kinesic state. To test this principle, note your own respiratory patterns when going to sleep or resting, listening to music, or watching a movie.

In Chapter 4, we noted that the suspect who has a labored respiratory pattern or continually hyperventilates during the discussion with the interviewer/interrogator is under a tremendous amount of stress. The respiratory pattern referred to here simply denotes the neurolinguistic channel that the suspect is using.

The respiratory pattern is also reflected in the individual's voice. The person who is in a visual mode generally speaks quickly and has high-pitched tones. This type of speech pattern is often heard in witnesses who have just observed a crime or significant incident. Because of the emotional impact of the recent observation, the witness clearly visualizes the incident in his mind and processes the information on the visual channel. When an individual is in an auditory mode, the voice is rhythmic and very clear. In contrast, when an individual enters a kinesic pattern, the voice takes on a slow, deep quality. This is often expressed when an individual is extremely tired and the voice becomes slow, and low, as the individual feels the weariness of his body.

When the interviewer uses the elements of mirroring, physiology, and verbal neurolinguistic techniques to establish rapport, he has the ability to quickly achieve the rapport necessary to communicate with the victim, witness, or suspect. These techniques are clearly evident in the day-to-day interaction the interviewer has with family, friends, and business associates. Paying attention to the body language and words spoken by other individuals will allow the interviewer an opportunity to assess their modes of communication and utilize mirroring to establish rapport. By paying attention to your body positioning as you talk to other people, you will begin to identify similar gestures and posturing with the person to whom you are speaking. The next time you go out to lunch, look around at the postures and positions of the others in the restaurant. How many have their legs crossed at the ankle or knee or have the feet planted closely together. By examining the emotional state that you are in at this point, you can begin to make an assessment of the other's emotional state.

### Case Example

As an example of the behavioral mirroring, the auditory and kinesic channels can be demonstrated though an earlier example,"Barb," the sister in the $73,000 loss who was asked to come to the personnel office for an interview. This interview was conducted three days following the discovery of her sister's involvement in the theft of the $73,000. As previously stated, Barb was a long-term, valued employee whose work record at the company was unblemished.

On her arrival for the interview, Barb was defensive and mildly uncooperative. Behaviorally, her body was closed and tense. When she was interviewed, the interviewer shook hands as she arrived and he told her that he was sorry that he had to meet her under such a difficult set of circumstances.

At that point, Barb sat down and crossed her legs and arms. The interviewer modeled this same behavior and opened the conversation by discussing the positive work record that Barb had at the company. During this discussion, she used words that indicated the kinesic channel was dominant.

The interviewer began by discussing how Barb must feel about her sister's involvement, then asking how she felt when she first learned of her sister's problem. After about five minutes, the interviewer opened his arms and uncrossed his legs. Because the sister had now established a strong rapport with the interviewer, she behaviorally followed by dropping her arms to the side of her chair and uncrossing her legs.

At this point, the interviewer leaned forward and began to ask questions regarding her sister. Barb sat forward and began to talk in animated terms about the shock to herself and the family. She went on to relate how she felt personally, and the embarrassment she felt. It was plain to see the relief she felt when she began to talk about the theft and her sister. The interviewer leaned to the side and put his hand to his chin and Barb followed suit, placing her hand to her cheek in the same manner. The interviewer was leading and Barb was behaviorally following because of the rapport between them. Her need to maintain rapport with the interviewer caused her to unconsciously follow his lead and move from a defensive posture into one of cooperation.

The value of establishing rapport with the suspect, victim, or witness cannot be underrated. In the preceding discussion, we have seen that neurolinguistics, mirroring, and communication can form a bond with the person being interviewed. The establishment of rapport results not from merely being pleasant, but rather from the establishment of both a verbal and physical communication that enhances the relationship and responsiveness of the person interviewed.

During the victim's, witness's, or suspect's narrative, the interviewer should begin evaluating the verbal and physical behavioral patterns of the person he is interviewing. The interviewer should attempt to establish a behavioral norm for the individual. Consider the person's voice pattern, word choice, attitude, and the physical behavior as well. By establishing this behavioral norm when the suspect is in the rapport-building phase, the interviewer will have access to clues to deception or informational areas with which the person is uncomfortable.

## Selling the Interview

Once the interviewer has established rapport with the person to be interviewed, the next step is to sell that individual on the benefits of cooperation. Similar to the salesperson who presents the benefits of his product, the interviewer begins the interview by making a general benefit statement. The general benefit statement contains two distinct parts. First, the interviewer must describe an assumed need of the person being interviewed. This could vary depending on the individual's background and/or the circumstances of both the witness and the case. For example, when investigating a burglary, an interviewer might talk about the need to resolve the incident so that other homeowners in the neighborhood are not victimized in the same way. The need to avoid victimization of neighbors is thus established.

Another example might be the interviewing of a witness who is reluctant because he has reported a crime that was never resolved, owing to, in his mind, inaction of the police. In this case, the interviewer could state the assumed need that everyone wants the person who did this to be caught. The need to catch and punish the responsible person is thus established.

The second part of a general benefit statement is providing a benefit to the witness that addresses his expressed or assumed need. In the second example above, the interviewer needs to state a benefit to address the perceived need that the person responsible for the present crime be caught and punished and that perhaps that this investigation could also encompass the interviewee's previous complaint. To provide the benefit, the interviewer must explain the building of a case and the development of information. This will allow the witness to understand that the quality of the information he might provide can help resolve the case with an arrest.

If a witness shows open skepticism regarding the interview, the interviewer must begin by restating the benefit, offering proof of past cases that were resolved by witness cooperation and then expand on that benefit to the case at hand. Obviously, if the person being interviewed is being cooperative and shows no signs of reluctance or skepticism, the interviewer can proceed without a lengthy sale of the reason for the interview. The difference between these two types of approaches can be illustrated using the analogy of a car salesman. If a customer comes in the door and expresses interest in a particular car and shows a willingness to buy immediately, the salesman immediately attempts to close the sale. However, in instances where the customer is only beginning to shop, the salesman must handle customer concerns, identify customer needs, and establish in the customer's mind the benefits of purchasing the particular vehicle his dealership has for sale.

As with the salesman who discovers that his customer is reluctant to buy, the interviewer must determine the reasons for the witness's or victim's reluctance to cooperate in the interview. As we touched on earlier in this chapter, a witness may be reluctant to cooperate in an investigation for any number of reasons. It is the interviewer's job, in the earliest stages of the interview, to establish a belief within the victim or witness that their cooperation in the interview is a correct action, and provides a benefit to him. The benefit may take many forms. It may be the apprehension of the individual responsible for the incident, it may be the recovery of their's or a neighbor's property, or it may be even as simple as doing civic duty and supporting the criminal justice system.

Investigators everywhere know that the likelihood of success in resolving any crime is based upon the quality of the information that is provided by victims or witnesses. That information is directly related to the skill and intuitiveness of the interviewer.

## Allowing a Narrative

Once the interviewer has established rapport and sold the individual on the need to cooperate in the interview, the third step is to allow the individual to make a narrative response concerning the incident. The interviewer generally begins the interview by using open-end questions that encourage the free flow of dialogue from the victim, witness, or suspect. By allowing the victim, witness, or suspect to complete the story that he has to tell, the interviewer can develop an understanding of what the individual may know and what areas require further exploration.

During the preliminary narrative, the interviewer has an opportunity to begin to establish the circumstances surrounding the incident and ascertain what, if any, crime was committed and the elements necessary to prove the violation. In many instances, victims use incorrect terminology to describe a particular event. For example, the citizen will often say that he has been robbed. By establishing the facts of the case, the interviewer may determine that it was in fact a robbery, either armed or unarmed. However, it may not have been a robbery in which a suspect, by the use of force, took an item of value from the victim, but rather a break-in in which someone broke into his vehicle or residence and removed the item. In this instance, a burglary, rather than robbery, was committed. A third possibility might be that the person left the item on a chair when they got up to get a drink of water and returned to find the item was missing. In this case, a theft has been committed that may or may not be a burglary, depending on the location of the theft.

During the narrative, the interviewer can encourage a continued dialogue by nodding his head in agreement at appropriate points in the suspect's story. He can further continue the individual's dialogue by using noncommittal sentences such as, "What happened next," or, "I understand, then what?" These types of noncommittal responses by the interviewer show that he is actively listening and interested in what the victim or witness has to say. The interviewer also may find during the narrative that the individual is getting off track into unrelated areas. The interviewer simply needs to put the individual back on track by returning to the point where the interviewee began to branch off. Simply saying, "Going back to what happened at the garage, what went on from that point?" This allows the interviewer to reorient the victim or witness to the story line without interrupting the flow of information.

The narrative by the victim or witness allows the interviewer to continue to establish the bond of rapport. This happens because the victim or witness feels that he has valuable information to give and it is being appreciated by the interviewer.

## Hearing the Untainted Story

In addition to allowing the victim, witness, or suspect to give an overview to the interviewer, the interviewer also has an opportunity to hear the story in an untainted form. By listening to and observing the story in its untainted form, the interviewer may find a number of valuable clues to the mindset of the person being interviewed. The interviewer may be able to ascertain perceptual or social biases on the part of the victim or witness that will taint the credibility of information given by him. In addition, the interviewer also has an opportunity to hear the story told by the witness or victim who places his own emphasis on the information. The interviewer can now begin to listen closely and plan the direction of the follow-up questions he will use. In many instances, it will become evident that a victim or witness is manufacturing information based upon assumptions instead of observations. By listening closely, the interviewer can plan for the follow-up questions and decide which areas to explore more fully. Probably the biggest failure in interviewing is the failure to plan the direction of the interview and follow-up questions.

In some cases, as the interview progresses, the individual may become uncooperative or reluctant to give further information. By having allowed the individual to proceed with essentially an uninterrupted narrative, the interviewer has had an opportunity to gain significantly more information than he would have by simply questioning the suspect.

The interviewer, who now has the victim or witness's narrative from beginning to end, can begin to test the truthfulness and consistency of the story. As any experienced investigator knows, it is not beyond the realm of possibility for individuals to manufacture stories for their own reasons. By evaluating the consistency of the story in both its direction and detail, the interviewer can evaluate its truthfulness. The interviewer will also have had an opportunity to observe the verbal and physical behavioral clues given during the interview. These behavioral clues will assist the interviewer in identifying areas of sensitivity.

On occasion, when a victim or witness is extremely cooperative and credible, the interviewer may, prior to his scheduled appointment, ask the individual to make notes of the circumstances surrounding the incident for later discussion. By having had time to consider the information surrounding the incident, the individual will often be able to give a greater amount of detail regarding the circumstances. For those witnesses who might be reluctant or less than helpful, the location of the interview should be a more formalized setting of the police station or loss prevention office. In cases where several witnesses were present at the scene of the incident, it is beneficial to separate them so that the more forceful observer does not dominate and taint the stories of the other witnesses.

The interviewer must also remember that information provided may be less than credible. While eyewitness testimony has been attacked for years by certain psychologists as unreliable due to the passage of time and stress associated with the incident, other psychologists have found that the memory was accurately and vividly recalled even after the passage of time. In assessing the individual's story, we, the interviewers, should not discount its validity simply because of incorrect details such as the color of a vehicle or inaccurate physical description. These may be individualized perception problems on the part of the interviewee. Later in this chapter, we will discuss a method of using behavioral provoking questions to elicit behavior that is specifically related to truth telling or deception. However, this method is generally used in the latter stage of the nonaccusatory interview to eliminate truthful people from the investigation.

## Evaluating Neurolinguistic Eye Movement

Earlier in this chapter, we discussed the neurolinguistics of verbal communication. The visual, auditory, or kinesic channels were typified by the style, speed, word usage, and even physiology of the individual. Similarly, the eyes are used by each of us as we begin to recall or create information from one of the previous channels. While observing the interviewee, the interviewer should recognize the value of eye movements and the information they can give the interviewer. By determining which representational system the victim, witness, or suspect is using, the interviewer can ascertain whether or not the information is being recalled or created. In our business, information created is usually a lie.

Part of the time that the interviewer was observing the suspect during the narrative, he was establishing behavioral norms relating to the verbal and physical patterns of the individual. In addition, the interviewer was also observing the pattern of eye movements during the rapport-building and the narrative portion of the interview.

To illustrate this neurolinguistic eye movement point, answer the following questions and note the positioning of your eyes:

What was the color of the car you first learned to drive?

What would the offspring of an elephant and zebra look like?

Who is the first person who spoke to you this morning?

What did that person say to you first this morning?

How would it feel to sit in a tub of warm Jell-O?

The pattern of eye movements that you noted is related to the diagram in Figure 6.2.

In response to the first question, you probably looked up to the left, recalling the color of that first car you were able to drive. This response is typical for all but approximately 10% of the population. In most instances, when we recall something visually that we have actually experienced, the eyes go up and to the left. When we are recalling something that we have actually heard, the eyes move to the left and straight across. In instances where we are creating visually, the movement of the eyes will move up and to the right. For example, in response to the question of how the offspring of an elephant and zebra would look, your eyes probably moved up and to the right as you visually created the image asked about in the question. If you were asked to imagine a siren that sounded like a bellowing elephant, your eyes would probably go to the right. It would be there that most people move their eyes when creating a sound. If you were asked to imagine what it would feel like to touch a piece of newly sanded wood, your eyes generally would move

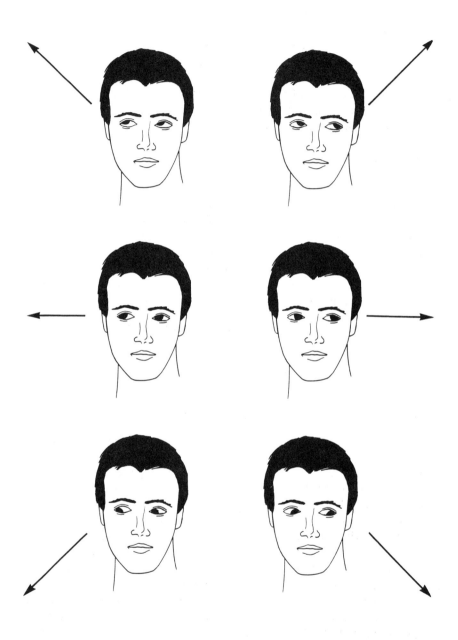

**6.2.** (**Top left**) Individual is creating visually. (**Top right**) Individual is recalling visually something that he actually experienced. (**Middle left**) Creating an auditory memory. (**Middle right**) Recalling sounds actually experienced. (**Bottom left**) Kinesic or touch position. (**Bottom right**) Internal dialogues, getting in touch with one's feelings.

into a kinesic mode as you created this thought in your mind. Often, a person's memory can be enhanced by having them position their eyes in the proper representational location.

The observation of the eye movements takes considerable skill and concentration by an interviewer. Remember that in approximately 90% of individuals, the eyes to the left indicates their recalling something that they actually experienced and the eyes to the right is creating. Also, remember that the eye movement may be very slight and incorporate a number of different positionings in response to a particular question. Many of the 10% who do not respond typically are left-handed people who simply reversed the clues. However, neurolinguistic eye movement can be the same for both right- and left-handed people.

The following exercise will help you begin to watch neurolinguistic eye movements. The easiest place to begin to observe the neurolinguistic eye movement is in one's everyday social context where the interviewer is cognizant of his own eye movement in response to questions and feelings that he has during a conversation. In addition, by utilizing mock interviews to watch the pattern of eye movement, an interviewer can gain experience, understanding and confidence that the technique has validity.

One position not yet discussed is moving the eyes to the left and down. The eyes in this position generally indicate an internal dialogue within the suspect, victim, or witness. Often this is the position of the eyes when a suspect is in submission during an interrogation and about ready to confess. At this point, the suspect is weighing the consequences of confessing and making a decision. This internal dialogue is represented by the head tilted forward and down with the eyes down to the left. In social situations, when we are being asked to respond to emotional situations, the eyes may go down and to the left as we debate what our response should be. Children being disciplined by a parent often position themselves in this way.

### Case Example

The following example illustrates the value of observing neurolinguistic eye movements:

A jewelry company had $60,000 in loose diamonds shipped into their distribution center. Shortly after the diamonds were received from United Parcel; they were discovered missing. Because of the security controls at the facility, suspicions centered on two particular individuals, the receiving clerk and the clerk who would next have access to the diamonds.

In evaluating the background of the two individuals, it was learned that the receiving clerk was a male in his late twenties who had been with the company less than six months. His work record was unsatisfactory, he was disgruntled, and he was generally dissatisfied with the company. He had had some minor brushes with the law relating to disorderly conduct and traffic offenses. The second employee was female in her early twenties and had been with the company just over one year. Her work record was also less than satisfactory and she had an attendance problem. Rumors among the employees claimed she was dating a man who was reputed to be the largest cocaine dealer in town. Further investigation revealed that she had been observed by other associates using drugs while on the company's property.

During the interview with the female clerk, it was determined she was not involved in the theft of the diamonds; however, based on her behavior, she probably was involved in using drugs during working hours at the company. Her neurolinguistic eye movements had been observed previously and helped elicit the confession to drug use. The interview questions were formulated in response to her eye movements.

*INTERVIEWER:* Mary, let me ask you, what types of drugs have you ever just experimented with at any time in your life?

*SUSPECT:* Uh, well, I tried cocaine, marijuana, and PCP and some LSD back in high school.

During her recollection of the types of drugs that she had used, her eyes went up and to the left as she visually recalled the different types of drugs that she had used.

*INTERVIEWER:* Mary, let me ask you this... When was the very last time that you used any type of a drug during working hours here at the company?

*SUSPECT:* (Pausing, eyes up and to the right, she looks back at the interviewer) About six months ago.

*INTERVIEWER:* And what kind of drug was that?

*SUSPECT:* (Eyes up and to the left) Marijuana.

From these questions the interviewer was able to ascertain that the suspect was in fact a drug user and had used marijuana on the job. However, the admission about the last time being six months ago was created and very possibly a lie.

*INTERVIEWER:* Mary, when was the very last time? You know, sometimes it's hard for a person to remember exactly the last time, because it's not like doing heroin or something?

*SUSPECT:* (Mary's eyes drift to the right and up, creating a response. She begins to speak.) Well...

*INTERVIEWER:* No, Mary, that wouldn't be true. I mean the very last time, no matter how recently.

*SUSPECT:* (Eyes drop down to the left, move up and left.) This morning before the interview.

*INTERVIEWER:* What did you use this morning?

*SUSPECT:* Marijuana.

The interviewer, during this sequence of events, was able to ascertain that the suspect had used marijuana on the job, but the time mentioned was most likely a lie. By watching the eye movements and recognizing that the suspect was going to again create a lie regarding the time of her drug use on the job, the interviewer could anticipate her response. By anticipating the lie and cutting it off, the interviewer was able to elicit an admission from the suspect of illegal drug use just before the interview.

The reader, being aware of his own eye movements and watching for the pattern of eye movements in social situations with others, will learn to assess the reliability of information based upon these neurolinguistic movements.

## Leading the Interview

Once the victim, witness, or suspect has completed the narrative portion of his story, the interviewer now returns to the beginning to lead the individual back to areas that need exploration. The interviewer will do this using closed-end questions that require specific answers. A closed-end question would require that the suspect respond specifically with details or a yes or no answer. The question "Who was in the room with you at that time?" focuses the suspect's attention to a particular detail to which he must either lie or tell the truth.

In interviewing and interrogation, the interviewer must often conceal the areas in which he is particularly interested. This is especially important when he is dealing with the reluctant or hostile witness. This individual is attempting to obtain as much information from the interviewer as the interviewer is from him. This information may be passed on to the perpetrator or to protect himself, should he later be identified as the individual responsible for the incident.

The interviewer conceals the areas of real interest by asking questions directly about the areas of particular interest to the interviewee. Much the same thing is done during an investigation. Although he could not avoid having it be known that he was investigating, the interviewer does not reveal the target of the investigation. The interviewer can do the same thing by focusing on less relevant areas of the story before bringing the suspect back to a point of particular interest.

At this point in the interview, the interviewer may also ask the victim, witness, or suspect to produce evidence or documents that may help the case. In these situations, the interviewer may also ask specific questions regarding the evidence or documents that will establish the elements of the crime he is investigating. In the event that the interviewer receives evidence or documents from a victim or witness, proper cataloging and chain of evidence procedures should be used to preserve the evidence's admissibility. Many departments give receipts for any documents or evidence received. In certain instances where the identification of a suspect is contemplated, the interviewer should have previously arranged a photo lineup that meets the legal criteria established by the courts.

## Challenging the Untruthful Witness, Victim, or Suspect

The interviewer may also choose to explore discrepancies in the suspect's story. These discrepancies may have been omissions, evasions, what appeared to be conflicts, or outright lies. The suspect's level of cooperation will determine whether or not the interviewer will challenge the suspect regarding his truthfulness. The decision to confront an untruthful victim, witness, or suspect may be directly related to the preinterview strategy that the interviewer decided to follow. If the strategy was to keep the lines of communication open by not confronting the individual, a plan for reinterviewing should be prepared. The information provided by the individual should be thoroughly investigated prior to the next interview. In the event that the victim, witness, or suspect has lied, any subsequent interviews should take place in a less supportive and more controlled environment.

### Case Example

In a recent kickback investigation, a vendor was identified as having been contacted by the buyer in an attempt to elicit a kickback. Credible evidence that this conversation had taken place was developed during previous interviews. The interviewer scheduled an appointment to meet at a local restaurant with the vendor. The interview was scheduled in this manner because all indications were that the vendor was honest in his previous dealings with the company and had no outward reasons not to cooperate in the investigation.

During the interview, the vendor was evasive, omitting information that was previously known from the investigation. His physical behavior gave further indication he was withholding information. Because of the interview environment, the suspect was not challenged about these evident deceptions. In this case, a decision was made to reinterview the vendor when a more formal setting could be arranged.

However, the second interview generated no incriminating admissions primarily because the suspect was prepared and became increasingly uncooperative. In this instance, the location of the first interview directly related to its lack of success because the interviewer could not confront the suspect on his falsehoods immediately.

## Using Rationalizations

With particularly weak suspects, an interviewer may be able to obtain additional information by indirectly probing the area that the victim, witness, or suspect is lying about. This indirect probing needs to be combined with rationalizations that allow the victim, witness, or suspect to save face about his inability to tell the truth the first time. Like the suspect in an interrogation, a witness who is withholding information needs to have support and a face-saving rationalization that allows him to feel better about himself. If the interviewer merely confronts the witness about a falsehood, the witness now has to admit that he withheld information and that it was improper for him to do so. Utilizing the process of rationalization in the interview, a skilled interviewer removes the second stumbling block to the suspect's telling the truth. Now the individual has to merely acknowledge that he "forgot" to tell something. The rationalization process also allows him to save face with the interviewer because he believes the interviewer does not believe he "intentionally lied."

## Shifting to Interrogation

The second possibility an interviewer must consider is whether or not a direct accusation of untruthfulness should be made and an interrogation be conducted. In this method, the suspect is confronted with his lies and the interviewer begins to dominate the conversation using rationalization to minimize the seriousness of the lies or involvement. The ultimate goal is to elicit the truth from the reluctant victim, witness, or suspect.

With that change, the interview has moved into an interrogative phase where the interviewer begins to offer reasons and excuses why the individual did what he did and thus encourages the suspect to confess by allowing him to save face. Further discussion of the tactics utilized in an interrogation will be discussed in detail in Chapters 7 through 11 of this text. The decision by an interviewer to confront the suspect should be soundly based on several factors:

1. Preinterview strategy
2. Completeness of the overall investigation
3. Location and timing are conducive to an interrogation—that is, it is private and nonsupportive for the suspect
4. The interviewer's reasonable certainty that he can elicit the information from the suspect and that this confrontation will not affect future cooperation

In a situation where the interviewer has ascertained that the individual being interviewed is being deceptive, the interviewer should consider postponing a confrontation until the completion of the investigation, which may uncover the reasons for the individual's deception. The ability to reinterview should not be underestimated. The time and effort expended by the interviewer to establish rapport with the person in the initial interview can be used as a springboard for any follow-up interviews. In these follow-up interviews, after additional investigation has been conducted and relationships in the investigation are more clearly defined, it may become evident why the suspect lied about a particular portion of his story.

At any rate, the ability of the interviewer to ascertain a suspect's deception can often lead to new investigative leads, even though the suspect lied. For this reason, it is often preferable to keep a suspect talking in an interview format rather than interrogate. If an interrogation is unsuccessful, it may close all lines of communication between the interrogator and the suspect.

## Using Cognitive Interview Techniques

During the directed fact-gathering portion of the interview, an interviewer may decide to use cognitive interviewing techniques. These techniques were systematized to enhance the recall of information by victims or witnesses under a grant by the National Institute of Justice, United States Department of Justice. Any experienced investigator recognizes that victims and witnesses have little or no time to memorize details that they observed under less than ideal circumstances. The techniques used in the cognitive interview have been used in whole or in part by investigators for many years. However, this is the first time that the technique has been quantified in a study to show that it is an effective method for obtaining information from eyewitnesses. Studies have shown that the information elicited from a witness through the cognitive interview technique can be more correct than information from someone who is interviewed under hypnosis. Thus far, the cognitive interview has successfully avoided the pitfalls hypnosis has faced in the courts. Additional research studies have shown that the cognitive interview technique reduces the impact that leading questions have on feeding information to witnesses. Finally, it was also shown that using all four parts of the cognitive interview together, as explained below, enhances the eyewitness's ability to recall information more significantly than when they are used separately.

The four techniques incorporated in the cognitive interview are utilized to enhance the recollection of the victim and witness are

1. RECONSTRUCT THE CIRCUMSTANCES OF THE EVENT: The interviewer begins by asking the witness to reconstruct how the incident began and the circumstances surrounding it. The interviewer instructs the witness to think about what the environment looked like from weather, to lighting, to the cleanliness of the room.

In addition, they also ask the victim or witness to recall their emotional mindset at the time of the incident.

2. INSTRUCT THE EYEWITNESS TO REPORT EVERYTHING: The victim or witness is informed not to omit any details, no matter how small. The interviewer explains that even very minor pieces of information may be important to the investigation.
3. RECALL THE EVENTS IN DIFFERENT ORDER: The interviewer may instruct the eyewitness to start from the middle or end and move either forward or backward through the story at a number of different points.
4. CHANGE PERSPECTIVES: Ask the witness to change roles with another person in the incident and to consider what he or she might have seen. Ask them to mentally change their position and ask what they might have seen from their new location.

The cognitive interview's basic value is that it reconstructs the circumstances in a number of different ways in the witnesses mind. The non-law-enforcement person rarely has an idea of what may or may not be of value to the investigator, and the small details obtained by this method often lead to other details being remembered.

The cognitive interview also developed five specific techniques to develop specific items of information.

1. PHYSICAL APPEARANCE: The witness is asked to think about the suspect in terms of "Did he remind you of anybody?" and "why?" "Was there anything unusual about his appearance or clothing?"
2. NAMES: If the suspect spoke a name during the incident, what were the number of syllables or what was the first letter of the name.
3. NUMBERS: If a number was involved, was it a low number or a high number, how many digits were in the number, were there any letters that were in sequence. This is especially valuable in attempting to remember license plate numbers.
4. SPEECH CHARACTERISTICS: Ask the witness if the voice reminded him of anyone and why was that. Was there any unusual accents, words, or tone of voice used by the suspect.
5. CONVERSATION: The eyewitness should be asked if there were any reactions to what was said, if any of the reactions were unusual, and if there were any unusual words or phrases included in the conversation.

## Using the Selective Interview Technique

The selective interview technique can also be incorporated as part of a fact-gathering interview to determine the truthfulness of the individual being interviewed. In the selective interview, a series of behavior-provoking questions are asked in a nonaccusatory manner. These questions are designed to solicit interpretable behavior that is typical of either a truthful or untruthful person. This interview is especially beneficial when questioning several suspects regarding a specific incident such as an arson or theft at a warehouse.

It is important to remember that in order for these interview questions to be effective in soliciting interpretable behavior, the interviewer needs to ask the questions in a sincere manner. Each question should refer to the specific issue or incident under investigation. This constant reference to the incident minimizes the possibility that an outside issue will cause concern or behavioral changes in the suspect. For example, if a suspect were asked, "What do you think should happen to someone that would take something from the company?" the interviewer would not know if a typically guilty response was the result of the specific incident or a side issue. By changing the wording of the question, the interviewer can reduce the level of concern of an individual who is only responsible for a side issue, like the unrelated theft of a small amount of merchandise. The questions should be asked, "What do you think should happen to the person who stole the missing $2,000 deposit taken from the safe?"

## Questions Asked

A sample of the types of questions asked during the selective interview are as follows:

Who do you think started that fire in the warehouse?

Is there anyone you know well enough to vouch for? In other words, say in your opinion that person is above suspicion and wouldn't do anything like steal that $2,000 deposit?

Before we go any further, let me ask you, did you start that fire in the warehouse?

Do you think that $2,000 deposit was stolen?

Who do you think would have had the best opportunity to start that fire if they wanted to? I'm not saying he did, but if someone wanted to?

Is there any reason that you can think of that someone would say they saw you take that $2,000 deposit out of the safe?

What do think should happen to that person that started that fire in the warehouse?

Did you ever just think of doing anything like stealing that $2,000 deposit?

How do you feel about our conducting this investigation into this fire?

In addition to these questions, the investigator may elect to ask additional investigative questions that he feels are appropriate.

In interpreting the verbal and physical responses to each of these questions, it is important to apply the rules and principles that were discussed in Chapter 4, Interpretation of Verbal and Physical Behavior.

Remember that people who are telling the truth about the issue under investigation are more likely to give direct answers during the interview. In addition, they are often helpful and cooperative in their responses. On the other hand, people who are not telling the truth are not as specific, direct, or helpful. In many cases, their responses are vague, too elaborate, short, or evasive.

In order to test the validity of truthful behavior observed during the interview, the interviewer asks a control question. A control question is a question similar in nature, but not directly related, to the issue under investigation. For example, while investigating a theft of a deposit from a company, the investigator might ask the suspect, "Did you steal that missing $2,000 deposit from the safe?" The suspect denies his involvement and the interviewer responds with the control question. "Did you ever do anything that could be considered a violation of company policy?" The theory is if a suspect is displaying "truthful" behavior during the interview, he should show some concern or behavioral change to the control question. If the suspect does not show any concern or behavioral change to the control question, it should put the interviewer on alert in that the suspect might be attempting to control his deceptive behavior. If the suspect shows more concern to the control than the issue question, it reassures the interviewer that the suspect is probably telling the truth to the issue under investigation (see Figure 6.3).

### Case Example

The authors conducted an investigation with a bank that had a $3,500 deposit missing. During one of the interviews, a male employee displayed behavior that was typical of truthful people. However, when he was asked the control question, "Did you violate any bank policies that you would not want your supervisor to find out about?" he did not show any concern. This made the interviewers cautious, because they knew the suspect had violated bank policy by writing two checks when he had nonsufficient funds in his checking account. The interview went as follows:

*INTERVIEWER:* Before we go any further, let me ask you, did you steal the missing $3,500 deposit?
*SUSPECT:* No. (Calm, direct)
*INTERVIEWER:* Have you ever taken any money from the bank?

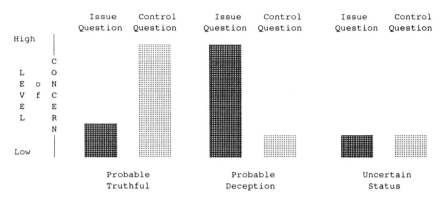

6.3. Generally, if a suspect responds behaviorally more significantly to the control than the issue question, he is telling the truth. However, if a suspect reacts to neither the issue nor the control question, he may be attempting to control his behavior and should not be eliminated as a potential suspect.

*SUSPECT:*  No.
*INTERVIEWER:*  Did you violate any bank policies that you would not want your supervisor to find out about?
*SUSPECT:*  No. (Calm, direct)

There was no significant change in this suspect's demeanor. Therefore, the interviewer believed that this suspect was capable of displaying truthful behavior even when he was not telling the truth. An interviewer confronted with a "good liar" should never eliminate him as a suspect on the basis of behavioral responses alone. Those individuals capable of controlling their behavior are more difficult to identify and the control question allows the interviewer to test the credibility of the suspect's behavior.

As noted in Chapter 8, Reducing Resistance—Rationalizations, it is important to identify an individual's motive for committing the crime and his resulting fears of a confession. If the interviewer believes that the suspect he is questioning might be involved in the issue under investigation, he may decide to ask questions that may evoke the motive of the crime: "Why do you think someone would have started that fire in the warehouse?"

If the suspect responds that perhaps the individual was mad at the company, the interviewer can postulate that the fire may have been started for revenge or because he was not treated fairly at the company: "Let me ask you a hypothetical question, Bob. If you had taken the missing $2,000 deposit, what would be the biggest reason you would not want to tell the truth?"

If the suspect responds by saying that he would be concerned about his parents' finding out, the interviewer can hypothesize that embarrassment may be the suspect's hurdle. During the interrogation the interrogator can attempt to overcome the suspect's primary hurdle.

In conclusion, the selective interview is a good investigative tool that can be used while investigating an incident that could have been committed by any one of several people. Using structured questions and evaluating the suspect's verbal and physical responses will allow the interviewer to eliminate truthful individuals from the investigation while focusing on those responsible. However, remember that these interviews, like any other investigative tool, are not infallible. The purpose of these interviews is to enhance the interviewer's ability to identify the innocent and focus the investigation on the guilty suspect.

## Using Questions of Enticement

An enticement question is a behavior-provoking, nonaccusatory question that entices a suspect to change or consider changing his original story. This question can be used during either an interview or an interrogation.

### Purpose

The interrogator uses the enticement question in an attempt to identify the true status of the suspect. The guilty person is more likely to be accurately identified with an enticement question than a truthful individual. The enticement question can be used during an interview to offer the suspect an opportunity to change his story. Whether the suspect actually changes or merely considers changing his story, the interviewer/interrogator can observe the delay as the guilty person weighs his options. This delay is highly indicative of a deceptive individual. During the interrogation, an enticement question can also be used to overcome weak denials or to enhance the interrogator's ability to develop the admission of the suspect.

The origin of the enticement question is uncertain. However, the presentation of fictitious evidence certainly has been used by investigators for hundreds of years. One of the first actual references to this type of a question can be found in the book *Police Interrogation* by Captain Kidd[2] of the Berkeley, California, Police Department. Published in the 1940s, this is one of the earliest comprehensive texts on interrogation.

---

2. Kidd WR, New York: R.V. Baguino, 1940.

## Presentation of the Question

Before an enticement question can be used effectively, the suspect should be pinned down on the details of his alibi. Once the suspect has committed himself to the details, the enticement question can be presented in an attempt to shake the suspect's story. The enticement question must be presented to the suspect in such way that he must consider that there is evidence of his guilt. The interviewer/interrogator should preplan the type of enticement question that will be most effective. The enticement question can be used when referring to real evidence developed during the investigation or to fictitious evidence that could logically have been uncovered. This real evidence might be the observation of the crime by a witness, fingerprints, tire tracks, or other physical evidence found at the scene of the crime.

Regardless of whether the evidence is real or fictitious, the interviewer/interrogator only implies the evidence's existence. This is preferable to a flat statement that the evidence exists because it allows the interviewer/interrogator a way out if the suspect demands proof of its existence. In cases where real evidence of the suspect's guilt exists, it may not be in the interviewer/interrogator's best interests to present it as an enticement question. Implying the existence of evidence frees the interviewer/interrogator from having to reveal it.

The enticement question is usually worded, "Is there any reason why ...[your fingerprints, your tire tracks, your picture] were found at the scene of the burglary?" If an interviewer/interrogator uses an enticement question such as, "Is there any reason that a witness would say that they saw you at the drug store just before the clerk was killed?" and the suspect immediately denies his presence, and, furthermore, demands to face this accuser, the denial may or may not be deception. Regardless, the interviewer has no current interest in presenting a witness, but has left himself a way out. The interrogator can reply that the investigation is continuing, with numerous individuals being interviewed, but if there were a reason why the suspect was present in that store sometime during the day, he would prefer to talk about it now so that the interviewer/interrogator need not inconvenience him again.

Prior to the interviewer/interrogator's using an enticement question, the suspect should be locked into his story or sequence of events. The enticement question should also take into account the method used to commit the crime. For example, an enticement question such as, "Is there any reason why your fingerprints would be present at the scene of the burglary?" may or may not be effective. The question's effectiveness is dependent on whether the suspect wore gloves during the perpetration of the crime. The guilty suspect, because of his intimate knowledge of the circumstances surrounding the burglary, can immediately discount the evidence presented by the interviewer/interrogator because he wore gloves. Because of the suspect's certainty that this evidence could not exist he can quickly make a denial. However, if the interviewer/interrogator had presented an enticement question such as, "Is there any reason that you can think of that a witness to the burglary would have identified you as being responsible?" then the suspect has to consider the possibility that he was observed while he entered or left the burglary. He must also consider whether he was implicated by an informant, whether he should admit being in the area but not being responsible for the burglary, or whether he should stick to his original story. If the suspect changes his story, the interviewer/interrogator now recognizes the suspect's guilt. In other instances the guilty suspect must consider whether or not the evidence alleged by the enticement exists, and what his options are. This results in a delay while he considers his alternatives, which delay the interviewer/interrogator in turn recognizes as deceptive behavior and indicative of probable guilt.

The interviewer/interrogator must make sure, however, that there is no legitimate reason why the suspect may agree to the possibility of some alleged evidence linking him to the crime. For example, if the suspect does go into the safe at certain times while performing his duties, it would serve no purpose to ask if there is any reason his fingerprints would be found in the safe.

The following are examples of some commonly used enticement questions. The interviewer/interrogator is limited in an enticement question only by the inventiveness of his mind. For example, a rape suspect was apprehended approximately three blocks from the scene of the rape. The victim was almost positive in her identification of the suspect as the person who raped her. During a subsequent interview with the suspect, the interviewer asked, "Is there any reason that you could think of why the arresting officer would say your zipper was open when he arrested you?" The suspect paused and considered this statement before responding. Then snapping his fingers, he said, "Oh yeah, earlier in the day I did break my zipper while I was running so that's maybe what he saw." The guilty person's frequent attempts to explain away damaging evidence lead him to invent alibis or admit to fictitious evidence.

## Examples of Enticement Questions

### Implying an Eyewitness

Katherine, as you know, we will be talking to everyone here today regarding that missing $600. Is there any reason that you can think of that any of the people we will be talking to would say that you took that missing $600?

### Implying Handwriting Evidence

Pat, as you know, anytime we do an investigation, we will use the services of outside experts. For example, if a situation involves handwriting, we retain the services of a handwriting expert. What we do is send the handwriting expert samples of the individual's writing so he can compare the individual's handwriting with that of the handwriting found on the _____[check, contract, etc.]. Pat, is there any reason you can think of that the handwriting expert would say that your handwriting matches the handwriting found on that _____ [check, contract, etc.]?

### Implying Physical Evidence such as Fingerprints, Footprints, Tire Tracks

Jennifer, in many situations like this, we will take the fingerprints of the individuals to see if their fingerprints match any fingerprints that may have been found at the scene. Is there any reason that you can think of that they would find your fingerprints_____[inside of the safe, at the house, on the gun, etc.]? If you have to go into the safe for some reason, that is important to know in case they may find your fingerprints.

### Implying Closed Circuit Camera Evidence

Kelly, as I mentioned to you before, we use closed circuit video cameras quite extensively throughout the store to watch what both customers and employees do. When we review that video tape, is there any reason you can think of that we would see you taking money out of Carolyn's cash register?

### Asking the Suspect to Remember

Jonathan, do you think it is possible you could have been on Forest Avenue at the dock at the time of the burglary even though you don't remember? The reason I ask that is we will be talking to residents and I don't want anyone to say they thought that you may have been involved because they saw you nearby at that time, especially if you had a reason for being there.

## Obtaining the Suspect's Biographical Information

At the conclusion of the interview, the interviewer should obtain biographical information of the person he interviewed. Attempting to obtain this information at the beginning of the interview contributes to the possibility that the witness may become reluctant to give information simply because he does not want to be involved in a prosecution or termination. The correct spelling of names, dates of birth, social security numbers, and residence addresses are important to the overall investigation. Many interviewers fail to ask for additional phone numbers for work or other family members in case it should be difficult to locate a critical witness. The interviewer should also obtain the correct spelling and addresses of all the company's referred to during the interview.

## Obtaining a Written Statement

In some cases, it many be useful for the interviewer to obtain a written statement from the witness. This may be done in a narrative form, question and answer, or by video or audio cassette tape with permission (check your local and state statutes). An alternative to the written statement may be to have the witness initial the field notes of the interviewer to confirm their accuracy. (For additional discussion of this topic see Chapter 12, The Statement.)

## Closing Professionally

Before leaving, the interviewer should restate what was said by the victim, witness, or suspect so that it is clear to both what was said. The interviewer should ask if what he repeated was accurate or if there was anything else the victim, witness, or suspect recalled. If any other information given, it should be explored before the interview is terminated.

Regardless of the outcome of the interview, the interviewer should remain friendly and supportive. This way the lines of communication will remain open in the event a reinterview is necessary. The reinterview will more likely occur under pleasant terms because the rapport remains unbroken. In almost any case, it is in the best interest of the interviewer to thank the suspect and remind him that you may need to ask additional questions later on. By doing this, the interviewer gains the individual's agreement to cooperation in another interview.

How the question asking for a reinterview is phrased is critical to obtaining an affirmative response. Since the interviewer wants the person to agree to another interview, the use of an assumptive question that directs the proper answer is often used. The interviewer might ask, "I'm sure you wouldn't have a problem talking with me again if it were necessary, would you?" By asking the question this way, the individual is encouraged to say they would not have a problem with a latter interview. This agreement is essential because once an individual has agreed, it increases the likelihood that he will go through with another interview.

Finally, it is in the best interest of the interviewer to leave a business card or phone number where he can be reached should the witness recall any other information. It is not unusual for a victim or witness to recall additional details of the incident after he has had time to reflect. Inviting the individual to call if he should remember anything pertinent allows him to feel that he should continue attempting to remember other details. By leaving a card or number, the interviewer has made it easy for the victim or witness to call and identify the interviewer. If a victim or witness has any difficulty in identifying and contacting the interviewer, it often results in the information not being relayed.

# Establishing Credibility/
The Accusation

7

*Many of the problems faced by interrogators
during an interrogation have their origin during
the opening moments of the accusation.*

The accusation is the last step in the investigative process. The interviewer has conducted an investigation that developed the necessary evidence to believe the suspect is involved in the issue under investigation. The interrogator has prepared a plan and considered the room setting as part of his overall plan for the interrogation.

The interrogator should consider the different accusations available and the different ways he may establish the credibility of the investigation. In establishing the credibility of the investigation, the interrogator must establish a belief by the suspect that his guilt is known for certain. A failure to convey this belief to the suspect will result in a more difficult interrogation and probable denials by the suspect.

This chapter will deal with the different ways to begin an interrogation. The interrogator should realize that each method of beginning the interrogation has benefits and pitfalls. It is often the opening moments of the interrogation that dictate its success or failure. Many of the problems faced by interrogators during an interrogation have their origin during the opening moments of the accusation. Suspect denials or a difficulty in developing an admission are often problems created by the interrogator himself because of his choice of accusation. The interrogator should consider the impact of the accusation he intends to use in light of later potential problems.

## Positioning

The interviewer should have selected the witness and arranged the chairs prior to the suspect entering the room. This will minimize any distractions to the suspect. The chairs should be spaced three to four feet apart with no desk or table to separate the participants. This separation is a comfortable distance for both the suspect and interrogator. However, if the interrogator is more comfortable using a desk during the interrogation, he should position the chairs so that only the corner of the desk separates him from the suspect.

## Attitude

The interrogator's attitude is that of a mediator seeking the truth rather than that of a dominant, authoritative figure. Taking the role of a mediator instead of an opponent will allow the interrogator to allay some of the suspect's fears.

The interrogator should also exude confidence, both in his approach and word choice. This show of confidence will often help conceal any mistakes the interrogator may make during the interrogation. In addition, the interrogator should display professionalism (not superiority, however).

## Introduction

The interrogator should consider how he wants to present the accusation. As discussed earlier, the interviewer can sit behind a desk to give him additional authority, stand if he wants to come across as even more authoritative, or sit directly across from the suspect. Each of these positions will give the suspect a different feeling toward the interrogator. Ideally, since the interrogator wants to reduce the suspect's level of defensiveness, positioning the chairs directly across from each other or slightly off to one side will lessen the confrontational feel of the meeting (see Figure 7.1).

## Impressions Given by the Interrogator

The interrogator must consider the role that he is to play. To a certain extent, the interrogator is an actor in a play and the role that he chooses serves to satisfy the needs of the suspect. The interrogator should consider his dress, language, professionalism, and the impact that each of these might have on the suspect. A professional impression will enhance the interrogator's ability to successfully handle the case and increase his stature with coworkers.

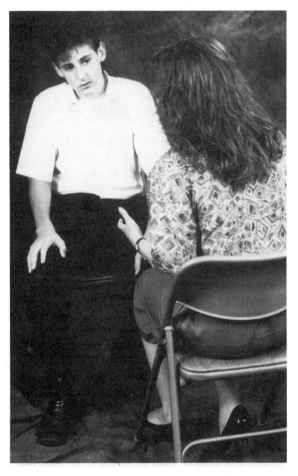

7.1. Remove any barriers between the suspect and the interviewer/interrogator.

## Selection of the Accusation

Once the interrogator has considered his image, positioning, and attitude, he should now consider the different methods of beginning the interrogation. The choice of a particular accusation is dependent on many factors—the type of case and the suspect's personality and criminal history should be considered. The case facts and the certainty of the suspect's guilt also play a role in determining which approach will be successful in obtaining the suspect's admission.

## Factual Approach

One common method of accusation is the *factual approach*. The suspect is locked into his story or alibi in great detail by the interrogator. Once a suspect has committed to the details of the case, the interrogator uses the evidence developed during the investigation to disprove the suspect's story. Initially, the interrogator gives the appearance of believing the suspect's story, which encourages the suspect to tell more and more lies. The suspect becomes overconfident and begins to embellish his tale. This will prove to be his undoing.

Following the suspect's story, the interrogator presents evidence that establishes the credibility of the investigation and convinces the suspect that his guilt is known. The factual approach to an interrogation can be quite successful in those instances where a massive investigation has been conducted. The factual approach works best when clear, overwhelming evidence of the suspect's guilt can be presented. However, in instances where the evidence is only suggestive, rather than conclusive, of the suspect's guilt, the interrogator may find that the suspect will attempt to explain away the incriminating evidence.

Public law enforcement often uses the factual approach to convince suspects that their guilt is provable and that they should cooperate in the investigation. Sting operations and homicide investigations are good examples of when to use a factual approach. Inviting a suspect in to discuss his involvement and being able to present wiretap or video documentation of his involvement can often result in a suspect's willingness to cooperate in the investigation or give testimony.

In major case investigations, when the key participants have been identified, the interrogator may approach those individuals with a peripheral involvement in the case to cooperate in the investigations. These individuals are often given an opportunity to bring counsel with them so that they will be more likely to make a rational rather than emotional decision when confronted. However, counsel for the suspect should only be invited to meetings where the evidence of his client's guilt is so overwhelming that it will immediately convince him of the benefits of his client's cooperation. A meeting of this type is generally conducted in conjunction with the prosecutor, who will usually ask for the suspect's testimony to support other portions of the case in return for a plea arrangement.

The interrogator presenting evidence in this type of case need not be aggressive or condescending but instead simply can be a mediator who is dealing from a position of power. During this approach, the case is built systematically and overwhelmingly to convince the suspect that it is in his best interest to cooperate with the investigators. Imagine the suspect who has repeatedly denied knowing another individual, and suddenly must face photos of them together or recordings of their conversations. Overwhelmed by this evidence, the suspect often offers his cooperation in the investigation.

The factual attack, however, is clearly less effective in cases where overwhelming evidence of the suspect's guilt is not attainable. In many investigations, the evidence developed is circumstantial and open to interpretation. When the evidence is circumstantial, it often encourages the suspect to deny simply because he is under the mistaken belief that circumstantial evidence is not conclusive or cannot convict. In many cases, circumstantial evidence, when presented alone or piece by piece to the suspect, does not have the emotional impact of direct evidence such as wiretap or fingerprint evidence.

In the majority of instances, the factual approach only creates problems for the interrogator who now must convince the suspect that the total picture of the evidence does indicate his guilt. The suspect, however, may offer other plausible explanations for the incriminating evidence and is less likely to accept the interrogator's belief in his guilt because of the evidence's circumstantial nature.

Often, the factual evidence of a suspect's guilt may be merely one specific observation, for example, of a cashier's taking $20 out of the register and putting it in his pocket, or of the suspect in the area of the robbery. Although each of these observations may have value in the presentation of the overall case, it may not be sufficient in and of itself to convince the suspect that his guilt is known for certain. The cashier who has placed the money in his pocket may counter that he merely placed it there until he could get change and intended to put it back later. The suspect who has been observed on a street near the robbery may manufacture a story that explains away this observation. Lying about his alibi, however, may later prove to be his downfall.

It is thus only when significant, irrefutable evidence of a suspect's guilt is available that a factual attack can be easily used to overwhelm the suspect and convince him that he should confess. The interrogator who attempts to use a factual approach without sufficient facts runs the risk that the suspect will recognize the case weaknesses and not confess because he believes that his lies cannot be disproved. Also, using a factual approach on a specific issue may reduce the likelihood of the interrogator's being able to expand the suspect's admissions into other areas of involvement.

## Direct Accusation

An accusation commonly used by interrogators is the *direct accusation*. The direct accusation is generally used in a single-issue case where the incident is clearly defined. The directness of the accusation allows the interrogator to tell the suspect exactly what he is being accused of having done. The interrogator is interested in obtaining an admission on a specific incident and must focus the suspect's attention on that single issue. To focus the suspect, the interrogator must use the very direct accusation.

This direct accusation is more suited for public law enforcement than for the private sector. The public law enforcement community are generally more likely to be focused on a specific incident, whereas the private sector often interrogates on a pattern of merchandise or money theft. The private sector also has to be concerned about employee morale and the company image. This concern generally precludes the use of the direct accusation on a regular basis.

In public law enforcement cases, the suspect may invoke his rights under *Miranda*. Should he do so, the interrogation must stop immediately or any resulting confession could be rendered inadmissible. The police interrogator should avoid tactics that will cause a suspect to invoke his rights.

The direct accusation can also elicit additional behavioral clues from the suspect. These additional behavioral clues may help the interrogator to eliminate an innocent suspect from the investigation. For example, a direct accusation might be helpful when the investigation has focused on two suspects who might possibly be involved in the incident, but it is unlikely that further investigation will develop conclusive proof of either's guilt. An interrogator's use of a direct accusation can often identify the person responsible for the issue.

Interviews with the two suspects may only give the interviewer behaviors indicative of deception but not identify which of the two suspects was actually involved. One of the suspects may have behaved deceptively because he was involved in the incident, but the other suspect's behavior may be a result of a related side issue or knowledge of who is really responsible. The suspect's denials resulting from the direct accusation can be evaluated by the interrogator. These denials can give the interrogator direction as he probes for the truth.

Another use of a direct accusation is to refute denials voiced by the suspect during the interrogation. Whenever a denial is used by the suspect, the interrogator must reaccuse with an equal directness. This directness may be as strong as the following:

*SUSPECT:* I didn't do it.

*INTERROGATOR:* Bob, just a minute. There is no question from the investigation that you are responsible for the break-in.

However, the interrogator's reaccusation might be much weaker if the suspect's denial is weaker.

*SUSPECT:* But...I...I didn't do it. (Spoken weakly)
*INTERROGATOR:* Bob, that's just not true.

The problem with the direct accusation is that it invariably elicits an emphatic denial from the suspect. This is especially true in the earliest stages of the interrogation when the suspect is strongest. The interrogator, because of his directness, has now forced the suspect to defend his contention that he was not involved in the incident under investigation. Because of the directness of the interrogator's accusation, the suspect generally takes the path of least resistance and thought. He lies, using a denial.

The interrogator must now overcome two problems in order to enable the suspect to confess: first, the suspect's unwillingness to admit his involvement, and second, the fact that the suspect has now lied to the interrogator and must tell additional lies to defend that position.

The preferred sequence to use during a direct accusation follows.

*Relate the Issue.* The first part of the direct accusation is an introduction. The interrogator introduces himself and his witness, if one is used. The interrogator then tells the suspect that an investigation has been conducted and reveals the issue they will discuss in the interview/interrogation. At the beginning of the direct accusation, it is important to focus the suspect's behavioral responses specifically on the issue under investigation. The interrogator makes sure that the suspect understands that the discussion is about a single incident and is not a general inquiry.

By identifying the reason for the interrogation, the interrogator focuses the suspect's attention directly on the issue and away from any side issues. For example, consider the mindset of the suspect who has over the last six months been burglarizing vehicles in and around the town. The interrogator mistakenly believes the suspect is involved in a residential burglary. The suspect, although innocent of the residential burglary, may show deceptive behavior when questioned about the residential burglary because of the thefts from vehicles. This deceptive behavior is related to the side issue of the vehicular burglaries rather than the residential burglary.

The following is an example of the opening statement:

Bob, my name is Detective Humer, with the City Police. As you might be aware, we have been questioning individuals regarding a burglary to a residence at 1237 Holly Court in the city. During the break-in, some jewelry and electronic equipment were stolen.

The interrogator has clearly stated the reason for the meeting and what was stolen. The suspect's behavioral responses should now be reflective of his role (if any) in the residential burglary rather than of any side issues.

*Make Clear, Simple Accusations.* The interrogator must make a clear simple accusation to the suspect. This accusation must have only one meaning and must be direct enough so the suspect is not confused by what the interrogator means. The purpose of this statement is to throw the suspect off balance by its directness and demand a denial from him—a denial that can be interpreted by the interrogator as being truthful or deceptive.

The following is an example of a direct accusation:

> Bob, it is clear from our investigation that you are responsible for the break-in at 1237 Holly Court in the city last night.

*Pause.* Once the interrogator has made the direct accusation, he should allow the suspect an opportunity to respond. In almost all instances, the suspect will make an emphatic denial to the direct accusation. The interrogator can then evaluate the strength of the denial and its content. This evaluation will help the interrogator to eliminate the suspect from the investigation or focus on him as the primary suspect.

The following is an example of the denial from a truthful and deceptive individual:

> *TRUTHFUL SUSPECT:* You're crazy, I didn't break into any house last night!" (The suspect's denial is direct, spontaneous, and physically he leans forward.)
>
> *UNTRUTHFUL SUSPECT:* (Clears throat)...I'm sorry, you've got the wrong guy. It wasn't me. (Weak voice, no eye-to-eye contact, slumped in the chair).

*Repeat the Accusation.* Once the suspect has made an emphatic denial in response to the direct accusation, the interrogator should cut off further denials and repeat the direct accusation. Even during this early stage of repeating the accusation, the interrogator should begin to minimize the seriousness of the issue under investigation.

The following is an example of the softened reaccusation:

> Bob, just a minute. There is no question about the fact that you went into the house on Holly Court but, my concern is...

The interrogator must confidently reaccuse the suspect to let him know that the investigation indicates that he is involved in the incident.

The interrogator attempts to stop any other denials and moves on to the rationalizations he will present the suspect.

*Lead into Rationalizations.* Following the reaccusation, the interrogator begins to use the rationalizations which he believes will minimize the seriousness of the incident and allow the suspect to save face. These rationalizations will be based on the suspect's background, motive of the crime, or other issues that will be discussed in the section on rationalizations.

*A Problem with Direct Accusation.* The primary problem with the direct accusation is that, because of its directness, it encourages the suspect to lie using a denial and then forces the suspect to defend the position he took with additional denials. Although interrogators can overcome the suspect's denials and obtain a statement of guilt from the suspect, it generally results in a more difficult interrogation than was necessary. In certain circumstances, the direct accusation, even though it results in denials, is effective in identifying the individual not responsible for the particular incident. This allows the interrogator to eliminate an innocent suspect from suspicion.

The interrogator should never use this form of interrogation to eliminate suspects from an investigation unnecessarily. It is generally used only in those circumstances where an investigation is stalled and is unlikely to clear or convict a suspect of involvement. The choice is to interrogate each of the two suspects in the hope of clearing one through the interrogation and focusing on the second suspect, or to let the investigation wither and die. In some cases, this may be the only method to resolve the case.

The interrogator assesses the initial denial from the suspect and attempts to determine whether the strength of the denials is increasing or decreasing, as the denials continue. The interrogator assesses the strength of the initial denial and continues to offer rationalizations to the suspect. As the interrogation continues, the interrogator attempts to determine whether the denials are increasing in strength, which would be typical of the truthful, or decreasing in strength and frequency, which would be typical of the deceptive (see Figure 7.2). The initial difficulty for the interrogator is that even the guilty may respond strongly at first, but as the rationalizations have their effect, the guilty suspect will deny less frequently and becomes more docile. The opposite is true of the truthful individual. The truthful suspect increases the strength of his denials and takes control of the interrogation.

## Introductory Statement Approach

Another approach to beginning the interrogation is the *introductory*

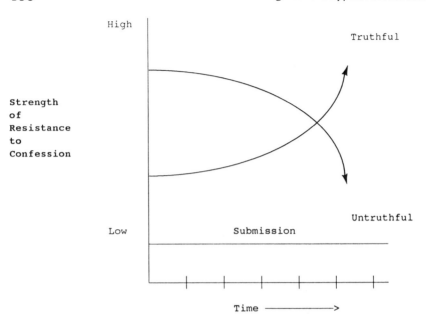

**7.2.** This chart illustrates the resistance of truthful and untruthful suspects. The truthful suspect's resistance to a confession increases as time passes in the interview, whereas the guilty suspect's resistance lessens until he is ready to confess.

*statement.* The introductory statement uses a factual component and an emotional appeal that allows the suspect to save face. The interrogator builds the credibility of investigative process in the early stages of the interrogation and uses a process of rationalization to minimize the seriousness of the suspect's involvement in the issue.

This particular accusation has a tremendous flexibility. It can be used with or without a nonaccusatory interview. It can be used where there is direct evidence of an individual's involvement in the incident or in situations where the suspect has been implicated but is not linked by direct evidence to the crime.

The interrogator has the best of both worlds, factual and emotional, by using an introductory statement. The introductory statement allows the suspect to make a rational decision to confess rather than an emotional one. In the direct accusation, the directness of the interrogator's statement encourages most individuals to quickly deny. However, the introductory statement makes no accusations initially, which allows the suspect to listen to what the interrogator has to say.

Although an emotional approach can be used for a large percentage of suspects, the emotional approach generally has little impact on the street-sharp, experienced individual. Using both a factual and an emotional component allows the introductory statement to be more effective on any type of suspect. The introductory statement allows the interrogator to discuss the process of investigation and establishes the credibility of the investigation, that is, the belief by the suspect that he is caught. Establishing the belief that one has been caught can help obtain a confession even in the experienced, street-hardened suspect. About 95% of those who ever would confess are susceptible to a combined factual–emotional approach. The remaining 5% will not confess unless the interrogator presents proof of their guilt. While not directly accusing the suspect of anything, the interrogator utilizes his own behavior to tell an underlying story to the suspect. This underlying story conveys a separate message to the suspect, telling him about the real reason he is present.

Prior to beginning the introductory statement, the interrogator may find it beneficial to review some biographical information with the suspect. The review of the biographical information allows the interrogator to establish rapport with the suspect and calm his own nervous feelings. In addition, it also allows the interrogator an opportunity to evaluate and develop a set of baseline behaviors for the suspect. Utilizing these "behavioral norms," the interrogator can assess changes in the suspect's behavior as he begins to discuss the case at hand. Furthermore, it begins to let the suspect know an investigation has been conducted.

*Interrogator's Behavior.* The interrogator is telling two stories during the course of the introductory statement. On the surface, he is telling the police or loss prevention story. The introductory statement is spoken in nonaccusatory tones and in an offhand manner. The interrogator will use subtle variations in voice and eye contact to tell the secondary story.

The underlying secondary story is how the suspect actually was involved in the incident and the methods that he used to commit the crime. By being indirect, the interrogator can avoid having the suspect make any form of a denial that would make the interrogative process more difficult.

If the introductory statement is presented to a truthful individual and an untruthful individual, their reactions to it are markedly different. The truthful suspect listens closely and enjoys being told about the police or loss prevention story. The guilty suspect's reactions to the same words results in a different reaction, "I've been caught!"

*Suspect's Behavior.* The suspect's behavior during the introductory statement can be interpreted as truthful or deceptive. The truthful individual has a relaxed, open posture. His face remains relaxed and interested.

The guilty suspect often has a stiffness to the body and moves in a

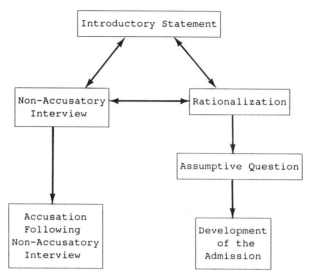

**7.3.** The introductory statement establishes the credibility of the investigation in the suspect's mind, while allowing the interrogator to change strategies in response to the suspect's actions.

jerky, abrupt manner. The face takes on a fearful, hunted look as he realizes that his involvement in the incident has been discovered. The guilty's nodding of the head is also often abrupt and mistimed.

*Introductory Statement Options.* The interrogator has a number of options when using the introductory statement (see Figure 7.3). The introductory statement can join with rationalizations and lead to the assumptive question. If the interrogator is uncertain of the suspect's guilt after using the introductory statement, he can use a nonaccusatory interview to elicit additional behavior typical of innocence or guilt. If the interviewer begins the encounter with a nonaccusatory interview, he can slide into the interrogation by following the interview with the introductory statement. The introductory statement then leads to rationalization and the assumptive question.

## Construction of the Introductory Statement for Loss Prevention—Private Sector

The basic construction of an introductory statement does not differ between the public and private sectors, although modification of terminology and subtle changes of technique may be required. This first example is a standard introductory statement used in a theft case in the private sector. For a law enforcement introductory statement, see Chapter 10.

*Explanation of the Interrogator's Role.* In the first part of the introductory statement, the interrogator identifies himself as a member of the loss prevention staff and defines his role in the company. It is in this first part of the statement that the interrogator lets the employee know that the employee is the most important asset that the company possesses. The interviewer will also describe the three factors that relate to shortage within the company. These factors are: 1) paperwork errors, 2) shoplifting, and 3) employee's taking things.

The interrogator also relates to the suspect that the loss prevention department's primary concern must be with those employees that would be causing tens of thousands of dollars in cash or merchandise losses rather than something of a minor nature. This statement is the interrogator's first attempt to begin minimizing the seriousness of the suspect's involvement in a theft.

As the interrogator talks to the suspect, he consciously attempts to avoid causing the suspect to deny. For example, if the suspected employee was stealing cash, the employee would be more likely to make a denial if the interrogator worded his opening statement this way.

> Bob, my name is Dave Zulawski. I'm a member of the loss prevention staff here at the company and it's my job to protect the assets. Assets of the company are money, merchandise, building, fixtures, and our most important asset is our employee.

In this example the interrogator put the word money first in the list of the company's assets. A guilty individual might make a denial to protect himself and it would not sound unusual if the denial came immediately after the word money. However, when the interrogator attempts to avoid denials, he positions the word money at the end so the suspect is unlikely to make a denial because he failed to deny taking any of the other assets. For example:

> Bob, my name is Dave Zulawski. I'm a member of the loss prevention staff here at the company and it's my job to protect the company's assets. The assets of the company are its building, fixtures, merchandise, money, and our most important asset is our employees.

By putting the word money almost last in the sentence, the suspect is less likely to deny because he did not deny stealing the building, fixtures, or merchandise. When money is finally said, it would appear out of place for the suspect to only deny money, so he remains quiet.

*Explanation of How Losses Occur.* During the second part of the introductory statement, the interrogator details how losses occur due to internal theft. The purpose of this second point of the introductory statement is to tell the suspect indirectly how he is stealing without the interrogator's being so direct that the employee can make a denial. This is generally done by placing the theft activity that the employee is engaged in about midway in the explanation. The same strategy of placement, as previously discussed, is used to avoid denials. A denial to the properly positioned known theft method would seem out of place, even to the guilty. The method of theft thought to have been used is placed in the middle rather than at the end of the second part of the statement so that the suspect cannot be sure what his exposure is in the case. Placing the suspect's method of theft at the end of part two would help the suspect to identify how much the interrogator may know about his theft activity. For example, if the suspect was stealing money by failing to ring sales, the explanation of how losses occur might be as follows:

> An employee might cause losses by taking money right out of the register. They might write up fraudulent credits or voids. They might fail to ring up sales. They might pass merchandise off to friends or carry merchandise out themselves.

The interrogator's eye contact in the early portions of the introductory statement can be effectively used to emphasize the points an interrogator wishes to make. For example, after saying, "failing to ring up sales," the interviewer should subtly pause and make eye contact with the suspect. This short pause and eye contact sets "failing to ring up sales" apart from the other examples of theft. The pause and eye contact, however, should not be so long that the suspect has an opportunity to make a denial.

The second purpose of the explanation of how losses occur is to elicit behavior from the guilty suspect regarding his involvement in other methods of theft. Often, an investigation will identify only one of several methods of theft an employee is using to steal from the company. This section allows the interrogator to obtain deceptive behavior from the suspect when he mentions a particular type of theft activity the suspect is engaged in. The resulting stress as the suspect mentally recreates in his mind another method of theft he used often results in a noticeable behavioral change. These behavioral changes might be as subtle as an on-time blink of the eye or as obvious as a large shift in the trunk of the body.

Regardless of the behavior, the interrogator should recognize that there was a reason that the suspect felt more stress on passing merchandise off to friends than he did on writing fraudulent credits. The interrogator should mentally file this information away for use during development of the admission. The known method of theft utilized by the suspect should be positioned somewhere in the middle of the statement. Interestingly, asking a guilty suspect how a theft might be committed by an employee will result in the suspect offering the method he actually used to steal from the company.

*Explanation of How Investigations Are Conducted.* The third part of the introductory statement is an explanation of how investigations are conducted. This section describes investigative techniques, which may or may not have been used, in the investigation. The explanation of how the investigation was conducted must be in sufficient detail to convince even the street-sharp individual that an in-depth investigation has been conducted.

Although many types of evidence could be developed during an investigation, it is generally most effective for the interrogator to discuss techniques that would develop direct evidence of a suspect's involvement (i.e., surveillance, shopping service, undercover agent, or videotape recording) versus circumstantial evidence of his guilt (i.e., register audits, computer reports or charting of register shortages).

The interrogator speaks in general terms regarding the investigation and never gives any details or evidence. It is inappropriate for the interrogator to give the suspect any specific information at this time. In any of the three sections discussed thus far, the comments made by the interrogator should never be focused directly on the suspect, but rather be of a general nature discussing overall employee theft activity.

The interrogator should avoid words that are threatening to the suspect or too descriptive. For example, an interrogator might say "customers' taking things without paying for them" rather than "shoplifting." The word shoplifting recreates the seriousness of the activity and attaches connotations of punishment. Saying "customers' taking things without paying for them," describes the same activity in a much less threatening way.

By now, the interrogator has conveyed the underlying message that the suspect is present because of "employees' taking things." The suspect is also probably aware that it may be the result of "failing to ring up a sale" and that an in-depth investigation into losses has been conducted. If this message has been successfully conveyed to the guilty, he realizes that there is a strong likelihood he has been caught; however, the interrogator was never direct enough to allow the suspect to initiate a denial.

*Discussions of Why Employees Make Mistakes—Rationalizations.* During the fourth part of the introductory statement, the interrogator begins to rationalize the suspect's actions. These rationalizations focus the suspect's attention on resolving the incident rather than on the consequences of his actions. In the next chapter, Reducing Resistance—Rationalizations, we will discuss methods to reduce a suspect's resistance to confessing.

The rationalizations used in the fourth part of the introductory statement are presented using third person pronouns. The interrogator constantly refers to others—they, them, people, individuals—and never uses words like you or the suspect's first name. By talking about others and the reasons why they became involved in an illicit activity, the interrogator can offer rationalizations for the suspect's behavior without inviting him to deny.

Most suspects will not make a denial at this point because the interrogator has not been direct enough for them to feel threatened. As the suspect listens to the rationalizations, his behavior will begin to change as the rationalizations begin to reduce his resistance. The interrogator will note behavioral changes by the suspect who will begin to open his closed body posture and relax some of his muscular tension. Once the interrogator has reduced the suspect's resistance sufficiently, the interrogator can make a transition statement.

*Transition Statement.* Once the interrogator believes that the suspect is behaviorally close to confessing, he offers the suspect a transition statement. The transition statement makes it evident that the rationalizations the interrogator had previously been using directly applied to him. The interrogator makes this evident by using the suspect's first name and second person pronoun, you or your. The following is a basic transition statement made by the interrogator:

> Mark, the problem is that we don't know the problems you face outside of work.

*Soft Accusation/Assumptive Question.* Once the interrogator has observed the behavioral clues indicating the suspect's susceptibility to confessing, he uses a soft accusation or an assumptive question. The assumptive question bypasses the question, "Did you do something?" and requests information about some aspect of the crime such as, how many times a suspect did something or when the first or last time was that he did it. The following are some examples of assumptive questions:

> What would be the greatest amount of money that you took from the company in any one day?

> What would be the largest amount of merchandise that you took from the company in any one day?

> When was the very first time that you took any money from the company, no matter how recently?

What was the most expensive piece of merchandise that you ever took from the company in any single day?

Whenever a suspect behaviorally reacts in a way that indicates he is going to give an admission, the interrogator immediately uses a follow-up question.

*Follow-up Question.* The follow-up question is a question directly related to the soft accusation. The follow-up question is an exaggeration of what the suspect could have actually done. This exaggeration continues to minimize what the suspect has done and encourages an admission.

*INTERROGATOR:* Bob, let me ask you this. What is the greatest amount of money that you took from the company in any single day?
*SUSPECT:* (Pause, looks away)
*INTERROGATOR:* Was it a whole day's receipts in any single day?
*SUSPECT:* Geez, no.
*INTERROGATOR:* Great. I didn't think it was that much. Would you say that it was more or less than $1,000.00 in one day?
*SUSPECT:* Less.
*INTERROGATOR:* Okay. How much was it?
*SUSPECT:* $20.00.

The interrogator immediately supports the denial as an admission letting the suspect know that he has confessed. The suspect now realizes that he has made an admission and is drawn into a dialogue, which develops his admission.

## Length of the Introductory Statement

In almost all interrogations, it will take some time for a suspect to feel comfortable in confessing. With the introductory statement, the interrogator should not anticipate receiving an admission of guilt before approximately fifteen minutes (see Figure 7.4). The graph in Figure 7.4 illustrates the frequency with which individuals made first admissions versus the amount of time they were interrogated. This graph resembles a bell curve.

What this means is that very few individuals in the opening moments of the interrogation will give an admission; however, as the interrogation continues, the number of suspects giving an admission increases until approximately one hour, after which the number will diminish very rapidly. There exists approximately a half-hour window during the interrogation when using an introductory statement when most individuals will confess if they are susceptible. This half-hour window occurs between fifteen and forty-five minutes into the interrogation. Although some suspects will confess before fifteen minutes of interrogation, the interrogator should time his presentation of the soft accusation or assumptive question based on the half hour of high probability and the suspect's behavior.

Generally, the interrogator should spend five to seven minutes talking about the first three parts of the introductory statement—1) who we are and how we do our job; 2) how losses occur; and 3) how we investigate. It is this section that establishes the credibility of the investigation and forces the suspect to consider the fact that he has been caught. The fourth part of the interrogation, why mistakes are made, justifies and rationalizes the suspect's behavior. The interrogator should plan to spend a minimum of ten to fifteen minutes justifying a suspect's actions before he attempts a soft accusation or assumptive question.

## Participatory Accusation

Another form of accusation that the interrogator can use is called a *participatory accusation*. This accusation tends to be somewhat more difficult to use simply because the suspect is invited to participate in a decision making process leading to the confession. This type of accusation generally takes longer to complete than the introductory statement or the direct accusation because the interrogator allows the suspect to talk while leading him in the proper direction. However, it does provide the interrogator with some positive benefits. In many ways, the participatory accusation begins as more of an interview than an interrogation because of the amount of talking the suspect does. In addition, it allows the suspect an opportunity to define the boundaries of his job, his actions, or present an alibi before any actual accusation is made by the interrogator. In this way, the participatory accusation limits the ability of a suspect to explain away any incriminating evidence.

In a police case, the alibi a suspect might attempt to use to cover his tracks should be obtained first before an interrogation. This may increase the likelihood that the suspect will lie about his alibi, and even if he does not confess, these lies may become key evidence in his prosecution. Because the interrogation is nonaccusatory in its earliest stages, the suspect typically cooperates by giving the required information and details. Once the details have been established, the interrogator can begin the process of moving into an accusatory format.

In the private sector, the interviewer/interrogator is often interested in whether or not a suspect knew he violated a particular policy. For example, in some companies an employee is offered a discount on merchandise he purchases for himself and immediate family members. Employees who violate this policy often will claim that they did not know or understand the policy. For an employee to be terminated for the violation, the interrogator must prove two elements. First, that the employee acted outside the specific guidelines of the policy, such as receiving money for the purchase of a piece of merchandise by someone who was not an immediate family member, and second, that the suspect understood and knowingly violated the policy.

The participatory accusation affords the interrogator an opportunity to have the suspect define his understanding of the policy before he ever gets into an interrogation of the actual violation. By approaching the interrogation in this manner, the interrogator has eliminated an often-used explanation for the suspect's action.

The participatory accusation works extremely well in police cases where a suspect's alibi may be the key to breaking the case. In addition, this type of accusation is extremely effective against upper level management or in complex kickback cases. This accusation forces the suspect to define the boundaries of his decision making process. By defining these boundaries and disclosing that he makes decisions based on certain criteria, he can no longer hide in grey policy areas. Before the suspect recognizes what the interrogator is interested in, the interrogator has gotten him to commit to a specific sequence of events. If he offers any exceptions to the way he does things, the interviewer/interrogator follows up by determining the frequency and circumstances surrounding the exceptions. This effectively commits the suspect into an alibi, story, or decision making process with which the suspect must live.

## Construction of the Participatory Accusation

The construction of the participatory accusation is a multi-step process.

*Introduction.* The interrogator identifies himself to the suspect and makes some preliminary rapport-building remarks. The interviewer/interrogator begins by developing a behavioral norm utilizing the suspect's responses to questions about his background. Once the interrogator feels comfortable with the suspect's behavioral norm, he can then move on to the next portion of the accusation.

*Establishing the Suspect's Alibi and Actions on the Job.* Here the interrogator asks the suspect to define the boundaries of the interrogation. The suspect's alibi is developed in detail including times, places, and names. It is critical to lock the suspect into his alibi moment by moment so that in the future, he is unlikely to change his story. In the event he does change his original story, the original alibi can be used to refute his truthfulness in subsequent alibis.

In situations where the interrogator is reviewing the suspect's decision making process or training, a detailed description of how he does his job is developed. By developing this detailed description of his activities in handling transactions, purchasing, or other tasks, the interrogator locks the suspect into a sequence of events. Now, even weak circumstantial evidence can become damning evidence. Up to this point, because the employee had not committed to a sequence of events, he could explain away any deviation from the norm by simply saying, "Well, sometimes we do it that way."

**Case Example**

In a case where a company's director of transportation was suspected of receiving kickbacks from a vendor, the only evidence was an excessive amount of expendable income, far exceeding his salary.

The director of transportation was questioned about how he handled his day-to-day activities. The director then discussed how he handled financial matters within his department. Once these details had been defined, the director was asked to describe why he gave so much business to a particular company when it seemed to violate the parameters he had described. Had the interrogator approached this differently, the suspect could have given any number of reasons why he chose to do what he did. However, because the interrogator did not let the suspect know what he was investigating, the suspect defined the actual boundaries of his activity. The circumstantial evidence showing he violated his own policies became even more damning in the suspect's eyes.

*Promoting Cooperation through a Story.* During this section of the accusation, the suspect joins the interrogator in developing a story that promotes the cooperation of the guilty. The suspect joins the interrogator in developing a story where certain decisions must be made regarding losses to an imaginary company owned jointly by the suspect and the interrogator. The interrogator and the suspect have, in this story, become partners in a business, one that has suffered significant losses at the end of the first year. The interrogator asks the suspect how they might resolve the large shortage in their business.

The interrogator points out to the suspect that certain employees in their business have violated policy and procedure by taking money and merchandise. In the story the interrogator asks the suspect to decide how he would feel toward an employee who cooperated and talked about the reasons he made his errors as opposed to an employee who has not cooperated in the investigation.

The conclusion reached by the suspect is that you feel better about an individual who cooperates than one who lies or stonewalls the results of an investigation.

*Discussing How Investigations Are Conducted.* Once the suspect has come to the conclusion that it is good to talk about a problem and the reasons why it occurred, the interrogator begins to draw the suspect into a discussion of how investigations are conducted. This may be done in one of two ways. If the suspect is particularly responsive, the interrogator may ask him how he would investigate a particular incident. As the suspect offers investigative avenues, the interrogator expands upon them describing the types of information that can be obtained using that method.

In some instances, a suspect will not be responsive and the interrogator will simply describe different investigative methods and the types of information that could be obtained from them.

It is particularly important for the suspect's alibi to be known before discussing the investigation in this interrogation. For example, in a residential burglary, several young males were identified as being responsible. In discussing how the investigation could be conducted, the interrogator discussed latent fingerprints. One of the youths replied that he had been in the house visiting recently and had probably left his fingerprints on or around the stove. Although this admission put the youth in the home, the interrogator had not yet established an alibi and the suspect explained away any physical evidence that would have indicated his involvement.

The investigation section, like the investigation section in the introductory statement, is designed to establish the credibility of the investigation in the suspect's mind. It is here that the suspect is forced to recognize that his guilt is known. This is even more evident to a suspect who offers methods of investigations because he soon realizes that if he could think of these methods certainly law enforcement professionals had thought of them.

*Creating Rationalizations.* Rather than offering reasons and excuses for the suspect's behavior, the interrogator questions the suspect about the reasons why someone might become involved in the incident. The interrogator allows the suspect to offer excuses and then expands on them. In the event that the suspect does not offer reasons or excuses, the interrogator must now take a more active role in offering justifications to the suspect.

As in the introductory statement method, the early stages of rationalization are done in the third person to avoid placing a suspect in a defensive position where he might offer denials. By having the suspect offer his own rationalizations for an action, the interrogator is more likely to hit upon the justification most favored by the suspect. Once again, the interrogator must watch the suspect for behavioral clues to tell how long the process of rationalization should continue. At some point, the interrogator must make the decision to personalize the rationalization through the use of a *transition statement* that applies everything that has been talked about directly to the suspect.

*Offering the Soft Accusation/Assumptive Question.* Once the interrogator believes that the suspect is behaviorally receptive to making an admission, he prepares to offer the soft accusation. The soft accusation is an assumptive question that addresses some detail of his involvement. The assumptive question makes it clear that the suspect is involved and avoids the last defensive barrier the suspect might have.

## Transcript of a Tape

The following is a transcript of how this interrogation could be developed. Although this particular example deals with the private setting, only minor changes are necessary to make it applicable to public law enforcement officers.

*FRED:* Good morning, Doug. I'm Fred Marks from the corporate office. I just wanted to cover a few areas with you regarding the store. What do you think of the training you received here? Do you think the training is good?

*DOUG:* Not really. The only training I've ever had is when Mr. Thompson, the District Supervisor, brought in a little VCR and played it when the store was slow, but it's better than what I've had before.

*FRED:* Do you think you pick things up pretty quick?

*DOUG:* Yes.

*FRED:* How do you handle a check sale?

*DOUG:* A customer comes in to make a purchase. They ask if I'll ring up the sale and sometimes I will ask beforehand if it is cash or a check. If they say it is a check, I will say fine. I will tell them the amount, they would write out the check and give it to me, and I then say I need to see your driver's license.

*FRED:* Yes.

*DOUG:* Then I write down the driver's license number and the state that it is from.

*FRED:* Where do you do that? On the face of the check, back of the check?

*DOUG:* Oh, it should be on the back of the check.

*FRED:* Oh, is there a stamp or something you should use?

*DOUG:*   Yes.

*FRED:*   Do you always do it that way—I mean, do you do the same thing the same way all the time, you're consistent when you do the job and you always do it the same way when you take a check?

*DOUG:*   Yes.

*FRED:*   So you always do it that way?

*DOUG:*   Yes.

The suspect has now committed to doing a certain job the same way all the time.

The interviewer may also cover charge sale or other types of transactions.

*FRED:*   How about like another sale. A cash sale, how do you ring up a cash sale?

*DOUG:*   Customer comes in and they give me the item. I then ring in my sales number, then I ring in the number on the ticket, and then the amount.

*FRED:*   OK—and then the customer gives you a $20 bill and then what do you do?

*DOUG:*   Then I give him change for it.

*FRED:*   Do you ring that $20 bill into the register?

*DOUG:*   No, I ring up the sale.

*FRED:*   As the amount tendered—$20 amount tendered?

*DOUG:*   Oh, yes.

*FRED:*   And then when you count the money back, do you count it once, double count it, do you count it as it is coming out of the till and then count it again when you're giving it to them or what?

*DOUG:*   Well, if they give me a $20 bill, I put the $20 bill right on top of the register.

*FRED:*   Yes.

*DOUG:*   And let's say it's a $5.50 item and the register obviously shows that there's $14.50 in change. Then, I'll take out the bills and the 50 cents and then I'll count out their change to them again.

*FRED:*   OK, and you always do it that way? I mean you do the same job. You sound like a guy that does the same thing the same way all the time.

*DOUG:*   Yes.

*FRED:*   OK, let me do this another way. Say you and I own a store, OK, Doug and Fred's Shoe Store. We had this store and we open it up and after a year we really watch the overhead, we watch the rent, we watch how much we're paying for the merchandise, we watched our advertising costs, we watched everything, I mean, you and I really busted our bottoms to really go and do a good job here and make a lot of money. At the end of the year, what happened was instead of making money, we lost money. We take the inventory and all that stuff and it turns out we lost $30,000. What would you do?

*DOUG:* Probably have a heart attack, I mean...

*FRED:* Try and find it?

*DOUG:* Yes, I mean I'd...

*FRED:* Hire a bookkeeper or something, maybe hire an auditor to try and find it or...

*DOUG:* Well, I don't know if I'd do that. I'd go back and I'd review my sales, and I'd review the paperwork and a...

*FRED:* Are you an accountant?

*DOUG:* No.

*FRED:* Neither am I. If I was a partner in the business, we'd hire auditors. OK—so say we had the auditors and they came and looked at all the books and all the records. They then said, you know, there's a couple of things where you're receiving the merchandise here and you're not counting it right. There are some markdowns here and they're not taken care of, all of them, the proper way. Therefore, there is a little more of this shortage. There are also a couple of other things that I saw that really bothered me. I mean, I'm an independent auditor talking to you and I have to tell you, Doug, I saw you take a couple of bucks out of the cash register and buy milk on the way home when I rode home with you that day. It's your store and you had a right to, but it sets a bad example for your employees. And Doug, you know, you got these guys that keep coming in and you keep giving them discounts all the time. It's your store, you have a right to do it, but it causes shrink and it sets a bad example for your other employees. Furthermore, I've got to tell you that I think your employees are probably responsible for most of your loss. And we say there's no way. He said yes, I'm pretty sure that it is. I can't prove it, but I think it is. What would you do?

*DOUG:* Well, if I'm paying the auditor for his advice, obviously I have to change my procedures, so I'm not setting that bad example. Hopefully, I can turn the profit picture around.

*FRED:* But he brought up something else. I mean we ask him what to do? You're telling us we got this problem and what we do about it. He says here's what you do, hire some consultants. These consultants come in and they put a video recorder over the front cash register and record everything for three months. They also put a video recorder in the back with time and date generator over the back door. They have a couple of investigators that do surveillance and look at everybody that comes in and what they're bringing when they come in and what they're leaving with when they take it out. They then pull the documentation and go through the detail tape and make sure that everything was rung up and paid for. They gather all of this documentation and after three months, they come into you and give it to you and they say, yes, we found that your niece is taking cash and my nephew is taking merchandise, what would you do then?

*DOUG:* Boy, I don't know. If you could prove it, I would probably have to sit down and talk to him about it.

*FRED:* They've got it. They have the documentation. That's the case. You can do anything with the case that you want to do. You can take it to criminal court, you can take it to civil court, you can do anything in the world that you want with this case. The case is cast in concrete. There's not a question of whether they did it or not, you know they did it. You've got the tape. You have the tapes and you watch them take the money, all right?

*DOUG:* OK.

*FRED:* And not record the sale and put the money in their pocket. You have the detail tape to show that they didn't record the sale and you have the videotape to show the shoes went out and you have the videotape that shows the guy handing the money to the sales person and putting it in his pocket. I mean it's not whether they did it or not. They did. You have it on tape. You have the detail tape. You have the whole thing.

*DOUG:* OK.

*FRED:* So that isn't the issue. The issue is what do you do about it?

*DOUG:* Well, I'd still want to find out why they did it.

*FRED:* Why, is that important?

*DOUG:* Well, yes. I mean, if there was reason.

*FRED:* Sure. I can understand that because there are a lot of reasons why people do things. So you sit down and talk to them?

*DOUG:* Yes.

*FRED:* OK, you talk to the niece and you say, "Niece, I understand that you've been taking some cash out of the cash registers," and she says sure. Nothing wrong with that, I saw you do it. You took $2 out of the register and bought milk on the way home; and Doug, he's been giving discounts to friends. I didn't think there was anything wrong with it—what would you do?

*DOUG:* I guess it probably depends on how much she's done or I don't know...I don't know what I would do.

*FRED:* Well, at least she was honest right?

*DOUG:* Yes.

*FRED:* I mean, that means something.

*DOUG:*  Sure.

*FRED:*  I mean do you suppose that if you and I changed our ways and if we set some black and white examples and we followed those examples ourselves, she might make a good employee in the future?

*DOUG:*  Yes, she could—I would hope so.

*FRED:*  Well, let's go the other way, we talk to my nephew and say nephew, you've been taking merchandise out the back door and he says "No, I haven't." I say, listen, you know I'm as embarrassed by the situation as you are, but you've been taking merchandise out the back door and he says screw you—OK, what would you do with him?

*DOUG:*  I'd probably say screw you back to him and I'd probably have to get rid of him.

*FRED:*  I'm the director of loss prevention for the company and my responsibility is protecting the company assets. Now the niece is somebody that wants to work for herself. She's being honest and straightforward and you can deal with her and the nephew you can't. You see what I mean?

*DOUG:*  Yes.

*FRED:*  Which brings us down to the reason that we're here today. We had to conduct an investigation in the store, and I am aware of the fact that you know that you're responsible for some of the inventory shortage here. What I'd like to do is clear up the amount and see whether or not you want to work with me on the thing or not.

*DOUG:*  What are you talking about?

*FRED:*  What I'm talking about is I'd like to ask you when's the last time that you failed to record a sale and kept the money?

*DOUG:*  I never have.

*FRED:*  Doug, let me explain the way we do an investigation. What we do is... I'll talk about the last one. It's one that I just finished up yesterday. We had a case where I got a call from the store manager and she says listen, I have something that happened. This happened a couple of months ago. She called me up saying this happened and I just can't believe it. I've been working with this assistant manager, we're good friends, we've been working together for a year. The other day, I worked from 8 until 5 and she worked from 1 until closing. That afternoon, we got in some merchandise. There was this pair of sandals, a hot seller on the market. I ordered a case and I only got one pair in each size. I know that because when I got them, I marked them myself. I put them out. I was just fuming that I only got one in each size. I left at 5 o'clock and then I came back that night because this store was in the mall and there was a theater in the mall and I went in the store. This gal and I have been trading each other's make-up all along. She's got permission to go into mine and I have permission to go into hers. Anyway, there's this bathroom in the back of the store that we use, and I noticed I didn't have my make-up, so I went into her purse to look at the make-up. The bottom line is there's a brand new pair of these sandals that were still ticketed, that I ticketed, in her purse. The manager says to me, "I couldn't believe it." I went up to the registers to look at whether or not they had been rung up. They hadn't been rung up, so I went back into the stock and a pair was missing from the stock and they were a pair that I had just received, so I stayed until we closed that night to see whether or not she took them out or paid for them or anything. She didn't, I could still see them bulging through the purse. What would you do if you were me and you got that call?

DOUG:  I'd have to go and investigate it.

FRED:  What would you do?

DOUG:  Talk to her.

FRED:  You'd go talk—so you talk to her and you say listen, you know, you took that pair of sandals last night that you didn't pay for and she denied it. Then finally you convinced her that you knew and could prove the truth and so she finally said OK, I took the pair of sandals. Now you ask, have you ever done it before? And she said no. Is she telling the truth?

DOUG:  I don't know.

FRED:  You don't know—so you know what we did was put a video camera and recorder in the back stockroom and we saw her take three pairs of pumps, two pairs of sandals, fourteen different cans of shoe polish and the last thing that she took was with her boyfriend. She put a case of shoes out in the trash and picked it up later in a '57 Chevy and drove it over to the garage. So when I talked to her, I talked to her about that case of shoes. I didn't even let her know how the thing started, OK. I just talked to her about the last thing and I explained to her about the case of shoes and she said that she didn't. She finally understood that we had it sealed up tight and she said, "Yeah, OK I did it." And I asked her if she'd ever done anything before and she said no and then you know after a little conversation I convinced her, and she said OK, this is what I've done. She told me about this, this, this, this, and this. Then she told me more than I knew about. I'll tell you that right up front, she told me more than I knew about. She told me about every single thing that I knew about over that three month

period of time without me having to coach her. Is she telling me the truth?
*DOUG:* Yeah.
*FRED:* She probably is, right?
*DOUG:* Right.
*FRED:* That's the way we do it here. This isn't something where anybody flies out 2,000 miles to talk to somebody about if one little iffy deal happened. It's not a question of whether or not something is or isn't probable or whether it is or isn't just one time. You and I both know the extent of this and the only question is whether you want to resolve it here or not. I think that you do. You know it's like when I go home and I find cookie crumbs around my son's mouth and I say Mark, you been in the cookie jar and he says no I haven't—I mean I got a problem there. It's my own son, I can't work with him. I can't believe what he's telling me because I know the truth—I got the proof. With him, it's the cookie crumbs—with this, it's something else. I go home and say you been in the cookie jar and he says, yes dad, I'm sorry I didn't get lunch and I couldn't wait till supper and I was hungry. That's a whole different ball game. I'm able to deal with that one. I really would like to resolve this one with you today.

Now, Doug, when was the last time you took money from the store? No matter how recently?

## Interrogation Time Limit

Although individuals still confess after one hour of the confrontation, the odds of obtaining a confession drop rather dramatically that late in the interrogation. However, in especially emotional cases such as a homicide, it may require more time to reduce the suspect's resistance. There is no absolute time limit to an interrogation, but the interrogator should use his good judgment in deciding when to stop. Unless the incident is a particularly heinous crime, most interrogators will conclude their interrogations at a maximum of one and one-half to two hours without gaining a first admission. It will be the "totality of circumstances" surrounding the interrogation that will determine if the time length is excessive. In complex cases, where the development of the admission is difficult, a number of hours following the first admission might be required to document the admission. That extra time would not be considered unusual.

In the private sector, most interrogators will begin to back out of an interrogation where no admission has been gained beginning at about an hour and fifteen minutes. An interrogator's good judgment and assessment of whether or not he is likely to get an admission from the suspect should identify the point where the interrogation should be concluded.

## Countering Suspect Interruptions

The guilty suspect may attempt the tactic of trying to rush the interrogator into playing his hand early. The interrogator should avoid taking this bait. By allowing the suspect to control the interrogation, the impact of the introductory or participatory statements is lost and the interrogator's ability to obtain an admission will be hampered.

Suspects who tell the interrogator to "Get to the point!" or ask "Are you saying I stole?" are attempting to draw the interrogator into a premature direct accusation. The interrogator who immediately gets to the point and makes a direct accusation, plays into the suspect's hand. The direct statement allows the suspect to make a denial.

Some suspects will repeatedly ask the interrogator to get to the point. When it is obvious that the introductory statement is not having the desired impact, the interrogator may simply use a direct accusation and move to rationalizations handling the suspect's denials as he proceeds.

The interrogator should attempt to put the suspect off without directly answering his question. This might be done by simply saying: "Just a minute, let me finish what I'm telling you and I think you'll see exactly what my point is."

It is the inclination of most interrogators to directly accuse a suspect who interrupts with these questions, but by doing so, the interrogator can create a more difficult interrogation. The interrogator should recognize that a suspect who attempts these types of tactics is giving additional evidence of his guilt. It is unusual for a truthful suspect to interrupt an interrogator telling "the police or loss prevention story."

# Reducing Resistance—
# Rationalizations

8

*Rationalization is the engine that drives an emotional interrogation.*

The driving force behind an emotional approach to interrogation is the process of rationalization. Rationalization is usually a one-sided discussion, presented to the suspect by the interrogator, offering excuses or reasons that will minimize the seriousness of the crime and make it easier for the suspect to confess by allowing him to save face. The rationalization is an integral part of the introductory statement method and the participatory accusation method. In each of these openings to an emotional interrogation, they allow the interrogator to offer excuses or reasons that minimize the seriousness of the crime and make it easier for the suspect to confess.

Contrary to the practice of many interrogators, the emotional appeal requires that the interrogator do almost all the talking until the suspect gives an initial acknowledgment of guilt. The suspect is never questioned why he did something, but rather he is offered reasons or excuses why he did it by the interrogator. This one-sided discussion by the interrogator allows him to control the direction of the interrogation much more easily than using questions directed at a suspect. An interrogator who attempts to question a suspect by using direct questions is often lead astray by a suspect who is attempting to stall, sidetrack, or deceive the interrogator.

The interrogator who offers rationalizations to a suspect is not asking about investigative facts to further the interrogation. Instead, the interrogator discusses the reasons why the suspect became involved. If the interrogator chooses to discuss the factual elements of the case, the suspect could take issue with the interpretation of the evidence and attempt to explain it away. However, in the emotional interrogation, the interrogator simply says, "You did it," ignoring the circumstances surrounding the how and concentrating on the reasons why. By concentrating on the reasons why the suspect became involved, the interrogator can offer any number of reasons for the suspect's actions either real or fictitious.

Rationalization is an integral part of each of our lives. In almost everything that we do, we justify or rationalize reasons why we do what we do—consider the driver who goes 64 miles per hour in a 55 mile per hour speed zone because he believes that police officers do not write tickets until the driver is going 10 miles over the speed limit, or the office worker who takes pencils home because he can justify his actions by the fact that he does some office work at home, or by the fact that the company has plenty and they do not cost much. Another employee can justify taking saleable merchandise but not cartons of merchandise or any money; and yet another employee can justify taking cartons of merchandise and money as long as he does not go into the safe and touch the deposit. In the progression of rationalizations, still another individual can justify taking anything as long as he does not physically harm another person, some other person can justify taking anything as long as he does not kill anyone, and so on. Each person, through their parents, church, and society has developed moral guidelines that justify his actions. These guidelines form the basis of our day-to-day decision making. When we violate a guideline, we use the process of rationalization to bring ourselves back into equilibrium with our moral guidelines.

## Concept of Rationalization

The process of rationalizations allows the interrogator an opportunity to develop a relationship with the suspect. This relationship is one of an understanding mediator rather than an adversary. It allows the suspect to view the interrogator as an understanding individual who faces problems and turmoil in his everyday life just as the suspect does.

The process of rationalization also allows the interrogator to transfer guilt to someone or something other than the suspect. This guilt transference assists the interrogator in minimizing the seriousness of the suspect's offense. It makes the suspect a victim of circumstances instead of the initiator of the incident.

Rationalizations also allow the interrogator to focus the suspect's attention on the resolution of the incident rather than on the consequences he may face as a result of being involved. This refocusing of the suspect's attention is fundamental to allowing a suspect to believe that it is in his interest to confess his involvement in the incident. The suspect who continually focuses on the consequences of his actions and the impact these consequences will have on his life is less likely to confess than the suspect who focuses on the future and puts the incident behind him.

Finally, the process of rationalization allows the interrogator to overcome the hurdles or fears the suspect has in confessing. Typically, a suspect must reconcile his fears of the consequences before he will make an admission. Generally, most suspects have one or more of the following hurdles standing in the way of a confession:

Fear of arrest and prosecution

Fear of embarrassment

Fear of termination

Fear of restitution

Fear of bodily harm to himself or family

The interrogator is like a salesman. He must understand and answer the objections the potential customer has before the customer will buy the salesman's product. Once the salesman understands the customer's objections, he then offers benefits of his product that overcome the customer's reluctance to buy. If the product's benefits outweigh the customer's objections, the customer will make a purchase. The salesman handled his customer's skepticism by stating and restating benefits, offering proofs, and expanding on the benefits. For a customer who is potentially indifferent, the salesman uses closed probes to uncover needs and offers benefits to handle these needs.

The needs of the customer may be complex. There may be his personal needs and corporate needs as well that the salesman must fulfill before the customer will purchase. In the same way, the interrogator must recognize that the suspect has a complex group of needs. Image, financial, and family needs all come together to form the basis of the final hurdle that the interrogator must overcome for the suspect to confess.

The interrogator should understand the concept of hope as it applies to interrogation. Hope is really the cornerstone of an interrogator's understanding of the suspect. The suspect hopes that if he does not say anything, the interrogator and investigation will not have developed information sufficient to terminate or arrest him. If the investigation has not developed sufficient evidence, then the suspect will not have to be embarrassed or pay restitution. The interrogator must, through establishing credibility of the investigation, take away the suspect's hope that he has not been caught. The process of rationalization returns hope to the suspect, that his life will not be completely devastated as a result of confessing. In instances where the suspect says, "Well, I don't care, just lock me up," he has given up hope. The interrogator must first renew his hope through rationalization before he will be susceptible to an admission of guilt.

## Determining Which Rationalization to Use

There will be a number of factors that the interrogator should consider prior to selecting the rationalization to use during the interrogation. The interrogator must consider the motive, background of the suspect, and the suspect's receptivity to any rationalizations he presents. In most interrogations, the initial rationalizations selected by the interrogator are educated guesses based upon the case facts, possible motive, and background of the suspect. The selection of the most successful rationalization will be decided on by the suspect himself during the interrogation. The interrogator offers the rationalizations and observes the suspect's behavior to determine which rationalization seems to have the greatest effect in reducing the suspect's resistance.

### Motive of the Crime

The motive behind the incident will often lead the interrogator to the proper rationalization. In many cases, the motive of the crime can be accurately guessed based upon the investigation and the background of the suspect. In the early stages of an investigation, a suspect's motive may not be evident from the limited facts available. The more common motives for a suspect are theft, revenge, sex, and curiosity.

The theft motive could be the result of a true or perceived financial need of the suspect or his family. This need may be a result of bankruptcy or overlimit credit cards that caused the suspect to have or believe he had an immediate need for money. In many cases, simply having an opportunity to steal might have been a sufficient temptation for the suspect to steal. In some corporate environments where theft is common, even the most honest individuals might steal because it is the norm of the group. Some studies indicate that as much as 30% of the population would steal if given the opportunity; however, only 10% of the population would still steal if they had to look for a way to do it. This base 10% are often motivated by greed and are typically the more hardened, experienced criminal element.

A second motive, revenge, can play a part in a number of different crimes. It may justify the theft of a deposit to make a supervisor look bad. Revenge might be used to justify sabotage to get even for a real or perceived insult. It might even justify the killing of another individual. The need to get even can burn like a fire inside an individual, weakening the moral fiber until it breaks.

The third motive is sexual in nature. This motive can justify anything from theft to the killing of another. Many people become involved in theft to steal for lovers when their salaries will not support the gifts they want to give. Sexual deviance can also account for the torture and killing of victims. Sexually motivated killings often tend to be vicious, brutal acts by sexually deviant suspects.

Finally, curiosity or thrill-seeking can also be a motive in the crime. These may start an innocent adventure, but the temptation overcomes the suspect's good sense and he does something that he should not. Youngsters often shoplift out of curiosity to see if they can get away with it or simply for the sense of adventure. Once they see how easy it was to shoplift from the store, this motive is generally replaced with the theft motive. Now, the youths take expensive items they could not otherwise afford.

The previous motives were discussed as individual reasons for committing the crime, but a suspect's actual reasons are often more complex. It may have begun as a theft because the suspect needs cash, but it culminates with a rape because the suspect had an opportunity and inclination to do so. This sexual urge, however, may be complex in and of itself. The sexual act is often secondary to the need to denigrate the female because of some past experience.

Thus, the interrogator recognizes that the motivation for any incident may be simple to complex. Often, it is only after evaluating the case facts and background of the suspect that a true motive becomes apparent.

## Background of the Offender

The background of the offender can give the interviewer/interrogator direction in selection of the proper rationalization. A suspect's educational, financial, and social situations all may help to indicate the proper rationalizations to use.

The interrogator should consider what might cause him to confess were he in the suspect's position. Often, such role reversal will give the interrogator an insight into the suspect's mindset that will indicate a proper rationalization. However, the interrogator should not place too much emphasis on this role reversal because of the different moral and ethical values a suspect may have. Consider an example in which the background investigation of a suspect indicates that his financial problems might be the reason for committing the crime. These financial problems include having his car repossessed, wage assignments, and being in the process of being evicted from his apartment. Although most people would consider that they are having financial difficulties, the suspect views the situation only as a momentary cash flow problem. He has $20, a date for Saturday night, and he sees the situation in an entirely different light from most people. Remember that each person justifies how he spends his money individually. Some individuals will not own a credit card or will pay the balance on the card off at the end of each month, whereas others carry a small balance and pay it off as soon as possible. Still others run it up to the limit and then obtain another credit card. Each of these individuals has a considerably different financial perspective.

The interrogator, reviewing the background of the suspect, is looking for the suspect's value system. By understanding how the individual thinks and what is important to him, the interrogator can present rationalizations that coincide with the suspect's thinking.

Consider the rationalization used on a teenager who was the second child in the family. The suspect's older brother was a straight-A student, letterman on several school teams, and one of the most popular boys in his class. His brother was an average student, with average performance in scholastics, sports, and social relationships. The interrogator used the rationalization that the suspect became involved because he was calling out to be noticed by his parents. Although this approach may seem clichéd, the effect on the suspect was significant. The rationalization was developed along the following lines.

> You know Bob, I think the reason that this happened was not because you're a bad person, but rather to call out to your parents and say, notice me, too. For years you have had to walk in the shadow of your brother who is lucky enough to be a straight-A student, be the most popular kid in class, and it's got to be awfully hard to follow someone like that. You know, moms and dads often begin to focus their attention on the child who does the best. It does not mean they don't love you, but, sometimes it does not seem like it. I think what has happened here is not so much that this happened for money or anything like that, but I think it was a call to your parents to say, notice me, I'm a person, too.

By considering the motive of the crime along with the suspect's background, an interrogator can often make an educated guess as to why a suspect became involved. Consider a case of a nurse who has administered lethal doses of medication to her patients. Why might this woman have killed these individuals?

These types of cases are seen in hospitals and nursing homes. The interrogator must consider the background of the suspect in relationship to the possible motives. Some motives in this situation could be

The nurse was simply lazy and trying to reduce her workload.

She had a mental apparition.

She saw this as a way of reducing the suffering of the patient.

She saw this as a way of reducing the hardship and suffering of the family.

The nurse was influenced by another individual to do this.

Considering these and other potential motives to commit the crime, the interrogator should begin to look at the background and decision making process of the suspect. Although the background alone may not indicate which motive directed the suspect's action, the interrogator can often make an educated guess at what the most likely motive for the crime was. Once he has considered the most likely motive, it is then that he begins to consider what he might say that would justify the suspect's actions, recalling that the interrogator's primary goal is to transfer guilt and overcome the hurdles of the suspect.

## Behavior of the Suspect

While presenting the rationalization, the interrogator must study the suspect's behavior to determine whether or not it is having the desired impact. The behavior of the suspect will indicate whether or not the rationalization should be continued or other rationalizations should be tried. Receptive and nonreceptive behavior by the suspect are discussed below.

*Receptive Behavior.* If the suspect accepts the rationalization presented him by the interrogator, he will display receptive behavior. The receptive behavior of the suspect will include warm, accepting eyes. The muscles around the corners of the eyes will relax and the eyes will begin to moisten. The suspect allows the interrogator to look below the surface and into his eyes as the rapport deepens.

The suspect may occasionally nod in agreement and the overall physical tension of the body will begin to relax as he accepts the interrogator's rationalization for his actions. The closed defensive barriers of the arms and legs will begin to open and the shoulders will lose their tension and begin to slump. The suspect's denials will become less frequent and finally will cease all together as he moves towards a submissive posture.

*Nonreceptive Behavior.* Nonreceptive behavior by the suspect can consist of cold, hard, unaccepting eyes. The nonreceptive suspect's eyes take on a flat look that does not allow the interrogator's gaze to penetrate below the surface of the eye. The muscles around the eyes tighten into an unaccepting frown. The suspect may roll the eyes to amplify his disbelief of the interrogator's statements.

The suspect's body will maintain its tension and closed defensive posture. The suspect's denials will continue unabated during the rationalizations that do not meet his needs. The frequency of the suspect's denials will increase as he reacts negatively to the unacceptable rationalizations.

The interrogator who recognizes the behavioral clues of acceptance and nonacceptance will modify his rationalization to meet the suspect's needs. An interrogator can be eloquent while relating rationalizations, but if the rationalizations do not meet the suspect's needs, they will fall on deaf ears. Consider the following case example and the suspect's comments following the interrogation.

### Case Example

The director of training for a convenience store operation was interrogated regarding the theft of cash from franchise owners. The suspect had surgery approximately a year prior to the interrogation for a brain tumor and had recently been rediagnosed as having another tumor. The suspect was under a severe financial strain because of the expense of his operation and the medication. The suspect was well liked by coworkers. The most likely motive for the suspect's stealing was financial problems. Investigators suspected that the stolen money was used to pay medical bills and for his medication.

The interrogator used an introductory statement to establish the credibility of the investigation and followed it with rationalizations that placed the blame on financial problems. During the rationalization of financial problems, the suspect showed receptive behavior and began to open his body posture. The suspect had uncrossed his legs and positioned his feet flat on the floor, opening his arms to the sides of the chair, indicating that he was near submission. The interrogator, in the final stage of the rationalization, attempted to focus the suspect's attention towards the future rather than the present by saying, "When a problem occurs we have to put it behind us and look down the road where we'll be at five or ten years from now. While right now it may seem like the most important thing in the world, as the years pass, it becomes less and less significant."

The suspect immediately crossed his legs and arms indicating that he did not like what he was hearing. The interrogator dropped this line of rationalization and returned to the financial problems as a reason why people make errors in judgement. After a short period of time the suspect uncrossed and opened his legs once again nearing submission.

The interrogator now attempted to minimize the seriousness of the incident by talking about the size of the company and the amount of sales it had. Then the interrogator said, "The company is looking for some common ground to begin a discussion so that they can understand the reasons why this happened." As this was said the suspect once again recrossed his legs and folded his arms across his chest. The interrogator recognizing the suspect's disagreement immediately returned to a discussion of the financial reasons for the crime. Shortly thereafter, the suspect went into submission and confessed.

During a discussion with the suspect following the interrogation, he related that there were two things that the interrogator said that just didn't ring true. The first statement the suspect said he disagreed with was looking down the road to the future. The suspect said, "I have no future. The doctors have discovered another tumor and I'll be lucky to be alive a year from now." The second area of disagreement was establishing common ground. The suspect related, "When you talked about common ground, there is no common ground. Two weeks ago another director was caught stealing and I'll be lucky if I'm not arrested like he was."

The post-interrogation interview with the suspect revealed the reasons for the change to a nonreceptive body posture. Although the interrogator was not sure specifically what the suspect's objections to these rationalizations were, it was evident from the change in his physical behavior that he did not like what he was hearing. When an interrogator observes nonreceptive behavior, he should immediately change rationalizations and attempt to use other face-saving justifications.

The important thing for the interrogator to realize is that the rationalization offered to the suspect does not have to be the real reason or motivation behind the suspect's activity. What the interrogator is attempting to do is look for excuses that the suspect can accept. It may be the real justification the suspect made to himself, or it may simply be a reason that he thinks others might accept to justify his behavior.

Remember that the interrogator presents the rationalizations in the third person because it is less threatening to the suspect. Using the third person is much less of a direct attack on the suspect than saying directly, "You are having financial problems." Often the suspect may not be sure the interrogator is talking about him and so he withholds any denials. Once a suspect has begun to deny, an interrogator can use the second person pronouns you, your, or the suspect's name. These, however, may cause additional denials by the suspect because he feels the need to defend himself.

The interrogator may offer several different rationalizations to the suspect. As he presents each of these different rationalizations or reasons for the suspect's actions, he observes the suspect's behavior to see which one the suspect most readily accepts. When the interrogator discovers a rationalization that the suspect accepts, he should begin to talk more and more about the acceptable rationalization and omit the others. This will enhance the rapport the suspect feels with the interrogator and will further reduce the suspect's resistance to confession.

An interrogator may use the same rationalization a number of times during the interrogation. The appropriateness of the rationalization and its effectiveness in overcoming the emotional resistance of the suspect depends on the suspect, the interview, and the interrogator.

## Minimizing the Seriousness of the Offense

The interrogator also minimizes the seriousness of the crime during the interrogation. Minimizing is playing down the seriousness or the scope of the suspect's involvement.

The interrogator might assist the suspect in minimizing the seriousness by saying, "And sometimes it's really nothing more than an error in judgement, a mistake," or "What is important here is that a person doesn't get blamed for things he hasn't been involved in, just because people often think the worst about others," or "Everyone can make a mistake in judgement."

Minimizing the seriousness of the suspect's involvement is a twofold process. First, the rationalizations begin to justify the reasons behind a suspect's actions and second, the interrogator begins to contrast the incident with more serious crimes. The interrogator discusses a robbery, but compares it with a robbery where the victim was shot or killed to minimize the seriousness. For example, the interrogator might say, "All we're talking about here is taking some money. I mean nobody was shot, nobody was hurt, and I think that's important here. I'm glad that this thing didn't get out of hand."

## Focusing the Suspect's Attention on the Future or Past

The interrogator can also attempt to focus the suspect's attention on the future or the past. Using positive statements about his past performance or his future draws the suspect's attention away from his present situation. The interrogator who focuses the suspect's attention on the past might highlight the good that a suspect has done. This good may be raising a family, job performance, or any other skill that the suspect has. The suspect needs to feel that the incident he is being interrogated about is only a small portion of his life.

Often, an interrogator will focus a suspect's attention to the future. Whenever anyone makes a mistake, that mistake, because of its immediacy, seems to be the most serious error that was ever made. However, the interrogator, by focusing the suspect's attention into the future, can minimize the seriousness of this error. He might say something like,

Remember when we were kids and we didn't study for a test. It seemed like the most important thing in our life at that moment because we knew we weren't going to do well? But you know, looking back on that test now, it really wasn't that important. What was really important was what we learned from that mistake. We went on and studied for other tests and did better as a result of learning from that mistake.

With individuals who have been extremely responsible or have significant job responsibilities, it is often to the benefit of the interrogator to point out past successes and the good things that happened before the incident. The interrogator highlights the fact that all the good things that they have done should not be forgotten and that the suspect just made an error, an error that should not outweigh all the positives he had done in his life.

## Offering a Positive Outlook

The interrogator might also offer the suspect a positive outlook during the interrogation. This positive outlook makes the suspect aware that there may be benefits to his making an admission. The interrogator does not tell the suspect that things are going to turn out well, nor does he offer to help the suspect when offering a positive outlook. In the short term, the interrogator is there neither to help nor to have things turn out well for the guilty suspect. That does not mean, however, that the cooperation a suspect shows in making an admission does not have benefits. It might be the benefit of feeling better because he talked through a problem that he thought could not be resolved and put it behind him. The lifting of an emotional weight is a wonderful feeling. It could also be the perceived benefit of being understood by family, coworkers, or others by explaining the reasons why the suspect became involved in the incident.

This positive outlook shows the suspect that others are capable of understanding his problems. It also allows him to consider what potential benefits he might derive from confessing. Many suspects focus only on the negatives of confessing without ever considering what positive benefits they might derive from making an admission.

These methods of showing understanding are crucial to the interrogator's success in reducing a suspect's resistance. The interrogator's warm, conversational tone of voice is important in developing rapport and trust with the suspect. The interrogator should present his rationalizations or other methods of showing understanding to the suspect in a sincere, positive manner. The interrogator sells the belief that it is good to talk through problems and to resolve them. A persuasive argument can help the suspect develop these same feelings.

## Relating Personal Stories

The interrogator might use personal stories from his own life to illustrate the rationalizations. It is a rare individual who has not at one point or another in his life been short of money and under some financial pressure. This financial pressure might have occurred only when you were a child and wanted to buy that very special toy but did not quite have the money to do it. How did it feel? What impact did this have on how you dealt with others during this time? Personal stories by the interrogator illustrate the rationalizations and their impact on everyday life, and they help portray the interrogator as a human being who has faced adversity in his own life. The interrogator should never let himself appear dishonest to the suspect. Saying something like, "When I was 16, I was a burglar and look at me today," only detracts from the professionalism and trust the interrogator is attempting to achieve. Simple stories about children and life, but ones that do not necessarily relate to dishonesty, are most effective in showing understanding.

An interrogator could discuss his feelings when his friends wanted him to start smoking. He did not have any desire to smoke, but ultimately he took a cigarette. Now today, he is a nonsmoker, but at that point in his life, his friends influenced his decision and he did something that on his own he would never have done.

Children make wonderful stories for illustrating the rationalizations.

My son Jonathan, when he was three years old, cut up our bedroom blanket with his scissors. Now I know my wife didn't do it and I didn't do it. He is the only three-year-old running around the house with a pair of scissors. I can't change the fact that the blanket has been cut up and ruined, but what is important is that he learns from his mistake. As a parent, I have to make him understand that what he did was wrong and that he can't just go around just cutting up things around the house anytime he wants. It's important that he learns that there is a right way to use the scissors and a right time to use the scissors. Now, this does not mean that he wasn't punished, but the important thing is that he learned from his mistake so he never makes that same error again.

## Illustrating with Current Events and Publications

Rationalizations can also be illustrated by newspaper and magazine articles. Current events or topical news items often make excellent illustrations for the rationalizations. The interrogator might ask the suspect to consider famous people and the reasons why they might have made the mistakes. Showing the suspect that even the rich and famous can make an error often helps in minimizing the seriousness of the suspect's actions. The error does not make them a bad person, just someone who has made a mistake. By transposing a suspects feelings to others who have problems helps the suspect feel less isolated and fearful about how he will be viewed.

## Avoiding Threats or Promises

The interrogator should never threaten or promise any suspect anything during the interrogation. Promises made to a suspect should not be made unless they can be carried out and the promise is one that would not be likely to make an innocent person confess. To tell a suspect that if he confesses, he will maintain his job or not go to jail might under certain circumstances make an innocent person confess just to get out of this situation. Threatening physical harm to a suspect might also cause an innocent person to confess.

The interrogator should be cautious about any promise he might make during an interrogation. Promising a suspect to "tell his side of the story" is acceptable, but promising that a suspect will not be prosecuted when the interrogator knows that a prosecution will occur, is not, in our opinion, acceptable. The interrogator needs to maintain an ethical outlook on the process of interrogation. The interrogator who believes that it is okay to "lie to a liar" or that "he [the suspect] is just getting what he deserves" soon becomes no better than the criminals with whom he is dealing.

It certainly is acceptable to make promises to a suspect to obtain his cooperation. The state's attorney who offers the suspect immunity or a lesser sentence for his cooperation does so only with strong evidence of the suspect's guilt. An interrogator might trade a prosecution for the return of money or property when a prosecutable case is unlikely or weak. In the private sector, the recovery of company's assets are in many cases more important to the company than a prosecution.

For example, an employee of a small fast food restaurant stole an $8,200 cash deposit from the safe. Other than the suspect's confession, there was no additional physical evidence to tie him to the crime. The suspect was identified because of his deceptive behavior during an interview. His primary fear was prosecution. The interrogator entered into a negotiation to recover the money from the suspect. The owner authorized the interrogator to promise he would not press a criminal complaint against the suspect as long as the money was returned. The suspect returned over $7,600 in cash and a motorcycle he had purchased with the remainder of the stolen money. To a small business, the loss of over $8,000 could be a crippling blow. To the company, the promise of no prosecution made business sense. However, the interrogator must be careful to avoid any perception that the money is being extorted from a hapless victim. The proper witnessing of the suspect's statement with careful attention to the agreement to pay back the funds should avoid any problems.

## Examples of Rationalizations

The following are examples of rationalizations, minimization, focusing on the future, and positive outlook. The interrogator must remember that the process of showing understanding to reduce the suspect's resistance may take some time. It might require that the interrogator talk for fifteen to thirty minutes or longer using rationalizations, personal stories, and other justification tools to reduce the suspect's resistance sufficiently so he is able to make an admission of guilt.

### *Job Pressures*

There are a lot of reasons that people do things that they wouldn't ordinarily do. Sometimes a person might feel under tremendous pressure because of his job, because he has ambition and wants to get ahead. He might want to look good at work and make a good impression. Sometimes things like this happen because of that.

### *Financial Pressure*

Sometimes people do things because of financial pressures. You know it's awful easy to get credit these days. Almost everyday I get an offer for a credit card in the mail with a $5,000 line of credit to spend just like that. The next thing the person knows, his monthly payments on the credit card is way more than he can afford. It sure seems simple at first, but paying it back can be real difficult.

### *Minimization*

I think we all have made a mistake or an error in judgement at one time or another. Nobody is perfect. A lot of times, our mistakes seem a lot bigger than they probably are. Maybe you had a time in high school where you asked this girl out for a date and she turns you down. It seemed like your whole life was ruined, but you got up the next day and it still hurt but as time went on you put it behind you and went on with your life. There were other girls that you asked out, girls who accepted, fun times that you had and your life went on. That was one small moment in your life. Years later it doesn't seem very significant.

## Focusing on the Future

You know, Bob, I think it's important that we all learn from the mistakes that we have made in our lives. It would be a terrible shame if we didn't. We would be doing the same things over again at fifty, making the same mistakes we made in our teens. It's an important part of growing up, making mistakes. We should do it while we are young so we can learn from them so that later on we're not making those same errors. Look at the auto insurance industry. The rates are real high when we're young, and after we turn twenty-five, they go down. Why? Because we are better drivers and we don't make the same errors we did when we were young. And now we're better drivers as a result.

## Positive Outlook

You know, think about two kids playing baseball in the living room. One of them throws a ball and breaks a lamp. Now, you're the parent who is responsible and you ask them if they were playing baseball in the living room and broke the lamp. One of the kids says, "Hey, we didn't do anything, it wasn't us." You go to the other child and he says, "I'm sorry. We were playing ball in here, I threw it, it bounced off the wall and broke the lamp." He explained exactly how it happened and why. Which one are you going to feel better about? The one who said he was sorry and talked to you about it? Or the one who said he didn't do anything wrong when you know that he did. Doing something wrong doesn't make us a bad person, but when we do make a mistake, it's important to get it cleared up and go on with life.

## Examples of Rationalizations with Choice Questions

The following are examples of rationalizations along with choice questions that logically work well with them. An interrogator often reviews at least the broad topics he will discuss before he meets the suspect. This section may prove helpful during the preinterrogation review.

Remember that the rationalizations presented to a suspect do not have to be the real reasons he committed the crime, but rather an acceptable alternative that merely allow the suspect to save face when he confesses.

## General

Bill, frequently we find that the people we talk to are basically honest people who at some point in their lives find that events beyond their control caused them to do something that is out of character. Medical bills, family problems, and financial pressures are things that can push a person into doing something he never dreamed he could do. We all have our breaking points. Decisions have to be made about what to do with the evidence gathered during this investigation. It is very important to know as much about the person as possible before making any final decisions. Certainly, someone who has been under severe pressures and was forced into doing something is a much different person from someone who had ill intentions from the very beginning. It's very important that we understand your side of what happened, especially if a personal crisis was the motivation behind these mistakes. We know much of *what* happened from the investigation, but what we now must learn is equally important—*why* it happened.

## Suggest Accident

I can see if this was an accident and you didn't intend on...

*Use.* This rationalization can also be effectively used in some homicides, batteries, or incidents where the injury or damage inflicted could be explained as an accident. One difficulty in using this rationalization is that it removes the element of intent from the suspect's actions. If the rationalization is used, the interrogator must often confront the suspect again to establish the element of intent. In other circumstances, the facts of the case may establish the intent. For example, the suspect agrees that he started the fire accidentally, not intentionally. The physical evidence indicates five points of origin and an accelerant being used to spread the fire. The suspect's intent can be inferred from the physical evidence developed by the investigation.

### Choice Questions

Did you plan on this happening or was it just an accident?

Was it for no reason at all, or was it to show them where they went wrong?

Did you mean for this to happen, or did it just get out of hand?

## Suggest Impulse

If this just happened on the spur of the moment without your thinking about it...

*Use.* This rationalization can be used for theft or damage to property cases. It is also effective in cases where the suspect reasonably might have made an impulsive decision without thinking through the consequences of his action. Even if a homicide was planned out by the suspect, an interrogator might use an "impulse" rationalization to reduce the seriousness of the crime. Most people view mistakes made under pressure very differently from a planned event. The suspect who impulsively decides to rob a store because of pressure is viewed differently from the individual who coldly calculates a robbery.

### Choice Questions

Did you plan this out, or did it happen on the spur of the moment?

Did you take the job here with the intention of doing this, or did it happen on the spur of the moment?

Had you planned on doing this all along or did you just suddenly decide without thinking it through?

## Blame Victim (Company or Supervisor)

Bob, if this happened out of frustration because of the way your boss picked on you...

Use. This rationalization can be used for theft or damage to property. The victim can be blamed in almost any crime from a homicide, to a sex crime, to theft. The guilt is transferred to the victim by the interrogator who portrays the suspect as a victim of circumstances. The suspect became involved because the victim dressed or acted a certain way, flaunted their wealth, or made advances to the suspect. The interrogator can even blame a child victim of a sex abuse for appearing older and tempting the suspect. In the private sector, the company or supervisor can be blamed for lack of security or poor working conditions. However, the interrogator should be careful about placing blame on the company or supervisor because of personnel considerations and employee morale. In some cases management may not understand the interrogator's efforts to shift blame from the suspect and be concerned that the interrogator was focusing on real inadequacies of the company or supervisor. On occasion, this shifting of blame can create problems with a management team who fails to understand the process.

### Choice Questions

Was this planned out or just out of frustration?

Did you want to hurt the company or was it just to bring attention to the problems?

Did she come on to you or did you start this whole thing?

## Blame Poor Pay

Cindy, I don't know how you can make it on just $5.00 per hour...

*Use.* This rationalization can be used for theft, robbery, burglary, or embezzlement cases. The interrogator blames an insufficient income for causing the suspect to steal. Generally, the interrogator uses examples that show the high cost of living in today's economy. Discussing the price of eating out or just clothing children illustrates the impact of low pay. Personnel managers often dislike this rationalization because they consider that the pay rate is fair for the skill level and responsibility of the position.

### Choice Questions

Were you going to sell it for a profit, or was it just for yourself?

Did you use the money for a bad purpose like booze and drugs, or was it to pay bills?

Did you need the money for bills or was it just to party?

## Blame Fellow Worker or Friends

I don't think this would have ever happened if everyone else wasn't doing it too...

*Use.* This rationalization can be used in cases where someone else other than suspect is involved in the same issue or when other people have done the same thing before. The idea for becoming involved in the incident is transferred to another and the suspect was just following the pack. People usually view the one who had the idea as being more guilty than those who just followed along. An interrogator who transfers the idea to another helps minimize the seriousness of the suspect's participation in the crime.

### Choice Questions

Was this your idea, or someone else's idea?

Was this your idea or did you get involved only because others were doing it too?

Did he come to you or did you approach him to do this?

## Blame Poor Security

I think the company's the one to blame since they didn't have good security in the first place...

*Use.* This rationalization can be used in most types of cases. The interrogator expands on the idea that the victim (person or company) was tempting the suspect because they did not take the necessary precautions to safeguard their property. The victim's failure to safeguard his property was like asking to be ripped off.

This rationalization works well with the "blame victim" rationalization. "If they had lights and a decent set of locks this certainly wouldn't have happened. What do they expect when it's so dark around the building?" Effectively, the suspect was put into a tempting situation that left him almost no choice in the matter. If the victim had been security conscious, the suspect would never have been tempted to get involved. A personal story could be about a mother who bakes a cake and leaves it on the counter only to have the family eat it while she is out. The cake was for a bake sale, but she didn't leave a note or hide it to protect it. She just left it on the counter to tempt her hungry family.

*Choice Questions*

Did you go looking for the [item] or was it just laying around?

Did you think of doing this all along or was it only because security was so bad?

Was the door locked or did they leave it open?

## Blame the Economy (Politicians, Creditors)

All you have to do is look at how the cost of everything keeps going up...

*Use.* This rationalization can be used during any type of theft or economic gain case. This rationalization works well with the rationalization of low pay. The interrogator blames rising costs for the suspect's money not going as far as it used to. The economy can be blamed for the suspect's losing his job or being unable to find a job that pays wages decent enough to have kept him out of trouble. Consider articles about the rising costs of business and plant closings, which make wonderful illustrations for the interrogator to use as examples. Relating the rate of inflation to pay raises the suspect has received show the suspect in a very personal way how these changes affect his daily life.

*Choice Questions*

Did you take the money for a bad reason or a good reason such as paying bills...?

Were you paying for your family's needs or were you just going to party?

Did this happen because you were looking for trouble or because you couldn't find a job?

## Blame Peer Pressure

If what happened is that your friends kept pressuring you to do this...

*Use.* This rationalization can be used in cases where others may also be involved. The interrogator shifts the blame for the idea to friends or family members who pushed the suspect into becoming involved. The interrogator can also refer to indirect pressure the suspect has felt of wanting to dress like his friends and go the same places they go. The pressure the suspect feels because of his need to belong to a group is often an acceptable rationalization for a suspect. This is especially true of younger suspects or individuals belonging to gangs. This rationalization works well on suspects from broken homes who have replaced family with their peers. The difficulty in using peers is the loyalty shown toward friends. This can often be overcome by not attempting to identify the friends until after the suspect has confessed. To attempt to have the suspect implicate others too early might result in an increased resistance to confessing.

### Choice Questions

Did you want to do this all along or was it because the others pushed you into it?

Did you go out and offer to do this, or did they just ask you?

Did you make money selling this, or did you only charge them the same amount? (Private sector: very useful in cases involving discount abuse)

Does this happen all the time, or just a few times?

## Exaggerate Loss, Frequency, or Seriousness

It appears the loss could be a lot more now...

*Use.* This rationalization can be used for cash register shortages and/or inventory shrinkage. It is also a useful method to minimize the seriousness of the incident by exaggerating the frequency or size of the loss. This can be effectively used during the development phase to make the suspect's involvement less significant.

While interrogating a burglary suspect who had stolen loose gems and jewelry, the interrogator exaggerated the loss and blamed the homeowner for trying to get more out of the insurance company. The suspect denied the large loss, claiming he had only stolen a smaller amount during the burglary. This rationalization was used along with peer pressure to shift the blame to his accomplice and the homeowner.

*Choice Questions*

Are you responsible for all the things [money or merchandise] missing or only a small part of it?

Are we talking dozens of times or just a few?

Could it have been thirty or forty thousand dollars or a lot less?

## Propose Loss of Control

I don't think you had any intention of this getting to the extent it did...

*Use.* This rationalization can be used for thefts over a long period of time. It can also be used for crimes of violence, sexual harassment, or damage to property. The suspect "saves face" by admitting having something go too far even though he did not intend it to happen.

The interrogator portrays an innocent situation that gets out of hand and goes further than anticipated. In a beating, it could have started out as a simple fight that escalated into a homicide when the suspect struck the victim's head against the curb repeatedly. The use of this rationalization might require the interrogator to reinterrogate to establish the element of intent. Intent might make a significant difference in how a person is charged criminally. The suspect's lack of intent might even make it difficult to terminate the employee in the private sector.

*Choice Questions*

Did you use the money for illegal things or was it for expenses?

Did you think it was going to be this much, or did it just get out of hand? (Theft or damage)

Did you know it had gotten this bad or did it just get out of hand?

Did you mean for it to go this far or did it just happen too fast?

## Blame the Use of Alcohol/Drugs

I think it was the drugs that caused you to do things that you normally wouldn't do...

All you have to do is look around and see that most people try...

*Use.* These rationalizations can be used for thefts, accidents, or damage to property, or rape, child abuse, and homicide when it is known that the suspect has a problem with drugs or alcohol. Other crimes can also be attributed to the use of drugs or alcohol. The interrogator can discuss how addictive even cigarettes can become, and how people are almost driven to fulfill this need. This rationalization may create some difficulties in the private sector, where management might wrestle with the issue of rehabilitating the employee through drugs or alcohol treatment programs. This issue may also raise questions in the private sector about termination, because drugs and alcohol in some cases fall under state or federal disability acts that preclude discriminations because of a disability (i.e., drug/alcohol dependency).

*Choice Questions*

Can I tell them that you will stop taking the drugs/alcohol?

Did you realize what you were doing or was it only after it happened?

Did you use the [drug] during working hours, or was it only during breaks?

Was it to get high, or just to relax?

Were the pills for yourself, or were you going to sell them at work?

## Emphasize Borrowing

If you planned on paying the money back all along...

*Use.* This rationalization can be used for theft of money or some types of property. The interrogator minimizes the loss by focusing the suspect's attention on "loan" rather than on theft. Although the loan was unauthorized, the suspect is allowed to save face by agreeing that he had intended to return the money or property. The intent to permanently deprive can be established by the frequency of the unauthorized loans and the failure of the suspect to have repaid this loan. Intent can also be established by the amount of time that has elapsed between the suspect's taking the loan and the confrontation with the suspect. It will be difficult for the suspect to convince anyone that he intended to repay the money when he concealed the loan and a significant period of time elapsed between the loan and its discovery. However, the suspect often takes comfort in the rationalization that he intended to repay the money. Many embezzlers start with borrowing and actually repay some of the money at first, but gradually these repayments fall further and further behind, before they cease all together.

## Choice Questions

Were you going to keep the money all along, or were you going to pay it back?

Were you going to keep that item or did you just want to borrow it so you could have some time to see if you wanted to buy it?

## Play One Against the Other

I would rather see you get your side of the story in first before...

*Use.* This strategy and rationalization can be used when it is known or believed that two or more suspects are involved in the issue under investigation. The interrogation is often easier when multiple suspects are involved in the incident. When only one suspect is involved, he is totally aware of his position and can accurately assess his exposure. When multiple suspects are involved, a suspect can only guess what the others have said that might incriminate him. Generally, these types of cases are easier for the interrogator to resolve because he can drive a wedge between the suspect and his coconspirators obtaining a confession from one, with others falling like dominos.

In one interrogation, two cousins were being confronted about the theft of merchandise from a jewelry store. Finally, one of the women admitted stealing two Timex watches worth about $60. The second suspect continued to deny any involvement. The interrogator of the first woman entered the second interrogation room and told the second suspect that her cousin was getting the matter cleared up and that she needed to cooperate. He also told her that her cousin had told him about the watches. She responded, "That bitch, I can't believe she told you about the Rolexes!" What followed was an admission to the theft of two diamond Rolex Presidentials with a combined value of almost $25,000.

It is not uncommon for a suspect to reach an incorrect conclusion and think the worst has happened. In presenting the evidence to the suspect, the interrogator should be specific enough to have the desired impact, but as in the previous case, vague enough to let the suspect make the mistake.

### Choice Questions

Was it your idea or someone else's idea?

Did you realize he was going to do this all along or did you think he was kidding?

## Identify the Hurdle

On occasion, during the latter stages of the interrogation, a suspect might become submissive but still be reluctant to confess. There seems to be a stumbling block holding the suspect back from a confession. The interrogator should ask the suspect what he is afraid of or concerned about. Generally, the suspect will not answer and simply sits silently. If this is the case, the interrogator should present a hypothetical situation to the suspect, then ask the suspect to speculate on what great fear might be keeping the individual in the story from telling the truth about the incident.

Once the suspect has pointed at a particular hurdle, the interrogator should restate the hurdle and announce that he believes that is the suspect's greatest fear as well. The interrogator then begins to overcome the hurdle by again showing understanding and refocus the suspect on the future or past.

> *INTERROGATOR:* Let's say another person was in the same situation you are. What do you think would be his biggest concern about telling the truth? Don't tell me you did anything, but just your best guess why this person wouldn't want to talk about what he did.
>
> *SUSPECT:* He'd be afraid of friends finding out.
>
> *INTERROGATOR:* Afraid of people finding out, I'm sure that's what you're concerned about too. These are the kinds of things that we want to handle as quietly as possible. No one is here to embarrass anyone unnecessarily.

By specifically confronting the suspect's fear, the interrogator works to reduce the hurdle in the suspect's mind. A suspect who fears termination can often be convinced to confess by discussing if the company could terminate him even without a confession. Once the suspect realizes that his hope of maintaining his job is gone, even if he continues to deny involvement, he will often confess his involvement.

## Correcting the Rationalizations

The interrogator should consider what problems his choice of rationalization might cause the case. As pointed out earlier, certain rationalizations might remove the intent necessary to prove a violation of the law or a policy. If an interrogator elects to use the rationalization, it might be necessary to correct it after the first admission. After the first admission, the suspect is much less resistant to a confession and usually will go the next step to correct the intent.

Sometimes the introduction of a second interrogator who expands the admission and corrects the intent issue is helpful. This second interrogator is not bound by the previous rationalizations, nor is the suspect embarrassed changing his story because he has not lied to the new interrogator. A factual presentation of evidence that establishes the suspect's intent is often all that is necessary to obtain the suspect's additional admission. Factual evidence becomes even stronger as the suspect's resistance to a confession weakens. Even circumstantial evidence can become more damaging in the suspect's mind as he weakens emotionally.

An interrogator's failure to correct a rationalization that removes intent may result in difficulty terminating an employee or establishing probable cause for the suspect's arrest. Knowing what is necessary to prove the crime enables the interrogator to recognize deficiencies in an admission before he obtains the written statement.

# Denials

# 9

*No matter to what extent the interrogator*
*attempts to avoid denials, he will on occasion*
*still have to face them.*

In Chapter 5, we discussed the causes of denials and strategies to avoid offering a suspect the opportunity to deny. Unfortunately, no matter how much the interrogator attempts to avoid causing denials, they cannot always be avoided. The more difficult suspects especially will attempt to deny so that they can defend their position of noninvolvement. The very strong-willed suspect will on occasion simply make a blanket denial, telling the interrogator he has never done anything. Typically, this suspect is not going to allow the interrogator an opportunity to use an introductory statement or participatory accusation, but rather makes a blanket denial as his opening gambit.

Most suspects will be polite and wait for an opportunity to enter the conversation and make a denial. Since the interrogator is doing all the talking, this should limit the suspect's ability to enter into the conversation. Avoiding long pauses or silences can also assist in deterring denials. Silence during rationalizations invites the suspect to enter the conversation and make a denial.

## Types of Denials

The interrogator should recognize that there are two unique styles of denials that he will face during the interrogation. Although both denials refuse to acknowledge involvement, they are dramatically different in how they occur and how they must be handled.

## Emphatic Denial

Any response from a suspect that refuses to acknowledge the truthfulness of the accusation is an emphatic denial.

"I didn't do it."

"You're wrong, it wasn't me."

## Explanatory Denials

Any response from a suspect that offers an excuse or a reason why he could not or would not be involved in the incident is an explanatory denial.

"My mom and dad didn't raise me that way."

"My father's a policeman."

## Where Denials Occur

Denials occur at a number of points during an interrogation. The primary difference between the handling of denials in an interview and in an interrogation is that during the interview, the interviewer allows the suspect, victim, or witness to voice the denial. During an interrogation, the interrogator will attempt to control the conversation to avoid the suspect's making a denial.

In an interrogation, the first place an interrogator is likely to encounter a denial is after the accusation. In rare instances, the interrogator may encounter denials by a dominant suspect even before he makes any formalized accusation. In general, the suspect who is going to deny involvement will do so in response to the direct accusation of an interrogator. Those suspects who are offered an accusation before their resistance has been reduced to a level permitting an admission will also make a denial.

The second place that an interrogator can expect denials is during rationalizations. Typically, the interrogator will find that suspects will attempt to interrupt the rationalizations with denials and protestations of their innocence. In general, denials tend to diminish the longer an interrogator rationalizes the guilty suspect's involvement. In the early stages of rationalizations, while the suspect is physically and emotionally strong, he will offer more and more denials to protect his position. If the interrogator is offering rationalizations that do not meet the needs of the suspect, he can expect that denials will surface more and more frequently. As the suspect begins to weaken and have less resistance to making an admission, the numbers of denials tend to decrease.

The third place during an interrogation at which denials can surface is at the presentation of the choice question. The interrogator offers a choice, an acceptable versus unacceptable choice such as, "Did you use the money for bills or for drugs?" The suspect's response is, "I didn't use it for either," a denial. The denial surfaces because the suspect's resistance to a confession was still too high. The presentation of the choice question was asked before the suspect was in a submissive posture and all his denials had stopped. The interrogator who elects to use the choice question to test the suspect's susceptibility to making an admission should expect that it will encourage an emphatic denial if the suspect is not ready to confess.

Finally, denials occur during development of the admission. Denials that occur here may be truthful or untruthful. The interrogator may find that the suspect will have made an admission to the theft of merchandise from his employer, but denies the theft of money because he did not do that. The copycat killer may make an admission to some crimes, but deny others because he had no involvement in those homicides. During the development of the admission phase of the interrogation, the interrogator needs to be especially conscious of evaluating denials for their truthfulness.

## Emphatic Denials

Emphatic denials by a suspect are essentially a defensive posture with which the suspect hopes to hold the interrogator at bay. In the early stages of interrogations, the suspect will typically use the emphatic denial to defend himself. To use the metaphor of a gladiator fighting another gladiator, the emphatic denials are the shield and the explanatory denial is the gladiator's sword. At first, the suspect merely uses his shield to deflect the rationalizations offered by the interrogator.

### Suspect's Behavior

The suspect makes emphatic denials in two ways, verbally and physically. The interrogator can anticipate a denial by recognizing the verbal and physical behavior associated with it. By anticipating the emphatic denial, an interrogator can often control it or even stop it from even being verbalized.

*Physical Behavior.* The suspect about to make an emphatic denial will physically manifest a number of behaviors that will be observable to the interrogator. The most prominent behavior observed will be the suspect shaking his head "no." This emblem of the word no is learned behavior and almost always precedes a denial. The suspect may not make a full movement of the head from side to side, but rather make only a partial movement. This partial emblem will be an abrupt quick shake of the head to one side before the head moves slightly towards the interrogator as the suspect speaks the denial. The emblem, shaking the head "no," shows the suspect's disagreement with what is being alleged by the interrogator.

Other facial characteristics can also be noted in conjunction with the emblem of shaking the head "no." Because the suspect is disagreeing with the interrogator, typically, the brows will pinch down and together in a frown. The muscles around the mouth will begin to tighten to form the initial words the suspect will speak. As the mouth tightens, the interrogator can often hear an intake of breath that prepares the suspect to speak as soon as an opening in the interrogator's dialogue occurs. Finally, although eye contact may break momentarily while the suspect makes the denial, generally, his eyes will make contact with the interrogator's eyes as the denial is spoken. In the later stages of the interrogation, the eye contact may not be present as the suspect's resistance to confessing weakens. Just before the suspect enters submission, he may not make any eye contact with the interrogator.

The interrogator has five identifiable behaviors that will allow him to anticipate an emphatic denial. These behaviors are

1. Shaking the head "no," either a full or partial movement
2. Frowning brows
3. Tightening mouth
4. Taking breath
5. Making eye contact

*Verbal Behavior.* The suspect may also give a verbal clue that he is about to make an emphatic denial. The emphatic denial is generally spontaneously delivered in response to a statement with which the suspect does not agree or to a pause in the conversation. The suspect may also attempt to interrupt the interrogator while he is rationalizing to make an emphatic denial. These interruptions to deny are often preceded with permission-asking phrases. A suspect who attempts to interrupt by saying, "but," "can I," "may I," "please, sir," will generally conclude these phrases with, "I didn't do it." An interrogator who hears this type of verbal clue should anticipate an emphatic denial.

## Handling Emphatic Denials

The primary concern of an interrogator handling the emphatic denials of the guilty is to avoid a "did too–did not" exchange with the suspect. This is the kind of argument we had as children that was generally never resolved. Unfortunately for the interrogator, an interrogation that deteriorates into a "did too–did not" exchange is a stalemate. In interrogation, stalemates are won by the guilty.

The second important consideration in handling emphatic denials is to recognize that an emphatic denial is significantly different from the explanatory denial. The interrogator not only handles the emphatic denial differently, but recognizes that an explanatory denial means he is making progress with the suspect.

The interrogator can use a number of conversational techniques to control a suspect's emphatic denials.

## Use the Suspect's First Name

The use of the suspect's first name is an effective means of stopping an emphatic denial. An individual, upon hearing his name, immediately stops what he was about to do or say and pays attention to the speaker. As we grew, when people called our name, we realized that we were doing something inappropriate or that somebody needed us. This learned behavior causes most people to at least pause in their attempt to join the conversation. An interrogator's use of a suspect's first name can be used at several points during the interrogation when he needs to gain the suspect's attention or momentarily cause him to stop what he is doing.

## Discuss Important Areas

In any interrogation, the suspect is torn with a desire to leave and a desire to stay and resolve the issue. On the one hand, the suspect is denying involvement, but on the other hand, he stays because he is curious to see what information the investigation has revealed about him.

The suspect's desire to know the amount of information that has been developed can be used by an interrogator to get the suspect to be quiet and listen. The interrogator tells the suspect that the information he is going to present is important because the suspect is going to have to make an important decision. The suspect generally interprets this statement to mean that the interrogator will be discussing specific evidence that proves the suspect's involvement. The interrogator, however, has no intention whatsoever of discussing specifics, but rather returns to rationalizations to minimize the seriousness of the suspect's involvement.

The suspect now pauses to hear the expected evidence so he can make up a story to explain it away. However, as he waits for the evidence to be presented, the rationalizations begin to reduce his resistance to confessing.

## Tell the Suspect That He Will Have a Chance to Talk

Especially in the early stages of the interrogation, a suspect may continually interrupt the interrogator with denials. Telling the suspect that he will have a chance to talk as soon as the interrogator is finished often appeases the suspect so that he will do the socially acceptable thing and maintain silence while the interrogator talks. The suspect's silence has the effect of allowing the rationalizations to chip away the resistance of the suspect. Even momentary silence by the suspect allows the interrogator to show understanding and establish a rapport that moves a suspect closer to submission. More dominant suspects will continually interrupt, attempting to talk over the interrogator.

If the interrogator is unable to get the suspect to wait it is sometimes effective to offer them an opportunity to speak. The interrogator tells the suspect to go ahead and say what he has to say. The suspect usually says, "Well I didn't do it." The interrogator then asks if there is anything else he would like to say. The suspect generally will respond, "Just that I didn't do it." The interrogator should acknowledge the suspect's position and immediately take control of the conversation and begin rationalization again.

The suspect who continually wants an opportunity to speak rarely has much to say beyond an emphatic denial, "I didn't do it." He has no prepared presentation other than to discuss specific evidence. Since the interrogator has avoided presenting specific information, the suspect is at a loss for words and the interrogator can again take control of the conversation. However, if the interrogator has presented his evidence too early, the suspect will have much to say on the subject as he begins to make explanations and excuses for the incriminating evidence.

## Advise the Suspect That It Is Better to Say Nothing Than to Lie

One of the more effective techniques in the stopping of emphatic denials of the guilty is to tell them that it is better to say nothing at all than to lie about the incident. The interrogator relates that, "To have the investigation be able to show that they lied only makes things look worse for them." The interrogator should tell the suspect that it enhances his position to say nothing rather than to make unnecessary denials. Denials that do not match the investigative results will make people question his sincerity. Surprisingly, many suspects will discontinue all denials in response to this interrogation tactic.

## Interrupt the Suspect and State the Denial for Him

Another effective method of handling the denial is to cut off the suspect's verbal denial, and then state it for him. The interrogator might say, "Bob, just a minute. You're probably thinking I should say I didn't do it. That is often the first reaction we have in a situation like this. The problem is that saying I didn't do it, doesn't match with the investigation and only makes people wonder." The interrogator has kept control of the dialogue, and expressed understanding about the suspect's motivation to deny. This establishes rapport but does not allow the suspect to feel he has to protect a position because he did not actually say, "I didn't do it."

## Use Behavior to Control the Interrogation

The interrogator can also, to a certain extent, control the suspect's emphatic denials through his own verbal and physical behavior. The interrogator can use his gestures to tell the suspect that he does not want him to speak. The use of commonly observed emblems and conversational reactions allows the suspect to recognize that it is inappropriate for him to enter the conversation. Upon observing the suspect's attempt to deny, the interrogator employs the emblem "stop," raising the hand, palm out, to tell the suspect he is not permitted to speak. In conjunction with this, the interrogator turns his head and breaks eye contact looking away, telling the suspect indirectly, "I don't want to hear this" (see Figure 9.1). However, these two gestures in the early stages of the interrogation are insufficient by themselves to stop the denial. The interrogator must use his behavior in conjunction with the preceding ploys to help stop the suspect's denial. For example, the suspect might attempt to do the following:

*SUSPECT:* But... (shaking head) ...no.
*INTERROGATOR:* Bob, just a minute. There are some important things that we need to discuss. (Hands up in "stop" gesture turning head away.) The important thing here that I think you need to understand is that... (returns to rationalization)

As the suspect's resistance to a confession lessens, the suspect becomes less aggressive and the interrogator can control any emphatic denials simply with the emblem of "stop" and turning the head (see Figure 9.1).

The interrogator should also use the conversational ploy of increasing the speed of his words and his volume slightly. This is the same thing that individuals do during conversations when they are interrupted. They tend to talk just a little bit faster and a little bit louder to talk over the person attempting to interrupt them. In the same way, the interrogator talks over the suspect who attempts to interrupt him to give an emphatic denial.

**9.1.** To stop a denial, the interrogator turns his head and uses the stop emblem to control the suspect's denial.

## Change the Psychology of the Room

With especially difficult suspects, it may be necessary to change the psychology of the room. As the interrogator approaches forty-five minutes in the interrogation and has still made no significant headway with the suspect, it may be necessary to change the psychology of the room. This is done by the interrogator's physically changing positions. Up to now, the interrogator has been seated across from the suspect with several feet of space separating him from the suspect. The interrogator, recognizing that the suspect has significant resistance to confessing, may want to challenge the suspect's resolve.

There are several ways to change the psychology of the room. The first method is for the interrogator to stand as if he is going to leave. As the interrogator stands, he expresses exasperation with the suspect's inability to cooperate and tell the truth. He might say something like, "Bob, I just can't believe that we can't get this straightened out. You act like you don't care and I just don't believe that." The movement by the interrogator is not meant in any way to be physically intimidating to the suspect. Rather, it is designed to challenge the suspect who believes he can wait out a persistent interrogator. The movement of the interrogator often will result in a change of posture by the suspect. The interrogator, as he rises, continues to talk to the suspect, but does not raise his voice as he allows exasperation to creep into his tone. The interrogator should challenge the suspect by saying,

> You know, Bob, I'm not here to aggravate you, I'm just here to get this thing straightened out. If you don't care, then that's fine. The investigation has already resolved the issue. The only reason for talking to you was to get your input and your side of the story. If you don't care, then that's fine. The investigation can be handled without you participation.

The interrogator then expresses his belief that this is not what the suspect really wants. The interrogator tells the suspect that he is sure the suspect does want it to get straightened out. Then the interrogator returns to his seat across from the suspect and continues the process of rationalization. As the interrogator stands and then reseats himself, the suspect often changes positions in his chair. This shift of position by the suspect is the result of the interrogator's movement in the behavioral zones of the suspect. Many times, this postural shift by the suspect will move him into a less defensive position that makes the rationalizations more effective. The interrogation should be conducted while seated. Unnecessary standing or movements during the interrogation can disrupt the smooth flow of the interrogation.

In certain instances, the more difficult suspect may not change posture and continue to defy the interrogator. The interrogator, who is now standing, tells the suspect that the meeting is over and that they are going to leave. As he does so, he continues to express disbelief in the suspect's lack of cooperation. Once he has gotten the suspect to stand, the interrogator returns to the process of rationalizations. After a moment or two, the interrogator suggests that the suspect sit down because there are "a couple of other things" that he needs to discuss with him. Once seated, the interrogator immediately returns to rationalizations.

The benefit of getting the suspect up and moving him around is that he may return to his chair in a different posture in which he is more receptive to the interrogator's rationalizations. This tactic is used only in those circumstances where the suspect is not responding to the

emotional appeal after forty-five or more minutes. Having the interrogator or suspect move around when the emotional appeal is reducing
the suspect's resistance often has the effect of increasing the suspect's
resistance.

The final way to change the psychology of the room is to exchange
roles with the suspect. An interrogator who is making little or no
headway with a suspect may change roles with him and allow the
suspect the opportunity to interrogate the interrogator. This might be
done by asking the suspect to ask the interrogator if he has a pen in his
pocket. The interrogator places a pen in his pocket and asks the suspect
to ask him if he has a pen in his pocket. Once the suspect asks if the
interrogator has the pen in his pocket the interrogator denies that the
pen is there. Most suspects will challenge the interrogator telling him
that the pen is there. The interrogator again denies the pen's existence.

This exchange goes on for a moment or two until the interrogator
picks the pen out of his pocket. He then asks the suspect if he believed
that the pen was not in the pocket just because the interrogator told him
it was not there. The suspect will respond that he did not believe the
interrogator. The interrogator should say,

> Exactly—you and I both know the pen was there. We could see it and
> it's the same way with this investigation. The investigation is very
> clear. Simply saying no, that you didn't do something is not sufficient
> to convince anyone. The problem that we face with the investigation
> is that it doesn't tell the reason why...

and then immediately return to the process of rationalization.


## Use an Enticement Question to Stop a Suspect's Denial

Under certain circumstances, an interrogator might use an enticement
question to break the cycle of denials. The enticement question, discussed in Chapter 6 of this text, is a question that presents either real
or fictitious evidence to a suspect that causes him to change or consider
changing his story. In Chapter 6, the question was used during an
interview and the suspect was allowed to respond, either by changing
his alibi or by pausing to consider changing his story. The question is
used differently, however, when an interrogator is attempting to handle
a suspect's emphatic denial.

The interrogator still implies that he has evidence by using the
introductory phrase, "Is there any reason...," but he does not pause for
the suspect to respond at the end of the question. Instead, he immediately stops any response from the suspect.

*SUSPECT:* But, I didn't take it. (Weakly said)

*INTERROGATOR:*    Pat, is there any reason that you can think of that... [interrogator selects one enticement that best fits the case facts: a) there is a videotape of you taking the money? b) that your fingerprints were found in the safe? c) that you were observed taking the deposit?] Wait a minute before you answer that. That wasn't fair and I shouldn't have said anything. But you know its better to say nothing than to deny and have the investigation show the opposite. I think the greatest concern is not that this happened, but why... [Interrogator returns to rationalization]

Using an enticement to stop a denial generally works best when the suspect is only weakly denying involvement. Sometimes, an interrogator who uses an introductory statement will find that the suspect will make a tentative, weak denial to the soft accusation. A partial enticement question can often stop the denials from continuing past the first one. This type of question can only be used once to stop a suspect's denials. Its repeated use dilutes the enticement impact and may even cause a suspect to question whether this information exists. The interrogator, in stopping the suspect's response and immediately returning to rationalizations, does not allow the suspect time to evaluate the question fully. This may cause the suspect to believe the evidence actually exists.

Regardless of which method the interrogator uses to control the suspect's denial, it is imperative that he immediately return to the process of rationalization. The rationalization is the driving force that reduces the suspect's resistance to confessing and the interrogator returns to it as soon as he has regained control of the conversation again. Especially in the early stages of the interrogation, the interrogator must be prepared to handle the emphatic denials of the guilty. The hands of the interrogator are generally out in front of him so that all he has to do upon seeing any of the behavioral clues of a denial is to raise them into a stop position (see Figure 9.2).

## Truthful Emphatic Denials

The interrogator should always be alert for truthful suspects who may have been identified inadvertently as guilty by the investigation. This generally occurs in investigations that develop only circumstantial evidence that may misidentify a suspect.

Truthful denials are spontaneous and direct. The suspect has good eye contact and gets progressively stronger as time goes on. The truthful suspect continually interrupts the rationalizations with protestations of his innocence, and his denials sound spontaneous and genuine. As a

9.2. The interrogator uses his hands to gesture and also to control the suspect's attempts to deny.

general rule, truthful suspects stay to convince the interrogator of their innocence and do not walk out.

The guilty may deny, but they often leave before they have convinced the interrogator of their innocence. By contrast, their eye contact is tentative and gestures are overdone and dramatic. Finally, the positioning of the suspect's body, when he makes a denial, can be an indicator of his truthfulness. The truthful suspect is up in his chair, leaning forward aggressively, defending his position. The guilty suspect who is making a denial slumps, with the trunk of his body back in the chair, and uses his legs as a barrier to keep the interrogator away. Once the interrogator recognizes that the emphatic denials may be coming from a truthful suspect, he should change the direction of the interrogation. The interrogator may discuss specific evidence against the suspect or interrogate him on a secondary issue. For example, if a suspect were to be suspected of stealing money from a register, the interrogator might begin an interrogation about the theft of merchandise from the company. Similarly, if the suspect were to be suspected of a robbery and his denials appeared to be truthful, the interrogator might go to a secondary issue of his involvement in theft or burglaries in the area of the robbery.

The interrogator should remember that the suspect's behavior during the interview initially was indicative of deception. Although this is not always a total guarantee of the suspect's involvement, there generally is a reason why the suspect appeared deceptive. In this case, it was not the primary issue the suspect was to be interrogated about, but rather an involvement in a secondary issue, that created the deceptive behavior. Generally, when the suspect is confronted on a secondary issue on which he is guilty, the denials will be less emphatic and delivered from a more reserved submissive posture. An interrogator, comparing the denials to the main issue and secondary issue, often sees and hears a dramatic contrast. This contrast in the strength of denials leads the interrogator in the correct direction and can be helpful in convincing the interrogator of the suspect's truthfulness in the main issue.

## Explanatory Denials

An explanatory denial is the first offensive stroke by the suspect. It is the gladiator's sword, as the emphatic denial was his shield. In general, the explanatory denial is most likely to be a truthful statement that is most often made by the guilty suspect. The suspect is attempting to sidetrack the interrogator by having him challenge what is often a true statement. The explanatory denial, "I wouldn't do that because my father is a policeman," if challenged by the interrogator, might bring a response such as, "Well, go ahead and call the Barrington Police Department and ask them. You'll find my father is working right now."

Although the suspect's statement is supposed to sidetrack the interrogator and show his truthfulness, it is also telling the interrogator a direction to proceed with his rationalizations. The suspect, on the one hand, has been repeatedly denying his involvement, while, on the other, attempting to think of reasons or excuses that would show the interrogator why he would not be involved. The interrogator, recognizing that the introductory phase for the explanatory denial is different from the emphatic denial, asks for an explanation.

The explanatory denial is often preceded by introductory phrases that cry out for the interrogator to ask for an explanation. Introductory phrases preceding the explanatory denial might be, "I wouldn't do that. It's impossible. It couldn't have been me." To which the interrogator responds, "Well, why is that Bob?" In response to the interrogator's query, the suspect may make any of a number of explanatory denials:

The security is too good here.

I wouldn't want to jeopardize my job.

I don't want to go to jail.

I don't need the money.

I'm a born-again Christian.

I love my wife.

I'd never hurt a fly.

The interrogator accepts the explanatory denial as a true statement and turns it around as another reason for the suspect to confess. The interrogator expresses excitement that the suspect has joined him in resolving the problem. The interrogator responds with something like:

I hope that is true!

I was hoping that you'd say that!

I'm glad you mentioned that!

Exactly, that's great!

Good, that's one more reason to get this cleared up!

The interrogator delivers the preceding statements with excitement. This excitement and the statement itself has a number of functions. First, it allows the interrogator to once again dominate the conversation. He has invited the suspect to give his explanatory denial in a sentence or two but does not want the suspect to continue talking. By being excited, he can talk over the suspect's statement and again take control of the conversation. Second, by being excited about what the suspect has said, the interrogator discourages the suspect from bringing it up again. The suspect is reluctant to return to this statement because it was received so positively by the interrogator. Instead of being the knockout blow the suspect had intended, it was turned back against him. Finally, the statements of excitement by the interrogator afford him an opportunity to think about what he is going to say next in response to the suspect's explanatory denial. The following is an example of how to handle the explanatory denial:

*INTERROGATOR:* Sometimes these things happen because we feel that we are not being treated fairly. We do the best we can, but it is recognized instead...

*SUSPECT:* I wouldn't do that.

*INTERROGATOR:* Why is that, Bob?

*SUSPECT:* I don't need the money. I've got plenty of money in the bank.

*INTERROGATOR:* I'm sure that's true. I don't doubt that for a second that you've got money in the bank. That tells me a lot about you as an individual. It says that this wasn't something that was plotted out over a long time, but rather was probably done on the spur of the moment. A response to a pressure that I'm not even aware of. You know, I think there are several things that we should consider...

The interrogator begins a new rationalization playing off the fact that the suspect has money in the bank. The suspect has told the interrogator that the reason he did it was not economic in nature. The interrogator now uses rationalizations that would justify the suspect's behavior on the basis of something other than an economic reason.

Although an explanatory denial is generally a true statement, and typically the interrogator accepts it and turns it to his benefit, this is not done if the suspect attacks the interrogator racially or sexually. A suspect who says, "You're only saying this to me because I'm [Black, Puerto Rican, Oriental, Native American, etc]..." should be confronted immediately by the interrogator. The interrogator should handle these types of statements by saying,

> I can understand how you might think that, but that is the reason why we do an investigation. An investigation doesn't have anything to do with whether a person is black or white. It only deals with the facts and the facts of this case are irrefutable. An investigation doesn't care about the race or the sex of an individual, it only deals with facts. In the past, I'm sure there have been abuses at one time or another, but that's the reason that we're required to conduct an investigation that is both thorough and extensive, to develop these facts so there can't be any abuses of power. You know, I think that the one thing that is important that you understand here is this... (Interrogator returns to rationalizations.)

If the interrogator fails to handle an explanatory denial, the suspect will immediately recognize that the interrogator did not deal with his statement. The suspect who recognizes that the interrogator could not refute his statement will immediately press his advantage. He does this by repeating the explanatory denial again. If the interrogator still does not handle his explanatory denial, the suspect will become more forceful in stating his position, "But I've already told you, I've got plenty of money in the bank. I don't need it." If the interrogator still doesn't handle the explanatory denial, the suspect will recognize that the interrogator cannot overcome this statement and will focus his defense in this area to counter any claims made by the interrogator.

If the interrogator attempts to take exception to the suspect's explanatory denial, the suspect now can prove his position or at least sidetrack the interrogator.

*SUSPECT:*   But I love my wife.
*INTERROGATOR:*   That's not true. You didn't love your wife.
*SUSPECT:*   Of course I did. Just the other day I bought her flowers. You don't buy flowers for somebody you don't love.

The suspect has now sidetracked the interrogator into a position where the interrogator can be defeated because the suspect can now talk about degrees of love and the instances where he showed it.

In handling the denials, the interrogator should recognize the differences between an emphatic and explanatory denial. He should also recognize the differences in handling these two types of denials. On the one hand, the emphatic denial is stopped, hopefully before it is ever spoken by the suspect. However, to handle the explanatory denial, the interrogator asks for an explanation and turns the explanation around after accepting it as another reason why the suspect should confess.

# Obtaining the Admission

# 10

*If the interrogator has sufficiently reduced the immediacy of the consequences in the suspect's mind, the suspect will be prepared to make an admission of guilt.*

During any interrogation, the most difficult point for the interrogator to ascertain is when the suspect is ready to confess. The behavior of a suspect can often give subtle clues to his susceptibility to making an admission. The interrogator observing these clues still may not know exactly when to ask for the admission.

It is at this point that the interrogator will attempt to bring the suspect into the conversation with an admission of guilt. The suspect has emotionally accepted the fact that he has been caught and has worked through the risk–benefits scale realizing that he must face the consequences of his actions. The interrogator has offered rationalizations that allow the suspect to save face and has focused the suspect's attention on the future, rather than on the consequences at hand.

## Mindset of the Suspect in Submission

As the rationalizations begin to have their effect and the suspect begins to accept his fate, he begins to withdraw emotionally. The suspect becomes quiet and withdrawn. All the suspect's denials stop. As the suspect enters the submissive phase of the interrogation, he reaches the lowest ebb psychologically that he will reach during the course of the interrogation. In this phase of the interrogation, the suspect's eyes may begin to tear up or he may even cry as he wrestles with the realization that he has been caught and must face the consequences. The suspect is still searching for a way out that will allow him to save face or reduce the consequences.

In this phase of the interrogation, the suspect is unable to give narrative responses to questions. An interrogator who asked the suspect to answer open-end questions such as, "Why did you do it?" will only be answered with silence as the suspect grapples with a response to this question. On the other hand, the suspect may have clearly in his mind the actual reason he did become involved, but he is also weighing accepting the face-saving devices of the rationalizations offered by the interrogator. An interrogator's questions should only require one-word responses from the suspect at this point in the interrogation.

## Behavior of the Suspect in Submission

The interrogator can recognize the behavioral keys of submission in a suspect. As the suspect withdraws emotionally, eye contact reduces to almost zero. For most suspects, the head drops down and looks toward the left knee, as the suspect begins to have an internal conversation with himself, discussing the pros and cons of confessing. As he does this, the trunk of the body often tilts forward and the shoulders slump as the tension drains out of the muscles. The interrogator may notice the suspect's eyes begin to moisten and tear. In a few suspects, crying may occur at this point. The suspect looks much like an athlete who has just lost the biggest game of his life, slumped over, head down, teary eyed, and defeated (see Figure 10.1).

## Shortening and Repeating Rationalizations

As the interrogator recognizes the submissive behavior of the suspect, he begins to shorten the rationalizations and repeat them more often. As the suspect withdraws emotionally, he begins to listen to less of what the interrogator is saying. The repetition of the rationalizations is important to continue the process of acceptance by the suspect, who is now only partially listening.

The interrogator selects the rationalization that seems to have been most effective in allowing the suspect to save face. If the interrogator has been using rationalizations that focus on peer pressure and financial problems to allow the suspect to save face, he now selects the one that seemed to have had the greatest emotional impact. As the interrogator focuses on the rationalization that seems to be the most effective in causing the suspect to go into submission, he becomes repetitive so that he will still be able to communicate with the withdrawn suspect.

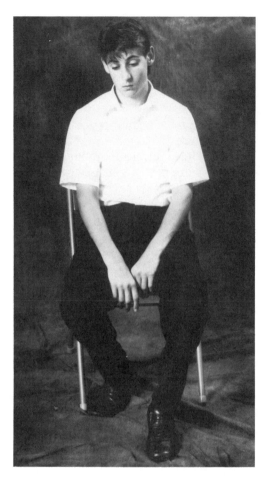

10.1. A suspect in submission is slumped over, withdrawn, and defeated. All verbal denials have stopped as the suspect begins an internal conversation to decide if he should confess.

## Closing Physically with the Suspect

As the suspect begins to withdraw emotionally and breaks eye contact with the interrogator, the interrogator can begin to close physically. In the early stages of the interrogation, the interrogator was slowly closing the gap between himself and the suspect. This movement toward the suspect was slow and deliberate, covered by the movement of the hands as they begin to occupy the space closer to the suspect. As the suspect becomes used to the hands' being positioned closer to him, the interrogator can lean slightly forward and occupy that space with the trunk of his body. As the interrogator does this, he slowly inches his way forward on the chair using his hands to gesture and occupy the suspect. When the interrogator reaches the edge of the seat of his chair, he merely pulls the chair up under him and begins the inching process again.

In the early stages of the interrogation, this movement typically is a slow process because the suspect is neither physically nor emotionally ready to allow the interrogator into his space. However, as the suspect withdraws into submission, the interrogator can accelerate his closure with the suspect. The suspect is no longer watching the interrogator and has emotionally withdrawn, which makes this closure more acceptable. The interrogator moves closer physically to increase the intimacy of the conversation with the suspect. The suspect, as he reaches the final decision to confess, will in most cases place both feet on the floor and open the arms, reducing any barriers to the interrogator. The interrogator continues to move closer until his chair is right next to the suspect. Sometimes female suspects may not uncross the legs as they enter submission. Women, because of their instruction as children, are often more comfortable with the legs crossed than uncrossed.

## Controlling the Suspect

The interrogator has recognized the emotional susceptibility of the suspect to confess. He has observed the suspect's barriers dropping as the suspect's legs uncross and the arms unfold and go to the sides of the chair. He observes the head drop as the suspect begins the internal conversation with himself. The interrogator shortens his rationalizations, repeating them over and over. The interrogator is now sitting close to the suspect and attempts to develop eye contact. If the suspect is left for too long in submission, he will get stronger and he may elect to deny again. The interrogator must now make direct eye contact with the withdrawn suspect and ask for an admission.

One way to gain the suspect's attention is to achieve eye contact. This eye contact may be achieved by having the suspect look up at the interrogator. Using the suspect's first name will often cause him to look up at the interrogator. When the suspect looks up, the interrogator holds the suspect's eyes with his own. This will allow the rationalizations to have a greater impact and prepare the suspect for the first admission. In some cases, when the suspect has withdrawn significantly and begun to cry, it may be necessary for the interrogator to lean over and look up at the suspect to make eye contact (see Figure 10.2).

## Avoiding Physical Contact

The suspect who has reached his lowest level psychologically is defeated and at an emotional low. Physically touching the suspect can form a

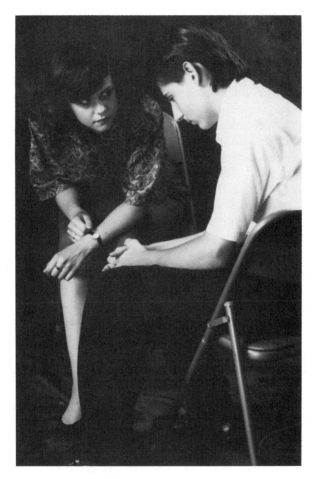

**10.2.** Once the suspect is in submission, the interrogator moves closer, shortens his rationalizations, and attempts to develop eye contact with the suspect.

bond between the interrogator and the suspect. This touching is similar to going to a funeral and placing one's hand on the shoulder of the grieving widow to console her. Although this is an effective technique for a suspect in submission, the current legal climate makes this an unwise choice for the interrogator. An interrogator who touches the suspect may later be accused of the crime of battery. Battery is defined as touching another in an offensive manner. Although the suspect at this point in the interrogation may not find the interrogator's touch offensive, the interrogator may later be accused of touching the suspect offensively, or in the case of a woman, touching her sexually.

The current legal climate makes physical contact an unacceptable method to support the suspect; however, it can be an effective means of consoling a suspect in submission. The key lies in the partial gesture. The interrogator reaches out to place a hand on the shoulder but never completes the touch. The hand is left approximately an inch above the arm and never makes physical contact. This nonthreatening supportive gesture is recognized by the suspect and it cements the bond he feels with the interrogator, but the interrogator does not expose himself to a potential battery charge.

The interrogator should anticipate that any movements or gestures he makes in the interrogation may be later questioned in criminal or civil court. As such, the interrogator should be conservative in any movements or gestures that might be interpreted as threatening to the suspect. The partial gesture by the interrogator solves this problem and still allows for the benefits that physical contact can achieve, without the liabilities.

## Using the Assumptive Question

The assumptive question used by the interrogator is based on the rationalizations the interrogator has offered during the interrogation. The questions always assume that the suspect was involved in the incident, but avoids questions like, "Did you do it?"

The interrogator also avoids incorporating any harsh language into the question he is asking of the suspect. The interrogator, through the use of rationalization, minimizes the seriousness of the suspect's involvement and focuses the suspect's attention on the future. By using harshly realistic words like steal, embezzle, fraud, kill, rape, the interrogator can undo all the work he has done up to this point. These words recreate in the suspect's mind the incident's seriousness and bring to the forefront the consequences of his actions. Using these types of words during the interrogation can rekindle a suspect's need to deny and set the interrogation back significantly.

## Testing the Waters

The timing of the question to obtain the first admission is a difficult moment for the interrogator to identify. If the interrogator asks the question before the suspect is ready, the suspect will make a denial. If the interrogator waits too long, and the suspect emotionally recovers from submission, the interrogator is likely to get a denial. Before the interrogator asks a question designed to elicit the first admission, he should first have a sense that the suspect is ready to confess. For this reason, the interrogator tests the waters with the suspect to determine his susceptibility to confess. Testing the waters can be done in several ways.

## Transition Statement

During the early stages of rationalization, the interrogator spoke in the third person, using them, they, he, etc., when discussing the reasons why people make mistakes. This allowed the suspect to internalize the rationalizations without having to face the reality that it was him the interrogator was talking about. The transition statement is used to test the waters when the interrogator recognizes behavioral clues that the suspect is in submission. These behavioral clues include break of eye contact, open body posture, feet flat on the floor, and shoulders in slumped position. The interrogator now uses the suspect's name and directly applies all the rationalizations he has been talking about to the suspect. He might use a statement like this: "Mark, the problem is that the investigation doesn't show what type of problems you're facing."

This statement focuses all the previous rationalizations directly on the suspect. The interrogator, as he makes the transition statement, watches for the suspect's reaction. If the suspect makes eye contact, tightens, and leans slightly back, it means that he was not quite ready for an admission. If the interrogator observes such behavior, he controls any denials that the suspect may make and immediately goes back rationalizing in the third person.

However, if the suspect does not make eye contact or slowly nods yes, the interrogator recognizes that the suspect is susceptible to a confession and moves to use a choice question or soft accusation to obtain the suspect's first admission.

## Choice Question/Soft Accusation

Another way to test the suspect's susceptibility to an admission is to ask the choice question or make the soft accusation. Generally, when these are asked prematurely, they elicit a denial from the suspect. However, the interrogator can present these questions to the suspects periodically to determine his resistance to answering with an admission.

In the very earliest stages of the interrogation, presentation of a choice or assumptive question to the suspect will result in an immediate denial. The interrogator, expecting the denial, is ready to stop it and return to the rationalization/justification process. As the suspect becomes less resistant to giving an admission, he responds less emphatically and spontaneously to these presentations. Occasionally, asking these questions of the suspect is like periodically putting your finger under the tap to determine the water's temperature. When you feel the temperature is just right, it is only then that you put your hands in to wash them.

The difficulty with this use of the choice question or soft accusation lies in the probability that if it is presented at inappropriate times, it may begin a cycle of denials by the suspect. This may create a more difficult interrogation because the suspect has now denied his involvement.

### Suspect's Behavioral Shift

If the suspect is in submission with no eye contact and all denials have stopped, then he is having an internal dialogue with himself. Often, as this internal dialogue concludes, the interrogator can observe a behavioral shift by the suspect. This behavioral shift may occur at the point where the suspect has made his decision to confess. As a general rule, this shift occurs in the trunk of the body or the hand may lightly slap the thighs, as though to say, "What the heck, go for it." The interrogator, observing these behavioral clues should immediately respond with a choice question or soft accusation to obtain the admission.

The interrogator should remember that submission by a suspect can vary from the most withdrawn and defeated look to a more emotionally calm appearance. The variability of the behavior associated with submission is due primarily to the emotional state of the suspect. In the most dramatic form, evidenced by the suspect's beginning to cry, the communication between the interrogator and the suspect is like that between parent and child. The suspect responds as a child by emotionally withdrawing and finally acquiescing to the parents wishes. Less emotionally submissive is the communication between two adults, with the suspect reaching the decision rationally after weighing his options. If the interrogator has successfully used the introductory statement to establish the credibility of the investigation and provided rationalizations that justified the suspect's actions, he will often actually come to the conclusion that it is best to cooperate. In situations where the interrogator has to overcome denials of the suspect during the classic emotional interrogation, the behavior associated with the submission tends to be more pronounced.

### Asking Assumptive Questions

An interrogator's use of assumptive questions leapfrogs the final defensive barrier that a suspect has erected to oppose the confession. The suspect is often prepared to answer the question "Did you do it?" with a denial. This final defense barrier can be breached by the interrogator using the assumptive question. An assumptive question assumes that the suspect did, in fact, do it, and asks for an admission regarding some aspect of the crime. There are two general types of assumptive questions that are effective to use at this point in the interrogation.

## The Soft Accusation

The soft accusation is generally utilized at the conclusion of the introductory statement or participatory accusation. The soft accusation generally asks for an admission about some aspect of the crime. It is a one-sided question that is broad enough to cover a number of issues.

One of the difficulties that an interrogator faces in interrogating is not knowing exactly what the suspect is thinking. For example, during the introductory statement, the suspect is thinking he has been caught taking money out of the register. However, the interrogation is really as a result of the suspect using fraudulent documents to steal. The interrogator could lose an admission from the suspect if he were to ask a narrowly focused soft accusation such as, "What was the most amount of money that you took using fraudulent credits since you worked at the company?" or "When did you plan to take his car?"

The suspect may make a denial because the introductory statement led him to believe that he had been caught taking money directly from the register. The suspect, recognizing the error in his thought process, may quickly deny because he never considered it a possibility that he was caught using the fraudulent documents. If the interrogator had asked the question more broadly, he would have avoided this problem. For example:

> INTERROGATOR: Bob, let me ask you, what was the most amount of money that you took from the company in any single day?
> SUSPECT: $20.00.
> INTERROGATOR: And how did you do that?
> SUSPECT: By just taking it out of the register.

The interrogator can now take advantage of a miscalculation by the suspect. In fact, this admission may be a complete surprise to the interrogator who did not know about the missing $20.00 from the register. By approaching this question broadly, it allows the suspect to make the mistakes and the interrogator to profit from them.

*Construction of the Soft Accusation.* The suspect has been listening only partially, so it is necessary to alert the suspect that something different is about to happen. To do this, the interrogator uses the suspect's first name to gain his attention. Then, the interrogator tells the suspect that he is about to be asked a question to which a response is necessary. "Bob, let me ask you..." Alerting the suspect that he will be required to respond enhances the likelihood of an admission from the suspect because he is listening closely.

*Wording of the Soft Accusation.* The soft accusation is presented to the suspect in a slow, deliberate voice by the interrogator. The interrogator now uses the soft accusation to address some aspect of the crime. Some examples of soft accusations would be as follows:

> What would be the greatest amount of money that you took from the company in any one day?
>
> When was the first time you considered buying the gun?
>
> What would be the largest amount of merchandise that you took from the company in any one day?
>
> When did you begin to plan this out?
>
> When was the first time you used an illegal drug?

The interrogator makes direct eye contact with the suspect toward the end of the soft accusation. The suspect will begin to respond behaviorally as soon as the question's meaning becomes evident to him. In the first soft accusation example, the question's meaning becomes clear only after the interrogator says the word "took." "What would be the most amount of money that you took from the company in any one day?" The suspect who is going to deny will often begin shaking his head at this word. The behavioral differences between an admission and a denial are very marked (see Figure 10.3).

*Suspect's Response to Soft Accusation.* If the suspect uses any form of behavioral denial, the interrogator immediately attempts to stop the denial and returns to the techniques for reducing resistance. If he shows signs of behavior relating to an admission, the interrogator immediately uses a follow-up question to cause the suspect to confess.

The suspect will respond to the interrogator's question in one of three ways.

1. He may deny.
2. He may make an admission.
3. He may pause to consider his options.

The interrogator must be prepared to handle a suspect's denial any time he asks a question that attempts to elicit an admission of guilt from the suspect. Recognizing the behavioral clues of a denial as differing from the behavioral clues of an admission is critical in anticipating the suspect's response.

10.3 (A) The suspect is about to make an admission. The head drifts to the side, the brows arch, the eyes are averted, the lips are pursed or go slack. (B) The suspect is about to make a denial. There is an intake of breath and fighting of the mouth along with eye contact and frowning brow. The head often shakes no, and the hand may make a stop emblem.

*Follow-Up Question.* A suspect may also pause to consider his answer. This pause by the suspect signals the interrogator that he is susceptible to making an admission. The interrogator immediately fills the pause using a follow-up question that exaggerates the seriousness of the suspect's involvement. Examples of the follow-up question might be:

1. What would be the greatest amount of money that you took from the company in any one day? Was it a $1,000.00 in one day?
2. When was the first time you considered buying the gun? Was it the first day that you met him?
3. What would be the largest amount of merchandise that you took from the company in any one day? Was it more than $5,000.00 in merchandise in one day?
4. When did you begin to plan this out? Did you begin to plan this a year ago?
5. When was the first time you used an illegal drug? Was it five years ago?

Generally, when the suspect is presented with these exaggerated questions, his immediate response will be a denial. The exaggerated follow-up question used by the interrogator shocks the suspect before he can make a decision about what to say. As the suspect pauses to consider his response, he is thinking about two things: First, how much did he steal in any single day, and second, should he confess his involvement. The interrogator, recognizing that the suspect is considering his answer, immediately asks an exaggerated question about an amount that is far above what the suspect could have been involved in. Since the suspect has not had time as yet to consider the wisdom of responding, he immediately makes a denial, which is, in fact, an admission of guilt.

*INTERROGATOR:*   Was it as much as $1,000 in one day?
*SUSPECT:*  No way!
*INTERROGATOR:*   Great. I was sure it wasn't that much. How much do you think it was?

The interrogator recognizes that this denial is an admission of guilt and supports the suspect, letting him know that he has confessed.

*INTERROGATOR:*   That's great, Bob. From the investigation I didn't think it was anything like $5,000. How much was it? Would you say it was more or less than $2,500?
*SUSPECT:*   Less!
*INTERROGATOR:*   Good! Well then how much do you think it was?
*SUSPECT:*   $20.00.

Recognize that the first admission of guilt from the suspect is most probably a lie that minimizes the seriousness of his involvement. However, the suspect is now over the most difficult part of the interrogation, that being the first admission. The first admission, be it for $10,000 or 10¢, is the most difficult one to achieve because the suspect has acknowledged his dishonesty. It is no longer whether he is an honest or a dishonest individual, but rather, how dishonest is he? The interrogator will attempt to discover this during the next phase of the interrogation, development of the admission.

## The Choice Question

The choice question, like the soft accusation, is assumptive and asks about some aspect of the incident. The choice question differs by offering the suspect two incriminating choices from which to choose. The choice question is an extension of the rationalization previously offered to the suspect. It generally incorporates a good, acceptable and a bad, unacceptable choice in the question. Selection of either the acceptable or the unacceptable choice is by the suspect's first admission of involvement.

Some examples of choice questions are

Did you use the money for bills or was it for drugs?

Did you plan this thing out or did you do it on the spur of the moment without thinking?

Did you mean to do this or was it an accident?

The presentation of the choice question should take place only when the suspect has shown the behavioral signs of submission and all denials have stopped. The only exception to this rule is when the interrogator elects to use the choice question as a method of testing the suspect's susceptibility to making an admission. The choice question increases in effectiveness when the interrogator is able to close with the suspect physically, thereby increasing the bond between himself and the suspect.

The interrogator should reach a peak of sincerity when presenting the choice question. Like the soft accusation, he uses the suspect's name to draw the suspect's attention to the question. The interrogator becomes repetitive as he attempts to encourage the suspect to make a decision and select one of the two choices he has presented. The repetition is important because of the suspect's withdrawal. In addition, the interrogator encourages the suspect to select one of the choices by emphasizing the good over the bad choice. The following are examples of how to emphasize the good or bad choice.

GOOD CHOICE:   I'm sure it was to pay bills, wasn't it, Bob? If it was, that proves we're talking about something anybody could have done...It was for bills wasn't it? It was, wasn't it Bob. It was for bills, right?

BAD CHOICE:   If the money was used to buy something like drugs, then we're wasting my time. That's a whole different story..., but that doesn't seem right, I can't believe it was for drugs, Bob. It wasn't, was it? I'm sure it wasn't...

By encouraging the suspect to take the more acceptable of the two choices, the interrogator continues the process of face-saving. The interrogator should understand that the suspect's selection of the more acceptable choice does not necessarily correspond with the real reason that the suspect became involved. However, in most cases, the reason why the person did it is less important than the fact that he did do it. In general, it does not make a difference to the case whether the suspect used the money for bills or drugs. Merely intending to permanently deprive the owner of his property is sufficient to prove theft. However, in certain cases such as in arson, the use of a choice question such as, "Did you start the fire by accident or was it on purpose?" might create problems in a prosecution. This choice of "by accident" lacks the intent that is a necessary element of the crime of arson. The acknowledgment that the suspect started the fire might be sufficient when combined with the physical evidence of an accelerant being used and multiple points of origin to obtain a conviction.

It should be noted, however, that the easiest way to encourage a suspect to admit starting a fire is by saying it was an accident. After the initial admission, the interrogator can then go back and reconstruct with the suspect the facts and get an admission showing the intent. Remember, the hardest part of any interrogation is getting the first admission. Afterwards, the suspect is more likely to give a complete confession.

## Acknowledging Acceptance of the Assumptive Question by the Suspect

Once the suspect has acknowledged his involvement, the interrogator must support the suspect's decision. The suspect may have admitted to the choice question by either nodding his head in agreement or using a one word answer, "Yes" or "No." Rarely is a suspect able to respond with a full narrative at this point. Once the suspect acknowledges his involvement, the interrogator must let him know that he has confessed. Often, the suspect does not even realize that he has made an admission of guilt.

### Case Example

A gang member was being interrogated regarding the theft of a handgun from under the register at a liquor store where he worked. The interrogator utilized rationalizations that the suspect had taken the gun to protect himself and family members against threats from other gangs.

During the rationalization the suspect went into a head-and-shoulder slump and his eyes began to tear up. The interrogator narrowed the rationalizations to the choice question of, "I'm sure you didn't take the gun to do anything bad, it was just to protect your family. It was, wasn't it?" The interrogator observed the suspect subtly nod to the choice, but neglected to support the suspect's admission by letting him know that he had confessed. Instead, the interrogator attempted to go back and rationalize for a moment longer. At this point the suspect realized what he had done and immediately recrossed his arms, sat up, and a mask of coldness dropped across his face.

The admission was lost because the interrogator failed to let the suspect know he had confessed by supporting his admission. Any delay

10.4. Individual recalling visually as he considers a response. This behavior often occurs during the making of an admission.

on the part of an interrogator in supporting the suspect's admission of involvement can lead to a retraction.

## Observing Behavioral Clues of an Admission

The behavioral clues that an interrogator can observe when a suspect is about to make an admission are significantly different from those observed when a denial will be forthcoming.

During an admission, the suspect's face tends to be relaxed. The eyes break contact and unfocus, drifting away. The suspect's lips either purse tightly or go slack. The suspect's eyebrows arch as he considers a

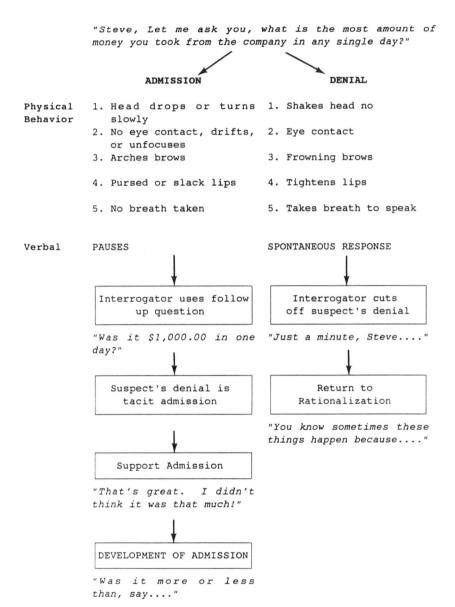

*"Steve, Let me ask you, what is the most amount of money you took from the company in any single day?"*

ADMISSION                                    DENIAL

| Physical Behavior | 1. Head drops or turns slowly | 1. Shakes head no |

1. Head drops or turns slowly        1. Shakes head no

2. No eye contact, drifts, or unfocuses        2. Eye contact

3. Arches brows        3. Frowning brows

4. Pursed or slack lips        4. Tightens lips

5. No breath taken        5. Takes breath to speak

Verbal        PAUSES        SPONTANEOUS RESPONSE

| Interrogator uses follow up question | Interrogator cuts off suspect's denial |

*"Was it $1,000.00 in one day?"*        *"Just a minute, Steve...."*

| Suspect's denial is tacit admission | Return to Rationalization |

*"You know sometimes these things happen because...."*

| Support Admission |

*"That's great.   I didn't think it was that much!"*

| DEVELOPMENT OF ADMISSION |

*"Was it more or less than, say...."*

**10.5.** This chart illustrates the behavioral differences between a suspect making an admission and one making a denial.

response to the question. Since the suspect is not intending to speak, he does not take a breath. The positioning of the head is also significantly different in an admission than in a denial. When making an admission, the head may slightly drop toward the chest or drift toward the left side of the body. In general, the eyes become unfocused as the suspect considers the response to the choice or soft accusation (see Figure 10.4).

In contrast, the suspect who is going to deny tends to make eye contact with the interrogator and shake his head no. The shaking of the head is an emblem response that almost always precedes a spoken denial by the suspect. Because the suspect is not accepting what the interrogator is saying, his eyebrows frown as he prepares to make a spontaneous denial. As soon as the interrogator finishes his sentence, the spoken denial will start. To prepare to speak, the suspect begins to tighten his lips and takes a breath so he will be able to speak as soon as there is a break in the dialogue. Figure 10.5 illustrates the behavioral clues an interrogator should look for to tell whether a suspect is going to make an admission or denial with the proper follow-up procedure for an admission or denial.

The interrogator should recognize the behavioral clues of submission and their importance to the susceptibility of an admission by the suspect. The use of an assumptive question, either the soft accusation or choice question, affords the suspect an opportunity to begin his dialogue with the interrogator. The interrogator recognizes that the suspect is emotionally unable to answer open-end questions but is capable of responding to closed-end probes such as the soft accusation or choice question. Acceptance of either one of these questions by the suspect is not the confession but merely his first acknowledgment of guilt. Once the suspect has acknowledged his involvement, the interrogator moves into the next phase of the interrogation, development of the admission.

The following are sample introductory statements for both loss prevention and law enforcement personnel.

## Sample Introductory Statements

## Loss Prevention

### Part One: What We Do and How We Do It

Hello, Cindy?

I'm David Zulawski with the loss prevention department here at the company. It is my job to protect the assets of the company. These assets are the building, fixtures, merchandise, cash, and the employees that work for us. The employees are certainly the most important asset in the company.

As you may know, there has been a fairly high shrinkage in the department here. We know that at one time or another everyone makes mistakes. That's just human nature. We also know that shortage, or shrinkage as we call it, consists of a number of things. This shrinkage figure consists of customers who take merchandise by carrying it out without paying for it, and it certainly consists of the errors in paperwork that are part of our everyday jobs. It's also employees taking things [pause, eye contact]. The major concern that the company has is those employees that would be taking trailer loads or cases of merchandise or $10,000 out of a safe. Things that would add up to thousands and thousands of dollars worth of property or money. Because every employee is a valuable asset here at the company, we feel it is important to sit down and discuss the results of an investigation that we have conducted.

## Part Two: How Losses Occur

As I mentioned, besides customers taking things and paperwork errors, employees sometimes take things. There are many ways that an employee could take money and merchandise from the company. For example, an employee could use fraudulent credits to take money. They could use phony voids and void out sales and then keep the money. They might work directly out of an open register and not be ringing up sales. It is also possible that some employees might just take money right out of the register and cause a shortage in that manner.

[The interviewer should pause and make direct eye contact after the explanation that he believes is most likely how the suspect is stealing. The manner of theft that the suspect is involved in should be positioned in the middle of the examples given.]

Of course, there are many other ways that an employee could cause losses to the company besides just money. For example, they could wear merchandise out of the store, they could give a customer more merchandise than that customer paid for, it's possible that the employee could just pass merchandise off to a friend or conceal it on their person and carry it out after they're done working for the evening.

[The interviewer should watch for behavioral changes during the examples offered the suspect. The changes may be the result of stress that might indicate involvement in that method of theft.]

## Part Three: How Investigations Are Conducted

You're probably not familiar with the manner in which security investigations are conducted at the company. We use any number of avenues to generate information that will bring the investigation to a satisfactory conclusion. It is only at the very end of that investigation where we have evaluated all the evidence that we have accumulated that we'll sit down and talk with any of the employees. Since you may not be familiar with how these investigations occur, let me just discuss some of the ways that we gather information. Many times in evaluating a high-shrinkage department, we'll place an undercover employee into the department. This undercover employee is looking for a number of things like errors in paperwork, errors in procedure that may occur, employee dishonesty [pause—eye contact]. These undercover employees will then file reports concerning their findings here in the department. Another way in which we will continue the investigation is actual surveillance by members of the loss prevention department. This surveillance may be conducted by the investigators' concealing themselves in the area or simply walking through the department.

Additionally, we use a shopping service in which we have people come in to make controlled purchases from various registers and store personnel. It is during these purchases that the shopper is determining if correct cash-handling procedures are being followed, if the register is being rung properly, if paperwork is being filled out, and the shopper is looking as well at the general demeanor and courtesy with which the employee is treating the customer. We will also, on occasion, stop customers as they are leaving the department and question them as to how they were treated and, at the same time, check to determine if their merchandise that they purchased matches up with the sales receipt.

On many occasions, we will also use video cameras that use pinhole lenses to conduct a surveillance of a particular area or register in an attempt to determine exactly what the procedures, and perhaps problems, are occurring at that register. We may also, at the same time, monitor that register to determine exactly what is being rung and in what departments.

There are many other ways in which we get our information and conduct an investigation. These include receiving help from other employees, audits, salting registers, sending out credit and refund letters to determine if they actually were received, to name but a few.

[This area usually has greater impact on the suspect if the interrogator uses examples of investigative techniques that could develop direct rather than circumstantial evidence, i.e., videotape of theft rather than patterns showing an employee's being present at all incidents.]

## Part Four: Discussion of Why Mistakes Are Made

There are many reasons why employees might make a mistake in judgement and take something from the company.

[Expand on several rationalizations for an employee's being involved in theft at the company, i.e., peer pressure, financial pressures, or impulse. Part Four may account for up to two-thirds of the time spent on the introductory statement. The rationalizations should be at least ten minutes in length or longer depending on the suspect's behavior.]

### Impulse

Cindy, you know, I think this whole thing really just boils down to advertising. When we're talking about doing something on impulse, that's really one of the big things that advertisers try to play on. We do the same thing here in the store when we try to display merchandise or when we try to put it together in such a way that it's pleasing to the eye—so pleasing that it becomes a fad to wear that particular item.

In a lot of cases with the prices that we are charging, and with the pressures that we put the associates under in the store, it becomes difficult for them to fight off that temptation to do something they know isn't right. But yet, we are in a situation that people at school are wearing particular items or we're held in better regard because we wear a particular garment, and all of a sudden, we do something that we probably shouldn't do because we do it on impulse without thinking the consequences through.

I think that's important when we're talking about a situation such as we're dealing with here. The worst thing in the world in this business is having to deal with that person who's really premeditated things. Who's thought things through. Who came with the company with the idea that they were going to get as much as they could, for as long as they could, and they don't care about anything.

That's entirely different from the associate who comes here, who works around the items day in and day out, and finally temptation takes over. I think that's totally different.

You know, when I was a kid, I can remember that my dad told me, "Don't touch the candy on the table," and he put a big bowl of candy there, my favorite kind of M & Ms. I love M & Ms. He said, "Don't touch them—you're not to have any," and then he walked out of the room.

Well, I sat there and looked at those M & Ms and thought about how good they were. When I got up that morning I didn't think to myself, I'm going to run out and I'm going to get as many M & Ms out of the kitchen as soon as my dad turns his back.

But, what happened to me was that the temptation just overcame me and I just took a few. Who was really at fault? Was it me, or was it my dad? Obviously I disobeyed him, but on the other side of the coin he put me in a position where I couldn't win. If he had stayed in the room and enforced that rule, or if he had taken the bowl of candy and put it away so it was out of view, I would have been able to deal with that a lot better, but the problem is that I was put into a situation where I couldn't win.

A lot of times, especially when we're young, we make errors in judgment. We do things without really thinking them through, either because we don't have the experience that an older person might have, or we've never been exposed to it, or whatever. Look at, for example, insurance rates. When are the insurance rates on your car the highest? It is up until the time you're twenty-five. Why is that? That's because that's the time most people have accidents—they make mistakes—they're reckless because they're driving too fast because they haven't seen the consequences of driving fast yet.

These things can happen over and over again and I think that's what happened here. I think that this is a situation where it was done on impulse.

## Peer Pressure

You know, Cindy, I think almost everybody has heard the term peer pressure and understands what it means. There are a lot of situations we're put into in our lives because of our peers, our friends, and how they think. We do things that maybe under ordinary circumstances we wouldn't do. But, because we have our friends, or we have other people who think in a particular way, they tend to force our thinking in a direction that we may not consider as appropriate.

I can give you a perfect example. When I was a kid back in high school, I never smoked, and my friends said, "We're smoking cigarettes, come on and have one." I really didn't want one, but finally I said OK and I tried one. Today I don't smoke cigarettes, my parents don't smoke cigarettes. I was put in a position where everybody was doing it, and it became very, very difficult for me not to go along with the group.

I think what's really happening here, is just that. When we're dealing with a situation like this, it's not your idea, but rather a group idea. You hear "We need to keep up with the Jones'," or "You gotta wear the right clothes, certain types of jeans or jackets or sweaters." You know they're popular and if you don't wear them, you're not a good person.

Well, that's crazy, letting the clothes decide. However, that's the way people are, especially people who feel that wearing the right clothes or keeping up with the Jones' is important. If they do that, and if they feel that's important, then it tends to go over, putting pressure on their friends.

If what has happened here is that this situation was brought to you, rather than you going out and soliciting, I think that's very important to know. In a lot of cases, people or friends of associates will come into the store and say, "Listen, give me this at a discount," or, "I'm not going to pay for this," or, you know, "Don't say anything, I'm going to carry this out."

They might have really put you in an awkward position. They put you into a position where they either force you not to charge the right amount, or they force you to let them walk, or do something that under normal circumstances you wouldn't let anybody do.

The key here I think is not so much that it's happened, but rather it's, did you go out and say to people, "It's OK, come on in, you can take as much as you want," or did they come to you and say "This is what I'm going to do," and put you on the spot? Because, if that's what happened, I think its important that we understand that. If I thought for a second that you were going out and telling your friends, "Hey, just come on down, you can take anything when I'm working," I don't think I could deal with that, but I don't believe that's the case. In most situations that I deal with, it's not an associate but rather those friends coming in and putting them on the spot that causes them the biggest problems.

*Financial Problems*

Cindy, I think that we set people up for problems simply because of how much we pay them. Probably one of the most difficult things to do, is to work around beautiful items that are real expensive and yet you're not being paid $30 to $40 an hour. You're making pretty close to minimum wage, I would imagine. The thing is, once you start being around nice things, it's only natural to want them for yourself.

This also happens with friends, I mean, if you've got friends who perhaps have some money and they're suddenly wearing fancy jeans that cost $40 to $50 a pair, they're wearing skirts that may cost $100, you can rest assured they can afford these things. You're working hard for the money that you earn, but maybe you don't have as much as they do at home. All of a sudden, they're treating you differently, simply because you don't have the same things they have. You want them, too.

You wouldn't be human if you didn't. But yet, you're not making enough to pay for it even though you're diligently working, you're taking very few days off, and you're doing a good job, but yet, you can't buy those things.

And you know, we also expect you to look good. I mean, you're the image of the company. You're the person that the customer sees. You're our representative, and we don't want you coming in here looking like a slob. We want you to dress nice, look sharp. We'd like you to wear our clothes because you're a walking mannequin. You're a walking advertisement for how good our clothes can look on a person. If you look good people think, "Boy, I'd like to look like that," or, "I would like my wife or my girlfriend to look like that." Then they go ahead and buy it.

We'd like you to look nice, but do we turn around and say "Here's money for clothes," or, "Here's a raise." No, we don't! So we have to recognize that part of the situation is a result of how the company views itself and what it considers important. The thing that I don't want to see is, somebody put into a position of doing something because of peer pressure, frustration, low pay, or making an error in judgement that's causing them to do something that under normal circumstances they wouldn't do. I think that's the key here. A lot of times people do things because they need the money. I think that's important, because, if there was a need, a legitimate need, that's something that every one of us can relate to.

We all have bills, whether they're phone, heating, rent, car payment, or insurance. We all have things that we have to pay. There are times where we have extra money and there's times when we run short. Sometimes, when we're put in a position where we don't have an alternative. We need to do something that maybe we weren't raised to do, or we wouldn't do under normal circumstances, however, we're put into a position where we have a need.

We're not going out and blowing the money on drugs or booze or good times. We're using it for the necessities of life, to keep our head above water, and I think that's important. If that's the case, then I think this all can be settled and done.

During any investigation, many things are uncovered and known absolutely. But oftentimes, it's the reason why mistakes are made that don't come out. These things are important to the company to show why things happen and to show also that the employee cares. This is why at the conclusion of every investigation, we sit down with the employee and discuss the results and to assess really the attitude of that employee toward the company.

## Part Five: The Soft Accusation/Assumptive Question

*INTERROGATOR:*   Cindy, what was the most amount of money that you took at any one time from the company?
[If the suspect delays and looks away, immediately ask]
*INTERROGATOR:*   Cindy, did you ever take something like $1,000 in a single day?
*CINDY:*   Oh no!
*INTERROGATOR:*   That's great, I knew from the investigation that it wouldn't be that much! Would it be more or less than $900 in one day?
*CINDY:*   Less!
*INTERROGATOR:*   What would be the most amount of money that you took in any one day?
*CINDY:*   $5.00.

Interviewer enters the development of admission phase.

## Law Enforcement

The following is a sample introductory statement that could be used in the investigation of a burglary. The suspect was to be questioned because his vehicle was observed parked several blocks from the scene of a burglary to a gas station at approximately 2:00 A.M. The suspect's vehicle was observed by a patrol officer, who noted it in his log. There is no other direct evidence that links the suspect to the incident.

## Part One: Who We Are and What We Do

Hi, Jack, my name is Detective Humer and I'm with the City Police. I appreciate your taking the time to come in and talk to me today.

[If the suspect is to be taken into custody at the conclusion of the interrogation, it may be necessary for the law enforcement officer to give the suspect his Miranda rights prior to any interrogation. If the suspect will be free to leave following the interrogation, even if he admits his involvement, the Miranda rights may be omitted. Officers should consider any special departmental guidelines or requests from the prosecutor's office before omitting Miranda warnings.]

Jack, I'm sure you're aware of what a police department does for a community. Really, our job is to protect the community, its homes, businesses, and citizens from any type of criminal activity. To do that, we get involved with a number of different complaints.

For example, some might be traffic problems or safety problems that we have to deal with on a daily basis. Other times, we have to deal with business or home owners who are filing false reports in an attempt to obtain a fraudulent insurance settlement. Then we have those instances where someone is genuinely a victim. The department's primary concern obviously has to be with the most serious type of incidents: homicides, rapes, rather than something of a minor nature like a small item being taken or someone driving over someone's grass.

## Part Two: Different Types of Crimes

As investigators, we're asked to look into any number of different types of crimes. I am sure you are aware that our community, like any other community, has its share of problems. Those problems range from homicide, to rape and arsons, to people breaking into buildings, [pause, eye contact] taking things out of cars, or even out of homes.

## Part Three: How We Investigate

Now when we discover or we receive a problem or a complaint from a citizen, the case is assigned for investigation. Now, when it's assigned for investigation, we'll use any number of different techniques to attempt to establish who was responsible for the incident under investigation. For example, if the case calls for it, we may utilize latent fingerprinting. Now I'm not sure how familiar you are with latent fingerprinting, but what we do is go to the scene of a crime and begin by dusting those areas that will hold a fingerprint. In using these types of techniques, we're able to develop latent prints and can often determine who was responsible as a result.

Now, in some areas, an individual will be careful not to touch any type of a smooth surface but may touch a piece of paper and the oils and perspiration from the fingers are actually absorbed into the fibers of the paper and can be held there for years. By using special techniques such as lasers the crime lab is able to develop prints that can be used for comparison purposes.

In other instances, we'll locate a particular tool that may have been used as a weapon, or as a means to gain entry to a building. This is particularly important to us, because by using scientific techniques, we can establish the unique marks a tool makes and compare those to the pry marks at the building. This establishes that a particular tool was used to gain entrance or as a weapon.

We also recover physical evidence, like hair samples. With these hair samples the lab can do a DNA analysis. Like a fingerprint, it is unique and can identify a person.

As investigators, we'll also attempt to talk to people or other officers who are constantly patrolling the streets, asking them if they saw anybody or observed anything unusual in or around the area of a particular incident. In this way, we can often initially focus our investigative efforts in a particular direction.

As does any department, we have informants who supply us with information that helps us resolve any number of crimes during a year. Some of these informants are paid for their services. Others do it to obtain a reward or simply to stop what they think is an improper activity.

These, as well as many other different types of investigative techniques, help us to identify the individual responsible and begin to develop the case. It may supply us with the information necessary to obtain a search warrant so that we can search a home, vehicle, or garage—wherever we believe we may recover additional evidence of the individual's guilt.

[The interrogator should watch for a behavioral reaction as he mentions places where evidence or missing property could be concealed. This will assist him during development of the admission or may give him additional investigative leads should the suspect fail to confess. The interrogator should modify the investigative methods described to those that, if they had been used, could have developed information pointing to the suspect's guilt. The interrogator does not say that he has fingerprints or other evidence directly, but rather infers that evidence may have been available because of the investigative efforts used. For example, if this was a forgery case, the interrogator should describe how a document examiner might be used.]

## Part Four: Discussion of Why Mistakes Are Made

[The interrogator should expand on several rationalizations that he feels may justify the suspect's actions. These rationalizations initially are based on background information or possible motives for the crime.]

The investigation, although it can identify a suspect and show that he was involved, rarely shows the reason why he did it. For example, when an individual is under financial pressure, perhaps having just lost a job, people sometimes do things to take care of their family that they wouldn't do under ordinary circumstances. These outside pressures and influences cause people to make decisions that, if they had plenty of money, they'd never even consider having to make.

In other situations, individuals are influenced by their friends, their peers, who have an idea and they press and press and press that idea until they get their way. Even if it's a bad idea, eventually this constant pressure on others around them can cause the other people to do what they never would have done on their own. Many times, the person who is put in this position is forced to judge between the friendship that they value and what they know is right and wrong. But, because of the environment that their friend puts them in, they make a decision on the spur of the moment to do something just so that they can keep him happy. This impulse decision is not always in their best interest, but still they make the decision to go ahead to appease their friend. If they had taken the time to think things through, they probably would have never done anything. But because of their friends, they made a decision on impulse, perhaps a decision that they later regret.

[The interrogator continues to rationalize until the suspect appears behaviorally ready to confess. Once the suspect has shown signs of submission, the interrogator should use a transition statement to focus the interrogation on the specific incident.]

Jack, as you know, we've been investigating the break-in at the [name of the business used previously] and the circumstances surrounding it. The difficulty, as I mentioned earlier, an investigation doesn't always reveal the reasons why something happens. Jack, the problem is we don't know what type of outside pressures you faced.

[The interrogator should assess the suspect's behavior after presentation of the transition statement. If the suspect tightens physically or begins to make a denial, the interrogator should control the denial and return to rationalizations in an effort to continue to reduce the suspect's resistance to a confession. If the suspect shows no outward signs of concern at this statement being made, the interrogator should proceed to the soft accusation.]

## *Part Five: The Soft Accusation/Assumptive Question*

*INTERROGATOR:*   Jack, let me ask you this, what was the most amount of merchandise that you took from the gas station last night?

*SUSPECT:*   (Delays, looks away)

*INTERROGATOR:*   (Immediately ask the follow-up question.) Did you take $10,000 in merchandise?

*SUSPECT:*   Oh, no!

*INTERROGATOR:*   That's great. From the investigation, I didn't think it was anywhere near that much. Would you say that it would be more or less than $5,000?

*SUSPECT:*   Less.

*INTERROGATOR:*   What would be the most amount of merchandise that you took from the station?

*SUSPECT:*   Just some cigarettes and oil.

Interrogator enters the development phase of the interrogation.

# Development of the Admission

# 11

*Development of an admission requires patience
and persistence by the interrogator.*

The suspect has just acknowledged his involvement in the issue under investigation by accepting one of the interrogator's assumptive questions. Although the suspect has acknowledged his involvement, this acceptance is not a confession, but merely the first admission in the development process. The interrogator takes the first admission that the suspect makes and develops it into a legally acceptable confession by having the suspect provide details of the crime. The interrogator then expands the initial admission into other areas of dishonesty or criminal activity within the community or company.

The scope of the development may be merely the details of the specific incident under investigation—answering the questions who, what, where, when, how, and why—or it may be much more. In the public sector, the interrogator will attempt to expand details of the suspect's involvement to other areas of criminal activity. In addition, the interrogator may attempt to develop information that will assist other investigations or attempt to turn the suspect into an informant to assist in other investigations.

In the private sector, expansion of the initial admission is used to make investigative decisions to recover assets, or to recover evidence that will allow prosecution. The expansion in the private sector may cover the theft of money and merchandise, knowledge of others involved in dishonesty at the company as well as secondary issues such as consumption, unauthorized discounts, and drug usage.

As part of the initial preparation for the interrogation, the interrogator should have considered in what other incident the suspect might have been involved. He should have taken into consideration the suspect, his background, patterns of activity, and intelligence or informant information.

The interrogator should be aware that often what is revealed during an investigation is merely the tip of the iceberg. Suspects are generally not apprehended until they grow bolder and become sloppy, not taking adequate precautions. As a development strategy, the interrogator should work under the premise that the suspect may have been involved in a number of incidents.

The interrogator should remember that the suspect's illegal activities may not have come to the attention of police or loss prevention. This conclusion seems obvious when one considers the case clearance statistics of police departments. Theft, burglary, and other nonpersonal crimes traditionally have a low clearance rate because often there are no witnesses to the criminal's activities. Personal crimes, such as rape, battery, robbery, or murder, generally have a higher clearance rate because there are witnesses and a focused investigation by the authorities.

In the private sector, the interrogator should consider that certain types of theft may not show up as a cash loss, but appear later as an inventory shortage. For example, a series of register shortages totaling $150, might indicate that the suspect has stolen $150 directly from the register. If the interviewer was to stop the development of the admission at this point, he might miss the fact that the suspect had also engaged in the theft of cash through voids and fraudulent credits. Additional losses might be later reflected as a merchandise shortage at inventory if the suspect was failing to ring sales and simply pocketing the money. The interrogator should remember that there are usually more questions than answers in an investigation. If you know one thing from an investigation, it is that you do not have all the answers.

## Acceptance of the Soft Accusation/Choice Question by the Suspect

Once the suspect has made an admission by accepting the choice question or soft accusation, the interrogator must immediately do two things. First, the interrogator must give the suspect a statement of support. The suspect has made one of the most difficult decisions of his life, to admit his wrongdoing, and the interrogator must support the suspect's decisions. The suspect is teetering and needs to be assured that he has made the correct decision by confessing. This can be done by the interviewer's simply saying, "That's great. I was sure from the investigation that we weren't talking about doing this because of drugs."

Second, the interrogator must present the statement of support immediately. The suspect must be supported as soon as he makes an acknowledgment of involvement. This lets him know that he has confessed and that he has made the right decision in doing so.

The suspect is emotionally withdrawn at this point in the interrogation. He is incapable of answering broad, open-end questions such as "Tell me how this happened." Because of the suspect's emotional mindset, the interrogator attempts to draw out the substantiation of the admission from the suspect using brief questions that can be answered with single words or nods of the head. These initial brief questions form the foundation of the substantiation of the admission and begin to draw the suspect into conversation.

The interrogator has spent much of his time up to this point attempting to minimize the seriousness of the crime and break down the suspect's resistance to confessing. After the suspect has made an initial admission, he is teetering at a point where he could conceivably back off and recant his admission. The interrogator, after supporting the suspect, must be sure not to use any harsh words or phrases that connote punishment. Using harsh phrases or words like rob, rape, or steal in the questions asked of the suspect recreates the seriousness of what the suspect has done and he may back off from the admission.

The initial questions used by the interrogators are closed-end questions that begin to extract the details of the incident or the circumstances surrounding it. These questions are questions of commitment that build the credibility of the statement. The purpose of these questions and the development process is to substantiate the suspect's involvement. The substantiation assures others who were not present during the interrogation that it was the suspect's confession and not the interrogator's creation. These questions of commitment supply the details and background of the incident that can only be known to the person responsible.

For example, these questions might elicit the time that the actual theft occurred, where the money was deposited, how the money was used, or how it was paid or transferred. These questions might also identify the location of additional evidence that could be recovered by an investigator—for example, the location of a murder weapon or the location of stolen property.

In most cases, the next step in an investigation is to go out and recover the additional substantiating evidence or documents. This evidence, for example, might be bank records, cancelled checks, or sales receipts, any of which could help substantiate the confession. The loss prevention investigator very often does not take this next step to recover additional evidence. Many times it is sufficient in the private sector simply to utilize the suspect's written statement to establish his involvement in the crime and allow for his termination and perhaps prosecution. It is more likely that a police investigator will attempt to recover additional evidence of the suspect's involvement to prepare a much more solid case for prosecution.

Although the suspect has made an initial admission, it is unlikely that the interrogator has yet established the elements necessary to prove the crime. During the development phase, the interrogator develops information and statements that establish the elements of the crime, the suspect's mental state, and proof of the suspect's intent. Sometimes, even innocuous statements made by a suspect during development may prove critical in the prosecution or termination of the suspect. The interrogator should note any statements that will help prove his case.

The interrogator has not taken any notes since the accusation was made; however, once the development of the admission is sufficiently under way, the interrogator should begin to make notes of the suspect's admission. The note-taking generally begins after the suspect has made a number of admissions and appears to be comfortable talking about his involvement. Once the interrogator sees the suspect becoming comfortable, he can make an offhand comment that he wants "just to jot a couple of notes" so that they don't keep going over the same topics or forget anything. This allows the interrogator to make notations that will be used as the foundation for a later written statement.

In a specific-issue case, the interrogator answers the six investigative questions of who, what, where, when, how, and why, focusing specifically on the incident in question. It is likely that the suspect will not tell the interrogator the complete truth even at this point in an interrogation. A suspect often withholds key elements that he feels will jeopardize his current story or create more serious problems. The suspect's deception even in the developmental phase may form the basis for impeaching his testimony at a later hearing or trial. The interrogator should consistently probe for the truth while recognizing that the suspect may not be entirely candid.

During the development phase of a specific crime, the interrogator is looking for additional investigative leads that can be followed up. These leads may allow the acquisition of additional information that will corroborate the suspect's confession and enhance the likelihood of a successful prosecution.

An interrogator should recognize that with the exception of homicide, many people involved in one type of criminal activity have often been involved in other types of criminal activity. The interrogator, while the suspect is in a state of reduced resistance, should attempt to identify other areas of the suspect's criminal activity. Although investigation into these other areas may not result in a prosecution, it may allow investigators to clear files by closing the case as solved but not prosecuted. In some cases, the suspect will make an admission that will enable the interrogator to link him to other crimes that may be provable. This may result in other prosecutions being brought against the suspect.

## Techniques to Expand the First Admission

In almost all instances, the interrogator should attempt to expand the suspect's initial admission of guilt into the full scope of his involvement. Although there may be some exceptions in certain cases, this will generally be the goal of the interrogator. The following techniques can easily be utilized to expand that initial admission.

### The Worksheet

The interrogator should prepare a worksheet for note-taking during the development phase of the interrogation. On the worksheet he should specifically note the elements of the crime under investigation that will be necessary to prove the suspect's guilt. In addition, he should have considered other types of criminal activity in which the suspect may have been involved. This evaluation may be based on a pattern of similar modi operandi (MOs), activities taking place in a similar geographic area, or other similar crimes. The interrogator may also note any behavioral clues he observed during the introductory statement that might indicate involvement.

The worksheet allows the interrogator to make sure that he has consistently covered each area of inquiry. It allows him an opportunity to take notes in a portion of the worksheet set aside for that particular type of crime. In addition, the worksheet can also contain background information on the suspect, suspicions or implications that the interrogator may want to remember to ask about.

### Resistance-Reducing Techniques

During development, the interrogator should return to the techniques that reduced the suspect's resistance to a confession. These techniques showed understanding through focusing the suspect's attention on the future instead of his current situation. They also minimized the seriousness of the suspect's involvement through the use of rationalizations, offering the suspect a positive outlook that gave him hope for the future after he resolved the incident in question. The interrogator may also use a change of perspectives to have the suspect look at the situation from another point of view. This is especially helpful during the development process, when the interrogator is attempting to get the suspect to detail his entire involvement.

Development of the admission requires patience and persistence of the interrogator. Although the suspect has acknowledged his involvement, he may not yet be willing to talk about all the details of the crime. Development of an admission is like rototilling a garden. Rototilling requires the gardener to go through a plot of land in different directions a number of times, constantly turning over the old ground looking for new clumps of dirt, before the soil is properly prepared. In the same way, the interrogator constantly reviews previous topics in an effort to uncover new information. An interrogator's decision to change topics does not mean he is no longer interested in that topic but merely that he has ceased making headway and so begins to probe a new area.

The interrogator should also make supportive comments that minimize the suspect's admissions. Being supportive during the development of an admission is critical to the expansion process. The interrogator who scolds the suspect by saying, "Why didn't you tell me that before? Come on, let's just get this whole thing cleared up. What's wrong with you?" is less likely to develop full admissions than the interrogator who is supportive. The supportive comments remind the suspect what a difficult time this is for him, and how hard it will be for him to remember certain details of the incident. This statement by the interrogator has a second purpose, which is to justify the interrogator's persistence during the development process. The interrogator tells the suspect he is not returning to the topic simply to annoy the suspect, but to help him remember during a very difficult time.

## The Assumptive Question

The use of assumptive questions by the interrogator during the development of an admission can enhance his ability to obtain additional information from the suspect. As discussed in previous chapters, the assumptive question skips over the issue of whether or not the suspect did something and addresses how often or when he has done it. Asking a question such as "Did you do it?" invites a denial from the suspect; however, the assumptive question with its follow-up question often leads to additional admissions. The delay of a suspect in responding to an assumptive question is a good clue that information is being withheld. The interrogator then utilizes an exaggerated follow-up question that results in a denial, which is actually an admission of guilt by the suspect. This very quickly leads to a specific admission and additional development paths, as the following dialogue illustrates.

INTERROGATOR:   Steve, what would have been the most number of radios that you took from the company?
SUSPECT:  (Pauses looks up and to the left.)
INTERROGATOR:   Are we talking like 100 or more?

*SUSPECT:*   Geez, no!
*INTERROGATOR:*   Great! From the investigation I didn't think
it was anything like that. How many do you think, more or less
than fifty?
*SUSPECT:*   Less, maybe three.
*INTERROGATOR:*   All right, great, but you know...

## Use of Exaggeration to Encourage Admission

The interrogator should always exaggerate what he is saying to the
suspect. Start high or with the more serious issue because this allows
the suspect to minimize what he has done. For example, if a suspect
who stole $20 from a register was asked, "Did you ever take a whole
day's receipts?" the theft of $20 seems insignificant by comparison. This
encourages the suspect to get closer to the truth because it does not seem
so bad. This same tactic can be utilized in a number of ways during the
development phase.

A second example might be attempting to expand the items taken
during a burglary:

*INTERROGATOR:*   Did you take as many as four TVs from the
house?
*SUSPECT:*   No way!
*INTERROGATOR:*   Good. I didn't think it was that many. How
many TVs did you take. Was it three?
*SUSPECT:*   No, it was only two.

During exaggeration, the suspect should be told that the interrogator
understands how difficult it is to remember everything immediately
because of the length of time since the incident occurred. The interrogator might illustrate this point by relating the difference between
somebody who would go into a safe and take $10,000 at one time versus
someone who took just a few little things over a long time that just
added up. The interrogator should offer that it would be easier to
remember something larger or serious than something of a minor
nature.

## Use of the Investigation as a Wedge

The interrogator should avoid any show of impatience with the suspect.
Showing impatience will play into the suspect's hands and shorten the
development process. Rather, the interrogator should empathize with
the suspect, reminding him that it is difficult to remember, but that
there are still things that he has not recalled yet about the incident.
During development, the interrogator should repeatedly assert that it is

important that the suspect tell the interrogator what the investigation has already discovered. By the suspect's confirming what is already actually known in the investigation, the subject will show his cooperation. Thus, the use of the investigation as a wedge can encourage the suspect to give additional admissions, hoping to substantiate what he believes the investigation has already uncovered. As the interrogator encourages the suspect to make additional admissions, he may use other techniques such as focusing on the future or changing perspective to illustrate his points.

In response to an interrogator's use of the investigation as a wedge, many suspects will respond, "Well, just tell me what the investigation has and I'll tell you whether it's correct or not." The interrogator should not reveal any evidence at this point in the interrogation. To do so will only compromise the interrogator's ability to develop additional admissions. The interrogator should counter the suspect's move by expressing understanding that the suspect does want to know what the investigation has revealed. The interrogator might say something like the following:

Bob, I understand what you're asking. I'd like to be able to just sit here and tell you everything that the investigation has revealed. But I can't do that. The reason that I can't do that is not to be a hard guy or to cause you any difficulty, but because I have to make some important decisions about how truthful you are being with me. I need to know whether or not you're cooperating in the investigation. One of the ways that I can assess your cooperation is by holding back what I already know, so when you tell me the things that I already know, I can feel comfortable that you are being straight with me.

The interrogator can explain that others who make the final decision, such as personnel, store management, or a prosecutor, will be asking a very difficult question. That question is, "How do you know the suspect has cooperated?" The interrogator then explains to the suspect that this question is the most difficult question to be answered. The question of whether or not something happened has already been answered by the investigation, but the only outstanding question is the level of the suspect's cooperation and truthfulness.

## Substantiation of Amounts

*The Length of Involvement.* The interrogator must establish the length of involvement in criminal activity during the process of substantiation. The time that a suspect has been involved in the criminal acts will give the interrogator a sense of the scope of the problem. The length of involvement can be expanded closer to the true time frame through the use of exaggeration as discussed earlier in this chapter. It is also beneficial for the interrogator to attempt to arrive at the true time frame for purposes of averaging amounts and estimating the total number of incidents.

An interrogator must recognize that suspects will often attempt to minimize the length of their involvement in criminal activity. A standard response from suspects is, "This is my first time." Only rarely do investigators apprehend someone the first time they do something. The interrogator, however, recognizing that the suspect will attempt to minimize his involvement, utilizes exaggeration to reduce the level of seriousness. For example, an interrogator might ask an 18-year-old suspected of breaking into cars, "How long has this been going on? I mean have you been doing this since, like, you were 11?"

This will generally result in a denial from the suspect and allow the interrogator to expand the length of activity. Some suspects may have been involved at age 11, so the interrogator should reduce the age further if the suspect's background is particularly bad.

*The Most Taken at Any One Time.* Often it is worthwhile to have the suspect identify the most amount of money or merchandise that he stole at any one time. This is particularly important in the private sector when attempting to develop the total amount of money or merchandise stolen from a company. This will also assist the interrogator in estimating the scope of the suspect's involvement. For example, if a suspect acknowledges stealing merchandise from the company valued over $300 on a single occasion, the interrogator should anticipate that the suspect's total involvement may be significant. Although this is not necessarily a true gauge of the suspect's overall theft activity, it can give the interviewer a sense of the upper limits of the dollar loss the suspect has caused.

*The Average Amount Taken Each Time.* In many cases where theft activity may cover months or even years, the interrogator may have to resort to averaging to determine the extent of the suspect's theft activity. Few suspects keep track of the items or cash that they have stolen. It is necessary for the interrogator to have the suspect give a best estimate. Generally, it is better to do the averaging after the interrogator has developed the length of involvement and the largest single theft activity. To do otherwise will encourage the suspect to limit the length of involvement and reduce the overall admission.

The suspect should be encouraged to give a total dollar figure that is both fair to himself and is as close to the truth as possible. One of the major difficulties faced by suspects who have been involved in ongoing theft activity is estimating a total dollar figure stolen. Suspects typically underestimate the value of the money and merchandise that they have stolen because they are only taking small amounts over a long period. An interrogator can illustrate how small amounts add up by having the suspect think about the cost of cigarettes, newspapers, or eating out over a year's time. Any of these calculations will assist the suspect in understanding how small amounts of money or purchases add up over a long period of time. Once again, the suspect needs to be supported by the interrogator during this calculation. The suspect must understand that the interrogator sees him as an entirely different person, as someone only taking small amounts that added up over time, instead of seeing him as someone who would go into a safe and take a large amount at one time.

The interrogator, in presenting the newspaper example, simply calculates the cost of a newspaper purchased each day and on Sunday. This amounts to perhaps $4.00 per week, or over $150 per year. If an interrogator attempts to develop an admission this way, he will overestimate the suspect's theft activity because he is not taking into account that the employee does not work every day or week of the year. The correction for this error can be made using averaging.

By having the suspect establish an average amount stolen and an average frequency of his activity, an interrogator should be able to arrive at estimates that are close to the suspect's actual involvement without being over. Averaging takes into account the days or weeks the suspect did not steal by locating the average between zero theft activity and the largest amount the suspect stole.

This averaging may take one of several forms, but it is most often used in general cash and merchandise thefts from companies. In this type of averaging, the suspect is encouraged to give a daily or weekly average amount stolen that can be calculated into a total monthly average and finally an estimated total theft figure.

By starting the average on a daily or weekly basis, it will encourage the suspect to arrive at a figure closer to his actual involvement. An interrogator starting out on a daily or weekly development strategy is giving the impression that the suspect's frequency is typical of the theft activity of other employees. Furthermore, this strategy tends to use smaller numbers that minimize the suspect's involvement until a grand total is calculated. These smaller unit numbers make this kind of totaling more palatable to the suspect.

*The List of Items.* In many cases, the suspect will be able to remember specific items that he has taken. It is beneficial for the interrogator to simply ask the suspect to recall all the different types of items he has stolen from residences, businesses, vehicles, or companies. The interviewer should continue to list these items without regard to the quantity or value. Once the suspect can no longer recall any additional items, the interrogator will return to the quantity and value and origin of the items.

When returning to the quantity of the items stolen, the interrogator should use the working assumption that more than one item was taken by the suspect. This is especially true in internal theft cases. The use of exaggeration once again will help the suspect to minimize his actual theft activity.

An example of exaggeration might be asking a suspect, "What would be the greatest number of shirts you have taken? Are we talking about fifty or sixty?" The suspect responds, "Oh no, just three or four." By exaggerating the total theft activity, the interrogator has minimized the seriousness in the suspect's mind and encouraged him to make an admission closer to the truth. Once the quantity has been established, the interviewer should now identify the particular items by value, style, or description. Once this has been done for all the items listed, the interrogator can calculate a total dollar figure for the suspect's theft activity.

In public law enforcement, the location of theft is the next most important area to cover. The interrogator attempts to establish the origins of all items so that they can be compared to robbery, burglary, or theft reports on file.

*The Total Dollar Figure.* The interrogator should have been taking notes during the later part of the substantiation process. It is preferable for the interrogator rather than the suspect to do the note-taking. If the suspect is allowed to make a list, he may recall what he has said previously with greater ease because of the notes of his admission. Also, allowing the suspect to list the items he has stolen reduces the interrogator's ability to test the suspect's truthfulness. By having the suspect go back and repeat the items from memory, the interrogator may find that the suspect unwittingly make additional admissions. Finally, allowing the suspect to write the list of the items he stole shows him the magnitude of the theft and may actually reduce the admission because he realizes the large dollar value of the merchandise. This can be quite a shock because the interrogator has been minimizing the seriousness each step of the way.

When the suspect can list no additional items of merchandise he stole, the interrogator totals the value of the items. Without telling the suspect the total that the interrogator has calculated, the interrogator should then ask the suspect what he believes is the total. Regardless of how the suspect responds, it is to the interrogator's benefit. If the suspect responds with a number higher than the calculated figure, the interrogator returns to the substantiation of that amount to determine how the suspect arrived at that figure. Often the suspect will make new admissions or increase the number of items to account for the difference.

If the suspect gives a figure substantially lower than the amount already substantiated, the interrogator must rationalize and support the suspect. The interrogator should tell the suspect that merchandise and money have a way of adding up over time. To illustrate this point he may refer to the mock calculations of the money spent on newspapers, meals, or cigarettes over a year's time. Once he reminds the suspect of this illustration, the interrogator should tell the suspect that the person who would take $1,000 at one time out of a safe is entirely different from one who takes a small amount over a long period of time that might add up to the same figure.

The interrogator should again ask the suspect what would be the most amount of merchandise he could have possibly stolen. If the suspect again gives a figure over and above the total calculated, the interrogator should return to the substantiation of amounts technique.

Sometimes, a suspect will set the amount of his theft activity at the approximate figure calculated from the items listed. The interrogator should then say, "That's approximately right based on what we have here, but there are some things that you have not remembered at this point based on the investigation." Here the interrogator continues the development by using the investigation as a wedge to get additional admissions. He also might support the suspect by reminding him what a difficult time this is for him, having to remember small things over a long time.

*The Repetition of Topics.* Patience and persistence are the interrogator's assets during development. The interrogator should return to each area previously discussed and attempt to gather additional admissions from the suspects. It can be frustrating for the interrogator to be spoon-fed small admissions by the suspect, who all the while is lying about his truthfulness. However, it is imperative that the interrogator not berate the suspect for failing to remember or for his lack of cooperation during development. The interrogator should empathize with the suspect by recounting that it is a difficult time and hard for him to remember things that have been done over a long time. The suspect should be repeatedly told that the interrogator believes he is cooperating and that he will remember additional items he took.

Upon returning to the previous topics to continue development, the interrogator should use an assumptive question like, "What else did you think of in this area?" When returning to the previous topics, it is often helpful for the suspect to relist items stolen and reestimate the frequency and length of involvement and other information already substantiated. By asking a suspect to repeat previously developed information, an interrogator will be able to determine whether the figures and information vary significantly from what he was previously told.

The liar needs a good memory. Suspects who are making up information during the development phase of the interrogation will rarely be able to recall consistently what they have previously admitted. An interrogator who discovers that the suspect is unable to recall what he previously admitted should anticipate that the suspect has not been entirely candid with him. This is generally a good indication that the suspect has not made a full statement of his activities as yet.

*The Mental Review of Places.* The interrogator, in an attempt to jog the suspect's memory regarding specific items stolen, should have the suspect mentally review his house, bedroom, and vehicle. Often, a suspect who mentally walks through his residence will recall particular items or incidents that need to be discussed.

This is also an effective technique for loss prevention representatives. Mentally have the suspect walk through the store or warehouse department by department in an attempt to identify items that he stole. As the suspect *mentally* walks through these areas, the interrogator should use educated guesses to expand the admission. The interrogator suggests items frequently stolen from the company or residences and observes the suspect's behavior. If the suspect pauses after a suggested item, the interrogator should use a follow-up assumptive question, "How many of those did you take?"

Interrogators often find it beneficial to suggest items that the suspect could have used personally. Individuals often begin their theft activity taking things they need or want and only later expand to stealing for profit or friends. It may also be helpful to ask the suspect to consider gifts that he has given to friends or family. These gifts were merchandise or property "liberated" at no cost to himself. In internal theft cases, a company catalog of merchandise may also be used to refresh a suspect's memory. This will also assist the interrogator as well, by determining specific descriptions and the prices of the merchandise stolen.

Finally, it is always to the interrogator's benefit to ask the suspect what else they should discuss. If the suspect's resistance to a confession has been reduced significantly, he may give additional information against his interests. Occasionally, the suspect mistakenly believes the interrogator has additional information and is merely testing him, so he makes another admission. Others just want the slate wiped clean so they have no ghosts in their closet and make admissions. But, for whatever reason they do it, the interrogator can derive additional admissions just by asking.

## Behavioral Peak of Tension

One of the difficulties in any interrogation is to establish an end point or direction for the interrogator. It is especially difficult when interrogating on pattern of theft activity or frequency of activity, some of which may not be identified. The behavioral peak of tension is a method for the interrogator to determine, through the suspect's behavioral responses, the extent of his involvement in terms of total dollar value or frequency. The interrogator asks:

> "Do you think the amount of money you have taken could be as much as _____?"
>
> "Do you think this happened as many as _____ times?"

The blank space is filled in with varying amounts beginning with what is believed to be a known truthful figure. The interrogator uses an amount that far exceeds any involvement the suspect could have. Asking a question with an amount that significantly exaggerates the suspect's involvement will compel the suspect to make an immediate emphatic denial. The interrogator has now established a behavioral picture of how the suspect looks when he is making a truthful denial. This further minimizes the seriousness of what the suspect has actually done. The key behaviors for the interrogator are the spontaneity of the denial and its strength along with the suspect's eye contact. When the suspect is truthful, the denial will be spontaneous and firm with no hint of hesitation. The suspect's eye contact is direct in meeting the interrogator's eyes. Once the interrogator has established what he believes is a known truthful response, he then pairs that response with a lower possible theft figure. For example, the interrogator might ask:

> *INTERROGATOR:* Do you think the amount of money that you have taken could be as much as say $20,000?
> *SUSPECT:* Absolutely not! (Spontaneous direct eye contact)
> *INTERROGATOR:* Great! From the investigation, I didn't think it would be anywhere near that amount. How much do you think it would be? I mean could we be talking about say $10,000 over the entire six months you have worked for the company?
> *SUSPECT:* No way! (Spontaneous and direct)

The interrogator, in assessing the suspect's truthfulness, recognizes that the behavioral response to the second amount is similar to the response to the $20,000 figure. Thus, the interrogator can conclude that the suspect is telling the truth at the second figure. That second figure now becomes a likely truthful amount and a third possible theft amount is offered.

*INTERROGATOR:* Okay, well, do you think you could have taken as much as $8,000 over the whole time that you have been here?

*SUSPECT:* No way! (Spontaneous and direct)

*INTERROGATOR:* You're sure? You're as sure as you would be at the $20,000 figure?

*SUSPECT:* Yes. (No hesitation, good eye contact)

*INTERROGATOR:* Well, would you say its more or less than $5,000?

*SUSPECT:* Less. (No hesitation)

*INTERROGATOR:* Well, do think we could be talking about say just $4,000? That's less than $1,000 per month.

*SUSPECT:* (Hesitates, looks away and says weakly) I don't think so.

This same scenario can be used when interrogating a person believed to be involved in several burglaries or armed robberies or multiple crimes.

The interrogator, using the suspect's behavior, has now identified an amount where the suspect is no longer certain. The hesitation, weak voice, and break in the eye contact register the suspect's uncertainty. This may not lead to a confession of $4,000, but the interrogator can use this information in several ways. First, he now has an end point toward which he can work. This is probably the highest level of the suspect's involvement. It is conceivable that the real amount could actually exceed this figure. However, if this technique is used in the final stage of development, after the suspect has talked through the items he stole, it is generally close to the truth.

Second, the interrogator can indirectly assign this amount of theft or frequency to the suspect under investigation. This can assist in making investigative decisions on the allocation of investigative resources on a particular case. For example, if inventory figures establish a $4,500 loss in a particular department, a suspect making an admission of $4,000 has in all probability been the significant problem in that department. However, if the suspect had admitted only $500 and the behavioral peak indicated that he was responsible for less than $1,000, then the interrogator should continue to assign investigative resources to that department to resolve the additional shortage. In the same way, police investigators can evaluate the size of a drug dealer's business by establishing amounts and frequency of sales. This will help focus a department's investigative resources in the most futile areas. Thus, this behavioral peak of tension can be effectively used to establish the frequency of activity, quantity of items, or dollar amounts that a suspect may have been involved in stealing.

This technique can also be effective in establishing a suspect's knowledge of other individuals' involvement. By asking a suspect to rank other individual's honesty from one to ten, with ten being the most honest, the interrogator begins with the most reputable people. In general, the suspect will respond to these people with the number ten. As other individuals' names are offered to the suspect, he may hesitate and give a lower number, such as six. This indicates that the suspect has reason to believe or has suspicions that the other individual may be dishonest or involved in similar activity. The interrogator should take advantage of this information using an assumptive question: "What is the single most expensive item that you have ever seen _____[name of person ranked six] take?"

The suspect will typically respond in one of three ways. First, the suspect may respond with a particular item that he knows the suspect has taken. Second, he might give a specific denial, "I have never seen Bill take anything," in which case the interrogator follows up with another assumptive question: "What is the single most expensive item that Bill has told you he has taken?" The specific denial of the suspect does not deny knowledge, but rather only the actual observation of Bill's having taken something.

Third, the suspect may ask if he has to answer the question. If the suspect responds in this manner, the interrogator should encourage him to be truthful. When a suspect responds this way, he is actually asking for permission not to tell you. In many cases, all the interrogator has to say is "yes," after which the suspect gives the item or name he has been withholding.

## Change of Interrogators

Generally, the primary interrogator should continue the interrogation for as long as possible. Changing interrogators before a suspect has made his initial admission of guilt only serves to strengthen the suspect's resolve. Changing interrogators is best accomplished in the latter stage of the development phase when a fresh interrogator can rework areas covered by the primary interrogator.

It may also be beneficial for the new interrogator to introduce new topics. For example, in certain types of cases, such as the theft of a deposit, an interrogator may have rationalized with the suspect that this was the first time anything like this happened. Once the suspect has admitted stealing the deposit, it is often difficult for that interrogator to expand into other types of theft activity because of the rationalization he used to gain the initial admission. However, the new interrogator is not bound by that rationalization and can introduce new topics to the development process in an attempt to expand the admission.

Sometimes, a suspect will withhold information simply because he is embarrassed about having lied to the first interrogator so many times. He lied and made an admission, lied and made an admission. Finally, he stonewalls and will not make any additional admissions to the first interrogator. The introduction of a new interrogator at this time often results in significant additional admissions. This is because the suspect was not unwilling to make the admission, but was simply embarrassed that he had not told the whole truth to the first interrogator. The introduction of a new interrogator has the advantages of fresh patience and persistence being focused against a weakened suspect.

In some situations, the second interrogator may have acted as the witness during the primary interrogator's interrogation. In this instance, the primary interrogator and witness simply switch positions. The primary interrogator now positions himself as the witness with the witness taking the role and seat of the primary interrogator. The witness should only be utilized as a second interrogator when he is competent and understands the process of interrogation. Allowing an unskilled interrogator to develop additional admissions often results in the suspect's recanting all or part of his previous admissions.

If during development of the admission, the suspect increases his resistance or begins to recant his admissions, the interrogator should return to rationalizations to reduce the suspect's resistance. However, if the suspect's resistance does not diminish, a written statement should be taken immediately, before any further questioning. This way, the interrogator is assured of a document containing incriminating admissions that can be used in court or to terminate the employee.

## The Use of Evidence/The Absolute Denial

An interrogator should not reveal his evidence until the final stages of development. Evidence used early in the interrogation typically results in a suspect's attempting to explain it away or admitting only to what is known by the interrogator. By withholding evidence until the final stages of the interrogation, the interrogator has reduced the suspect's resistance to a confession and strengthened even weak circumstantial evidence as a result. During the final stages of an interrogation, the suspect may make an absolute denial. The absolute denial is where the suspect absolutely denies the existence of any other criminal involvement or the existence of evidence to the contrary. Usually the suspect says something like, "That's it, that's all I've done, there is absolutely nothing else. I don't care what you or your investigations say." It is at this time that the suspect is most susceptible to the presentation of evidence. The suspect has now called the interrogator in on a game of cards and it is time for the interrogator to play his ace. By using the absolute denial, the suspect has left himself no room for an explanation of any evidence presented by the interrogator.

Once the suspect has made an absolute denial, the interrogator presents a piece of evidence that clearly refutes the suspect's statement. An interrogator who is able to present evidence that contradicts the suspect's absolute denial often finds that the suspect is susceptible to significant additional admissions. In theft cases, it is not unheard of for a suspect to change his admissions from a few hundred to several thousands of dollars simply because evidence has been presented at a key moment that refutes his protestations of innocence. For example:

SUSPECT:   That's all I've done, I don't care what you or your investigation says.

INTERROGATOR:   Mark, that's just not true. I'm going to give you one small piece of evidence to show you I'm not bluffing. I'm not trying to be a hard guy or trying to trick you, but I can tell you about the money you took an hour and a half ago if you want.

SUSPECT:   (Silence, withdrawn, physically shrinks as the evidence of guilt is presented)

INTERROGATOR:   Nobody want to put you in a bad spot, but it is important to be truthful. How much money did you take this morning?

SUSPECT:   $50.

INTERROGATOR:   Okay, lets go through this again and make sure...

Interrogator returns to techniques to develop the admission.

## Development of Knowledge

The interrogator should attempt to develop implications and investigative leads of other individuals involved in theft or criminal activity. The suspect is a vault of information from which the interrogator may be able to draw. The ability to generate implications will increase the productivity of an investigator by using the investigative resources in a direction that will prove most fruitful.

### Request for Names

The interrogator should ask the suspect for the names of others he knows are involved in criminal activity. The suspect may be somewhat hesitant to give information about another; however, the interviewer can overcome this resistance by offering the suspect limited confidentiality. In addition, an interrogator who is confident and expects the suspect to give an implication is often rewarded with a name.

The interrogator should ask the suspect for implications in a way that expects an answer. If the interrogator asks, "Could you tell me about anybody else taking things," it is likely the suspect will answer, "No." However, by asking the suspect firmly and confidently for a name, he will often respond with a name. One hurdle that individuals have in revealing another's identity is the fear of being discovered as an informant.

The interrogator should immediately tell the suspect that under no circumstances will the other individual be told of the suspect's cooperation, but this should be said only if it will be true. The interviewer should not tell the suspect that the information will not leave the room because that would be an untrue statement. The results of the information will certainly be shared with other investigators.

However, it is proper to tell the suspect that the implicated individual will not learn of the suspect's cooperation if the interrogator knows it can be kept confidential. It is at this point that the interrogator should attempt to determine the extent and value of a suspect's information about other criminal activity.

Trading pending criminal charges for a dismissal or reduced sentence in return for informant's help in penetrating another criminal organization is often accomplished now. For example, two youths were apprehended with a stolen handgun. During the subsequent interrogation, the suspects identified an apartment where gang members purchased and stored weapons. In exchange for their help in obtaining a search warrant, the interrogator offered to tell the prosecutor and judge of their cooperation in another case.

Suspects are often eager to help the interrogator solve other crimes and are full of grand promises of help. The motivation to help diminishes rapidly if the investigator does not maintain the leverage of sentencing or a criminal complaint on the suspect. The interrogator should work with the prosecutor before making any promises he may not be able to keep.

Once the suspect has given another individual's name, the interrogator should attempt to determine how he came by this information. It may be that the suspect knows this information because he was also involved in the incident. The interrogator should substantiate exactly who the other individual is and the circumstances surrounding the criminal activity. This will allow the investigator to initiate a new investigation into the circumstances given or provide the information necessary to interview the new suspect. In interviewing the new suspect, the interrogator now has information to help him construct either the introductory statement or the participatory accusation to begin the interrogation.

Once a suspect's name has been given, the interrogator should anticipate that there may be other suspects of whom the employee has knowledge. If an employee lacks direct knowledge, he should be asked for suspicions concerning other employees in the store. It has been the authors' experience that approximately 20% of employees will have knowledge of another's dishonesty at their company. In certain locations with higher theft activity, the knowledge of others may be significantly higher. In the public sector, the knowledge of other criminal activity is much more likely than in a limited company environment. The interrogator should anticipate that a suspect's friends may often be involved in same activities as the suspect. Friends tend to associate with one another because of similar interests, values, and backgrounds.

In many cases, a suspect is reluctant to give the interrogator the names of other people involved in thefts or other criminal activity. In those situations, the interrogator should attempt to gather certain information that will help identify who the suspect knows or believes may be involved. By discovering the individual's sex, race, marital status, and position of employment, the interrogator may be able to identify the person to whom the suspect is referring. If the interviewer/interrogator exercises patience at this time, he may be rewarded with the identity of other suspects.

# The Statement

# 12

*A statement is like the period at the end of a sentence—without it the job is incomplete.*

The final statement is a written document or audio/video recording, obtained from a victim, witness, or suspect, that encompasses the discussion that occurs during the interview or interrogation. The statement is not necessarily a confession although in many cases it may be. The purpose of this document or recording is to lock an individual into the details admitted or statements made during the interview or interrogation. Formalizing his admission in written or recorded form deters the suspect, witness, or victim from changing his story and reduces the possibility that evidence or testimony will be lost or manufactured later at a hearing or trial. For a victim or witness, it can also serve as a means to refresh their memory at a later date.

The written statement has value in a number of specific areas. The use of the statement at a civil or criminal hearing is well understood by most people. The statement, however, also has value in union arbitrations, company hearings, unemployment compensation hearings, claims investigations, and in terminations. The private sector can use the written statement as a loss prevention tool for management. By analyzing the methods of loss, management can effectively tighten operational controls to reduce the possibility of similar future losses.

In many instances, the written statement can also be used to establish loss for insurance purposes. This is especially important in the private sector where companies are protected by one or more types of insurance. The statement establishes that the employee breached his fiduciary duty to the company. This breach of trust is established in the statement by detailing the employee's dishonest acts. Second, the written statement also explains to the insurer the first time the loss occurred, total amount of loss, and the method used to accomplish the theft. By establishing these parameters, a company can often file a claim with the insurer.

The written statement also provides attorneys with an understanding of what a witness may testify to. These types of statements can be particularly effective in the early stages of a lawsuit when attorneys are developing information through interrogatories or depositions. By establishing the information that a witness or a victim holds, the opposing counsel can quickly ascertain the direction for his deposition and what specific information may be useful.

The statement also has another purpose, which is to act as evidence should a victim, witness, or suspect die prior to a hearing or trial. In certain instances where a witness is deceased, a statement given prior to the witness's death may be admissible in court or at a hearing. In the event that a witness is unavailable for a particular hearing or has become mentally incompetent, the evidence provided by his statement may also have some evidentiary value.

In both civil and criminal cases, the witness, who may be later asked to testify, may have to remember an incident that occurred several years before trial. Because the memory can be a tenuous thing, the witness's statement can often help recall the circumstances surrounding the incident. Especially in civil cases where it may be three or more years before trial, the statement can have considerable impact on their recall, and thus the value of their testimony.

A suspect's statement may take one of two forms. The first type details a statement made by a suspect who denies any involvement but relates his alibi or the circumstances surrounding the incident. Once this information has been documented, it is difficult for the guilty suspect to change his story. Should the guilty person later attempt to change his alibi or the circumstances of the incident, his original statement can be used to discredit his newly found information. By locking the suspect into the details of his alibi or the circumstances surrounding the event, the investigation can clearly focus on proving or disproving the information contained in the statement. At trial, a statement that can be proved false has almost as much effect on the judge and jury as a confession of guilt.

The value of the written statement and its usefulness in the investigative process can be underscored by the following:

### Case Example

Three males in their late teens were suspected of setting fires at three residences in the rural area of a county during a single evening. The police, through their investigation, obtained a partial license number and descriptions that matched the three youths and their vehicle.

The youths used each other to establish their alibi for the evening in question. Although the investigative information was sufficient to focus suspicion upon the three youths, it was insufficient to arrest or obtain an indictment for arson.

The three youths were interviewed separately and each was asked to give a detailed recital of the evening's activities with the other two boys. Initially, each of the youths gave broad, vague descriptions of the evening. However, the interviewers had each of the boys detail moment by moment where they had been, who they had been there with, and what had occurred. This was done in meticulous detail covering all aspects of the evening.

When the three statements were compared, it was evident that although certain elements of the evening were consistent, the details varied greatly. The youths differed in the type of vehicle that they had driven, the locations that they had visited, the order of the visits, the people that they had seen, and the times the events occurred. Even at points of general agreement the details varied significantly.

These differing statements, along with the information that the investigation developed, became the focal point for the interrogation of the three young men. As a result of the preinterrogation written statements from the three, the interviewers were able to take away the suspects' ability to use each other as an alibi. This ultimately helped in achieving their confession.

The second form of a suspect's statement is an admission of guilt. The details of a suspect's admission and the elements necessary to prove the crime are included in this statement. This type of statement serves as additional evidence of the suspect's guilt. If an interrogator fails to accurately reproduce a suspect's verbal admission in a permanent record, the job is only partially completed and successful. The written or recorded admission of guilt made by a suspect has a tremendous impact on the judge, jury, or hearing officer and their corresponding belief in the suspect's guilt.

In instances where multiple admissions are made to separate crimes, the interrogator should obtain a separate confession for each crime or incident. This is done in cases where the inclusion of other dishonest activity may bias the original confession, for example, as with a burglar who admits breaking into a home and removing cash and a TV set and who also admits stealing a car earlier in the year. The inclusion of this information in the written statement regarding the burglary may bias a jury and consequently cause the written statement to be excluded from trial.

## Types of Statements

There are a variety of different formats in which an oral statement can be put in writing. Some of these types are

Narrative

Question and answer

Formal

Audio or video recordings

The type of statement selected for use by the interrogator may be dependent upon the type of case, its seriousness, the resources at hand, and the time factor.

### Narrative

One of the most common forms of the written statement is the narrative. The narrative statement is usually a handwritten account by the suspect, using the first person to describe his activities in the incident. This narrative is generally in the form of a series of paragraphs, written on plain paper or on a form on which the opening and/or closing portions of the statement have been preprinted.

The suspect's narrative describes the incident and substantiates his involvement with details. The narrative contains the elements of the crime and in certain cases, his personal feelings about the incident or incidents. This narrative can also incorporate information relating to the suspect's state of mind at the time he committed the crime.

### Question and Answer

A second type of statement that can be obtained is the question and answer. In this type of statement, the interviewer hand writes or types a series of questions to which the suspect or witness makes a written response. The question and answer format allows the interviewer to ask for responses to very specific details of the incident. This type of question and answer format is also typically used in a recorded or formal statement.

An example of this format might be

QUESTION:   On December 31, 1991, did you kill John Jones?
ANSWER:   Yes.
QUESTION:   What did you use to kill John Jones?
ANSWER:   A Smith & Wesson .38 snub-nose revolver.

*QUESTION:*  Where is the Smith & Wesson .38 snub-nose revolver now?

*ANSWER:*  I dropped it down the sewer at Forest and Webster Lane in Des Plaines.

Sometimes, a suspect's written narrative statement may lack certain details or elements necessary to prove the crime. In these instances, the question and answer format can be used to supplement the written narrative statement by the suspect. The use of the question and answer format allows the interrogator to clarify points that were unclear in the suspect's narrative statement. The question and answer format is often helpful with a suspect who is evasive or makes significant omissions in his written narrative statement.

## Formal Statements

In cases where the seriousness of the incident or potential cost to a company is significant, a formal statement should be obtained. The formal statement utilizes a court reporter or stenographer to record the questions and the witness's or suspect's responses.

The use of a court reporter or stenographer in complex issues often facilitates a more detailed and complete statement. Very often, it reduces the time necessary to obtain a statement because the suspect does not have to actually write the information down. Having the suspect write can be a tedious process when he has difficulty writing. Witnesses and suspects tend to shorten statements because they are too long or difficult to handwrite. In shortening a statement, a suspect or witness often omits valuable information just so he can complete the statement. In complex issues, it is usually preferable to avoid the handwritten statement in favor of a formal typed document or recorded statement.

In cases where an upper level executive might be required to testify as a witness on behalf of the company, it is often in the interest of the company to spend the money to obtain a formal statement. Especially in civil lawsuits where the company's liability may be extreme, the formal statement can lock the employee into his testimony. This becomes important should the employee leave the company or be terminated because of some unrelated issue. Any resulting dissatisfaction with the company could taint the witness's future testimony. In cases that have the potential to go to litigation the statements should be formalized using audio, video, or stenographic recording to assure completeness.

## Audio or Video Recordings

With the expansion of technology has come the ability to clearly record statements by audio or video means. Many investigators successfully use these techniques to record a witness's or suspect's statement, which can later be transcribed and included in the case file. This technique is commonly used by insurance claims adjusters when they interview victims or witnesses of accidents.

The use of the audio or video recording of a suspect's statement or confession can make a significant impression at a hearing or trial. Because the recording shows the suspect at the time he confessed, the jury or judge is able to assess his emotional state and the voluntariness of the admission. In addition, his appearance is not polished for the courtroom, but rather is as it was at the time of his arrest. The believability of a confession when seen under these circumstances is enhanced; viewing it can leave a lasting image with the court. To hear a suspect describe the incident with his own words can be absolutely chilling.

The interrogator who elects to use this type of statement, however, may also wish to take a handwritten or formal statement as well. The interrogator should consider the pitfalls in obtaining an audio or video recorded statement. For example, interruptions of power may cause the recording to be incomplete. This stopping and starting of the tape due to electrical shortage or weakness in the batteries can cause the statement to be questioned at a hearing or in court.

In addition, the interviewer/interrogator should consider whether or not the audio portion of the recording will be clearly discernible to the listener. Airconditioning, heating, or other noises in the building can sometimes obscure the recorded dialogue. A suspect often has the tendency to speak softly or mumble when talking about the incident. The softness of the suspect's voice and his mumbling may cause the words to become garbled and indecipherable.

Voices can also become garbled if the interrogator and suspect both elect to speak at the same time. In audio statements, it may also be unclear who is speaking and thus be confusing to the listener. When a listener has to try to sort out who is speaking, he tends to miss the details spoken. In audio statements, for clarity, there should be only two people talking on the tapes, the witness or suspect and the interviewer/interrogator. Each of these individuals should be clearly identified at the onset of the recording.

Finally, the interviewer/interrogator should consider applicable state laws regarding recordings and eavesdropping before recording a statement. Several states require the consent of all parties involved if the conversation is recorded, whereas some states only require the consent of one person to make a recording.

Generally, for a recorded statement the subject's permission to record the statement should be obtained. The interrogator should also note the identity of the persons present during the statement along with the date and time it was obtained. Many video recorders have a date/time function that will allow the date/time to be superimposed on the video image.

## Interrogator Control

Regardless of the type of statement used, the interviewer/interrogator must continue to maintain control to assure a usable statement from the suspect or witness. To allow a suspect or witness to proceed without direction while making a statement is almost to assure that it will be unusable.

Although the interviewer/interrogator does not dictate the statement, he certainly controls the formatting of the document. Leading questions to the suspect will insure the inclusion of relevant details necessary to prove the elements of the crime and to substantiate the admission. The interviewer/interrogator should not leave the suspect alone to complete the statement. Leaving the suspect alone will likely result in either no statement being written or his failure to include pertinent information.

The interviewer/interrogator must sell the suspect on the need for a complete written or recorded statement. The suspect can be told that the statement will tell his side of the story and allow him to say he was sorry or to explain any mitigating circumstances. The interviewer/interrogator should tell the suspect that the written statement will accurately record the discussion between the interrogator and himself.

The suspect should be told that the statement will allow others to hear his side of the story so the others cannot blow the incident out of proportion. Similarly, a witness should be encouraged to give a statement because it may prevent his being inconvenienced with additional future interviews.

The interrogator also should consider the issue of custody. If the suspect has been in custody during the interrogation, then the Miranda warnings should be included in the statement along with the suspect's waiver of them, prior to the narrative or question and answer format. Regardless of the type of statement the interviewer/interrogator selects for use, he will find that the use of a standard statement format will enhance his ability to develop the information clearly, concisely, and in an orderly manner.

## Timing of Taking the Statement

The suspect's or witness's statement should be taken immediately at the conclusion of the interview or interrogation. The interviewer/interrogator has established a strong level of rapport and cooperation with the individual that should be exploited. Waiting to obtain a statement at a later date is rarely successful. More often than not, waiting results in a failure to obtain any statement at all. This failure to obtain a statement may impede the successful conclusion of the case when the witness or suspect rethinks the wisdom of making a written or recorded statement.

The interviewer/interrogator, having concluded the interview or interrogation, should obtain the written statement without leaving the room. Once the interviewer/interrogator has developed the information as much as possible, he should begin to introduce the idea of a statement. If the interrogator feels that an individual may be reluctant to write a statement, it may be prudent to have a witness hear the suspect's oral statement.

The suggestion of a written statement can be introduced to the suspect by calling it a statement of explanation. By calling the statement "an explanation," the interviewer/interrogator reduces the formality and consequences associated with the words confession or statement. This statement of explanation details what was talked about and the suspect's reasons for taking part in the incident. The interrogator may use questions that encourage a suspect to write a statement. For example, he may say, "I'm sure you'd be willing to write a statement of explanation detailing what we've talked about here, wouldn't you?" By using an assumptive question, the interrogator encourages the suspect to agree to write the statement.

Once the suspect agrees to write a statement, the interrogator should hand the witness or suspect the paper or forms necessary to complete it. Presenting these items to the suspect, the interviewer/interrogator simply states the date, for example, "Today is January 29, 1991." This statement by the interrogator encourages the suspect to place the date at the top of the paper.

In the event that preprinted opening and closing paragraphs are used, the interviewer/interrogator should review the information contained in the opening. Often, these opening and closing paragraphs have been written by attorneys and contain legal terminology that may frighten the suspect. The interrogator should minimize the seriousness of these formal opening and closing paragraphs and encourage the suspect to begin the narrative of his involvement.

In the event that the interrogator has decided to use a court reporter, stenographer, or audio/video equipment to record the statement, the suspect should be sold on the necessity for them in the same way as he would have been if a written statement was used. The interviewer/interrogator should briefly explain the necessity of the stenographer or recording to make sure that everything is recorded. It will also prevent the suspect from having to write all the information.

When a court reporter or stenographer has been retained to take a formal statement, it is beneficial for the interviewer/interrogator to brief him on the circumstances of the case prior to starting the statement. Having been briefed in advance, the reporter will be better able to follow the statement and will be less likely to be confused by names, places, or events. It is also helpful to provide the stenographer with the correct spelling of the participants, locations, or company names prior to the statement to help them accurately document the statement without interrupting the victim, suspect, witness, or interrogator.

If the interrogator has elected to use an audio/video recording, he can introduce it by saying that it will enable the suspect or witness to make his explanation in greater detail without having to make a written statement. In addition, the interrogator can remind the suspect that the sound of his words will reflect the truthfulness of his admission. These recordings are often transcribed for a later signature by the witness or suspect. This will allow them to correct any errors and sign the document at a later date. Many times the transcription is not actually signed but is rendered in a written form for use by attorneys or investigators.

## Potential Problems

Statements may be excluded from a hearing or trial for any number of reasons: the allegation of threats, use of leading questions, statements that are changed, mention of other convictions, or even the omission of circumstances favorable to the subject. Any of these may form the basis for the exclusion of a written or recorded statement. By considering and anticipating potential problems, the interviewer/interrogator can prepare the statement in such a way to avoid these pitfalls.

### The Suspect Alleges That the Statement Was Dictated to Him

Often, a suspect will say that the statement was dictated to him and that he just wrote what he was told. This allegation may be based on the interrogator's having helped to format the statement and having used leading questions to obtain the details. Other suspects will make this allegation simply because it might seem plausible to those not present. The style of the language, use of slang, and improper spelling by a suspect tends to negate the allegation that the statement was dictated. The interviewer/interrogator should avoid introducing words that would not be commonly used by the suspect. The interrogator should allow the suspect to spell and structure sentences in a way that is natural for him. This is not to say, however, that the interviewer/interrogator allows the suspect to omit the necessary elements of the crime or details that make the statement complete.

## The Suspect Says That He Cannot Read or Write

In some situations, a less educated individual will attempt to avoid writing a statement because he cannot spell or write well. However, some individuals may be functionally illiterate and legitimately unable to read or write. In these cases, the interviewer may elect to write the statement for the suspect or to use a stenographer or audio/video type of statement.

In the event that the interrogator writes the statement for the suspect, he should anticipate that the suspect may allege that he was just asked to sign a document he could not read. In an effort to avoid or defend against this allegation, the interrogator should make a number of mistakes while writing the confession. For example, he may put the biographical information concerning the street address where the suspect resides incorrectly. In the body of the statement, he may incorrectly put an amount or a direction that was incorrect.

When the statement is complete, the interrogator reviews it with the suspect. When the statement is read to the suspect, the interrogator will find that the suspect will discover mistakes in the details. In the event the suspect fails to mention an error, the interrogator should point it out and question its correctness. The suspect should be asked to cross out these errors and replace them with the correct information. These corrections should then be initialled by the suspect.

When the statement has been completed, it should be witnessed by someone not present during the interrogation or interview. The statement is witnessed by having someone read it aloud, stopping periodically to question the suspect about the details that have been changed. If this method is used, the suspect will have difficulty convincing judge, jury, or hearing officer that the statement was simply presented to him and he signed it without knowing the contents.

## The Recording of a Statement May Be Questioned

Interrogators who use electronic recording of the statement should anticipate that this may create problems in other cases. Attorneys may question why only certain confessions were documented using audio/video equipment. Although this question certainly can be handled with a simple explanation, the defense counsel may attempt to use this question to cloud the issue. Often an attorney will allege that the interrogator has something to hide because he failed to use electronic recording devices in the present case when he had used them in previous cases. The interrogator should anticipate this ploy and be prepared with an explanation.

## The Suspect Alleges That He Was not Advised of His Rights

On occasion, a suspect may allege that he was not advised of his *Miranda* rights. This is more common in situations where no written waiver was obtained from the suspect. In police cases where the suspect is in custody and *Miranda* is required, it should be incorporated as part of the written or recorded statement. By incorporating the *Miranda* rights and the suspect's responses as part of the statement, it further confirms that the suspect knowingly waived his rights and the statement was given freely.

## The Suspect Alleges Coercion in Writing the Statement

Many suspects will allege that they were coerced or forced into producing a written statement. This often plays on the public's fear and willingness to believe that third degree tactics are used to obtain confessions. Anticipating this allegation, the interrogator can overcome it in one of two ways. First, in the body of the statement, the interrogator can have the suspect respond that he was not forced or threatened in any way to write the statement. In addition, the suspect should also acknowledge that the information contained in the statement is true. This in and of itself, however, might still leave the potential for the suspect to claim that the statement was forced or coerced.

The second tactic employed by the interrogator is to use the individual who witnesses the written or recorded statement. During the witnessing, the interrogator should ask the suspect to acknowledge verbally that the statement is true, is his own, and has been obtained without the use of threats, promises, or coercion. Although a suspect may later still allege coercion or disavow the statement, it will be more difficult for him to overcome the credibility these tactics provide the interrogator.

The interrogator might also have the suspect include information about his treatment during the interview or interrogation. By documenting lunch, breaks, or bathroom use in the statement, the interrogator could help deter accusations of wrongdoing. By including these details in the statement, the judge, jury, or hearing officer has to consider how likely it was for a coercive interrogation to have occurred under these circumstances. Who serves coffee or lunch during a coercive interrogation? This tends to spoil the image of the suspect's having had a confession beaten out of him.

## The Suspect Refuses to Make a Written Statement

In some cases, a suspect may refuse to make a written statement for any number of reasons. It has been the authors' experience that suspects who refuse to make a written statement are often just embarrassed by their handwriting, spelling, or educational level. The interrogator in many cases can obtain a written statement from a reluctant suspect simply by offering to write the statement for the suspect. If the interrogator does write the statement for the suspect, he should use the preceding method to assure that the suspect does not allege that he merely signed the document without reading it.

In certain situations however, the suspect will refuse any type of written statement. Typically, they will say that their parents, friends, or an attorney told them to never write anything down. In these cases, it is critical that the suspect's oral statement be witnessed by others. It may be advisable to make an audio or video recorded statement as previously discussed.

If a witness was in the room during the interrogation, that individual will be able to testify to the suspect's treatment and verbal statement. It is usually in the interrogator's best interest to have an uninvolved participant rewitness the oral admissions of a suspect who refuses to write a statement. In the private sector, this might be the company official responsible for deciding whether or not to terminate the suspect's employment.

In rewitnessing a statement, the witness is brought into the room and the interrogator reiterates the admission in front of the suspect. Periodically the interrogator stops to ask the suspect about specific details of the admission. In doing so, he will bring the suspect into the conversation and eventually the suspect readmits to the incident in front of the uninvolved third party. The interrogator, in front of the witness, should also question the suspect regarding his treatment and the voluntariness of the confession. By having the suspect admit in front of an uninvolved witness that the statement was true and not coerced, the interrogator will help overcome any later allegations of his misconduct.

In addition, this readmission by the suspect will provide the necessary information for the company official to make a decision about the suspect's future employment with the company. The recounting of details by the suspect will also enable the company official to testify at hearings should the suspect file for unemployment compensation or a union grievance.

The police interrogator may also elect to have a third party witness the suspect's confession. Depending upon the seriousness of the incident, the interrogator may choose to use a prosecutor, female officer, or command personnel to witness the suspect's verbal statement. The selection of a witness in these types of situations should provide the most credible individual available to witness the admission. The use of a female officer or command personnel will enhance the believability that the statement was not coerced or forced in any way. In smaller departments where command personnel or a female officer are unavailable, the use of civilian personnel to witness the statement can be an alternative. Using a dispatcher, file clerk, or a secretary as a uninvolved third party to witness the statement may help overcome any later allegations of coercion or misconduct. The officer witnesses the statement by the method previously described and specifically asks the suspect whether the statement was a result of force or threats.

Upon completion of the oral statement the third party witness should make notes about the suspect's admissions to refresh his memory before testifying. These notes may be in the form of a written report or less formal handwritten notes. In either case, the notes or the report should be dated, signed, and maintained in the case file.

### The Interrogator Believes That the Suspect May Be Unwilling to Make a Written Statement

An interrogator often can anticipate a suspect's reluctance to make a written statement. This belief is based on the attitude and cooperation the suspect showed during the interrogation. In cases where the interrogator believes that the suspect may balk at writing a statement, he should have the oral statement witnessed by a third party. In the event the suspect does refuse to prepare a statement the interrogator has another individual who can testify to the admission. In addition, once the suspect has made the admission to yet another person, it provides an effective wedge to persuade him to commit his admission to writing.

Another effective tactic is to have the suspect initial the interviewer/interrogator's notes prior to the interrogator's requesting the written statement. The interviewer/interrogator asks the suspect to verify the correctness of his notes and initial those parts that are correct. If the suspect later refuses to write a statement, the initialed notes may be introduced as evidence. The initialing of the notes makes it even more difficult for judge or jury to believe the statement was coerced or dictated.

### The Suspect Avoids Admitting Elements or Details of the Crime

Sometimes a suspect will attempt to avoid including the details of his admission or the elements of the crime or will not define slang terms in the body of his statement. In the event this occurs, the interviewer/interrogator should prepare a supplemental statement by writing out a number of direct questions that include the elements of the crime, the details, or to define slang terms.

For example, a suspect may be reluctant to write or say that he killed the victim and instead says he "did him." That phrase is slang for a killing and is understood by law enforcement professionals, but it may lack the clarity necessary for an ordinary citizen to understand that the suspect murdered the victim. Using a supplemental question and answer format, the interrogator could specifically write down a question that clarifies the suspect's original admission: "On March 28, 1991, I killed Mike Smith." To this the suspect would write or respond "yes" and initial his answer. The interviewer/interrogator could also define any slang term using a question: "In your statement when you wrote, 'did him,' did you mean that you killed him?" Again, the suspect would respond "yes" and initial his answer. Used this way, the question and answer format supplements the suspect's statement. It provides the specific elements of the crime and clarifies slang terms or details included in the body of the statement.

## Statement Format

The interviewer/interrogator should become comfortable with a statement format that he uses for each and every statement that he obtains. Using the same format allows the interrogator to concentrate on the details of the incident rather than on what is going to come next in the body of the statement. In most statements, regardless of whether or not they are narrative, question and answer, formal, or recorded by audio or video means, a similar format can be used.

The statement can be broken down into five distinct parts:

Part One: Introduction

Part Two: Total admission

Part Three: Substantiation of the total admission

Part Four: Voluntariness of the admission

Part Five: Signature and correcting errors

### *Part One: Introduction*

In the introduction of the statement, the interviewer/interrogator asks the suspect to include biographical information about the suspect. Asking the suspect to include biographical information about himself is nonthreatening to the suspect and provides several benefits to the interviewer/interrogator. First, it clearly identifies the suspect who is giving the statement. The introduction includes the suspect's name, address, job title, and the location of the company where he is employed. Many interrogators also include information about the suspect's age, educational level, social security number, or other pertinent biographical information. The amount of biographical information included in the introduction is dictated by the interrogator or by department or company policy. In the private sector, at the least the suspect's name, position, assignment location, and company should be included.

The second purpose of this biographical information is to allow the suspect to get used to writing by beginning with nonthreatening information. The nonthreatening nature of the first several sentences breaks the ice and makes the suspect more comfortable with writing a statement.

In instances where the suspect is in police custody, the *Miranda* warnings should be incorporated in their entirety in the opening of the introduction. Many statement forms have a preprinted introductory paragraph that allows the suspect to fill in biographical information. These paragraphs also often cover part four, the voluntariness of the admission, either in the introduction or at the close of the document.

## Part Two: The Admission

The second part of the statement should be a blanket admission by the suspect that he committed the crime. The initial admission of involvement in the crime contains the element of proof but lacks the details of the admission. This is done for several reasons. First, having the suspect make a total overall admission to the crime sets the stage for later substantiation. It also gives the jury or hearing officer an opportunity to hear the blanket admission first; the blanket admission will grab their attention. Second, should the suspect balk at completing the statement, the interrogator has an overall admission to the crime even though it may lack the substantiation or details. Ideally, this blanket admission should also contain the element of the crime to which the suspect is confessing. This is done by the suspect's using words that include intent—for example, "I stole," "I killed," "I robbed," which show the intent of the suspect to commit the crime. The elements of the crime necessary to prove the violation should be incorporated again during part three, the substantiation of the admission.

## Part Three: Substantiation

In this section, the suspect is asked to substantiate his admission with the details of the crime. In the private sector, these details often relate to the theft of company assets. Here, the interrogator has the suspect detail the first and last time that he stole money or merchandise, the greatest amount of money or merchandise stolen at one time, the method of theft, what he used the money for, including any personal details of its use, and the location of any remaining merchandise or evidence.

For the police interrogator, the substantiation will generally relate only to the details of a specific incident. The police interrogator should often begin with details preceding the crime. For example, in a rape, the suspect may be asked to identify the location where he first saw the victim. This may include his thoughts during this first observation. Also incorporated in substantiation may be the suspect's identification of evidence, pictures, or documents. Sketches illustrate a particular portion of the admission. All these pieces of evidence should be referred to in the statement and reflect that the suspect dated and initialed the items to identify them.

The interrogator, regardless of whether he is in the public or private sector, should understand what will constitute proof of the suspect's guilt. In certain cases, it may be necessary to include in the substantiation the suspect's mental state at the time the incident took place. Understanding what is necessary to prove the crime will enable the interrogator to encourage the suspect to incorporate those details into the substantiation portion of the statement. For example, in a homicide, the fact that the suspect had had repeated arguments with the victim and had disliked him intensely for many years may provide a partial foundation for the suspect's premeditation of the murder.

*Part Four: Voluntariness*

Once the details of the incident have been included, the interrogator should begin to close the statement. This is done by asking the suspect if everything that he had written is true. The suspect will generally acknowledge that he has told the truth.[1]

The suspect should then be asked if he would include that in the statement. The suspect should also be asked if he is making the statement of his own free will without threats or promises. The suspect's affirmative response to this question can be included in the statement by simply saying, "Why don't you put that in, too." Once this admission has been included in the statement, the interrogator, who has been reading along as the suspect writes, makes a decision whether or not it is necessary to use an additional question and answer supplemental statement to clarify any points of the statement.

---

1. Note: If the suspect hesitates to admit that what he has written is true, the interrogator should return to the techniques used to reduce the suspect's resistance and attempt to develop the admissions further. Even while obtaining the final statement, the interrogator should probe for additional admissions or clarifications from the suspect. Many times the suspect's final reluctance to tell the truth is overcome by the actual writing of the statement.

## Part Five: Signature and Correcting Errors

When the suspect has completed the narrative portion of the statement, substantiated it, and acknowledged its voluntariness, it should be signed by the suspect, interrogator, and witness. The interrogator may ask if there is anything that the suspect would like to add to the explanation. Many suspects like to include that they are sorry for what they have done or the reasons why they became involved in the incident. Often these reasons were incorporated earlier in the documentation while substantiating the admission. Once the suspect and the interrogator are satisfied that the statement is complete, then it should be signed. The interrogator simply points to the place on the page immediately following the last paragraph and makes the statement, "Why don't you write your name here." Generally, the suspect will sign his name at the appropriate spot on the page.

If the suspect hesitates to sign his name, the interrogator may need to offer additional support to reduce this resistance. Encouraging a suspect to sign the statement may be simply done:

*INTERROGATOR:* Now everything that you put in here is the truth, right?

*SUSPECT:* Right.

*INTERROGATOR:* Well, if that's the case, then there certainly shouldn't be any problem signing it because all you're doing is attesting that in fact everything in here is the truth. I mean, you said you were sorry, right?

*SUSPECT:* Yeah.

*INTERROGATOR:* Well, then there certainly shouldn't be any problem signing it. Why don't you put your name right down there. (The interrogator again indicates the spot on the page where the suspect is to sign.)

Once the suspect has signed the document, the interrogator takes the last page and adds it to the other pages of the statement. At this point, page by page, the suspect is asked to initial any scratch-outs or corrections he made and sign each page of the statement. He is told that this is done to assure that he is the one that made the corrections and nobody else altered his statement in any way. At the same time he initials the corrections, each page of the statement should be numbered. This is done by noting at the top of each page, page one of three, page two of three, page three of three, and so on.

This page-numbering technique assures that no pages of the document are missing. Additionally, anyone reviewing the written statement immediately knows how many pages it should contain, and it is readily apparent which, if any, of the pages might be missing.

## Protection of the Statement

The interrogator has worked long and hard to obtain the confession and the written statement from the suspect. Sometimes a suspect may become reluctant to continue or will rethink the wisdom of his decision to commit the admission to writing. In some of these cases, the suspect may refuse to write any further or attempt to destroy what he has already written. Even a partial statement by the suspect has evidentiary value and should be protected.

As each page is completed by the suspect, the interviewer/interrogator should remove that page from the desk and conceal it in his case file to protect it from being destroyed. Statements left within reach of the suspect can quickly become damaged or destroyed. An interrogator who allows a suspect to tear up the statement generally allows this to only happen once in his career. In the event that the suspect does tear the statement up, the torn portions of the statement should be recovered and maintained as evidence.

On rare occasions, after beginning to write, a suspect will crumple the paper and refuse to go further. The interrogator should attempt to persuade the suspect to continue to write. However, if the suspect still refuses, the interrogator should attempt to obtain the partially written narrative. A suspect in this state of mind will often attempt to retain the partially written document. Sometimes the document can be obtained through the ruse of offering a waste paper basket for the scrap paper. Many suspects will, without thinking, throw the incomplete statement away. It can then be recovered later by the interrogator. In cases where the suspect is in custody, the interrogator may be able to obtain the partially written statement prior to the suspect's being returned to his holding cell.

Generally, a suspect who begins to write a statement will complete the document. However, the interviewer/interrogator should protect the statement page by page. Never leave it in the room with the suspect, should it become necessary to leave. Some suspects, upon completion of the statement, will attempt the ruse of asking to see it again so they can add something to the statement. The interrogator should never return the original statement to the suspect, except page by page for signature, but rather offer a clean piece of paper for the suspect to add whatever he feels necessary.

On occasion, the suspect may request a copy of his statement. This request can be granted unless it is contrary to department or company policy. The statement is available to the defense under discovery rules, so there is little danger of compromising the case. However, if there are other suspects to be confronted on the case at a later time, the interrogator may wish to delay turning a copy of the statement over until the other interrogations are complete.

## Transcription of the Statement

In those instances where a formal statement was obtained from the suspect using a court reporter or by shorthand, the interrogator should have the notes transcribed for signature by the suspect. In the event that shorthand was used, the secretary should be instructed to make several intentional errors per page on the typed document. While reading the typed statement with the suspect, these errors will be found, corrected and initialled by the suspect.

The tapes and/or stenographer's notes should be maintained in case of the necessity for assuring the accuracy of the transcription. The stenographer should date and initial the steno book or transcript to establish its authenticity. In the event an audio or video recording was made of the suspect's confession, a transcription of these tapes may be done as part of the preparation for trial or hearing. The original tapes should be marked and secured in such a manner that they cannot be taped over. In the event a court reporter was used to take the statement, he will return a formal document that can be reviewed and signed by the suspect at a later date.

## Witnessing the Written Statement

After the statement has been completed the document should be witnessed by the interrogator and a witness. The interrogator will sign his name to each page of the statement along with the date and time. The witness shall also place his or her name on the document immediately below the interrogator's signature.

In the event that the witness was not present when the written statement was obtained, the interviewer should bring the witness into the room to first witness the oral confession, then witness the written statement. The interrogator should have the suspect acknowledge that he did in fact write the statement, that the signature is his, and that the information contained within the statement is the truth. The interrogator also should elicit from the suspect several verbal admissions that confirm the substantiation contained in the statement. By verbally witnessing the suspect's oral statement and having the suspect acknowledge the truthfulness of his handwritten statement, the interrogator has now provided another witness able to testify to the suspect's admission.

## Completion of Other Documents

The written statement is not the end point of most investigations. The written statement may establish probable cause for a search warrant or develop other investigative leads that need to be followed up. The interrogator at this point in the case may find it necessary to search the suspect's residence, business, or vehicle. Although a written statement made by the suspect against his interests may provide sufficient probable cause to obtain a search warrant, the interrogator can often obtain the suspect's consent to search his home, business, or vehicle. The consent to search form outlines the locations to be searched and documents the suspect's authorization for the search. Like the written statement, the suspect's verbal and written consent for the search should be witnessed.

The interrogator should remember that a suspect can give permission to search only locations over which he has control. A son or daughter cannot give permission to search the residence of their parents. However, they may be able to give consent to search only their room within that residence. The interrogator should make every attempt to recover evidence indicated in the statement. Many prosecutors will not prosecute an individual on his statement alone without corroborating evidence. The recovery of evidence will bolster the statement's believability and add to the prosecution's case.

Another standard form commonly used is a restitution agreement. Many private sector interrogators obtain a restitution agreement from the suspect acknowledging his indebtedness to the company for the amount of the admission. The restitution form also establishes a payment plan to reimburse the company for the loss. Prior to accepting any funds, or obtaining a restitution agreement, the interrogator should determine whether it is the company's intent to criminally prosecute the individual. As a general rule, if the company elects to accept restitution from a suspect, they cannot also prosecute the individual.

Any other forms necessary to complete the termination of a suspect from the company should be presented at this point. In many cases, the company official responsible for the termination of the suspect's employment will have the suspect fill out the necessary forms. A suspect in police custody may have to complete an arrest report or other document to account for personal effects or an impounded vehicle.

## The Written Report

Whenever an interrogation has been concluded, whether it is successful or not, the interrogator should prepare a written report detailing the admissions and circumstances surrounding the interrogation. Any unusual requests or problems that occur during the interrogation should be fully noted and documented. In the event that the suspect was allowed to go to the washroom or was fed during the interrogation, this should also be duly noted.

Any documentation of the feeding of the suspect should also be retained. In many instances, a department will bring in food from the outside. It may be beneficial to have the suspect who is to be fed write his order on a menu or piece of paper and place his name on it. In this way, it can be added to the case file to substantiate that the suspect was not deprived of food or drink during the interrogation. This is especially important where the interrogation and case development takes a number of hours or even days.

The interrogator's notes taken during the interrogation should also be maintained in the case file. This is especially important should the suspect have initialled or made sketches on the interrogator's notes. Any sketches on other pieces of paper that illustrate the method of entry or theft or any other illustration should have been initialled by the suspect and maintained in the case file. Each of these may have significant evidentiary value, and should be safeguarded in the same way that the written statement was safeguarded.

# Ending the Interview

# 13

*The only interviewer/interrogator with a
100% confession rate is one who has
not yet talked to enough people.*

The final stage in any interview or interrogation is its close. In this final stage, the interviewer/interrogator's objective is to end the interview or interrogation in a professional and courteous manner, regardless of whether it was successful or unsuccessful.

Obviously, a successful interview or interrogation means that the interviewer/interrogator has obtained information that is helpful to his case. However, an interviewer/interrogator does not always obtain the necessary information, which can create an uncomfortable situation.

The interviewer/interrogator may be embarrassed or frustrated because he was unable to get an admission from an untruthful suspect. The professional interviewer/interrogator is the one who identifies when the process will end unsuccessfully. He then accepts the outcome, putting his own feelings aside, and changes from an accusatory to nonaccusatory tone. It is much easier for an interviewer/interrogator to accept success rather than failure. The professional interviewer/interrogator recognizes that he is not always going to be successful. The only interviewer/interrogator with a 100% confession rate is one who has not yet talked to enough people.

Each interview and interrogation can be a learning experience for the interviewer/interrogator. Assessing what he did correctly and more importantly, incorrectly, the interviewer/interrogator learns from talking with each witness or suspect. This practical experience cannot be gained in a book or classroom.

In this chapter, we will consider how to back out of an unsuccessful interview or interrogation as well as how to conclude a successful one. Finally, the ethical considerations of the interrogator will be discussed.

## Professional Close

Regardless of the reasons for the suspect's lack of cooperation, the interviewer/interrogator should close the interview on a positive note. By leaving the door open for future cooperation or meetings, the interviewer enhances the likelihood of gaining future cooperation or information from the witness. The interviewer who fails to close the interview professionally and courteously risks the possibility that the witness may not cooperate in this or future investigative efforts.

The interviewer who talks with a suspect but fails to gain an admission of guilt may have been successful in eliciting information that can be used later to the investigator's advantage. An important consideration for the interviewer is to close the encounter in such a way that the door is left open for the possibility of future cooperation.

The interviewer should leave a card with his name and phone number and encourage the victim or witness to call him if any other information comes to mind. In many instances, victims or witnesses will recall other significant details after the close of the interview. Although the initial interview failed to obtain these details, an individual who has been encouraged to call with other information may report the details to the interviewer. The interviewer should not be hesitant to recontact significant witnesses to determine if they recalled any other information.

At the close of the interview, the interviewer may want to take time to continue to establish rapport with the victim or witness by finding a common interest. Establishing a solid rapport often has far-reaching benefits for the interviewer that last long after the interview has been concluded. Taking time to make the victim or witness feel even more comfortable about giving information often ensures their later cooperation when the case reaches a hearing or court. The personal relationship established between the interviewer and the victim or witness often goes a long way in assuring their continued cooperation. Many victims and witnesses who are reluctant to cooperate in a hearing may do so because they do not want to disappoint the interviewer who has shown them consideration and respect.

## The Unsuccessful Interview/Interrogation

A more complex issue is backing out of an interrogation with a suspect. The reasons for the interviewer/interrogator's failure will vary from individual to individual and circumstance to circumstance. Regardless of the reason for the failure, the interrogator must back out of the interrogation and put the suspect back to work or release him from custody. The suspect has achieved at least a momentary victory, and the interrogator may be required to swallow his pride when releasing the guilty suspect. It is difficult for anyone to face a mocking, condescending individual gloating over his victory. It is even worse when that individual is a criminal.

In police interrogations, an abrupt halt to an interrogation comes when a suspect invokes his right to silence or counsel. Other reasons to back out are the amount of time the interrogation has taken and a suspect who is able to explain away incriminating evidence developed in the investigation. Although the reasons for concluding an interrogation vary, they require that the interrogator cease the conversation and conclude the encounter.

The best interrogators recognize that not all interrogations will be successful and understand that there is an appropriate time to end an interrogation. Although tempting, it is unwise for an interrogator to resort to desperate measures to obtain an admission in the closing moments of an interrogation. Resorting to desperate tactics in an attempt to gain an admission rarely results in an admission, but rather creates only an unfortunate situation. Attempting desperate measures to fix an interrogation is much like kicking a machine to make it work. Only in very rare instances will the properly placed blow result in the machine functioning properly. Generally, when an interrogator resorts to desperate measures to obtain a confession, it is of questionable value. Judges, juries, and hearing officers decide on the voluntariness of a confession based upon the totality of circumstances. The interrogator who interrogates a suspect for long periods of time in an effort to obtain a confession may damage an otherwise prosecutable case.

The interrogator should be professional and courteous even when he has been frustrated and embarrassed by his inability to obtain the confession. Calling the suspect names, yelling, screaming, or otherwise threatening and intimidating a suspect is never appropriate behavior for the interrogator. Although the interrogator may momentarily feel emotionally relieved by using these methods, they rarely cause a person to confess and are more likely to create significant problems later.

In other situations, the interrogator presses an interrogation too long and angers the suspect. It is unlikely that an interrogator who angers his suspect will obtain an admission of guilt. The suspect's anger can dominate an otherwise excellent interrogator simply because the suspect becomes aggressive.

Once the interrogator has concluded that the likelihood of an admission of guilt is unattainable, he should begin the process of backing out. The backing out process entails a subtle change in questioning that allows the suspect to enter the conversation. The interrogator may now present his factual evidence that indicates the suspect's guilt. The presentation of the evidence may break the suspect's resolve and result in an admission. However, if the suspect remains unaffected by the evidence and continues to maintain his innocence, the interrogator should begin to move into secondary topics. The interrogator changes direction from the specific issue to a secondary issue. This secondary issue could be the theft of other money or merchandise, a different crime, or the suspect's knowledge of who is actually responsible. If the interrogator obtains an admission, he begins the process of development with the suspect.

If he fails to gain an admission, however, he moves into the interview phase of the interrogation. In this phase of the interrogation, the interrogator begins to ask the suspect open-end questions that require the suspect to talk. Many of the facts or behavior-provoking questions noted in Chapter 6 of this text can be used in backing out of the interview. The interrogator may begin by asking the suspect if he knows or has an idea about who is responsible for the incident. The interrogation has now moved from confrontational tone to one of eliciting information from the suspect. Often, the information given by the guilty while backing out will be untruthful. The suspect may tell blatant lies while trying to cover his tracks. The interrogator should remain alert for statements that may further incriminate the suspect.

The change in who talks allows the suspect to enter the conversation. This provides several benefits for the interrogator. First, it allows the interrogator to present his evidence and have the suspect make his explanation. Second, the suspect can release some of his built up frustration at being accused. The suspect is going to want to explain his innocence. By letting the suspect talk, the interrogator allows the suspect to release his frustration. At the same time, the interrogator focuses on reasons why the interrogation took place. Finally, the interrogator shifts to asking questions that direct the suspect's attention on the future. Future-oriented questions might include these:

How do you see your future here at the company?

Where do you see yourself being in five years?

Do you have plans on returning to school?

What type of career path do you see yourself taking?

The interrogator should not apologize for confronting the suspect. Rather, he should shift the blame to the investigation and focus the suspect's attention on other areas of the incident or the future.

Regardless of the reasons for backing out, once the interrogator has neutralized the situation by changing the interrogation into an interview, he courteously indicates that the interview is at an end and thanks the suspect for his cooperation. At the conclusion of the encounter, the suspect should be told that the investigation is still open and ongoing. The interrogator should attempt to have the suspect agree to come back and discuss the case again should it become necessary. The suspect who agrees to return for another interview often does so. Many interrogators fail to obtain this agreement from the suspect and thus lose the opportunity of a later meeting.

There may be times when a suspect refuses to admit anything, but the evidence alone is sufficient to terminate his employment or to prosecute. In these situations, the interrogator should still professionally and courteously close the interview. If the suspect is to be arrested, then he is detained. If the suspect's employment is to be terminated, he should be asked to wait until the interrogator returns. The interrogator may offer refreshments or the use of the washroom to the suspect while he is absent. The interrogator should document the offers in his notes. This allows the interviewer time to present the investigative evidence to the individual responsible for making the decision to terminate.

In certain situations, the suspect may be returned to his job or released from custody when the interrogator fails to obtain an admission of guilt. If the suspect is returned to work or released from custody, the interrogator should review what was said during the interrogation and look for new information or investigative avenues that may have been revealed by the suspect. In situations where the suspect is to be released, the interrogator should let the suspect know that he can call the interrogator to talk. Only rarely does a suspect later call and confess his involvement, but it does happen.

Sometimes a suspect only needs time to consider the justifications and rationalizations offered by the interrogator. After he has had time to consider his alternative, he may elect to confess his involvement. As surprising as these later confessions might be, they do occur, although infrequently. The interrogator would never have had the opportunity to resolve these cases if he had closed unprofessionally with the suspect. By leaving the door open for communication and cooperation, the interrogator achieved a successful close to an otherwise unsolved case.

## Support for the Suspect

During and following an interrogation, the interrogator must recognize a suspect's emotional needs. The suspect is at a low point in his life and sees no hope for the future. The interrogator must support the suspect emotionally and attempt to focus his attention on positive aspects of the future, rather than his immediate situation. An interrogator who gloats or enjoys the suffering of the suspect is unprofessional and will not be respected by his peers.

## The End of the Interview

Once the suspect has given a complete admission of guilt and a written statement, the interrogator should prepare to make a presentation of the case's facts and admission to the prosecutor or person responsible for the termination of the employee. The interrogator should make the presentation of the facts and admission in a professional manner without gloating or making unnecessary harsh comments about the suspect.

Often there is a period following the interrogation when an awkward silence between the suspect and interrogator ensues. Many times a suspect would like to talk about something simply to get his mind off of his troubles. This is an opportunity for the interrogator to develop information about the tactics and techniques he employed to obtain the confession. The interrogator has an opportunity to talk with the suspect and get insight on the techniques from the suspect himself. Many times, the suspect will explain the feelings he had during the interrogation. These explanations often clarify behavioral patterns and observations that the interrogator made during the interrogation. This is an opportunity for learning that can be of immense value for the interrogator. This time also affords the interrogator an opportunity to continue to support the suspect emotionally as the realization of the consequences begins to become evident.

## Final Report

The interrogator should prepare a final report regarding the interview or interrogation while it is still fresh in his mind. Waiting clouds the memory and could result in the omission of pertinent statements made by the suspect. The interviewer/interrogator should clearly and concisely note the verbal statements made by the victim, witness, or suspect, as well as the circumstances of the interview. He should also note instances where the victim, witness, or suspect obtained refreshment or used the washroom. The suspect's mental state at the time of the admission may be important in evaluating the totality of circumstances. These notations may directly relate to the voluntariness and admissibility of the suspect's statements.

## Ethical Considerations

The interrogator should consider the moral and ethical guidelines that come with being a member of the law enforcement community. Many investigators feel a sense of frustration because they are restrained by court rulings or policy guidelines in their effort to resolve cases and identify the guilty. Often the lament of "Why should I play by the rules when they don't?" is heard. The interrogator should recognize that little separates the honest from the guilty. Often, it is merely the honest individual's adherence to the legal, ethical, and moral guidelines that separates the two parties. Following the rules is difficult, especially when the interviewer/interrogator has emotionally extended himself to resolve the case.

It is difficult for an interviewer/interrogator to reconcile the time and effort he puts in on a case with the end result. It is frustrating for an interrogator to see the criminal released from custody or put back to work when he knows that the person is guilty. By allowing himself to become emotionally involved, the interviewer/interrogator can easily make the bad decision not to play by the rules. The interviewer/interrogator and investigator must recognize that their job is to separate themselves and their work from the final outcome of the case. Although the final outcome is certainly predicated on the work that they have done, a court or hearing officer who does not convict the suspect is no reflection on the superb job done by the investigative community. Once the interviewer/interrogator recognizes that his job function is limited to the gathering of information and its presentation to the prosecution, the more emotionally secure he will be in the job he has done. The judge or hearing officer who refuses to accept the validity of the confession has to make his determination on case law and the information presented. An interrogator or interviewer who carefully prepares his case, recognizes the rights of the suspect, and follows the legal guidelines has done the best job possible.

The interview and interrogation of victims, witnesses, and suspects can be a frustrating and a rewarding task. The success or failure of the interviewer/interrogator is often a direct result of the insights and effort that he puts forth in resolving a case. Even a lifetime of study of the process will not enable an interrogator to have a 100% confession rate. However, by being aware of the needs of the suspect, the legal constraints, and the guidelines, the interviewer/interrogator can increase his success and the likelihood of a successful case resolution.

# About the Authors

David E. Zulawski is a 1973 graduate of Knox College, Galesburg, Illinois, from which he received a Bachelor of Arts degree. After graduating, Mr. Zulawski spent two years with the Chicago & Northwestern Railroad as a Special Agent. During that time, he investigated thefts from interstate shipments in transit.

Mr. Zulawski left the railroad to accept a position with the Barrington, Illinois, Police Department. As a police officer, his duties included patrol, investigations, and working as an evidence technician. In addition, he presented seminars on crime and rape prevention to groups in the Barrington area.

In 1978, Mr. Zulawski left the police department to attend the Reid College of Detection of Deception to become a polygraph examiner. He then joined the staff of John E. Reid & Associates as a polygraph examiner and later became the Director of the Police and Fire Applicant Screening Division of the company. Mr. Zulawski also instructed at the Reid College and the Criminal Interrogation Seminar, which is presented to law enforcement and private security personnel.

In October, 1980, Mr. Zulawski joined Reid Psychological Systems, an affiliate of John E. Reid & Associates that markets paper and pencil honesty tests, as a sales representative.

Mr. Zulawski is a licensed polygraph examiner in Illinois and Indiana and has personally conducted over 8,000 interviews and polygraph examinations. He is also a member of the American Polygraph Society, the Illinois Polygraph Society, the Special Agents Association, and the American Society for Industrial Security.

Douglas E. Wicklander received his B.S. degree from Athens College, Athens, Alabama, in 1971 and his M.S. degree in the detection of deception from Reid College in 1972.

Mr. Wicklander was employed by John E. Reid & Associates from June 1971 to October 1980 as a polygraph examiner and instructor at their school of polygraph and criminal interrogation. During this time, he was named Director of the company's Behavioral Analysis Interview Division. In this capacity, he worked extensively with John Reid in the development of the Behavioral Analysis Interview Division.

In October, 1980, Mr. Wicklander was assigned as a sales representative with Reid Psychological Systems, an affiliate of John E. Reid & Associates, which markets paper and pencil honesty tests for job applicants and existing employees.

Mr. Wicklander is a licensed polygraph examiner in the states of Illinois and Indiana. He has personally conducted over 10,000 polygraph examinations and interviews. He is a member of the American Society for Industrial Security, Special Agents Association, American Polygraph Association, and the Illinois Polygraph Society.

In May, 1982, Mr. Zulawski and Mr. Wicklander formed their own company, Wicklander-Zulawski & Associates, Inc. The firm specializes in the investigation of internal losses through the use of interview, investigation, and polygraph techniques. In addition, they conduct loss prevention surveys, preemployment background investigations, and training seminars. The firm is nationally recognized as the standard of the industry in conducting seminars on interview and interrogation techniques.

Mr. Zulawski and Mr. Wicklander produced an audio cassette program entitled, "Interview and Interrogation Techniques." In addition, they served as subject matter experts in the development of a comprehensive computer/interactive video training program entitled, "The Art of Interviewing—The Integrity Interview." This training program instructs the loss prevention/security professional on the complexities of interview and interrogation techniques. Furthermore, they wrote an in-house training program that companies use to train their own staff, in-house, on interview and interrogation techniques.

Since 1982, Wicklander-Zulawski & Associates, Inc. has trained thousands of individuals on interviewing and interrogation techniques. These seminars address the proper way to obtain legally acceptable confessions and the content and form a written statement should take. Mr. Zulawski and Mr. Wicklander have written several articles on the polygraph technique and interview and interrogation. They have lectured on these topics to professional and civic organizations throughout the country.

Wicklander-Zulawski & Associates, Inc., is licensed by John E. Reid & Associates, Inc., originator and developer of the method, to teach the Reid Method of Criminal Interviews & Interrogation.

# Index

**A**

Abdominal area
protection by knee, 80–87
protection of by untruthful suspect,
79–80, 85
Accident, as rationalization, with choice
questions, 216
Accusation
and attitude of interviewer/
interrogator, 171
by interviewer, 159
as last step in investigative process,
171–199
denial after, 228
direct, 175–179
as cause of denial, 122
introduction for, 177
problems with, 179
sequence to use, 177–179
use of to refute suspect's denials,
176–177
during interrogation, 9
factual approach, 174–175
participatory, 188–189
construction of, 189–192
and positioning of interviewer/
interrogator, 172
and rationalizations, 179
repeating, 178–179
selection of, 173–192
soft, 186–187
and use of follow-up question,
187
Actors, and deceptive behavior, 62
Adam's apple, quiver in untruthful
suspect, 92

Admission
behavioral clues of, 257–259
development of, 10–11, 271–289
first, techniques for expanding, 275–283
minor, tactic of untruthful suspect,
102
obtaining, 10, 243-270
in statement, 305
suspect about to make, 253f
use of exaggeration to encourage, 277
use of investigation as wedge to
encourage, 277–278
use of soft accusation to obtain, 251
as written statement, 292–293
Alcohol, as rationalization, with choice
questions, 221–222
Alcohol intoxication, and voluntariness
of confession, 40–41
Alcohol use
effect on suspect's behavior, 61
suspect denial based on, 127
Alibi
pinning suspect down on details of,
165–167
as written statement, 292–293
Appearance, of interviewer/interrogator,
142
Arm barriers, and untruthful suspect,
79-80
Assault, definition, 49
Assumptive question, 276–277
acknowledgment of by suspect, 256–257
use of by interrogator, 248, 250–256
Attitude, interrogator's, as cause of
denial, 115
Attorney, Sixth Amendment right to, 44

Auditory mode
neurolinguistics, 146
respiratory pattern, 147
voice characteristics, 147
Autonomic nervous system
and cold and clammy hands, 75
dry mouth response, 92
effects of self-preservation aspects of on
suspect's behavior, 64–65
increased heart rate and blood pressure,
92–93
and itching, 77
and responses in body, 73


**B**
Background information, obtaining prior
to interview/interrogation, 15–16
Battery
definition, 49
interrogator susceptible to charges of,
247
*Beckwith v. United States*, issue of
custody and Miranda rights, 37
Behavior
cautions in interpreting, 59–64
clustering of types and evaluation of
truthfulness, 56–57
consistency, 58–59
deceptive, and professional criminals,
actors, and politicians, 62–63
effect of cultural, ethnic, and geographic differences on, 61
effect of fear of detection on, 63–64
effect of fight or flight on, 64–65
effect of medical condition on, 61
effect of mental capacity on, 60–61
faking, 53–54
of interviewer/interrogator, 142–143
nonverbal, interpretation, 69–93
role of personal biases in assessing, 60
rules for evaluating, 54–59
suspect's, and choice of rationalization,
207–210
timing, 58–59
typical attitudes displayed by suspects,
66–69
use of to control interrogation, 233
verbal and physical, interpretation, 51–
108
when suspect is about to make
admission, 257–259
Behavioral norm, identification of by
interviewer/interrogator, 54–55
Behavioral zones, elliptical, surrounding
body, 114

Benefit statement, to sell witness on
benefit of interview, 149–150
Biographical information
including in suspect's statement, 304–
305
review of at beginning of interrogation,
181
suspect's, obtaining during interview,
168–169
Body position, and evaluation of emphatic
denial, 238
Body posture, suspect in admission, 244
Borrowing, as rationalization, with choice
questions, 222
*Brown v. Mississippi*, and third-degree
tactics, 34


**C**
Camera evidence, closed circuit,
implying with enticement
questions, 167
Carotid artery, observation during
interview/interrogation, 65
Case file, use of during interrogation, 17–18
Choice question
and denial, 229
after soft accusation, 254–256
Choice question/soft accusation, used to
test suspect's susceptibility, 249–250
Civil Rights Act of 1965, Title VII, as
applied to interview/interrogation,
44
Co-conspirator
and importance of obtaining
background information, 15
involvement of as basis for suspect's
denial, 128
Cognitive interview techniques, use of,
160–161
Collective bargaining agreement, and
right to an attorney, 44
Collusion cases, interview/interrogation
strategies, 28–29
Common ground, method of establishing
rapport by interviewer/
interrogator, 141–145
Common law, as applied to interview/
interrogation, 45–46
Competency hearing, and waiving of
constitutional rights, 40
Complaints, nature of in truthful and
untruthful suspects, 93–95
Confession
benefit versus consequence evaluation
of, 110

Confession [cont.]
 development of from admission, 10–11,
  271–289
 and Exclusionary Rule, 36
 importance of presence of witness for,
  300, 302–303
 legal decisions clarifying, 34–35
 must be voluntary, 302–306
 need for interrogator to offer acceptable
  rationalization to obtain, 118
 obtaining the admission, 243–270
 offer of leniency and admissibility of,
  41
 requirement of voluntariness, 35–36
 transition statement by interrogator
  when suspect is close to, 186
 use of assumptive questions to obtain,
  250–256
 and use of soft accusation/assumptive
  question, 186–187
 use of trickery or lying to obtain, 35–36
 voluntariness and alcohol or narcotics
  intoxication, 40–41
Congruence, definition, 52
Consequences, highlighting of may cause
  denial, 119
Consequences versus justifications,
  evaluation of by suspect as basis
  for denial, 127–128
Constitutional amendments, applying to
  interview/interrogation, 33–34
Constitutional rights, waiver of by
  youths and incompetents, 39–40
Control, loss of, as rationalization, with
  choice questions, 220
Control question, use of during interview,
  163
Conversation, information about
  developed by cognitive interview
  techniques, 161
Corporate sector, methods of establishing
  management rapport, 139–141
Counsel
 right to after indictment, 39
 suspect's demand for during
  interrogation, 38
Court reporter, for formal statement, 295
Credibility, establishing of by
  interviewer/interrogator, 171–199
Crime, reaction to differs according to
  nature of, 63–64
Criminal activity, substantiation of
  amounts of and involvement,
  278–283
Criminals
 professional, and deceptive behavior, 62

 violent, nature of behavioral zones
  surrounding, 114
Cultural differences
 as basis for denial, 126–127
 effect on behavior, 61
Current events, use of to illustrate
  rationalizations, 212–213
Custody
 issue of and Miranda warnings in
  statement, 297
 and suspect's Miranda rights, 36

D
Deception, verbal slip as indication,
  107–108
Defamation of character, and interview/
  interrogation, 46–47
Defensiveness
 and crossed-arm behavior, 80
 leg and feet positions, 80–87
Demeanor, of interviewer/interrogator,
  142
Denials, 227–242
 absolute, and use of evidence, 287–288
 based on cultural differences, 127
 based on drug and alcohol use, 127
 based on evaluation of consequences
  versus justifications, 127–128
 based on involvement of co-conspirator,
  128
 based on lack of rules, 126
 based on suspect's perception of the
  seriousness of the lie, 124–126
 causes of, 109–129
  compromised investigation, 121–122
  highlighting consequences, 119
  interrogator waiting beyond optimum
   point to obtain confession, 124
  interrogator's failure to reaccuse, 124
  interviewer/interrogator, 115–124
  poorly timed question, 124
  rationalization personalized too
   early, 119
  silence of interviewer/interrogator,
   119–120
 effect of environment, 113–114
  suspect's belief that interrogator
   cannot prove allegation, 121
 emphatic, truthful, 237–239
 explanatory, 239–242
 factors causing, 112
 forms of, 9–10
 increased likelihood of in supportive
  environment, 113–114
 questioning techniques as cause of, 122

Denials [cont.]
  as stall for time, 122–123
  statement of by interrogator for
    suspect, 232–233
  strength of in truthful versus untruthful
    suspect, 108
  truthful, 128–129
  types, 227–228
  use of enticement question to stop,
    236–237
Detection, fear of
  effect on behavior, 63–64
  physiological responses, 65
Dissonance, definition, 109–110
Distractions
  objects of potential use in punishment,
    21–22
  in room setting for interview, 20–21
  by suspect, 21–23
Documents, during interview, 157
Drug use
  effect on suspect's behavior, 61
  as rationalization, with choice
    questions, 221–222
  suspect denial based on, 127


E
Economy, as rationalization, with choice
  questions, 219
Edwards v. Arizona, and suspect's
  invoking right of counsel, 38
Emblem
  definition, 52
  during emphatic denial, 230
  use to control interrogation, 233
Emotion, during interview/interrogation,
  65–66
Emotional approach, interrogation, 2–5
  modified by factual component, 3
Emotional distress, charge of infliction,
  49–50
Emphatic denial, 9, 228
  handling by interrogator, 230–237
  truthful, 237–239
  use of by suspect, 229–230
Employee
  charge of emotional distress caused by
    interview, 49–50
  effect of interview on morale, 140
  employer's legal liabilities in interview
    of, 45–50
  rules for termination, 189
Employer
  decision to prosecute employee and
    malicious prosecution, 47–49

legal liabilities in interview of em-
    ployee, 45–50
  private, and Fifth Amendment rights of
    employees, 42–43
  public, and Fifth Amendment rights of
    employees, 42
Employment termination, as result of
  private sector investigation, 5–7
Enticement, questions of
  use of during interview, 165–168
  use of to stop denial, 236–237
Environment
  for interview/interrogation, 59–60
  role in precipitating denials, 113–114
  supportive
    and increased likelihood of denial,
      113–114
    value of in interviewing victim or
      small child, 113–114
Escobedo decision, and right to counsel,
  35, 39
Estelle v. Smith, and Miranda rights, 36
Ethical considerations, 318–319
Ethnic differences, effect on behavior, 61
Evidence
  considerations, 14–15
  developed as result of involuntary
    confession, 36
  during interview, 157
  presence of during interrogation, 17–18
  when to reveal during interrogation,
    287–288
  wrong or incomplete, use of by
    interrogator and suspect denial,
    120–121
Exaggeration, use of to encourage
  admission, 277
Exclusionary Rule, and evidence developed
  as result of involuntary confession,
  36
Excuses, premature, in untruthful
  suspects, 95
Explanation, premature, in untruthful
  suspects, 95
Explanatory denial, 9–10, 228, 239–242
  typical introductory phrases, 239
Eye contact
  differences in cultural, ethnic, and
    geographic groups, 61–62
  during emphatic denial, 230
  during truthful emphatic denial, 237–
    239
  interpretation, 90–91
  nature of in normal conversation
    versus interview/interrogation,
    57–58

Eye contact [cont.]
  poor, 90
  suspect in submission, 244, 250
  use of by interrogator, 184
  use to control interrogation, 233
  with suspect in submission, 246
  with suspect making denial, 259
  with suspect toward end of soft
    accusation, 252
Eye movement
  interpretation, 90–91
  neurolinguistic, evaluating, 152–157
  neurolinguistics of, 154f
Eyes
  bug-eyed, 90
  cold, 90
  flat look, 90
    indicative of nonreceptive behavior,
      207
    screening of by hands during deception,
      77
Eyewitness, implying with enticement
  questions, 167


F

Face-saving, offered to suspect after soft
  accusation, 255
Factual approach, interrogation, 2
Fair Labor Standards Act, as applied to
  interview/interrogation, 44
False imprisonment, and interview/
  interrogation, 46
Faniel v. Chesapeake & Potomac
  Telephone Company, and false
  imprisonment, 46
Federal statutes, applying to interview/
  interrogation, 44
Feet, position,
  flat on floor and truthful suspect, 85–86
  indicates when suspect is ready to
    leave, 83–85
Fifth Amendment
  and interview/interrogation, 33
  rights, of employees of public and
    private employers, 42–43
Fight or flight, effect of on behavior, 64–65
Financial pressure, as rationalization, 214
First name, suspect's, use of in obtaining
  admission, 246
Follow-up question
  to soft accusation, 253–254
  use of after soft accusation, 187
Foot
  circling or tapping, indication of
    impatience, 84

position in relation to interviewer/
  interrogator, 81
Formal statement, 295
Fourteenth Amendment, and interview/
  interrogation, 33–34
Fourth Amendment, and interview/
  interrogation, 33
Frazier v. Cupp, and obtaining confession
  with trickery and lying, 35–36
Fruit of the poisonous tree, 36


G

Gardner v. Broderick
  and coercion of statement from public
    employee, 42
  and rights of public versus private
    employees, 43
Garrity v. New Jersey, and Fifth
  Amendment rights of employees
  of public employers, 42
Geographic differences, effect on behavior,
  61
Geographic responses, and excessive politeness and respectfulness, 97–98
Gestures
  diminished during lying behavior, 76
  use to control interrogation, 233
Good guy/bad guy approach, 2
Guilt
  admission with offer of restitution in
    untruthful suspect, 105–107
  first admission, 10
  transfer
    as rationalization, with choice ques-
      tions, 217, 218
    by suspect through rationalization,
      202


H

Hand and arm positions, in truthful and
  untruthful individuals, 73–80
Hands
  cold and clammy, in untruthful sus-
    pects, 75
  message conveyed to interviewer/
    interrogator by, 77–79
  and screening of eyes during deception,
    77
  steepling, interpretation, 78
Handshake, evaluation of, 55–56
Handwriting evidence, implying with
  enticement questions, 167
Hanging sentences, in untruthful suspect,
  101

*Harris v. New York*, and Miranda rights, 36
Head
  back position, 89
  down position, 89
  neutral position, 88
  tilting, 88
Head and neck positions, interpretation, 87–90
Heart rate, during interview/interrogation, 64
Helpfulness, excessiveness, in untruthful suspect, 97–98
Hidden agenda, and importance of obtaining background information, 15
Hope, concept of in interrogation, 203–204
Hurdle, as rationalization, with choice questions, 223–224

I
Illustrators, definition, 52
Impatience, circling or tapping of foot as indication of, 84
Impulse, as rationalization, with choice questions, 216
Incompetents, and waiver of constitutional rights, 39–40
Incongruence, definition, 52
Interest, area of, value of concealing by interviewer, 157
Interrogation
  applicability of Miranda decision to, 36
  and change in psychology of room, 234–236
  definition, 5, 132–133
  emotional approach, 2–5
  establishment of end point, 284–286
  factual approach, 2
  good guy/bad guy approach, 2
  history, 1–2
  and Miranda warning, 36–38
  points at which denials occur, 228–229
  presence of evidence during, 17–18
  purpose, 4
  revealing evidence during final stages, 287–288
  shift of interview to, 159–160
  suspect's demand for counsel during, 38
  suspect's realization process in, 127
  time limit, 198–199
  use of behavior to control, 233
  use of case file during, 17–18
  use of introductory statement, 179–182

Interrogator
  advising suspect regarding lying, 232
  assessing truthfulness of suspect in establishing level of in criminal activity, 284
  attitude as cause of denial, 115
  avoidance of threats or promises, 213–214
  avoiding physical contact with suspect, 246–248
  behavior of, 181
  closing physically with suspect in submission, 245
  and concept of hope, 203–204
  control of statement from suspect, 297
  controlling of suspect in submission, 246
  countering suspect interruptions, 199
  development of the admission, 271–289
  development of suspect's knowledge of criminal activity, 288–290
  discussion of important areas with suspect, 231
  ethical outlook, 213–214
  exchanging roles with suspect, 236
  explanation of how investigations are conducted, 185
  explanation of role to private sector staff, 183
  failure to reaccuse can cause suspect denial, 124
  focus on emotionally significant issue, 125
  focusing suspect's attention on future or past, 210–211
  follow-up question to soft accusation, 253–254
  handling of emphatic denial by suspect, 230–237
  have suspect initial notes when suspect is unwilling to make written statement, 303
  impressions given by, 172
  introduction for direct accusation, 177
  and length of introductory statement, 187–188
  mental review of places with suspect, 823
  note-taking during suspect's admission, 274
  obtaining the admission, 243-270
  offering suspect positive outlook, 211
  perception of by suspect and denial, 117
  personality as cause of denial, 115
  poorly timed question can cause denial, 124

Interrogator [cont.]
preparation of written report, 310–311
questioning techniques as cause of denial, 122
reputation as cause of denial, 115
resistance-reducing techniques, 275–276
revealing strategy to suspect, 120
selection of strategy, 120
shortening and repeating of rationalizations to subject in submission, 244
statement of support to suspect, 272–273
stating denial for suspect, 232–233
supportive comments by to minimize suspect's admissions, 276
techniques for expanding suspect's first admission, 275–283
tentative and unconvincing behavior, 116–117
timing of taking of statement, 297–299
tone of voice as indicator of tentativeness, 117
and transition statement, 186
use of assumptive question, 248
to obtain confession, 250–256
use of choice question/soft accusation to test suspect's susceptibility, 249–250
use of enticement question to stop denial, 236–237
use of participatory accusation, 188–189
use of personal stories to illustrate rationalizations, 211–212
use of rationalization to reduce resistance, 201–225
use of soft accusation/assumptive question, 186–187
use of suspect's first name, 231
use of transition statement to test suspect in submission, 249
use of wrong or incomplete evidence, 120–121
use of wrong rationalizations by and denial, 118
value of changing during interrogation, 286–287
waiting beyond optimum point to obtain confession causes suspect denial, 124
Interview
allowing a narrative, 150–151
corporate sector, methods of establishing management rapport, 139–141

definition, 4–5, 131
effect on employee morale, 140
ending by interviewer/interrogator, 313–319
goal, 13–14
guidelines for private sector, 14
guidelines for public sector, 13–14
leading of by interviewer, 157
noncustodial stop-and-frisk, 18–19
as noncustody situation, 131–132
planned field, location of, 19
preplanning, 137, 138
purpose, 4
reluctance of witness to participate, 133
role of interviewer, 134
room setting, 19–21
selective technique, 161–165
selling witness on benefits, 149–150
shift to interrogation, 159–160
silence as effective tactic, 120
time and place, 133
use of cognitive techniques, 160–161
use of questions of enticement during, 165–168
Interview/Interrogation
and charges of defamation of character, 46–47
and charges of false imprisonment, 46
common law, 45–46
constitutional amendments applying, 33–34
developing the admission, 10–11
distractions during, 20–22
emotion during, 65–66
establishing credibility, 9
evidence considerations, 14–15
federal statutes, 45
information flow, 8f
interviewing, 7–9
language during, 24–27
legal aspects, 31–50
and malicious prosecution, 47–49
note-taking during, 27–28
obtaining admission, 10
obtaining background information on subject before, 15–16
overview of process, 7–11
as potential liability for employer, 47–49
preparation and strategy, 7, 13–29
privacy during, 18–19
profession close, 11
public sector rules, 34–35
reducing resistance, 9–10
rights of union members, 45
selective technique, 9

Interview/Interrogation [cont.]
  state laws applying, 45
  strategies, 28–29
  unsuccessful, 314–317
Interviewer
  challenging the untruthful witness,
       victim, or suspect, 158
  closing interview professionally, 169–
       170
  confronted by good liar, 164
  determining reasons for witness's
       reluctance, 150
  establishment of rapport with witness,
       139–149
  hearing the untainted story, 151–152
  obtaining biographical information of
       suspect, 168–169
  obtaining written statement, 169
  selection of, 16–17
  use of rationalizations, 158–159
  use of supporting tactics to help witness
       give information, 138–139
  value of concealing area of interest, 157
Interviewer/Interrogator
  appearance, 24, 142
  behavior, 142–143
  as cause of denials, 115–124
  cautions in interpreting behavior of
       suspect, 59–64
  continuing to establish rapport at end
       of interview, 314
  definition, 5
  delay in response to questions on, 98–
       102
  demeanor of, 142
  ending the interview, 313–322
  establishing credibility, 171–199
  establishing rapport with victim,
       witness, or suspect, 141–145
  ethical considerations, 318–319
  evaluation of suspect's handshake, 55–
       59
  final report, 318
  handling of lying by suspect, 58
  information gained from eye movements,
       152–157
  interpretation of nonverbal behavior,
       69–93
  interpretation of verbal behavior, 93–95
  interview behavior, 57–58
  making accusation, 171–199
  moving back into interview phase in
       unsuccessful interview, 316
  personal biases regarding suspect, 60
  positioning of in relation to subject, 114

  process of backing out at end of
       unsuccessful interview, 315–316
  role of, 23–24
  selling witness on benefits of interview,
       149–150
  support of suspect, 317
  use of language to justify actions of
       suspect, 26–27
  use of mirroring, 143–145
  use of silence may cause denials, 119–
       120
Interviewing, 131–170
Intoxication, alcohol or narcotics, and
       voluntariness of confession, 40–41
Introduction, of statement, 304–305
Introductory statement
  law enforcement, 266–270
  length of, 187–188
  loss prevention case, 259–266
  value to interrogator, 182f
Investigation
  compromised, as cause of suspect denial,
       121–122
  essential to factual approach, 3–4
  legal issues involved, 7
  levels of proof needed in private versus
       public sector investigation, 6
  private sector, levels of proof needed, 6
  public sector, levels of proof needed, 6
  public versus private sector approach,
       5–7
  use of as wedge to encourage admission,
       277–278
Investigations, explanation of how
       conducted, 185
Irrelevant points, focusing on by
       untruthful suspects, 96
Itch, fake, 77–78
Itching, autonomic nervous system
       response, 77


J

Job pressures, as rationalization, 214
Juveniles, and restrictions regarding
       interrogation, 40


K

Kickback cases, use of participatory
       accusation in, 189
Kinesic mode, neurolinguistics, 146
Kinesic pattern, voice characteristics, 147
Kinesic state, respiratory pattern, 147

## L

Language, during interview/interrogation, 24–27
Lansburgh's v. Ruffin, and false imprisonment, 46
Larynx, quiver in untruthful suspect, 92
Laughter, gallows, by untruthful suspect, 102
Law enforcement, introductory statement, 266–270
Law enforcement officials, off-duty, legal restrictions on interview/ interrogation, 32
Leakage, definition, 52
Legal aspects, interview/interrogation, 31–50
Legal issues, governing investigation, 7
Lego v. Twomey, and voluntary confession, 34
Legs, crossing method and defensiveness, 80–81
Legs and feet
  position in untruthful suspect, 82
  positions, interpretation, 80–87
Leniency, and admissibility of confession, 41
Libel, definition, 46
Lie, parameters for identifying, 53
Loss prevention
  case, introductory statement of interviewer, 266
  private sector
    and nonapplicability of Miranda decision, 43
    use of introductory statement, 182–187
  substantiation of amounts of and involvement, 278–283
Losses
  exaggeration, as rationalization, with choice questions, 220
  how they occur, 183–185
Lying, see also Behavior
  advising suspect regarding, 232
  belief in and behavior, 64
  benefit versus consequence evaluation of, 110
  and diminished movements and gestures, 76
  effect of on individual, 110
  fun coefficient, 110
  handling of by interviewer/ interrogator, 58
  justification of by suspect, 125

suspect's perception of seriousness of as cause of denial, 124–126
use of to obtain confession, 35–36

## M

Malicious prosecution, and interview/ interrogation, 47–49
Management
  corporate sector, establishing ground rules for interviews, 140
  possible role in wrongdoing and cooperation of, 140
Massiah decision
  and right-to-counsel, 35
  and right to counsel after indictment, 39
Mediator-negotiator, as role of interrogator/ interviewer, 23
Medical condition, effect on behavior, 61
Memory
  problems with in untruthful suspect, 104–105
  selective in untruthful suspect, 104–105
Mental capacity, effect on suspect's behavior, 60–61
Minimization, as rationalization, 214
Minnick v. Mississippi, and suspect's invoking right of counsel, 38
Miranda decision
  applicability to interrogation, 36
  and right against self-incrimination, 35
  role in investigation, 7
  and third-degree tactics, 43
Miranda rights
  and accusation, 176
  and presence of counsel during interrogation, 38
  in private sector interview/interrogation, 32
  and suspect's statement, 301
  suspect's understanding of, 38–39
  waiving of during interrogation, 37
Miranda rule, public safety exception to, 38–39
Miranda warning
  including in opening of statement, 305
  requirements, 36–38
  in statement, 297
Mirroring
  and rapport, 144f
  use of by interviewer/interrogator, 143–145
Motive of crime, and choice of proper rationalization, 204

use of by interviewer/interrogator, 143–
145
Motive of crime, and choice of proper
rationalization, 204
Motor coordination, fine, in untruthful
suspects, 75
Mouth
and created jobs, 91–92
dry in deceptive individual, 92
hand over, in untruthful suspects, 75–
76
positions, interpretation, 91–92

**N**

Names, information about developed by
cognitive interview techniques, 161
Narcotic intoxication, and voluntariness
of confession, 40–41
Narrative, allowing of in interview, 150–
151
Narrative statement, 294
National Labor Relations Act, as applied
to interview/interrogation, 44
Neck
interpretation of movements, 92
pulsation of arteries during questioning,
92–93
Nervousness
level of, relating to untruthful suspect,
55
in truthful and untruthful suspects,
68–69
Neurolinguistics
evaluating eye movement, 152–157
eye movement, 154f
physiological, techniques, 147–149
use of interviewer/interrogator, 145
verbal, techniques of, 145–146
New York v. Quarles, public safety
exception to Miranda rule, 38–39
NLRB v. J. Weingarten, Inc., and right of
union representation during
interview, 45
Nonresponses, types, 101–102
Nonverbal behavior
definition, 52
individualization, 54–55
interpretation, 69–93
Nose
and created jobs, 92
hand-to gesture to screen eyes and
mouth in untruthful suspect, 92
interpretation of movements, 92
Note-taking
advisability of, 27–28

importance of not having suspect do,
281–282
of interrogator during suspect's
admission, 274
Numbers, information about developed
by cognitive interview techniques,
161

**O**

Occupational Safety and General Health
Act, as applied to interview/
interrogation, 44
Offense, minimizing seriousness of as
rationalization, 210
Office, as room setting for interview, 20
Oregon v. Mathiason, and Miranda
warning, 37

**P**

Participatory accusation, 188–189
Pay, low, as rationalization, with choice
questions, 217
Payne v. Arkansas, and involuntary
confession, 34
Peer pressure, as rationalization, with
choice questions, 220
People v. Deborah C., and rights of public
versus private employees, 43
People v. Sleboda, intoxication and
voluntariness of confession, 40–41
Personal stories, use of to illustrate
rationalizations, 211–212
Personality, interrogator's, as cause of
denial, 115
Perspiration
during interview/interrogation, 64
in untruthful suspect, 73
Petty issues, focusing on by untruthful
suspects, 96
Physical appearances, information about
developed by cognitive interview
techniques, 161
Physical behavior, interpretation, 51–108
Physical contact, avoiding with suspect,
246–248
Physical evidence, implying with
enticement questions, 167
Physical force, renders confession
involuntary, 35
Police
interrogation room, 22–23,
items of authority as distractions
during interrogation, 21–23

Positive outlook
  offered to suspect by interrogator, 211
  as rationalization, 214
Posture
  change during emotionally significant
    question, 82–83
  defensive, 71
  interpretation of that of truthful versus
    untruthful suspect, 69
  slumping, 72
Preparation
  interview/interrogation, 13–29
  lack of in interrogator, and suspect's
    denial, 116–117
Privacy
  during interview/interrogation, 18–19
  emotional effect on suspect, 113
  zone of, 18
Private employers, and Fifth Amendment
    rights of employees, 42–43
Private sector
  compared with public sector approach
    to investigation, 5–7
  development of the admission, 271
  explanation of why employees make
    mistakes, 185–186
  interview guidelines, 14
  introductory statement in loss
    prevention case, 259–266
  legal aspects of interview/
    interrogation, 32
  methods to encourage witness
    cooperation, 139
  and rights of arrest, search, and seizure,
    32
  scope of case, 32–33
  selection of interviewer, 17
  use of introductory statement, 182–
    187
Professionalism
  of interviewer/interrogator, 11, 314
  and language use during interview/
    interrogation, 25–26
Promises, avoidance of by interrogator,
    213–214
Proof
  lack of perceived by suspect as cause of
    denial, 121
  levels needed in private versus public
    sector investigation, 6
Prosecution, as result of public sector
    investigation, 5–7
Psychology, of room, use of to control
    interrogation, 234–236
Public employers, and Fifth Amendment
    rights of employees, 42

Public law enforcement, and direct
    accusation of suspect, 176
Public safety, exception to Miranda rule,
    38–39
Public sector
  compared with private sector approach
    to investigation, 5–7
  development of the admission, 271
  interview guidelines, 13–14
  legal aspects of interview/
    interrogation, 31–32
  methods to encourage witness
    cooperation, 139
  rules applying to interview/
    interrogation, 34–35
  scope of case, 32–33

Q
Question
  assumptive, 186–187, 276–277
    acknowledgment of by suspect,
      256–257
    use of by interrogator, 248
  choice, after soft accusation, 254–256
  of choice, during submission phase, 10
  closed-end, used to lead interview, 157
  enticement, 165–168
    examples of, 167–168
    use of to stop denial, 236–237
  follow-up, to soft accusation, 253–254
  repeating of by untruthful suspect,
    99–100
  responding with by untruthful suspect,
    100
Question and answer statement, 294

R
Rapport
  continuing to establish at end of
    interview, 314
  and mirroring, 144f
  with witness, established by
    interviewer, 139–149
Rationalization
  basing assumptive question on, 248
  concept of, 202–204
  correcting, 224–225
  determining which to use, 204–210
  during submission phase, 10
  effect of on strength of denials in
    untruthful suspect, 108
  element of emotional approach to
    interrogation, 2–5
  examples, 214–215

Rationalization [cont.]
  explanation of why employees make
      mistakes, 185–186
  and focus on resolution of incident, 202
  illustrated by current events and
      topical news, 212–213
  illustrated by personal stories, 211–212
  minimizing seriousness of offense, 210
  need to individualize, 118
  and nonreceptive behavior of suspect,
      207
  and receptive behavior of suspect, 207
  shortening and repeating of to subject
      in submission, 244
  use of by interviewer, 158–159
  use of during interrogation, 10
  use of in participatory accusation, 191–
      192
  used with accusation, 179
  using to reduce resistance, 201–225
  with choice questions, 215–224
  wrong, use of by interrogator and
      suspect's denial, 118
Recollection, use of cognitive techniques
      to improve during interview, 160–
      161
Recording, audio or video
  for formal statement, 295–297
  of statement, 298–299
  questioning of, 300–301
Reinterview
  ability to, 159
  possibility of, 169
Repetition, during development of
      admission, 282–283
Reputation, interrogator's, as cause of
      denial, 115
Resistance
  reducing with rationalizations, 201–225
  truthful versus untruthful suspects,
      180f
Resistance-reducing techniques, 275–276
Resources, investigative, public sector
      compared with private sector, 6
Respectfulness, excessive, in untruthful
      suspect, 97
Respiration
  during interview/interrogation, 64
  pattern
    changes in deceptive individual, 73
    of as indication of dominant channel
        of communication, 147
    observation during interview/
        interrogation, 65
    of reflected in voice, 147
Restitution, offer of with admission of

guilt in untruthful suspect, 105–
      107
Restitution agreement, completion of
      after written statement, 309–310
Right-to-counsel cases, 35
Rogers v. Richmond, and involuntary
      confession, 34
Room setting
  distractions in, 20–21
  for interview, 19–21
Rules, lack of, as justification for suspect's
      behavior, 126


S

Search warrant, completion of after
      written statement, 309–310
Security, poor, as rationalization, with
      choice questions, 217–218
Selective interview technique, 9, 161–165
Self-incrimination
  rights of public employees, 42
  suspect's privilege against, 35
Silence
  as effective tactic in interview, 120
  by interviewer/interrogator, as cause of
      denials, 119–120
Sixth Amendment
  and interview/interrogation, 33
  right to attorney, 44
Skin, flushing and blanching, observation
      during interview/interrogation, 65
Slander, definition, 46
Smile
  interviewer/interrogator, 142
  phony, identification, 91
  sincere, identification, 91
  suspect's use of during interview/
      interrogation, 65–66
Soft accusation
  construction and working, 251–252
  follow-up question to, 253–254
  suspect's response to, 252
  use of to obtain admission, 251
Soft accusation/choice question, acceptance
      of by suspect, 272–275
Sources, uncheckable, reliance on by
      untruthful suspects, 95–96
Speech characteristics, information about
      developed by cognitive interview
      techniques, 161
Speech patterns, geographical differences
      in and behavior, 62
State laws, as applied to interview/
      interrogation, 45

Statement
  final, 291–311
  format, 304–307
  forms, 292–293
  importance of witness, 300
  potential problems with, 299–304
  protection of by interrogator, 308
  timing of taking, 297–299
  transcription of, 309
  transition, when suspect is close to
    confession, 186
  types, 294–297
  versus confession, 291
  witnessing of, 309
  written
    obtaining by interviewer, 169
    value of, 291–292
Stop-and-frisk interview, noncustodial,
  18–19
Strategy, interview/interrogation, 13–29
Street language, use of during interview/
  interrogation, 25
Subject, obtaining background
  information, 15–16
Submission, 10
  behavior of suspect in, 244
  behavioral shift of suspect during, 250
  mindset of suspect in, 243–244
Substantiation, in statement, 305–306
Supporting tactics, use of by interviewer
  to help witness give information,
  138–139
Suspect
  absolute denial and use of evidence,
    287–288
  acceptance of the soft accu-
    sation/choice question, 272–275
  accusation of, 171–199
  acknowledgment of assumptive
    question, 256–257
  admission and confession, 10–11
  admission during interview/
    interrogation, 10
  advisement of Miranda rights, 36–38
  alleges coercion in writing statement,
    301
  alleges he/she was not advised of
    rights, 301
  alleges that statement was dictated, 299
  allowed by interviewer/interrogator to
    enter conversation, 316
  attention focused on future or past by
    interrogator, 210–211
  avoids admitting crime, 303–304
  avoids elaborating details of crime,
    303–304

  background of and choice of
    rationalization, 205–207
  behavior, and choice of rationalization,
    207–210
  behavior during emphatic denial, 229–230
  behavior of, 181–182
  behavior of in submission, 244
  behavior when about to make admis-
    sion, 257–259
  behavioral shift during submission, 250
  cautions in interpreting behavior of,
    59–64
  claims that he/she cannot read or
    write, 300
  consequences versus justifications as
    basis for denial, 127–128
  definition, 5
  denial based on involvement of co-
    conspirator, 128
  details of alibi, 165–167
  development of commitment to
    admission with interrogator's
    closed-end questions, 273
  development of knowledge of criminal
    activity, 288–289
  distractions by, 21–23
  effect of drug/alcohol usage on
    behavior, 61
  effect of fear of detection on behavior,
    63–64
  effect of fight or flight on behavior,
    64–65
  effect of medical condition on behavior,
    61
  effect of mental capacity on behavior,
    60–61
  emotional effect of privacy on, 113
  encouraging cooperativeness of during
    admission, 277–278
  establishing behavioral picture of
    appearance when making
    truthful denial, 284
  establishing rapport with by interviewer/
    interrogator, 141–145
  evaluating against himself, 54–55
  evaluating against population, 55–56
  evaluation of behavior in context of
    situation, 56
  first admission of guilt, 10
  forms of denial, 9–10
  guidelines for interview of, 13
  guilty
    attitude of being defeated, 67
    and nasty and aggressive attitude
      during interview/
      interrogation, 67

Suspect [cont.]
  and outwardly unconcerned attitude,
    67
  overly polite and cooperative attitude,
    67
  identification of status through questions
    of enticement, 165–168
  interrogation of regarding internal theft
    in private sector, 184–185
  invoking right to silence or counsel, 315
  justification of lying, 125
  justifying actions, use of language by
    interviewer/interrogator, 26–27
  lack of rule as justification for behavior,
    126
  later confession, 317
  and minor admission, 102
  mirroring of by interviewer/
    interrogator 143–145
  obtaining biographical information of,
    168–169
  physical appearance when about to
    make admission, 253f
  position of feet indicates when ready to
    leave, 83–85
  positioning of interviewer/interrogator
    in relation to, 114
  posture in submission, 245f
  privilege against self-incrimination, 35
  promoting cooperation of in
    participatory accusation, 190
  and rationalization, 201–225
  realization process in interrogation, 127
  refuses to make statement, 301–303
  resistance of truthful versus untruthful,
    180f
  response to soft accusation, 252
  strongest at beginning of interrogation,
    123
  in submission, mindset, 243–244
  submission phase of interview/
    interrogation, 10
  substantiation of involvement in
    criminal activity, 278–283
  support for by interviewer/interrogator,
    317
  testing susceptibility of, 249–250
  timing and consistency of behavior,
    58–59
  truthful
    behavior in making denial, 258f
    behavior of, 66
    denial by, 128–129
    eliminated from suspicion with
      direct accusation, 179
    hand and arm positions in, 74

    head positions in, 87–88
    leg and foot positions in, 85–87
    mouth positions, 92
    and posture in chair, 70
    strength of denials in, 108
    verbal behavior, 93
  truthful and untruthful, attitudes
    common to both, 67–69
  typical attitudes, 66–69
  understanding of Miranda rights, 36–39
  untruthful
    admission of guilt and offer of
      restitution, 105–107
    and arm barriers, 79–80
    behavior during emphatic denial, 238
    behavior in making admission, 258f
    behavior of, 66–67
    challenging of by interviewer, 158
    changes in respiratory pattern, 73
    confrontation of interviewer by, and
      delay in response to questions,
      98–102
    dry mouth in, 92
    effect of rationalizations on strength
      of denials, 108
    emphasis on truthfulness, 103–104
    excessive helpfulness in, 97–98
    excessive politeness and respectfulness
      in, 97
    eye movements in, 90–91
    and fake itch, 77–78
    focus on petty issues, 96
    gallows laughter by, 102
    hand and arm positions in, 74–77
    hand over mouth in, 75–76
    hanging sentences in, 101
    head positions in, 89–90
    and level of nervousness, 55
    memory problems in, 104–105
    mouth positions, 92
    perspiration in, 73
    physical behavior to cover delay in
      response to questions, 99
    political answers tactic, 102–103
    and position of legs and feet, 82
    and posture in chair, 71–73
    and protection of abdominal area,
      79–80
    reliance on irrelevant points, 96
    reliance on uncheckable sources,
      95–96
    repeating of interview/interrogator's
      questions, 100
    responding to interviewer/interrogator
      with question, 100
    and screening of eyes by hands, 77

Suspect [cont.]
    strength of denials in, 108
    tactic of nonresponse, 101–102
    use of denial as stall for time, 122–123
    verbal behavior, 93–95
    verbal slips in, 107–108
    unwilling to make written statement, 303
    use of emphatic denial, 229–230
    use of smile to mask emotions during interview/interrogation, 65–66
    using interruptions against interrogator, 199
    and written statement, 11

**T**

Tension, behavioral peak during interrogation, 284–286
Tentativeness, interrogator's tone of voice as indicator, 117
Termination forms, completion of after written statement, 309–310
Theft, internal, private sector, 183–185
Third-degree tactics
    applicability of Miranda decision to, 43
    and *Brown v. Mississippi*, 34
Threat, physical force, renders confession involuntary, 35
Threats, avoidance of by interrogator, 213–214
Thumbs, and defensive attitude, 78–79
Time, limit on for interrogation, 198–199
Transition statement
    used to test suspect in submission, 249
    when suspect is close to confession, 186
Trickery, use of to obtain confession, 35–36
Truthfulness, emphasis of by untruthful suspect, 103–104

**U**

Union contracts, and legal aspects of interview/interrogation, 32
Union members, rights during interview/interrogation, 45

**V**

Verbal behavior
    definition, 52
    individualization, 54–55
    interpretation, 51–108

interpretation of by interviewer/interrogator, 93–95
Verbal slip, as indication of deception, 107–108
Victim
    establishing rapport with by interviewer/interrogator, 141–145
    untruthful, challenging of by interviewer, 158
    use of cognitive interview techniques to improve recollection, 160–161
Visual mode
    neurolinguistics, 146
    voice characteristics, 147
Visual representation mode, respiratory pattern, 147
Voice, respiratory pattern reflected in, 147
Voluntariness
    acknowledgment of in statement by suspect, 306
    requirement for confession, 35–36

**W**

Witness
    and concealment of information, 136
    definition, 5
    establishing rapport with by interviewer/interrogator, 141–145
    giving narrative during interview, 150–151
    importance of for suspect's statement, 300, 302–303
    inaccurate information provided by, 134
    and motive of revenge, 134–135
    rapport with established by interviewer, 139–149
    reasons for failure to cooperate, 135–136
    reliability of information, 134
    reluctance to be interviewed, 133
    and skepticism regarding the interview, 149–150
    for statement, 309
    untruthful, challenging of by interviewer, 158
    use of cognitive interview techniques to improve recollection, 160–161
Worksheet, for note-taking during development phase of interrogator, 275
Written statement, 11

**Y**

Youths, and waiver of constitutional rights, 39–40